THE IDEA OF THE
UNIVERSITY
OF CHICAGO

We look to you for friendship and understanding and if you have not understood us heretofore that is largely our fault—we have not talked enough about ourselves. We look to you for friendship and understanding and such other cooperation as you can easily infer and we, on our part, will use our best endeavors, constantly adding to that sum of human knowledge, the possession of which lifts the level of human life, constantly sending out into regions around about young men and women who have caught the spirit of research and of scholarship, dealing with questions honestly and on the basis of facts instead of on the basis of prejudice and ignorance, and giving out to the world from that university all the information we can get.

I thank you for your patient attention and invite your constant understanding and cooperation.

ERNEST DeWITT BURTON
27 February 1925
The Executive Club of Chicago

THE IDEA OF THE
UNIVERSITY
OF CHICAGO

Selections from the Papers of
the First Eight Chief Executives
of the University of Chicago from
1891 to 1975

Edited by
WILLIAM MICHAEL MURPHY
and
D. J. R. BRUCKNER

THE UNIVERSITY OF CHICAGO PRESS
Chicago and London

THE UNIVERSITY OF CHICAGO PRESS, CHICAGO 60637
THE UNIVERSITY OF CHICAGO PRESS, LTD., LONDON

Library of Congress Cataloging in Publication Data
Main entry under title:
The Idea of the University of Chicago.

Includes index.
1. Chicago, University—Addresses, essays,
lectures. I. Murphy, William Michael, 1947-
II. Bruckner, D. J. R.
LD906.5.I33   378.773'11   75-31570
ISBN 0-226-83608-8

CONTENTS

CONTENTS

*Photographs of the first eight chief
executives of the University of
Chicago follow page 160.*

FOREWORD

This is Bill Murphy's book. I employed him to make it. He proposed the method, chose, indexed and copied the papers, cut them up, pasted them down and fought over every elision, addition and rearrangement. His was a great labor of many months, and well done. All this time he was also working on his dissertation for a Ph.D. in history. His orderliness, imagination and candor have been an inspiration to a number of people working in the University's administration in a difficult time.

If it is Bill Murphy's book, then it must be William McNeill's too, for I called to him for help and Murphy appeared in my office, the appointed angel from on high.

It is, in a sense, Walter Blum's book too. In late 1972 I had told him I was reading the entire *University Record* from 1896 to 1933. He suggested that I assemble a volume of the speeches of the chief executives of the University, to find whether there might be a continuity of idea.

It is also Wayne Booth's, Robert Streeter's, and Warner Wick's book, for they read the first assembling of materials, and each made suggestions for improvements. What is more important, they all encouraged us to go ahead.

For me, it is always Edward Levi's book. Through the years, and especially after I came to work at the University of Chicago, he talked with me for many hours about the idea of this University, always referring to the other presidents in such a way as to arouse the curiosity that led me to the archives in the first place. When Bill and I began, Mr. Levi supported the project; he would stop by and ask questions which led to more exploration of the papers of the presidents, and which in many ways

vii

formed the long discussions Bill and I had about how to organize the volume.

Literally, it is his book and that of his seven predecessors; for it is entirely in the words of the first eight men who have been the chief executives of the University from its foundation. Each would have written a different book entirely, so, this is a book lifted from them. Whatever they talked about or wrote about in office, and a few before they were in that office, they were really talking about the living idea of this University. So, we read their papers with an eye for the different expressions of that one concern. In his preface, Bill Murphy explains how they were organized.

Each of the eight presidents—two had different titles at other times—was a powerful man. I think the power of the personalities comes through even this kind of mixture of their ideas. If you begin to read the papers of each separately, or to talk with the living ones, you can be amazed at the strength in them; and the papers themselves are full of worries, complaints, hopes, pleas, dreadful disappointments and, sometimes, bits of delightful rascality.

What is significant, then, is that the idea of this University continues to be expressed through such different men so clearly, and that it has continued to grow. Their language is symbolic, from the beginning, and thus a little frustrating; but it had to be symbolic to be truthful and faithful to the idea. Since the arrangements of excerpts in this volume is mostly chronological, the reader can see quickly how effective a teacher the University has been of its presidents, even of Mr. Harper.

The University is not entirely an idea, but the idea is its power. Even in these excerpts it is possible to see the changing circumstances and appearance of the place, but, somehow, the fact of it always seems evanescent. Perhaps that is because the idea is so resolutely pursued by all these men who speak of it as though it cannot be stopped in its growth and therefore can never be possessed. Mr. Burton, who was sixty-seven when he became president, said with clear amusement that the University of Chicago "is always becoming." I wonder whether his formula delighted the Platonists or the skeptics more in his original audience. The establishment of this University was a magnificent event in the world and, what comes through these papers is that its greatness has always rested on its fascination with and dedication to the enterprise of education; it is a living being with a powerful purpose.

If you read the excerpts aloud, you will begin to hear very different voices in a continuing conversation, and each voice carries the echoes of a thousand others; there are times when you seem to hear an entire faculty arguing. This is not the place to put down the biographies of the eight men who have been president. Someone should do that, one day. For three years, as I have read their papers and tried to hear the voices, the individuals have appeared in imagination in many ways: two were tall, two short, two fat, two very thin, four of middle height. Two were clergymen, but others were the offspring of clergymen and filled with the pastoral and preaching spirit; two were scientists, one an historian, two lawyers; only one was a professional administrator and only one served in the armed forces. All had been teachers, three of them in high schools, at some time before they became presidents and most taught here while they were in office. After Mr. Harper, three were elected from the faculty of this University, three from other faculties and one from this University's administration. Two died in office, five went on to or returned to other careers and only Mr. Judson retired to rest. All were married, some more than others, but members of the family of only one have become members of this faculty in later years. Each man was known, and could be known, as outstanding in some other work, but each took singular pleasure in being known as the President of the University of Chicago. The unity of their devotion, their concerns and their energetic pursuit of the idea of a real and singular university mark them apart from others. One who looks into their more private papers knows that the cost of their achievements was sometimes terrifying; in that respect, too, they are set apart.

Some had to give their energies to special purposes during their administrations. There are myths, among educators and especially in the Quadrangles of this University about each of them and his aims. Some of the myths are supported by these texts, others dispelled. Each of these men had that comprehensive understanding of the University which can only come from a real love and from the willingness to take on the moral load of being loved by a community of strong-willed, imaginative, imperious and sometimes simply perverse scholars. When

A. N. Whitehead said this place was more like ancient Athens than any place in the world, he meant proper praise, but those who know those old Athenians can feel the sting in the delight of it. One who looks through the archives of the presidents imaginatively and reflectively must be haunted by the notion that the University of Chicago is indeed a single living being of many members and no determinable age, which exalts, humiliates and consumes its leaders in a moment, and many times. It was Jean Cocteau who observed that men who become myths are burned by their admirers, not at the stake but in effigy.

But this collection is from these men, not about them; it is about the University. A real history of the University, it seems to me, would have to be an intellectual history, and this is not that. That may not be possible, though I think it should be attempted. This book is assembled for sampling, but it can be read right through, and I hope some people will read it through. These men can certainly be said to speak for themselves, but here they speak also for something much greater.

D. J. R. Bruckner

PREFACE

The excerpts which make up this book come from the official papers of the University of Chicago's presidents. Most of the views expressed in them were originally presented publicly, in speeches or articles, but a few were offered to a smaller audience, to the faculty, or to the Board of Trustees. In these excerpts, one can watch an idea of the University gradually unfold.

This book has taken its own peculiar shape because of the shape of the material itself. Our original idea was to select a few good speeches by each man which would reflect both his opinions and his style. Unfortunately, the presidents had not crafted their speeches with this book in mind. In fact, after some preliminary research, it began to appear as if they had written them with the specific purpose of preventing a book of this kind. Almost every speech had been written for a particular occasion and had covered far too specialized a topic for our purposes. Sometimes, too, a talk which clearly—even delightfully—presented a president's thinking about one facet of University affairs included uninspiring repetition of his well-known views on other matters. It simply was not possible to find well-written speeches which clearly reflected each president's thinking on the same broad range of issues within the University.

We solved the problem by collecting reports as well as published articles and speeches and by compiling an index to the material which we had gathered. The reports, if they were less eloquent, covered more ground than the articles and speeches. The index indicated which issues most interested the presidents —its 176 subject headings included such diverse items as "the University's identity and role," "fraternities," and "specialization vs. generalization"—and it assured that important expressions of opinion would not be left out. In selecting the excerpts, we tried to take from the original documents enough material to give a sense of the context without including very much that was extraneous. The text is entirely the presidents' own, as are the headings which appear in italics; the other headings are ours.

As the reader will probably have guessed, the final shape of this book has been a surprise, even to its editors. Its chapters, reflecting the different ways in which the presidents dealt with different topics, vary in format. The material within the chapters falls naturally into a chronological pattern, except where the exploration of a particular train of thought dictated a topical arrangement. The reader will find that, in a few such places, presidential opinions so diverge that the text takes the form of a serious debate over a period of many years. The constituent parts of this book vary in size and in shape. As a whole, they represent eight personal reports of a single compelling vision: the idea of the University of Chicago.

William Michael Murphy

ACKNOWLEDGMENTS

The central repository of papers of the Presidents of the University of Chicago is in the Special Collections section of the Joseph Regenstein Library at the University. Most of the papers from which these excerpts are taken have appeared in various publications of the University or the University of Chicago Press. Mr. Levi's address at the University of California Legal Center dedication, "The University, the Professions, and the Law," is reprinted by permission from the *California Law Review* 56 (1968): 251–59 (copyright © 1968, California Law Review, Inc.). Mr. Burton's "Baptists and Education," is reprinted from *The Positive Note in Christianity* (Philadelphia: American Baptist Publication Society, 1918) by permission of The Judson Press. We are grateful, in addition, to the following for permission to reprint: to WGN Radio (Chicago) for Mr. Hutchins' "Education and the University of Chicago," broadcast 2 January 1931; to Muskingum College for Mr. Harper's "The College President," from its centennial publications; to the Association of American Universities for Mr. Judson's "The System of Fellowships," from its *Journal of Proceedings and Addresses* (second annual conference), his discussions of papers by Messrs. Wilcox and Kinley (tenth annual conference), and for Mr. Hutchins' "The Chicago Plan and Graduate Study" (thirty-third annual conference); to the Executive Club of Chicago for Mr. Burton's "Business and Scholarship—What Have They to Do with One Another?" *The Exec-Club News*, 3 March 1925, pp. 4–8; to the Chicago Association of Commerce and Industry for Mr. Hutchins' pamphlet "Higher Education and National Defense" (1941); to the Los Angeles *Times* for an interview with Mr. Levi, "Chicago U. President Hits Expansion Trend," 6 July 1969; and to the Chicago *Maroon* for an interview, "Levi Speaks on Banfield and Funds," 23 and 26 April 1974, and for Mr. Burton's "President Harper—The Educator," *Monthly Maroon*, January 1906, pp. 142–47.

CHIEF EXECUTIVE OFFICERS
OF
THE UNIVERSITY OF CHICAGO
JULY 1891
TO
FEBRUARY 1975

WILLIAM RAINEY HARPER
1891-1906

HARRY PRATT JUDSON
1907-23

ERNEST DeWITT BURTON
1923-25

CHARLES MAX MASON
1925-28

ROBERT MAYNARD HUTCHINS
1929-51

LAWRENCE ALPHEUS KIMPTON
1951-60

GEORGE WELLS BEADLE
1961-68

EDWARD HIRSCH LEVI
1968-75

DEFENDERS OF THIS ANCIENT FAITH
The Idea of the University

It is the glory of the University of Chicago that, since its foun-
dation, in war and peace, in good times and bad, while chief
executive officers have come and gone, it has had a sense of its
mission. It has had an idea, a purpose. It has stood for some-
thing.

HUTCHINS

The importance of our University is that we are now, as we
have always been, somewhat out of step. We do not seek ful-
fillment in being a research institute, a collection of graduate
schools, or a liberal arts college. Instead, we are one university
committed to the discovery of knowledge and the transmission
of our cultural and intellectual heritage.

LEVI

LEVI

I am sure you wonder what kind of a university this really is,
and what the life of an undergraduate in it will be like. If this
is of any help to you, let me say I have often wondered what
kind of a university this is. It is an institution of many qualities
which, by its very nature, depends to a considerable extent upon
the quality of the individual who relates to it. I say this even
though I believe it to be true that this University knows more
about itself and is more determined about its own direction
than any other comparable university.

The original idea of this University is instructive. This Uni-
versity was not founded as a college, which then grew into a
university. That was the normal pattern until this University
was created in 1891, one of the major events in higher education
of that time. This University started both as an undergraduate
college and as a major center for graduate and professional
study. It placed its emphasis both on the liberal arts and upon
the overwhelming importance of investigation.

This combination of undergraduate and graduate work, of
teaching and research, was regarded as a bold but foolhardy ex-
periment—an attempt to put together the main attributes of the

1

English colleges and of the German centers of learning—and to do so in a most unlikely geographical place. Many of the experts were sure the experiment would fail. The parts of such an institution, it was believed, hardly could exist together. They would not make for a common strength. The place would fly apart. The institution was called a veritable monstrosity, "Harper's Bazaar," in wry reference to the first president's name.

And yet I believe all informed persons would agree that from the very beginning, this institution *has* found the closest relationship among its parts, and the greatest interaction among its scholars and between the disciplines. The University has honored the diversity of individual scholars and the structure of separate disciplines. But it has constantly searched for an understanding of a common mission. It has attempted to make pervasive throughout the entire institution, and at all stages, its dual emphasis on the liberal arts and on investigation. In short, it has never accepted the dichotomy which is supposed to separate teaching from research. It believes that discovery, itself, is the greatest form of teaching, and that mutual efforts to understand, whether in the classroom, the seminar, the laboratory, or the library, not only give the institution its unity, but link scholars over time and across national boundaries and disciplines. Mind you, I have not said utopia has been achieved, but rather that the idea has been deeply felt and is compelling. . . .

To its students the University will appear in different aspects from time to time. But you know a good deal about an institution if you can find the ideas to which it is responsive. The idea of teaching and learning as an adventure in discovery, with the unity which this implies, the belief in the actuality of discovery which will add not only to our knowledge but to the knowledge of mankind, and the emphasis on the individual scholars, are, in my view, central among these ideas. Alas, but perhaps fortunately, these ideas can all be stated differently. I have not claimed they are always realized—of course they are not—and the list is not exhaustive.

You find here an institution which always has had an outstanding record in research and in undergraduate and professional education. Some of the new sciences, such as sociology, found here their most creative period. Many of the faculty are making unique advances in man's efforts to understand, and they welcome students for their brightness, ability, tenacity to overcome obstacles and, in part, because students are where the future lies.

Class of 1975 Assembly, 26 September 1971

FIRST DAYS

HARPER

First days are always days of uncertainty and anxiety, but they are also days of peculiar interest and significance. The very uncertainty which attends them adds to this significance; for there is during this period of indefiniteness a possibility of development which no longer exists when fixity is once attained.

Our first days have seen little, perhaps too little, of this seemingly necessary uncertainty. From the beginning there has been a definiteness of plan which to some doubtless has appeared premature. Time will show—time indeed has already shown, that it is the definite conception which has power to move men to action; and if this conception is only sufficiently flexible, the possibilities of growth are not diminished by the definiteness.

Our first days have not been passed without anxiety. There have been weeks and months of serious solicitude. But, mark you, this solicitude has been occasioned by doubt, not as to what in the end could and should be done, but as to which of two or more things should be done in order best to secure the end. There has never been wavering, never despair; but there has been an appreciation of an ever increasing weight of responsibility, the appreciation of a burden growing heavier and heavier and one which in the nature of things must grow still more heavy as the work progresses.

We have met this evening together with our friends as members of the University to celebrate for the first time a day which we may confidently believe even a thousand years hence will be celebrated in the same spirit though in different form. Do we realize the meaning of it all? There is a feeling of uncertainty and anxiety connected with first days and the first doing of things. There is also sublimity and solemnity if the cause is high and holy and if being such the significance of it is appreciated.

3

This hour in which the University in its official capacity first comes before the public, is a sacred hour in the life of each one who is directly or indirectly connected with the University. It is an hour of serious importance to the city within whose confines the University is situated and to the great section of our country tributary to the city. For all of us, for the city, for the country, for humanity and for God, this night, this hour is heavy with significance.

In the holding of this convocation we have in mind three things;

1. To furnish an opportunity to bestow the proper awards for work accomplished, and to dismiss with all the honors which the University can confer those who have shown themselves worthy of such honor. And on the other hand to receive into the privileges of the University those who have shown themselves prepared to take advantage of these privileges.

2. To look back for a moment over the months of work completed, in order that an estimate may be formed of the progress made, or if such it be, of ground lost. And on the other hand to look forward to the opportunities and the necessities of the future, to note and select for effort those opportunities which seem most promising.

3. To bind together into a unity the many complex and diverging forms of activity which constitute our university life and work, and, thus united, to stand before the public in a way to show our appreciation of its good will and at the same time to show, if it can be shown, that we in turn are deserving of this same good will. . . .

Our first Convocation has come, and now is gone. Will not the students of the University receive from it new inspiration for that which lies before them? Will not the Faculties of the University take up again their work no longer new, but already old; a work the magnitude of which no man can estimate; will not our friends carry home with them clearer conceptions of what the University is, what it is trying to do, and what it needs to make the effort successful; and will not those men and women to whose liberality the University owes its existence recognize still more clearly than before, the greatness of the work undertaken, the divine guidance in it all, the fact that what they have done has been done for all eternity.

First Convocation, 1 January 1893

HARPER

To the God who is over all and in all we make acknowledgment of our gratitude, because he it was who prompted the founder's heart to undertake this gigantic work, because it was his spirit that inspired the hearty cooperation with which the donors entered into a participation in the work; because it was his overruling providence that created so widespread a sympathy and appreciation in the hearts of men who have everywhere become its friends. . . .

At the beginning of our work the mind of Chicago was engrossed with the thought of the Columbian Exposition. Before the close of our first year there had come a financial crisis which has perhaps grown more serious with every year until the present. The obstacles have been many, and the anxiety at times intense, but a merciful Providence has carried us through it all, and in every time of necessity friends have been raised up. There has been a feeling on the part of some that the institution has not conserved sufficiently the traditions of the past. These friends, if they are friends, have forgotten that it is in the nature of a university to occupy the advanced positions; that a university, if it will justify its name, must be a leader of thought, and that however cautious and conservative may be the policy of such an institution, the great majority of men are accustomed to follow far behind. It cannot be expected that such will sympathize with those whose responsibilities force them to the forefront in the great and continuous conflict of thought. And yet, to all who sincerely and earnestly point out what is thought to be a mistaken path and a misguided policy, we make acknowledgement of our gratitude, believing that the God who has established The University will guide and control it in all its history.

Does someone ask, What in particular does The University of Chicago represent? Upon what does it lay greatest emphasis? In what respect is it different from other institutions of similar character? What have been the distinctive features of policy adopted in the organization of The University? The answer may be briefly given: (1) Concentration on the part of student and instructor, as seen in the regulations which permit a student to take up at one time only three subjects, and which require the instructor, under ordinary circumstances to restrict himself to two subjects. (2) Accommodation to the special needs of students and instructors as seen in the regulations which make it possible for a student to be absent during any quarter of the year, or, if desired, to study during four quarters; as also in the regulations which permit an instructor by doing continuous work to secure vacation credits which, when placed together, make it possible to give up teaching for the purpose of travel or investigation in longer or shorter periods; still further in the regulations relating to summer instruction. (3) Individualism on the part of student and instructor as seen in the large liberty given each student in the effort to adjust the curriculum to his needs rather than to adjust him to a fixed curriculum; as also seen in the opportunity furnished instructors to specialize, not only in a single department but in subdivisions of that department. (4) Extension, as described already in the provisions made for university extension, technically so called, affiliations, cooperation and the University Press.

Quinquennial Statement, 1 July 1896

HARPER

The university is an institution of the people. It must, therefore, be "privileged" and, in many instances, supported by the people. In the latter case, it must be influenced by the changes which the people may undergo in their opinions. But the people must remember that when, for any reason, the administration of their institution, or the instruction in any one of its departments is changed by an influence from without, whenever effort is made to dislodge an officer or a professor because the political sentiment of the majority has undergone a change, at that moment the institution has ceased to be a university; and it cannot again take its place in the rank of universities so long as there continues to exist to any appreciable extent the factor of coercion. The state has no more right than the church to interfere with the search for truth, or with its promulgation when found. The state and church alike may have their own schools and colleges for the training of youthful minds, and for the propagation of special kinds of intelligence; and in these it may choose what special coloring shall be given to the instruction. This is proper, for example, in the military schools of the state, and in the theological schools of the church; but such schools are not universities. They do not represent the people; they do not come out of the people.

University of California Charter Day Address, 1899

PROFESSEDLY CHRISTIAN

HARPER

The position of the University of Chicago religiously has been definitely and professedly Christian. Any other attitude would have been false to the auspices under which the institution was established, and particularly to the hopes and desires of its founder. It is not forgotten that in the earliest days, when there was great question whether the first four hundred thousand dollars could be secured, the Jews of Chicago came forward, and by their splendid gift made the effort successful. A representative of the Jews has been on the Board of Trustees, several Jews are members of Faculties, large numbers of Jews have been matriculated as students; but in the large and true sense of the word "Christian" the University has maintained urgently and strongly its professed position as Christian. The various Faculties have contained members of almost every communion, and many who were not members of any church. The question of the religious faith of an officer has not been raised by the Trustees in connection with the appointment of any officer of the University. No one, so far as I am aware, has ever taken the trouble to make a calculation of the representation of the various denominations either in the Faculty or among the students. As the country of which we are citizens is a Christian country, so the University of Chicago is a Christian institution. The drawing of a narrower line than this would be fatal to the growth of the University. Here lies the distinction between a college and a university. The one may be controlled by the ecclesiastical or political spirit; the other may not be. . . .

During the first years a religious service was conducted every Sunday in the evening. This was after a while changed to the afternoon, and for several years the Sunday Vesper Service occupied a large place in the religious work of the institution. It soon became evident, however, that a service was needed which

7

would develop more definitely the spirit of worship, and after full consideration arrangements were made for introducing a regular Sunday morning service at which preachers officially appointed by the University should conduct the services and preach. A single year's experience has convinced all concerned of its value. It has been found that the most eminent preachers of the country are willing to visit the University and to give its members their service. The best results cannot, of course, be secured with the present lack of a proper place in which to hold the services, and this same difficulty presents itself in connection with all the other religious work of the institution. No one of the religious organizations has a place which can be called even respectable. Until such facilities are provided as are absolutely needed, the work will be seriously handicapped.

The daily Chapel Assembly—Monday for the Junior College students, Tuesday for the Senior College students, Thursday for the Graduate students, and Friday for the Divinity students— has contributed something toward the higher life of the University. At these meetings the greatest preachers of the country have addressed the students, and their words have been gratefully received. It is probably true that the religious life is as strongly marked in the University of Chicago as in any other institution similarly situated. It is an interesting fact that, so far as is known, no student has ever been arrested by a policeman for disorder or drunkenness. The moral life of the student body seems to be of the highest character.

I desire to make the following suggestions:

1. While the new Assembly Hall, erected by the kindness of Mr. Leon Mandel, will be used for the religious exercises as well as for other general exercises of the University, and will contribute greatly to the increased value of all such exercises, it remains true that the University should have upon its grounds a structure which should be used only for ecclesiastical and the highest academical functions. This building should be the most beautiful ecclesiastical structure in the Mississippi valley, and should cost not less than five hundred thousand dollars. In connection with it provision should be made for the headquarters of the various religious organizations, and no pains or money should be spared to make it the most magnificent building on the University grounds.

2. Some plan should be devised for bringing into closer relationship the various members of the Christian Union. It would hardly be thought best, under all the circumstances, to organize a church; but an organization as much like that of a church as possible should be effected, and all possible means should be employed to develop the community spirit in connection with its organization. It would seem probable that no more unifying factor could be suggested, and in a community like that of an urban University the greatest possible stress should be placed upon factors which produce the spirit of unity.

3. Although the work of the Settlement has been thoroughly successful, its influence has reached a small number proportionately of the University community, and it may be asked whether something may not be done which would bring a much larger proportion of the students and members of the Faculty into personal touch with this work.

4. No satisfactory arrangements have yet been provided for the residence of the University Preacher or for his office. Both of these matters demand immediate consideration. A large part of the effectiveness of the work is destroyed because of the lack of the proper facilities for doing it.

A DECADE OF CHANGES

It may be said that at least ten important experiments have been instituted in connection with the work of the University. Some of these may no longer be called experiments, inasmuch as the experimental stage has confessedly been passed. In other cases the time has not arrived at which the experiment may be called closed. Among the problems the solution of which has thus been attempted I may mention the following:

1. The establishment of work in the Summer Quarter as an organic part of the University year, in distinction from the Summer School work as it had formerly been conducted. The success of this plan is attested, not only by the large number of students in attendance—the largest, in fact, of any Quarter in the year—but also by the character of the students, a body made up of earnest men and women from every state in the Union. . . .

2. The continuous session of the University, including the Summer Quarter just mentioned—an arrangement by which the buildings and grounds, the libraries and equipment, of the in-

stitution are used throughout the entire year, in contrast with the prevailing custom of permitting the entire plant to lie idle during one-fourth or one-third of the time.

3. The distribution of service on the part of members of the Faculty throughout the entire year—a plan which requires that about 25 per cent of the officers of instruction shall be absent at any given time, and also makes it possible for the officer (*a*) to take his vacation at such season of the year as may be most satisfactory; or (*b*) to allow his vacation to accumulate until he shall be able to secure the privilege of spending six or nine months in a foreign land; or (*c*) to devote, if he so desires, only six months to instruction and to give the remaining six months to investigation—all of this flexibility being gained without extra cost of money or time. This arrangement, looked at from the student's point of view, permits students of all grades to enter the University four times a year instead of once, the adjustment of courses to this end having been found entirely feasible.

4. The graduating of students at four seasons of the year— that is, at the close of each of the four Quarters—a policy which is strictly in accord with the individualism of modern education, and serves to protect the student against many of the arbitrary arrangements ordinarily prescribed.

5. Specialization in administration, this being gained by distributing the work of various divisions of the University to special Boards and Faculties, and placing the responsibility of such service almost exclusively upon the Board or Faculty concerned. This might be put into another form: the abolition of the so-called General Faculty to which everything ordinarily must be submitted.

6. The policy of affiliating colleges and academies in accordance with a plan which makes the University responsible from an educational point of view, while it leaves the entire financial responsibility upon the local Board.

7. The plan of co-operating with high schools, emphasis being placed upon the individualism of the teacher, and the teachers recognized as University Deputy Examiners.

8. The separation of the work of the Freshman and Sophomore classes, called the Junior Colleges, from the higher work, and its assignment to an independent Faculty.

9. The House System described above, in accordance with which groups of students practically become self-governing un-

der the general supervision of a Head appointed by the President.

10. The plan of providing separate instruction for men and women in the Freshman and Sophomore classes, while allowing them to work together in the upper classes.

If the question were to be asked what two elements constitute the largest factors in controlling the organization and spirit of the institution, the answer might be made: (1) the principle of individualism, from the point of view both of student and instructor, which has been all-powerful in effecting the details of organization; and (2) the principle of flexibility, which is, after all, perhaps only a corollary of the first-named principle of individualism, to which everything has been made subservient.

Decennial Report, 1 July 1902

THE IDEA OF THE UNIVERSITY

Judson

We are discussing at this time the advisability of placing in the quadrangles some stately building which shall stand for all time as a memorial for our lost President. That such plan will be carried out I confidently believe; and yet, after all, the best memorial of Dr. Harper which can ever exist is the University which he founded. We must remember, too, that the University is not its lands, its buildings, its endowments alone. The University is the entire body of men and women, faculty and students, who compose the University community, who are here for the common purpose of attainment in a high intellectual life, with the common purpose of adding to knowledge by research. If we, then, wish to do our best to keep green the memory of the intellectual founder of the University, shall we not all of us, Faculty and students alike, unite in doing the best that within us lies to make the University all that Dr. Harper ever dreamed? To that end above all things we need to remember that we can do nothing without unity. Let us stand by one another; let us act as members of a common body, and let us never forget that we are members, above all, of the University of Chicago. And this implies, in the second place, a loyalty on the part of each

11

one of us which will make him cheerfully ready to give of his time, of his efforts, of whatever is needed to make the institution what it should be. It is by the sacrifice of time and thought and work that great things are accomplished in the world. The University can be maintained and extended; its life can be kept strong and vigorous and glowing through the years that are to come only by all of us putting in together our best efforts, our knowledge, our life, to that end.

Harper Memorial Student Body Meeting
15 January 1906

JUDSON

The modern university idea as we have developed it in the United States is different from that in our own country in past generations, and is different also in many respects from the idea as found in European institutions. In the American university there is always a college. The university would still be a university without the college. It seems, however, on the whole a practical convenience to maintain the American college in all its essentials in connection with university work. Besides the college the function of the university, as we understand it, is threefold: (1) Investigation on all lines of modern thought. (2) To train teachers for the higher form of institutions of learning. This last is a distinct function, in large part at least, of our Graduate Schools and is a very proper function of a specialized school for the training of teachers. (3) Education for the professions on the highest possible standards. It is in these three ways that the university seems likely to render the greatest service to education, to science, and to humanity.

Convocation, 12 June 1906

JUDSON

We may safely begin with the postulate that on the whole experience seems to show that education works from above down rather than from below up. In other words, in the development of educational activities it is the colleges which influence the development of secondary schools; it is the high schools which strongly influence the development of the common schools. Of course, any of these grades of schools might exist and in many

12

cases have existed with those above. The attractive influence, however, of higher institutions on lower has always been strong —indeed, irresistible. Within my own experience some years ago, the entire high school system of the state of Minnesota was so directly stimulated by the action of the state university that within a very few years the number of high schools was multiplied by ten and their efficiency was multiplied by even more than that. In other words, without the state university there would have been throughout the state a small number of high schools, a few strong and more feeble, and all lacking co-ordination and impetus. Under the influence of the university the state has many high schools definitely co-ordinated with a common purpose and common ideals and liberally supported.

In the light of this well-known fact we must consider at the present time what is the actual point of departure for educational advance. This I think undoubtedly will be found in the present day highest conception of a university. Of course we use educational terms loosely in this country, almost as loosely indeed as we give academic degrees. Still out of all the confusion there is emerging a very definite idea of a university which is quite different from the conception of that institution in past generations. From this point of view the university is not primarily, as in Oxford, a group of colleges. Nor again is it necessarily merely a group of professional schools. Again, it is not altogether and fundamentally a place for teaching. The two thoughts underlying the modern university are these: First, the institution must contain a faculty of specialists who are engaged in active production. In other words, they are busily investigating various fields of science and seeking to discover new knowledge. Ideally the university should cover the whole field of thought and should be composed of investigators in every field. Practically, however, it may easily be the case that in a given institution some fields are more strongly developed than others, while some fields may be wholly neglected.

In the second place, corresponding to this investigative and productive faculty of specialists, there is a body of students who in turn are learning to be specialists. This involves on their part the mastery of given fields of knowledge in the first place, and, in the second place, learning for themselves to become original workers within their fields. Obviously this body of students form on the one hand the advanced professional schools, and on the other the so-called graduate schools. By advanced professional schools of course I mean those which are not intended as short cuts to a profession, but those which, based on a thorough preliminary training, aim to develop only the strongest professional specialists. By "graduate schools" again we mean the aggregate of students who in like manner are becoming specialists in any or all of the various departments of knowledge outside of the different specific professions, like law and medicine. The term "graduate schools" has been used in this country as a mere practical convenience. It is perhaps unlikely that, in the natural evolution of our universities in the larger sense, this temporary designation will disappear, as the need for it is lost. A school of chemistry, of history, or of classics, planned for the development of the most advanced specialization, is no more and no less a graduate school than is an advanced school of law or medicine. The requirement of a baccalaureate degree is an incident in the more vital character of the work. . . .

The essence of the new education which is taking form under our eyes, then, I conceive to be four things: The first is flexibility in schemes of study—a breaking up of the old-time rigidity in curricula, and in the organization and interrelation of school, college and university. The second is special knowledge on some specific subject—the educated man should know some one thing, and should know it well. The third is the power of self-direction in getting at new ideas—in other words, the power to solve problems. Life, for the individual, and for the community, is a series of problems. He is well trained who meets them fearlessly and who solves them promptly and accurately. That, in science, is the immediate end of the university. That in fact is the ultimate end of all education. To that are tending the dissolution of old educational forms and the evolution of new ones, which so dismay some of us. The fourth is a keen sense of social obligation—no one lives to himself alone—every one should do his part to make and keep society clean and worth while.

Washington Educational Association (Seattle)
1 January 1908

JUDSON

It is this new and (nobler form) of social power to which the University is devoted. As tending to create such power, it may, if you please, be said that the University fosters an aristocracy—but it is in the true meaning of that term. The modern aristocrat is he who thinks clearly, works worthily and lives cleanly. The University with all its soul desires to form just such aristocrats—but none other.

The *basis* of a real university rests in the dual foundations of *culture* and *power*.

> "University Ideals." Date and occasion unrecorded
> From the H. P. Judson Papers in the
> Joseph Regenstein Library

LEST THE DESTINED WORK GO UNDONE

BURTON

Let me now add by way of exposition of what is implicit in this statement that a university which would really meet the demands legitimately made upon it in these days must make a careful study of what other universities, especially its near neighbors, are doing not so much for the purpose of imitating them or preparing to compete with them as to discover what they are not doing that it can itself properly undertake with a view to complementing their service and rounding out the task of the universities as a whole. And may I add also that a university that aspires to render the largest service to the country and the world must subject itself to a process of rigid self-criticism, discovering wherein it is weak in general policy and scope, in methods and in men, and courageously endeavoring to cut off what is superfluous, to eliminate duplications, to provide what is lacking and to substitute strength for weakness at every possible point.

I am sure that you will agree with me that this is a very large task, and I should rightly forfeit your confidence if I should undertake to answer now all the questions which such a study as I am describing would inevitably raise. This, as I have already intimated is not my purpose today. But as preliminary to the prolonged cooperative study by which alone we can hope to find the questions that are involved and discuss the answers to them, I should like to do three things.

First, to set forth in a purely tentative way certain ideals that I myself cherish; second, to indicate by way of example what these ideals would signify when applied to certain divisions of the University; and third, to ask your consent to the appointment of several committees which shall undertake the detailed and thorough study of certain large questions of policy and practice.

With your consent then, as one member of this body and for the purpose of starting the discussion I should like to set forth certain ideals that I cherish for the University. I am thinking not of what can be accomplished in one year or three, but of what will perhaps require ten or twenty years. Yet I am thinking of these things also as tasks to be begun at once. We do not move forward effectively without definite goals, yet goals are to be pursued without delay, not placed in museums for the curious to admire. Let me say further that I am not speaking in general terms and applying to the University of Chicago what I could equally well say of any other university of which I happened to be a member. I am thinking of our opportunity and our duty, and trying to define our specific task. I should like to paraphrase those words of Dr. Harper, "I have never doubted that God had given me a work to do that would go undone if I did not do it," and say of the University of Chicago that I am convinced that it has an opportunity and a task that belong to it alone, a work which will go undone if we do not do it.

What then should our University do and become?

I believe that from this time forward research should be the outstanding feature of the University of Chicago. Four considerations lead me to say this.

a. First the preeminent value of research, the things which it can achieve, as evidenced by what has already been achieved. It is research that differentiates our day from the middle ages and has been the cause of all the progress in education and of most of the progress in civilization that has been made in the last century. It holds the promise of all the progress that we can hope to make in the future. For the repetition of old opinions true or false it substitutes open eyed and resolute facing of the facts, and pushes its way on to reality. Before a popular audience it might be necessary, or it might be futile to argue these matters. Before this company the bare assertion is sufficient. Many of you know them far better than I.

b. My second reason for affirming that research should be the dominant characteristic of our University is that we have already made a splendid beginning in this direction. To call the roll of our research men by name might be invidious and certainly is superfluous. You all know in part—I doubt if any of us know in whole, the things that have been wrought in this University in Physics, in Chemistry, in the various departments of Biology, in Mathematics and Astronomy, and in the Social Sciences and in Theology. We have an enviable reputation for research throughout the world. It is our manifest duty and destiny to go forward and not backward.

c. My third reason for emphasizing research is that by it more than in any other way we may serve not individuals only or a local community only, but while doing both these things may also serve all other universities and colleges, our own land and all lands. The output of the research laboratory, the work of Michelson, of Moore, of Carlson, of Judd, to mention only a few examples of many that might be named are gifts to the race, are contributions to the future as well as the present. With no underestimate of other work the university that can do this ought to do it, and we can.

d. This brings me to my fourth and final reason for emphasizing research, viz. that very few other universities are in a position to give to it the first place to the extent that we are. I speak not in derogation of other institutions and for your ears only, but it is evident that a State University with its obligations to give a collegiate or technical training to the increasing numbers of the youth of the State, who are demanding it, responsive as it must be to the opinion and demands of a constituency to whom research means little or nothing, compelled to seek the money for its support from State legislatures in annual or biennial sessions, may indeed undertake research, but will find it practically impossible to give to it the place of first importance.

The Librarian of one of our largest and best State universities showing me recently the rooms set apart in the library building for graduate work, remarked, "Of course our graduates are practically all working for the Master's degree, the Ph.D. students are so few as not to constitute a problem for us." Even the under-graduate work of these universities is sometimes seriously endangered by the great numbers of students whom they do not feel at liberty to refuse. Under such conditions research has a hard task to live, to say nothing of flourishing. Over against this situation, we may, if Trustees and Faculty see their opportunity alike put our emphasis where we judge it wise; may choose the fundamental task of research, refuse to be overwhelmed by numbers of students. We are free to choose our own field of emphasis as few other schools in the West are. Moreover, Chicago is peculiarly well adapted to be the seat of a research institution. We share the sky and the air with other institutions, but we are in the midst of a great laboratory for the biological and social sciences, ready made to our hand. Even the eastern part of the country has few institutions so well situated and equipped for research as we. Traditional emphasis on undergraduate work, scattering of buildings and departments caused by the university far out-growing its original scope and plan, these and many other restrictions embarrass and hamper the work of research. We have absolutely no restriction that cannot be overcome if we really want to overcome it.

I do not dare say it so that any of our sister institutions can hear me lest they should judge that our hatbands are about to burst, but in this presence I do not know why I should not say in all seriousness that there is no university in the country that is so favorably situated to become the research university of the country.

The second element in my ideal for the university is that the spirit and practice of research should extend to all departments. I do not announce this as any novel doctrine. We have all accepted it as a matter of course. It may be that some departments have achieved a wider reputation for research than some others, it may be that some have given more time than others to the transmission of the acquired stock of knowledge, but none of us would admit that his department is not engaged in research. I mention this as a commonplace but especially for the purpose of emphasizing it in reference to education and pointing out what seems to me a necessary consequence of it as applied to education. For I think you will agree with me that there is no possible reason for not including education in the field of research. Certainly we shall not claim that we know all that is to be known in that field, or that it is less important to know and to know how in that department than in Physics and Chemistry or Biology, that the training of the mind is less important than the healing of the body, or that it is less important to pur-

18

sue investigations in the fundamental sciences which underlie education than to conduct research in those that underlie medicine. But if we grant this, then it follows, for me at least, that we must continue our policy of carrying on education all the way from the Kindergarten to the graduate schools and must include in the field of research not only the physical, biological and social sciences themselves, but the educational process as applied to those sciences and to pupils of all ages. To conduct research in education we need as our laboratories the elementary and the secondary school, and the college. We shall not say respecting any of these divisions of the university that they exist simply as laboratories for the research work of the School of Education. We shall not necessarily emphasize research as compared with the educational process itself equally in all divisions, but we shall affirm that even from the point of view of educational research itself, we need all these parts of the University.

This to my mind excludes the thought that we shall, as has been suggested in some quarters, make the University a super-collegiate institution, consisting solely of Graduate schools of research, or a Research institute analogous to the Research Institutes of Medicine and Social Science, only of broader scope. We shall continue to be a University, educating men and women as well as investigating subjects, and, for the purpose both of educating people and of investigating education, shall continue to carry on education from the Kindergarten to the graduate schools.

BEING CLOSE TOGETHER ALTOGETHER

The third element of my thought about our future is that we shall aim to keep all the essential elements of the University as an institution of research and education in close physical contiguity and in intimate intellectual relationship. We are extremely fortunate that though at the founding of the University, President Harper thought that our main quadrangle would be ample for all purposes of the University for all time, he early discovered his mistake, and with that farsightedness that was characteristic of him and Mr. Rockefeller, the means were provided to buy the additional land giving us the frontage on both sides of the Midway from Washington Park to Dorchester Avenue. This makes it possible for us to avoid the extreme embarrassment of Yale for example, which is hard put to find any suitable place for its new General Library building, and the unfortunate remoteness of the Medical School at Harvard and Columbia from the departments of the University which deal with the fundamental sciences and emphasize research, and even the less serious but irreparable misfortune of Johns Hopkins in that its Medical School is three miles from the University proper. It puts us in an altogether different class from the State universities of certain of our Western states which have scattered their departments in different cities hundreds of miles apart. We regret that the smokiness of Chicago necessitates our astronomers living and working in Wisconsin, but the separation of the observatory from the other parts of the University perhaps appropriately typifies the remoteness of the stars from the earth and is certainly less serious than would be the isolation of Medicine from Physics and Chemistry, or of Divinity from Philosophy and Sociology and Philology on which it is so largely dependent.

. . . In our emphasis on research, and on the physical contiguity and intellectual unity of the University we ought never to become academic or monastic. After all science is for men not men for science. Human beings may be the subjects of research, but the ultimate purpose is not research but human betterment. To *crescat scientia* we add at once *vita excolatur.* . . .

Two other elements of the ideal which I cherish for our University I should like to mention together, because of their intimate relation to one another and because they are alike in that they are most difficult to achieve by any set and ordained methods. I know no better names for them than the trite and familiar words, character and culture. Whatever else a student gains at the University these two at least he ought to carry away when he goes, and to the creation of them his residence at the University ought to make a large contribution. Yet neither of them can be set down among required studies; neither can be tested by a formal examination. They are something more than knowledge and something more than skill. They belong in the realm of attitudes and appreciations. They are the product of atmosphere, to which we all contribute, and for which we are all in our measure responsible. They are the result of companionships, among students and between students and teachers, of personalities, even in a measure of architecture and ceremonial, of the incidental and optional elements of University life. We have done much to create them in all these ways. Is it possible for us to do yet more?

... I have asked myself and I should like to ask you what we can do to make it more certain than it now is that with all the student's learning he will gain that indefinable something which we call culture and that indispensable quality that we call character. ...

In conclusion may I reiterate what I have already implied, that the responsibility and possibilities of our University are surpassed by none in the country. We are not as old as some, but youth has its advantages as well as its disadvantages and is besides the only defect that time is sure to cure. By our strong beginning, by our harmony of purpose, by the possession of space in which to grow, thus avoiding separating things that should remain together, by freedom of action given to us by the fact that we are independent of state control, by our liberty to subordinate size to quality and to emphasize whatever phase of work we judge wise, we stand in an exceptionally favorable position.

"The Future of the University"
University of Chicago Senate
24 February 1923

BURTON

Mr. Swift has spoken of my having already made two inaugural addresses. It would be more than superfluous, therefore, for me to inflict another upon you today. Yet I should like to say here again today, in briefest possible form, some of the things which I have said before, and most of all to express my profound conviction that the University of Chicago has at this time within its grasp an extraordinary opportunity of service to the cause of education and of human welfare. The solid foundations laid under previous administrations, the extraordinary devotion of the Board of Trustees to the interests of the University, the not less remarkable harmony of the Faculty, with an entire freedom from cliques, or even of unseemly rivalry between schools or departments, the great city at our very doors, an inexhaustible source, both of students to teach, and of means with which to endow instruction and research, our world-wide reputation and

21

relationships, the high ideals and broad vision which we may justly claim, characterize both trustees and faculty, constitute a combination of opportunities and of forces adapted to meet them, that quicken my imagination and stir my blood each time I think of them. It is true that many of the opportunities that I have in mind will require years in which to come to realization. Indeed, a University, like the world of the ancient Greek philosopher, is always becoming, never is. But this does not diminish the significance of these opportunities, even for me. For I long ago decided that anything that could be finished in my lifetime was necessarily too small an affair to engross my full interest. It is therefore with a joy but little dimmed by considerations based on the year of my birth, that I look forward with you to the future of the University.

Acceptance of the Office of President
Convocation, 31 August 1923

"LOVED SHE NOT TRUTH AND HONOR MORE"

BURTON

I want to speak to you today of some of the things for which the University stands and will stand in the future, and for which we hope you will stand.

The University will stand for scholarship. That is an essential characteristic of a University, without which it is a University in name only. A business house may stand for honesty and service and quality of goods. But it does not stand for scholarship. An amusement hall may stand for clean, healthful amusement, relaxation and refreshment of view. The University stands for scholarship, and it is no place for those who are not interested in scholarship.

But let me remind you what scholarship is. It is not pedantry. It is not dry-as-dust facts. It is primarily an attitude and secondarily an achievement. It is an interest in knowing things, a desire for truth, an insatiable curiosity, not about the trivial and the unimportant, but about the great things of the world and of human life. As an achievement, it is the acquisition of knowledge, and still more, a confirmed attitude of open-mindedness toward truth and acceptance of it.

You will learn to sing the Alma Mater and to say of the University:

> She could not love her sons so well
> Loved she not truth and honor

That is the spirit of scholarship and it is the spirit of the University.

The University will stand for the ideal of a symmetrical and well-balanced life. It is primarily a place for hard work. There is no room for the idler here. Amusement is not our principal business. I once asked a professor in a European University what it was necessary for a student to do in order to get a degree in his University. His answer was, only not to forget what he knew when he came. That is not our spirit—unless you have come here expecting to work hard you have come to the wrong place. But we do not expect you to spend all your waking hours in study. There is room here for social contact of student with student, time for you to look after your health, and the cultivation of your manners. We believe in Physical Culture and Athletics, we believe in social intercourse and recreation. But we believe in them all as agencies of education and as concomitants of the principal business of the place.

The University will stand—more I think in the future than in the past—for interest in and concern for the individual. We are determined to escape from the tendency to a mere mass education, which is so strong today and the almost inevitable result of the great demand for education. We do not expect to know you as so many hundred freshmen. We expect that in the case of each of you there will be at least one officer of the University who will know you as an individual and counsel with you as a friend whom he knows and understands.

On the other hand the University will aim to create a community consciousness. You are all individuals, each with an individual consciousness. But you are even more truly members of a community, parts of a social organism. You are not simply preparing for life; you are living, and preparing to live only as each stage of life is a preparation for the next. We hope therefore that you will feel yourselves responsible members of this community, and will take part in all phases of its life, learn to do team work, acquire the art of social living.

The University will stand for character—high moral character. I have said that scholarship is an essential characteristic of the University. But it does not follow that it is the most important element of its life. High character can never entitle the student to the University degree if there be not also scholarship. But neither can any amount or degree of scholarship atone for the lack of character. We are engaged in the business of producing men and women who can play honorably and efficiently their part in life, and we know they cannot do this without high character. Therefore we desire to create an atmosphere calculated to develop character. And we hope you will yourselves not only respond to such an atmosphere but will help to create it. We invite you all to take your part in creating and maintaining the moral standing of the University community.

Finally, the University will stand for religion. I shall not stop to define the relations between religion and morality. Suffice it to say that religion is something more than morality, and that the University will stand for both. Nor shall I stop to define the precise type of religion for which it will stand. In fact, it is not primarily concerned with that. What it is concerned with is that no life, whether of individual or community is complete or symmetrical without religion. I doubt if there was ever a time in the history of the world when the need of religion as an element of human life was more evident than it is today, or when leading minds were more frank to affirm its indispensableness. . . .

But it is not because it is the fashion of the hour that the University will stand for religion. It will stand for it because we believe that the whole history of the race shows, and never more clearly than now, that learning and religion can never be safely divorced. Each needs the other. Religion needs the free atmosphere of the University to keep it from becoming superstition or bigotry. Learning needs religion to keep it from becoming selfish and pedantic.

The University will therefore stand for both—not to prescribe for you the type or character of your religion—not to impose on you creed or ritual, but by its chapel and its Sunday service and in various other ways constantly to remind you that religion self-chosen, self-directed, unconstrained individual and social, is an essential element of the highest end of life.

It is in a University that will stand for scholarship, for a symmetrically developed life, for consideration for the individual, yet for the cultivation of a community spirit, for character and for religion—it is in a University that stands for these things that I welcome you to full membership, and I hope that every day you spend here will add to the richness, fullness and depth of your life.

Anniversary Chapel, 1 October 1923

BURTON

This, then, is what I am trying to affirm: that in this age of the world, characterized as none other has ever been by research, an age which by virtue of that fact has made greater progress in acquiring knowledge of the world and of how to live in the world than was made in twenty centuries before—in this age of the world in which commercial enterprises have the far-sightedness and breadth of mind to establish institutions of research, there is a place for the university and a duty to be discharged, which neither the college, nor the professional school of science or medicine or technology, nor the specialized research laboratory, can achieve.

Chicago Association of Commerce and the
University Club of Chicago, 1923

BURTON

What, then, is to be the future of our University, and what does it fall to us to do for the future? To this question the Faculty and Trustees have given earnest attention for the last year and a half, and we think now that we see the answer to it. A part of that answer I want to share with you this morning.

First, we shall continue the policy which we have followed from the very beginning, of combining research for the purpose of adding to the world's knowledge in various fields of learning, with instruction looking to the education of the young people who come to us as students. This is a relatively new conception

25

of the business of a university. There have always been teachers who have also been productive scholars, but it is only within less than half a century that, in this country at least, universities have definitely included research as a part of their function, and there are relatively few that do so now. This, however, has always been our conception of our business, and we shall continue to hold it.

In the second place, we are clear that the principal task of these next years is to make a better University. I think I may justly say that the University has always been supremely concerned for the quality of its work. But we have reached a time when that is practically our only concern. Once numbers were important to us; for we could not maintain the quality of our work without a reasonable growth in numbers. That is no longer the case. Serious decline in numbers might be serious, but not a stabilized number. It is for quality that we must now be concerned.

But there is another reason why we put all our emphasis on betterment. We are here not simply to educate the students within our walls. In various ways we have always aimed to extend our influence and our helpfulness far beyond our own quadrangles and to make a constant contribution to education in the country and even the world at large. But we can certainly do this most effectively by making our education better. Every institution that does a thoroughly good piece of work helps all its sister-institutions. To have larger classes carries with it no such benefit to others.

Moreover, the great need of this hour is not more education or education for more students, but better education. In no country or age of the world was there ever so large a proportion of young people in school as in America today. Perhaps we have pretty nearly reached the point of saturation so far as concerns numbers. But we are very far from having attained our goal in point of quality. It is here that we must exert ourselves now. And on this we shall lay our emphasis.

This effort at betterment we shall extend to every part of our educational work and to our research. We shall be continually trying to do all our work better for graduates and undergraduates, in the Colleges and the Graduate School and in the Professional Schools.

Anniversary Chapel, 1 October 1924

A BUILDING CENTRAL AND DOMINANT

BURTON

When in 1910 Mr. John D. Rockefeller, Sr., pledged to the University his final gift of $10,000,000 to be paid in ten annual installments, he stipulated that not less than $1,500,000 should be spent for the erection and furnishing of a University Chapel, and added, "As the spirit of religion should penetrate and control the University, so that building which represents religion ought to be the central and dominant feature of the University group." . . .

The erection of this beautiful and lofty building "the central and dominant feature of the University group" (of buildings) will not only afford the University a much needed place of worship and typify impressively the supreme place which religion fills in life and which the University accords to, but will be a contribution to the architectural development of the country not unworthy to be compared with that which was made by the World's Fair in 1893. Here in a building scarcely surpassed in dignity and charm by any old world cathedral, the University Community will gather on weekdays and on Sunday, to join in dignified and inspiring worship, to be uplifted by the great religious music of the ages, and to listen to the messages of the great living preachers. One cannot easily overestimate the contribution which this building will make to the higher life of the University. It will be the vital throbbing heart of our whole University community.

"The University of Chicago As It Should Be in 1940:
A Confidential Statement by the President," 1925

THE SOLE LORD OF LEARNING

MASON

One notes with interest the recent efforts at rating the higher institutions of learning throughout the country. You will be gratified to know that the Hughes report which has recently appeared gives the University of Wisconsin first place among state universities for scholastic achievement (Productive Scholarship) and the University of Chicago first place, running neck and neck with Harvard, and if we wished to be a bit snippy about it, just a bit better, among private schools.

Having spent my life with you Badgers, I address myself tonight in your hearing to our new Chicago friends specifically. We Badgers cannot speak too appreciatively of the spirit of service which motivated Chicago's founder, John D. Rockefeller, its first president, William Rainey Harper, his successors, the trustees, and the unselfish donors who have made its existence and continued growth possible. The spirit of freedom that characterizes the University, and the significance of this for the building up of right habits of thinking cannot be overemphasized. The contribution that it has made to the development of aesthetic taste, in part through the agency of its own architecture is not inconsiderable. Buildings were formerly constructed and ornamented afterwards. Now, beauty is recognized as the adaptation of structure to function. Just as the architect has found that beautiful design must be part of efficient use; so our education must be for use and not merely for ornament. Its ornamental character will result from its functional character—actual usefulness—fidelity to purpose.

The function of the University is the search for truth, and the training of men for this search. More Doctors of Philosophy are sent out from the University of Chicago than any other university in the country. They are the men who are adding to human knowledge. A harmony of knowledges, a reconciliation of contradictions emerges. . . .

In fact it is due to . . . these ardent research workers, that the great truths in natural science and social science are emerging, that life is being rationalized. From deeper insight comes a harmony of knowledge, a reconciliation of apparent contradictions.

Science and religion have at last recognized that one supplements the other and that the simple truths of science are as necessary to religion as the truths of religion are necessary to science. We are coming to an age of better understanding.

Alumni of University of Wisconsin and
University of Chicago (Milwaukee)
14 December 1925

MASON

However emphasis in subject may shift from decade to decade, the spirit of the work of the whole University will always be given by its traditions and ideals of high attainment in creative scholarship. In its Graduate Schools, and also in its Undergraduate Colleges, the University's effort is to educate for deeper insight, not to train in the practice of a formalism. The latter course is always tempting, as the easy way in classroom procedure, both graduate and undergraduate. In the graduate work and certainly in the Senior College as well, the students must study subjects, rather than take courses. The overemphasis on course taking is widespread, and many a college student seems to feel that he must die without knowing anything about a subject, unless he has taken a course in it.

Recent years have seen many expressions of dissatisfaction with the results of the American undergraduate colleges. We are in a period of wholesome self-examination and experimentation for means of vitalizing the intellectual life of the undergraduate. Under the leadership of Dean Wilkins much has been accomplished at Chicago, and the work will continue under Dean Boucher. The dominance of the University by the spirit of performance gives promise for the future, as the emphasis is placed still more on opportunity, and less on compulsion. Interest thrives on responsibility and opportunities for initiative, and in our Undergraduate Colleges, with a background of creative scholarship given by the Graduate Schools, we may well go far in abandoning any methods which seem to be based on the assumption that the undergraduate goes to college to resist an education. The American undergraduate shows great interest and energy in his self-managed extracurricular affairs—the so-called "student activities." Our goal will be reached when, in this sense of the word, the intellectual work of the College becomes a "student activity." Under such conditions the Undergraduate College will stimulate, as it is stimulated by, the work in graduate teaching and research.

The University, as its motto indicates, exists for the enrichment of life through the growth of knowledge. Man has undertaken the great adventure of discovery, and his knowledge of nature has grown by leaps and bounds through the technique of learning which we call the scientific method. By his application of pure scientific research he has gained control of vast forces, and is being rapidly released from physical drudgery. The success of the scientific method has been so striking that it has determined the very temper of our mentality. The body of detailed knowledge has become enormous. But the process is not that of heaping complexity on complexity. As knowledge grows, great simplifications appear.

The development of our knowledge of the physical universe is a startling example. But three centuries ago, Galileo dared challenge the authority of Aristotle, and appealed to experiment to initiate the science of the mechanical behavior of matter. With rapidity knowledge was gained in the great chapters of physics—mechanics, sound, heat, light, electricity, and magnetism. And as knowledge grew the great simplifications emerged. Sound was recognized as a mechanical behavior, heat as a molecular mechanical behavior. Magnetism became electricity, and light an electrical phenomenon. Then with a burst of speed came knowledge of the great unity. Matter itself is an electrical complex, and all behavior of matter describable as electrical behavior—one law in the atom and the universe. The universe itself a living unit, each atom, each electron, bound to every other.

And now man studies himself. Released from the prejudices of an extreme egocentricity, released from fear of the truth, he shall obtain self-mastery, through self-understanding, adequate to the direction of the forces of nature which are at his command.

We have faith that as self-knowledge grows, the result will again be, not the heaping of complexity upon complexity, but the recognition of underlying simplicities.

With a growing conception of the unity of the physical universe, and the essential unity of life, the conviction grows that man is traveling a true path toward the great goal—an understanding of the mystery of existence.

For no lesser purpose do mathematicians and biologists, psychologists and humanists, devote their lives in the quest for truth. For no other ultimate purpose does this University exist.

Convocation, 15 June 1926

MASON

Some years ago I looked up the definition of the word "humanist" and found the following in a rather old edition of Webster's dictionary: "Humanist: one who is versed in polite literature." I quote that today to indicate how rapidly the temper of mind has changed in regard to the activity of the humanist.

Today unity pervades all the activities of a great research institution like the University of Chicago. We may separate men into groups as humanists or as scientists, but they are closer than ever before in spirit of performance. They are making steps toward a common goal—the understanding of man and his place in the universe. The humanist today studies the works of man to obtain deeper insight into his mentality and evolution of his culture. The humanist studies by the aid of a technique that is thoroughly scientific.

The University of Chicago is dedicated to a program of the understanding of man and of nature. It is the hope of all connected with it that it be stimulated in all of its departments, undergraduate as well as graduate, by the spirit of investigation in the scientific manner, and that increasingly, year by year, its students may receive an education which is vitalized by opportunity to participate in the program of productive scholarship of the University.

Wieboldt Cornerstone Ceremony, 14 December 1926

"IT MUST BE OUTSTANDING OR NOTHING"

MASON

Chicago is the pioneer. It must be outstanding or nothing. There is no reason for its existence as just another university. We do not desire to do things that are new just because they are new, but to be unafraid and to do things that are new if they are for the best interests of research and education in America. There are no obstacles to such a program. I am deeply impressed by the truth of that statement. I was told it when I came. I have learned it in a new sense every week. I think that there is no other institution of anything like the magnitude of this University which in its component parts is so wonderfully unified, in spirit of performance and in direction of purpose. This great instrument is easily directed. We have the ability within this group to direct it, and if we will study our problems together with fresh viewpoints, with the feeling that we are literally unhampered by tradition, there is nothing impossible in research and education for this institution.

We must experiment. However carefully we may plan, we shall make mistakes, but we must keep trying. We are a fresh, young, vigorous group, with the inspiration of President Harper's genius as our tradition—a tradition to be without crystallized policies, a tradition of fresh vision, of new methods, and of courage.

There is plenty of research in American institutions. There is not enough really significant research. There are plenty of graduate schools in America, and the attendance in them is growing by leaps and bounds. Where lies our special function in research and graduate work? Evidently in a willingness to discount the mediocre, to have no interest in numbers of graduate students for the sake of numbers, to have no interest in amount of publication of the Faculty for the sake of the amount, but to have every interest in seeing that the best work of which the Faculty is capable is encouraged, is really produced, and is brought to its proper influence in America. We must see that the quality of our graduate school improves regardless of its quantity of students.

Trustee-Faculty Dinner, 12 January 1927

MASON

We shall not forget education. We all believe that in the combination of research, education, and service to the community there really does lie the basis of a wholesome existence of the University.

We in Chicago believe that the skeleton of it all is productive scholarship, and that as that skeleton is clothed with flesh it takes the outlines of a real education, a human education, an education in which through the solution of problems there comes the ability to meet the problems of life. We are not primarily an institution to perform civic service in the community, but that we must perform civic service to a certain degree is evident if we are to keep our contacts fresh, to keep our work in touch with real life, and to prevent ourselves from promoting a scholarship which is dead.

Trustee-Faculty Dinner, 12 January 1928

MASON

Chicago is a remarkable university—in process of becoming, let us hope, far more remarkable. We say the words often, but each week they come with a deeper meaning. There is a freshness about the institution, a frankness in communication between its members, a fellowship greater than I had ever observed elsewhere; and that is the necessary background for any achievement.

The first thing beyond this sort of feeling that struck me was the sanity of effort throughout the different divisions of the University. I think of a phrase in a letter of John Manly's that I received the other day. He said: "I am working at an authoritative text of Chaucer. That is not my goal or my aim; it is merely an incident in my curiosity." The phrase is good, and I think it illustrates the temper of mind of most of our workers. They are working with a purpose on problems that are incidents in their curiosity. But there does not fail here that synthesis by virtue of which the work receives constant rechecking. For value, tangible value, to human life there is only one final yardstick. In physics there are many different units—units of time, of length, of mass—but in the final evolution of human effort there is only one measuring unit—it is the unit of human happiness. Every bit of activity is to be measured in that unit. I am convinced that the measurement will be large, because of those two tendencies within the group—the tendency of reality of purpose in productive scholarship, with that of evaluation and synthesis. I hope it will always remain so.

We were met when I came here by the problem of expansion. We always will be met by the problem of expansion. It has been decided that the University of Chicago is to be always in a period of development. Effort must not be lacking in the manner which seems the most wholesome to secure understanding for the University in the community. The day is past for support by pressure. It is remarkable today to see the enthusiasm with which men not acquainted with the technicalities of scientific effort meet the presentation of the aims of science and become enthusiastic supporters of the work.

I believe that in the last ten years, and in the last five particularly, America has been waking up to the meaning of research work—the meaning of new knowledge—with a rapidity that is simply startling. That means much for this institution, an institution whose future depends upon the understanding by the community of its aims and purposes. Nothing can be substituted for that understanding; and everybody—not just a few—should have the problem particularly in hand. Every one of the Trustees and of the Faculty must feel that as a major responsibility on himself, that the spirit of scholarship may be made understandable to men competent of supporting this wonderful work, and to whom the support and the knowledge of the work will be a great happiness.

What, then, is the function of an endowed institution such as the University of Chicago? Evidently to do something different. The normal processes of democracy do not work with high efficiency. Chicago might be the dirty, ill-kempt city it always was; it could have left its broad planning to the officials of the city. But the Chicago Plan Commission, the Commercial Club, the Industrial Club, the volunteer organizations in this unusual community, have been the ones to lead, to press forward, and, unhampered, have made possible this great progress.

So it is with the endowed institution. It is a free institution. When it becomes not free, by virtue of its own inertia or its own traditions, it ceases to have its value. When it becomes merely another university it ceases to have its value. It must be a leader or stop. There is no excuse for the existence of any mediocre department in the University of Chicago. The Trustees and the departments are wasting valuable money if they merely do things in the same old way and do not show the leadership that their opportunities have given them.

Farewell Address to the Faculties, 1 June 1928

A SPIRIT OF INQUIRY IN EDUCATION

HUTCHINS

In addressing myself to the graduating class this morning I wish specifically to apply to you and to this University those familiar phrases which constitute all that can be said to a graduating class. It is far easier to talk about the economic crisis, about the political situation, or about the educational program of the University of Chicago than it is to face the dreadful task of uttering once again those ancient platitudes which from time immemorial have been showered on the heads of departing students. To tell you that you stand on the threshold of life, that this is commencement and not termination, that the University is a miniature of that great world in which everyone of you is expected to do his duty cannot be news to any of you. Yet all these things are true. Our business is to give them life and content by considering them in relation to the University of Chicago and to you, its graduates of today.

Devotion to Truth

This process requires us to ask what the distinguishing characteristics of the University of Chicago are. And we observe in the first place that the University has always been devoted to inquiry. When Mr. Harper was asked to be its first President he made it clear that he had no interest in the project if the founders proposed another college. If, however, their purpose was to establish a great university in the Middle West, he was prepared to devote his life to it. On the day on which the University opened it was obvious that it was and was to be a university. The character and interests of the faculty, the character and background of the students indicated that this was not simply another institution for the instruction of the young. It was an institution for the advancement of knowledge. We know the result. We know that the roster of great scientists, investigators, and discoverers is filled with those who either as teachers or as students have borne the name of this University. No institution in so short a time has made such contributions on so vast a

35

scale. The fact that today half its students are college graduates carrying on advanced work reflects the continuation since 1892 of that spirit of inquiry with which the University opened.

That spirit has informed the University's teaching. The changes that Mr. Harper introduced were the result of an attempt to inquire once again into the processes of the higher learning. The fresh view that he took of university aims and methods produced a reconstruction in educational institutions the influence of which is still felt. The business of taking a fresh view is one in which the University has been almost continuously engaged since Mr. Harper's day, and one in which it will always be engaged. Its new educational program is not, therefore, a violent eruption on its placid surface. It is the result of that spirit of inquiry in education which has characterized the University from the beginning. And so I hope that this present program will not be the last word the University will utter on education in America. It cannot be. The tradition of inquiry will compel the constant investigation of education as it has compelled the investigation of everything else.

A Declaration of Independence

Inquiry at the University of Chicago has been free inquiry. The University has been independent. From the outset it has been free from state or municipal domination. From the outset there was no religious qualification for membership in its faculty. The religious organization that founded it has now voluntarily relinquished its formal control. At no time has the denomination as such attempted to exert actual control. The constitution of the University therefore has given it independence. The attitude of the Trustees, the faculty, and the administration has been independent. At the beginning Mr. Harper left no room for doubt on this question: there could be no interference with freedom of thought, speech, or teaching as long as he was President. This attitude the University has consistently maintained in times of hardship and prosperity, in the face of criticism and pressure. The University has never had any ax to grind; it has refused to be a grindstone for anybody else.

That the University believes in independence is evidenced anew by its present educational scheme. The student is offered the realms of learning to explore at will. He is not required to do anything. At entrance he stops being taught and begins to learn. His education depends upon himself. He does not have to accept the views of his professors or conform to any social, religious, or political creed. The University believes in independence for others as well as for itself.

Determined to Do Something

The third characteristic of the University of Chicago is enthusiasm. The University has believed that something can be done. It has enthusiastically entered into the life of the community. It has enthusiastically developed or accepted new ideas. There has never been anything contemptuous, defeatist, or indifferent about it. It has never cared to be respectable, still less conventional. It was founded by young men in a hurry. The University has been unwilling to indulge in calm contemplation of a suffering world. At Hull House, at the University Settlement, in public affairs in Chicago, on national commissions, in surveys of school systems the country over, the members of the faculty have partaken of the woes and struggles of our people. Today you find them here and everywhere directing, advising, participating in movements designed to advance the welfare of mankind. The University's interest in ideas has prevented it from becoming a stronghold of reaction like the English universities in the eighteenth century, which, as Lecky shows, opposed every great step demanded by the English intellect. By the same token the University has declined to remain self-satisfied in the knowledge of its own deficiencies. When generations of experience have convinced the faculty that something ought to be done, it has done it, even though vested interests were dislodged and old idols destroyed. We have heard ever since I can remember, for example, that the credit system was the curse of education in America. I have never met anybody who had a good word to say for it. Nobody had ever done anything about it. Nothing could be done about it. The University of Chicago decided that if the system was bad it ought to be changed. The University abolished it. That great academic characteristic of suspended judgment, of not doing anything until nobody wants it done, or until it ought not to be done, or until something radically different ought to be done has not infected this University. This University has behaved as a pioneer university ought to behave. It has enthusiastically determined that something could be done, and it has done it.

The Object of the University

The fourth characteristic of the University of Chicago has been its perpetual agreement with Cardinal Newman that the object of a university is intellectual, not moral. This is not to disagree with the attitude that moral values, high ideals, and strong principles must be among the results of education. The history of the University and this building are the best guaranty of this University's belief in these things. But universities are founded as places where scholars and their students may develop or exercise their intellectual powers. In universities and only in universities may this be done on the highest level. A university provides its students with rigorous intellectual training at the hands of stimulating individuals, surrounded by able, industrious, and intelligent contemporaries. It sets a standard of intellectual attainment that can only be achieved through those qualities that are commonly called "character." Character is the inevitable prerequisite and the inevitable by-product of university training. A system of education that produced graduates with intellects splendidly trained and no characters would not be merely undeserving of public support; it would be a menace to society. In a real university, however, such a result is impossible. The business of education in a real university is too exacting, too strenuous, and puts too high a premium on character for the student to be affected intellectually alone. Consider the implications of the new Chicago plan. The student is now free, and to learn how to be free may be said to be the first duty of the educated man. The student who by his own efforts in the face of the distractions of college life and a large city has prepared himself for the general examinations under the new plan has had an experience that will do more for his character than years of lectures on character-building.

If we are to make our people understand what a university is we must insist on that intellectual emphasis which distinguishes it from all other institutions. The universities have only themselves to blame if the public confuses them with country clubs, reformatories, and preparatory schools. As long as the conversation of universities is exclusively about athletics, dormitories, and the social life of students, they can hardly expect the citizen to understand that these things are merely incidental to a university program and do not at all affect its principal task. Indeed I should go so far as to say that the reason why the universities are successful in developing character is that they do not

38

go about it directly. If a university informed the world and its students that it would improve the morals, inflate the physique, and enhance the social graces of all who entered there it would in my opinion fail in these undertakings and it would also fail to provide a sound education. Character comes as a by-product of a sound education. The university method of developing it is to train intelligence.

These are, I think, some of the distinguishing characteristics of your University. They are rather splendid characteristics. You could wish no better ones for yourselves. Devotion to truth, the courage to be independent, an enthusiastic interest in the community and in new ideas, an intellect rigorously trained and being trained—these things in law, in medicine, in teaching, in preaching, in citizenship, will distinguish you as they have distinguished your Alma Mater. These qualities have never been in such demand as they are today. We know that cowardice, selfishness, and stupidity have brought the world to its present low estate. In opposition to these forces your University offers you the example of those qualities which is has displayed from the beginning. They are the qualities of leadership. For lack of leadership the whole world is in despair. How can it ever hope to find it if honest, courageous, unselfish, inventive, intelligent men and women do not emerge from universities like this?

You will most of you become citizens of that great region of which this city is the capital. This is the Middle Empire. Its development has hardly begun. Its significance as a cultural area is not yet appreciated. But its influence already determines national policy and will continue to do so. Here the qualities of leadership will be most telling. Here their absence will be more damaging to the country and to the world. If in this formidable territory at this formidable time you are to do your part, the characteristics of the University of Chicago must become your own.

"The Characteristics of the University"
Convocation, 20 December 1931

THE AIR IS ELECTRIC

HUTCHINS

The University of Chicago has never cared very much about respectability. It has insisted on distinction. Neither its faculty nor its trustees would be interested in it on any other terms. If the time comes when it is impossible for this university to set standards in education and to make significant contributions to the advancement of knowledge, there is no reason for its existence. The country does not need another university. It needs leadership in education and research.

To supply such leadership is a much harder matter now than it was in the '90s. Then the University rose swiftly to imperial honors in a burst of deficits. The same lavish hand that paid deficits has scattered abroad funds that have built up universities almost as great as the one those deficits created. This faculty has trained men and women who have gone out to lend distinction to other institutions. You will find more than fifty of them at Ohio State, and more than forty at Minnesota. In the activity in which we were long indispensable, the education of scholars, Michigan and Wisconsin are now more active than we. I am not here raising the question of quality. I am simply pointing out that the strange phenomenon of two state universities in the Middle West producing more doctors of philosophy than we do shows that there has been a change in our relative position. No longer can we claim to be performing an essential service merely because we do graduate work.

"The Future of the University."
Trustee-Faculty Dinner
10 January 1935

HUTCHINS

What is at that makes the University of Chicago a great educational institution? It is the intense, strenuous, and constant intellectual activity of the place. It is this activity which makes the life of the student an educational experience. Presented with many points of view which are the results of the candid and courageous thinking of his different instructors, he is compelled to think for himself. We like to think that the air is electric, and that from it the student derives an intellectual stimulation that lasts the rest of his life. This is education. . . .

This is the principal, if not the sole, function of an endowed university, to establish ever-new frontiers of education and research. The state universities can and will carry on the bulk of the educational and scientific work of this country. The disappearance of distances and of denominational differences means that no institution can rest a claim for survival on its peculiar location or its peculiar religious flavor. You can now get to Urbana in about the same time that it used to take Mr. Harper to drive to the Loop. Few Baptist families insist on Chicago for their children because of its denominational ancestry. The state universities are excellent and are rising every year to new heights. But I believe that they would inevitably deteriorate if it were not for the example and the inspiration of a few strong, endowed universities. The influence of the University of Chicago on public education in the Middle West is a matter of historic fact. Its foundation transformed into universities state institutions that had been called universities because they were larger than colleges and had professional schools attached to them. It may be thought that these institutions are now so strong that they could go on from strength to strength without Chicago to support them. This is a vain hope. Even with the example of the endowed universities before their eyes the politicians of this country have halted and mutilated some of the finest state universities in the country.

Fiftieth Anniversary. Citizens Dinner, 26 September 1941

HUTCHINS

My observation leads me to think that happiness lies in the fullest use of one's highest powers. Of course it is folly to talk of the fullest use of a man's highest powers if he is starving to death. You are in little danger of starving to death, at least you are if a world catastrophe can be avoided. Your advantages are such that you have a decided superiority over the great majority of your fellow-citizens when it comes to the sheer business of staying alive. Your problem lies in the moral and intellectual realm, in achieving the feeling that you have made the most of yourselves, that you have done the best you could, and that you have not let down yourselves or your fellow-men.

Here I hope that you will follow the example of your university. I still think, as I have thought for many years, that the motto of the University should be that line from Walt Whitman, "Solitary, singing in the West, I strike up for a new world."

Farewell. Student Assembly, 2 February 1951

KIMPTON

And this brings me to the purpose of the University. The University ought to provide service for the community and service for the nation. This it tries to do. It must try to do it better. But ultimate service of the University is not to be merely a handy repository of facts, it is not merely to be a think factory to which citizens may turn to get a think job done.

It is not merely to answer the questions which society asks. Its ultimate duty, its more difficult and more important task, is to determine what questions ought to be asked. It has to concern itself, therefore, not merely with the means to ends but with the ends themselves.

Accordingly it must bring to our society a perspective broader than the views of the day. It must provide cool, objective, appraisal of our problems, and it ought to propose new ideas for their solution. I dare to say that this is the University's highest service, particularly in times like these when one problem presses upon another and when so many of us are so caught up with urgencies that we have neither the time, nor the freedom from our own interests, to give to these problems the thorough study and detached evaluation which their solutions demand.

To provide the intellectual stimulation which our times require calls for both a sense of going somewhere and a sense of being understood. It involves also the willingness to consider controversial subject matter, for almost everything that is important is likely to be controversial whether it be in the area of government, economics, social programs, or international relations. The fact that so many of these important subjects are controversial cannot permit the University to shirk its duty in bringing to them whatever light may be found in scholarship and objectivity. The task of the University and its staff is to find out what is true. In this task the University's staff members will and must dispute with each other and with those outside the University, for truth is seldom come by merely through inspiration. Most often it comes as an evolution in the exchange of ideas.

Any University that holds itself resolutely to its task runs the risk of being unpopular and misunderstood by a large mass of the people. For the truth, indeed the search for the truth, is long, difficult, and sometimes unpleasant.

But the University does need to be understood, in terms of its purpose and in terms of the means it uses toward that purpose; and misunderstanding is largely our fault. The University can do more than it has done to explain itself, perhaps over and over again. It can avoid the external irritations, the appearance of aloofness or indifference which sometimes characterizes the intellectual world. It can learn to communicate its purpose and its high dedication to the betterment of its community and the world. The University of Chicago has not lacked and does not lack for pioneering spirit. But it does not yet have the understanding, at least at home, which it needs.

Commonwealth Club of Chicago, 17 May 1951

Kimpton

It is the great virtue of the University of Chicago that it does not tiptoe around its shortcomings. Perhaps we inherit this open, roistering quality from the great city that lent us its name —the city on the make. The winds of freedom blew open our doors sixty years ago, and they have been banging ever since. When we decide to relocate the A.B. degree, we relocate it with a sound like the prospectors of the Klondike locating a new claim. When we make a decision to develop a center for nuclear research, there is an explosion that sounds like the first shot on the sands of the Alamagordo. And when, twenty-five years ago, we opened up the first full-time medical school, you would have thought that lightning had struck the house of Hippocrates. This is our tradition of sound and fury, but with us it signifies something. It means a dynamic, even dramatic university that sees what needs doing and gets it done. Our mistakes have always been those of commission, never of omission. What we are, we are by commission and self-criticism. Self-criticism has its role even upon an occasion such as this. By self-criticism, we testify to our faith in ourselves and our tradition, and seek out a future even more lustrous than our past.

Trustee-Faculty Dinner, 9 January 1952

UNITY AND ONENESS

KIMPTON

The present University of Chicago owes its origin to the zeal of a relatively small group of enlightened men, motivated by the desire to see the Baptists have a college in the city as an outpost in the expanding west. It must be confessed also that another motivation was to rival those heretical Methodists up in Evanston. For the impetus to get this project started, they turned first not to Chicago but to the east and to the almost legendary figure who was lighting the lamps of the world, John D. Rockefeller. It has even been suggested that the motto of the University of Chicago should be "Praise John from whom oil blessings flow." It has been suggested more recently that this motto should be changed to "How Ford a Foundation."

Women's Club (Chicago), February 1952

KIMPTON

The greatness of the University of Chicago has come about by its adherence to three principles which together constitute our tradition. The first is our spirit of pioneering, which has expressed itself endlessly through our sixty-one years in the freedom, the vitality, and the novelty of our University. The spirit of adventure has always been a part of this institution and has shown itself in countless experiments which have opened up new modes of thought and action. The second part of our tradition has been the unity and oneness of the University. This expresses itself administratively that it may flourish academically. We have no discrete empires, because the world of the mind knows no nationalism. The University is organized so that ideas, no matter how diverse, may be exchanged by men, no matter how specialized. Finally, our tradition is one of great men. The criterion of employment or of promotion is not one of length of service or administrative favoritism. "Is he good?" is the only relevant question, and always will be. It is for this reason that we have gathered from all parts of the world a great staff of teachers and scholars. This is the tradition of which your new Chancellor is the proud custodian. He will succeed if he can preserve it and solve within it the problems of our University in these troubled times.

State of the University. Address to Senate
14 October 1952

KIMPTON

Last year in my first report to you I said that when we take annual stock of ourselves we should have two questions uppermost in mind.

Have we sensed and properly evaluated the significant problems of the present? Have we, in solving our problems, been guided by the most luminous parts of our tradition? Thus, to report that we had encountered no significant problems during a year would be to report that we had died; and to report that we had found altogether new answers to our problems would be to report that we had never lived. As far as the state of a university is concerned, either would be bad, and neither will happen to us if all the coming years are like the past year, which was, objectively speaking, not without animation.

In fact, the newspapers have long since reported to the nation that in the year 1952–53 we were alive, had problems, and treated them in the best tradition of the University of Chicago, at least so far as rhetorical ornamentation is concerned. But that kind of reporting on the affairs of the University during the past year does not simplify our basic task today. For when we report to ourselves in retrospect we must do more than list the problems we have already confronted. We must do even more than give ourselves quiet assurances that these problems at the time were treated in the unsubdued style long-ago developed by the several debating societies of our faculty and students. Our basic task, I repeat, is to review the past year with two questions uppermost in mind. Did we sense the significant problems of the moment at the moment? Were we guided toward a solution of our problems by something larger than the moment—by the most intrinsic part of our tradition? We must ask these questions because the University is the result of something more than good fortune, industry, and talent. It has also been built upon a foundation of principles. . . .

From our community let us turn to our University. I ask you from time to time—as I ask myself frequently—not to forget its

45

distinctive purpose amid the pressure of its problems. As a great university in the great industrial city of America, we have the opportunity, such as no other educational institution has, to advance knowledge and to translate it into action that will affect all aspects of our way of life. This was the dream that Harper had both day and night, and we should see that each year brings it closer to fulfillment.

State of the University, 10 November 1953

EXCITEMENT, REBELLION, HUMANE VALUES

KIMPTON

There are times, I must admit, when life at the University is a bit too exciting; times when a little less stimulation would be welcomed by the Chancellor if by no one else. People at Chicago take every issue seriously—from the size of the orchestra at the Washington Prom, to the absurd statements made by the visiting Professor of Hittite at his Friday afternoon lecture. All concerned (and usually many who have no legitimate reason to be concerned at all) have volumes to speak on any subject. Faculty, students—even administrators and staff—at an energetic, productive, pioneering institution like ours tend to be people who are not content to "let George do it." I have been told that you can tell a Harvard man the minute he walks into a room because he acts as if he owns it; you can recognize a Yale man because he acts as if he doesn't care who owns it; in the same way you can spot a Chicago man easiest of all because when he walks in he immediately starts rearranging the furniture!

Now you can't do much furniture rearrangement without occasionally coming up with some unhappy combinations. You alumni have had—and occasions will surely arise in the future when you will again have—sound reason to get good and mad at your alma mater. When we make a mistake it is seldom just a common, garden-variety error; when we make a mistake it tends always to be—in the words of the late Mayor LaGuardia—"a beaut." I don't believe that this proves us to be uncommonly inept. The mistakes we make stem from the same source as our virtues. Our errors stem from our real concern for the real world; from our immense desire to learn, to know, to do; from our overwhelming curiosity; from our restless, impatient search for new ideas, new discoveries, new ways of interpreting and carrying out man's search for truth.

That concern and restlessness, however, is also the reason for our existence. The community has not established the University (and you don't support it) simply to confirm and mirror that which already exists. It is our job to go out on a limb; to encourage students to become free, self-reliant individuals; to provide an environment for those whose minds question every facet of our existence, analyze it, understand it, and produce new ideas about it. This is not an irresponsible search and Chicago is not an irresponsible university. Quite the reverse. Precisely because we feel so strongly our responsibility to you the alumni, to our students, to the Midwest and to the whole world of truth and learning, we are willing to take risks and depart from the well-worn paths in order to find something new and better.

Alumni Meeting, 9 May 1956

KIMPTON

A great university is also characterized by a particular kind of relationship to the society of which it is a part. If the role of a university is to meet the immediate or fancied needs of its community, as some professional educators would have us believe, then it becomes functional, vocational, and ultimately degraded, producing only useful gadgets and artisans and tradesmen. On the other hand, if the university is so cloistered that its teaching and research are without any relevance to the real needs of men and women, it is without impact and import. It is a fine line we walk, in careful suspension between heaven and earth, seeking out, with Plato's philosopher king, the clear form and beauty of the eternal ideas, but ever mindful of the shadows they cast upon the walls of the cave.

The great university must be efficient in an atmosphere of magnificent inefficiency. It must have an administrative structure instantly responsive to communication and productivity, and its administrators must rival those of industry in their ability to make quick, hard-eyed and correct decisions. Yet all of this structure and these people must be subordinated to a set of human and humane values that have nothing to do with efficiency and may seem to run counter to it. An economical university must be prepared to throw money away on things that do not seem to matter. It must be ready to make the big mistake, suspecting all the time that it is a mistake. It must insist on the dignity and rights of every man when often he is without dignity and deserves no rights. There was a member of this faculty who was to be dropped for incompetence at the end of his contractual period, but through a secretarial error he was made a full professor with tenure. And he was unaware to the day of his retirement of this phenomenal goof. A big university is big, for it has found that the petty meanness of immediate efficiency must yield to those larger human values that produce an ultimate efficiency.

The fourth thing that one always feels on the campus of a great university is an air of excitement, and I must say we have this in great abundance at the University of Chicago. A distinguished professor we were trying to hire recently told me he wouldn't dream of coming here because he would be so overstimulated that he would never get anything done. But if occasionally we lose a man on this account, we gain and retain many more. The quest for truth, like the chase, must be accompanied by baying hounds and tingling blood. And all this means at least two other things. The great university must be young, though this need not refer to chronology. It must be young in its ways and young in its thinking. It doesn't hurt to have a lot of kids around to help produce this spirit, but even the old in age must be young at heart. And what is more, an exciting university is not a particularly happy or well-adjusted institution. The great university, if it could be personalized, would be a fit subject for the psychiatrist's couch, and yet it would lose all its greatness if it were tortured into adjustment through analysis. It must always retain the excitement and rebellion, the maladjustment of youth, if it is to retain its quality. I have no idea where the general public gets the notion that behind the walls of ivy all is peace and quiet. A week without a revolution is a lost week, and if you don't believe it, look at the lined face and harassed eyes of the bedeviled administrator of one of these distinguished universities. For several reasons, it would be fitting to call them "mental institutions." But sedation is for sissies, and in the great universities chaos must continue.

There is a final characteristic that is a part of a great university, and I find it peculiarly difficult to put into words. The great university has a sense of direction, but you have to watch this one. It should not know too completely and too finally where it is going. There are no accurate road maps in the traveling that the mind must do, and any university that knows exactly where it is going is going no place. The final goals and ultimate objectives of education should be constantly redefined in the process of trying to realize them. A great university cannot be static; it is either moving forward or it is going in reverse. In the process of moving forward it must have a general sense of direction, but this has to be kept very general indeed. There are many roads that lead to Rome, and Rome always turns out to be a very different place from what you thought and also a place that is only a pause in the journey. The neat blueprint of a curriculum, the exact formulation of the objectives of a scientific experiment, the final meaning and value of a program in the humanities, are things that never happen in a great university. I don't mean, of course, that, like Leacock's hero in *Guido the Gimlet of Ghent*, we should ride wildly off in all directions, but the direction that we go, like the navigation of a ship, is subject to constant adjustments for wind and tide and magnetic deviation. And the voyage, all the way along, takes on new and unanticipated meanings and values, and the destination is always beyond the last horizon.

These are intangibles that make and keep a university great. And perhaps they differ only slightly if at all from the basic things that make life itself significant and productive. A life without freedom is intolerable, and personal freedom deeply obligates one to respect the rights and dignity of others. It is a good thing to have your roots in the solid earth, but leaves should seek the sun and air. The good life too is a big life, quick and efficient in accomplishment but only in a larger context of human values. And life, if it is to be worth living, must be a great excitement, renewing itself endlessly with the new. The happy and successful man remains forever young, with all the enthusiasm and discord and rebellion of youth.

Convocation, 7, 8 June 1957

A SERIOUS CONCERN FOR EDUCATION

KIMPTON

What is general education? What is specialized education? And how are the two put together to form something called "liberal education at the undergraduate level"? The great debates of the University have centered about this subject for the last twenty-five years. We have located, relocated, and redefined degrees; defined, redefined, and reworked curricula; and we still are not sure of the meaning of our Bachelor's degree. We have more confidence in our graduate program, perhaps because we are one of the inventors of it in this country. But, even so, many changes have occurred that have been recorded in these reports. Committees, centers, institutes, and even departments have been liquidated and have been created; and we are still not too sure about the objectives and content of the Ph.D., the meaning, if any, of the A.M., and the appropriate relationship that should exist between all the academic organizational devices that we have inherited or invented. The reports, too, record enormous changes among the professional schools. Medicine was great and became greater, Law has shown a meteoric increase, Theology reorganized and redefined its mission, the School of Social Service Administration embarked on a program of serious research, and the School of Business decided to do for business education what M.I.T. did some years ago for engineering. But with all these changes we are none too clear about the relationships between the professional school and the rest of the university and between the professional school and the profession. . . .

This is not the picture of an ordinary university. Its origins, its past, its present, and its destiny have always escaped the traditional norms for institutional behavior. Since the times of Harper our demands, determined by boundless enthusiasm and ambition, have always exceeded our supply, and this is as it should be. By standing at the forefront of new science and scholarship and teaching, we have had to invent novel organizational forms properly to express ourselves, and understandably we are not always clear about these relations. When the times are out of joint for an area of knowledge, we do not accept it with complacency; we continue to build, ignoring the times, for the world of the mind is eternal. The stature of this extraordinary university judged by any standard is great, and the length of the shadow of its trials and troubles is correspondingly great. Our taking stock fills us with a sense of pride in our University and with a renewed dedication to resolve the problems created by our eminence.

State of the University, 5 November 1957

KIMPTON

For the last half century at least, we in the field of education are the only ones who have taken our profession seriously. It was thought, of course, to be a fine thing for the young person to go to college, but parental concerns related far more to social prestige than to intellectual accomplishment. And the professor was regarded at best as a kind of amiable lunatic who knew far more than anybody ought to know about things that didn't matter very much. At worst, the professor was thought of as a dangerous fellow who was trying to mold the minds of the impressionable young in directions that ran counter to the interests of the established order. Sputnik has changed all this and changed it dramatically. Education has suddenly become important and educators suddenly have an audience hanging upon their words.

The University of Chicago is one of the places from which these words should come. Universities are often neatly ranked by arbitrary criteria that leave true greatness unmeasured. Our strength lies in an intangible thing. This University is alive. One part speaks to another not out of institutional courtesy but out of intellectual curiosity. Our faculty is not the largest among the universities, but I challenge any institution to show me men and women more sincerely and effectively devoted to the pursuit of truth. Our library is not the biggest, but I defy anyone to produce a collection of books more thoughtfully acquired or more heavily used. I can show you universities with pleasanter surroundings, but name one that lies more completely at the crossroads of our country or one more successfully dedicated to maintaining the quality and health of its environment. If one chooses to pursue happiness, he may well seek it elsewhere; but if he wishes the happiness of pursuit he shall find it here.

Trustee-Faculty Dinner, 8 January 1958

KIMPTON

As this report suggests, it is a pretty good university all right, and, perhaps, in a few areas, it is the best there is. But it is not so good as it was thirty years ago, either absolutely or relatively. Perhaps this distinction of relative and absolute is one without a difference, for the simple reason that there are a lot more good universities today than there were thirty years ago and that the number of great scholars and scientists has not increased in proportion to the number of present-day distinguished institutions competing for their services. These past thirty years have marked the rise of the state university as a major force in American higher education, particularly in the middle and far western parts of our country. For example, Indiana, Illinois, Wisconsin, Minnesota, Michigan, and California at Berkeley are today spending more money on their acquisition programs for their libraries than is Chicago; Harper remains a great library, but primarily because of materials purchased before 1925, which are no longer obtainable. It is a good thing to have the states take higher education seriously, but it creates a new and tough competitive situation for the private university.

It was this kind of musing that led me to the question: How can the University of Chicago remain a great university and indeed increase its stature in the time to come? The question is an obvious one, and the generalized answer is equally obvious: We have to do what we decide to do superlatively well. But, as we break this general answer down, its components are not so obvious or so easy to implement.

We need first to recognize that the University of Chicago is now and will have to remain a small institution. . . .

. . . The very fact that we are a private university, accountable to the law and our own conscience, gives us a real advantage over our public sisters. We are not obligated to establish a school of engineering because there is a local need for it, or a course in harbor management because of the St. Lawrence Seaway. And there is good reason why we should take a long look at some of the things we are now doing to see if they are worth doing or if we are doing them well. Mediocrity is the single intolerable thing; when we find it, we must eliminate it if we are to survive as a great university.

As a kind of footnote to this observation, let me give you some dangerous thoughts my musings led me toward. I, and a lot of other well-intentioned people, have long thought of the great private university as the pioneering, the innovating university. I still think so, but I also think it timely to inject a note of caution. Research is a patient, plodding, cumulative process, occasionally lighted by a flame of genius. Even the brilliant work of Darwin, which we commemorate this year, was built upon observations and thinking which long preceded him. And there is no substitute in great teaching for the learning and contagious enthusiasm of the teacher, though these fundamental virtues may be assisted by curricular and methodological innovation. Solid excellence must accompany innovation if it is to be significant, and that breathless breakthrough often turns out to be a gimmick or a gadget that briefly dazzles those who are determined quickly to save the world. . . .

Our greatest handicap is our competition. When Chicago was founded, it towered above all other institutions west of the New England Seaboard. One did not associate Nobel Prize winners and Guggenheim Fellows with state universities, but this is a commonplace today. Here again, though, there is a ray of hope if we can maintain our character as a small institution dedicated to pure research and high-level teaching. The states, whether out of pride or necessity, are continually increasing their commitment to higher education within their borders. They are building new junior colleges and creating or absorbing new four-year institutions; by 1965 they will be swamped by students at all levels whom they are obligated to train. The single great university of the state runs a serious risk of being weakened by the ambitions of the more specialized and localized public institutions within the state, which have been very successful in their appeals to the legislature based on local pride and service to the local constituency. From the over-all viewpoint of the strength of American education, this tendency worries me, but it reinforces my conviction that we at Chicago should go right on being what we truly are and doing what comes naturally.

What are the virtues of our character? First and most important, we are an institution dedicated to basic research, with all that that implies. This sets the tone and creates the atmosphere that is Chicago. The teaching loads are light, the committee assignments are minimal, and the demands of the University that would distract a man from his primary responsibility are few. There is an easy communication across departmental lines, making for interdisciplinary research and leading naturally to institutes and committees which draw together men of diverse backgrounds who share a common research interest. Our system of government, too, is a sensitive instrument which allows for the easy flow of intelligence and counsel between faculty and administration and provides privileged information for the entire faculty. I use "privileged" here advisedly to remind us that the frank and open discussions which so mark this University can be ruined by those thoughtless or malicious ones who release such information to the public. And we are a rich university as private universities go. We have enough money through endowment income, gifts, and tuition receipts to do the things we need and want to do so long as we have a care about the size of the institution and the peripheral activities we engage in. Our salary average is one of the best in the country, and we are determined to make it the best. The Humanities and the Library are soft spots in our budget, and these we propose to remedy. But most important of all is the air of freedom, even of magnificence, that pervades the place. These are wise and good men who surround us, dedicated to the search for truth and in easy and free communication with one another. These are our assets, and these we must preserve and indeed exploit in the future.

State of the University, 3 November 1959

KIMPTON

There is a value in the harsh discipline of research that is as essential for the teacher as for the investigator. Even if one's interests lie solely in teaching, he should have firsthand knowledge of what learning really is, and there is no way to find out without making, or at least trying very hard to make, a contribution to learning. Moreover, the specialist has been badly misunderstood in these flippant days when too often untutored people make fun of him by saying he knows more and more about less and less. The successful specialist is one who brings an enormous amount of general knowledge to bear upon what may seem to be a small problem, but out of the solution to this problem our knowledge is increased and the human lot improves—which comes very close, incidentally, to the motto of our University—Let knowledge grow from more to more; and so be human life enriched. . . .

A great university is forever innovating because she is forever young. And youth is a time of freshness, of novelty, of deep emotional commitment to good things and great deeds. Our University has perpetual youth because she always stands on the frontiers of new knowledge, flushed with the spirit of adventurous inquiry. Our final debt to our alma mater can be discharged by forever remaining, like her, young of heart, adventurous in spirit, and inquisitive of mind.

Convocation, 10, 11 June 1960

KIMPTON

. . . I would like very seriously to suggest that the life of the mind, what Matthew Arnold called the scientific curiosity and I would call "the scientific passion," is an end in itself; it need have no responsibilities beyond its own fulfillment. I don't mean to suggest that the scholar and scientist should be without moral commitment. But I question whether this moral commitment should take an evangelical turn, transforming all its passion and energies into a missionary zeal. The scientific passion is by its nature critical; it endlessly questions itself along with everything else.

And it is this quality of critical detachment, I further suggest, that gives it its greatest power, even though indirectly, over the world of action. I remember someplace in Plato's *Republic* a disciple asking Socrates if the ideal state could ever be realized. The ancient philosopher admitted that it probably never could, but that as a prototype laid up in heaven, it could forever guide the ways of men, as they looked first down and then up, seeking to approximate the eternal.

Perhaps it is symbolic that Plato in later years so forgot his master's teaching that he attempted to create an ideal state in Syracuse and, according to tradition, was sold into slavery for his pains. But we should remember the *Republic* was a product of the Academy, and for two thousand years has moulded the minds of men.

Convocation, 16 December 1966

"ON THE TOP INTELLECTUAL LEVEL"

BEADLE

Speaking in very general terms, one can say that it is the purpose of a university to preserve, evaluate, understand, and transmit to future generations the best of man's total accumulated culture—its history, religion, art, music, literature, science, and technology. Additions are, of course, constantly being made to all of these, both through rediscovery and through new discovery. If the processes by which human culture evolves are to continue unabated, it is of the greatest importance that new generations understand and appreciate the ways in which these additions are made. The most effective way I know to do this is for the individual to participate in the process—to experience the incomparable thrill of original discovery, even if this be in a modest way only.

Inaugural Address, 5 May 1961

BEADLE

We hold a special position in the Midwest as the only private university with a long-sustained record of excellence . . . We began with excellence of an order not previously known in this country, to provide a major demonstration of the university concept. We set so good an example that we are no longer unique; many of our neighboring state and private universities are so good, that we do not loom solitary in the Midwest as we once did. But we still have something that they don't have—a free-swinging, daring, and experimental spirit of willingness to try anything promising. That is a spirit we must cherish.

"Thoughts of a New President." Trustee-Faculty Dinner 10 January 1962

BEADLE

In writing about the University of Chicago for a small publication to go to friends of the University later this month, Provost Edward H. Levi says:

A great university is essentially a viable community of great scholars who have discovered the magic of working separately and yet together in the successful pursuit of knowledge. At the heart of the University of Chicago is the faith of its founders, Rockefeller and Harper, in the power of the unfettered human mind and in the wholeness of knowledge. The hallmark of the University has always been its interdisciplinary nature and its faith in basic research. The dialogue among its scholars has been continuous—so much so that Alfred Whitehead, after a visit to the University of Chicago, characterized it as the nearest approach to ancient Athens in the modern world.

However far short we may now fall of justifying that characterization—and I believe it is not far—we must continue to narrow the gap. I have said many times, if we cannot remain among the top three or four of the some 1100 senior colleges and universities in the nation, we have little excuse for continued existence. Anything less than a role of leadership in the Midwest and the Nation fails to justify the faith of which Mr. Levi speaks so eloquently.

State of the University, 5 November 1963

BEADLE

If this University loses the ability to deliver as a pioneer on the top intellectual level, then except for a kind of momentum which might tide it over short periods of dullness, it will be through. For this reason, the University throughout the years has given the highest priority to faculty strength, and, as a consequence, to faculty salaries. . . . In recent years, in addition to faculty salary support, we have emphasized considerable scholarship and fellowship aid to students, and major support for the library, in an effort to make up for the alarming deterioration which took place during a long period of financial stringency. These priorities are a manifestation of our central aims.

Student Assembly, 18 November 1966

BEADLE

All of these, plus numerous other activities and accomplishments of members of the University, symbolize our basic objectives: namely, to increase knowledge, understanding, and wisdom; to disseminate these attributes of human culture, and to transmit them to the generations that will succeed us; and, finally, to teach others how most effectively to do likewise.

Trustee-Faculty Dinner, 11 January 1967

BEADLE

Let me now say a word about the special role of private universities. In many respects we in the United States are blessed with by far the strongest system of higher education in the world. I am convinced it is so in large part because it is a dual system of state-supported and private universities—both components made stronger by the competition for excellence between them. I believe there are trends that now preferentially favor tax-supported universities. Costs of education at all levels are rising at unprecedented rates, and state universities seem better able than their private counterparts to meet them.

One factor is that Federal support for physical facilities, given on a matching basis, can be qualified for by tax dollars by a state university or college—tax dollars matching tax dollars—while in private universities, private dollars are required. In addition, Federal agencies have been directed to take geographical factors into consideration in making grants to institutions of higher learning—to spread support more evenly. They seem to be doing it. I do not make a value judgment on these policies. I report them and consider some of the consequences. Let me illustrate by trends reported recently in *Science* magazine. If one considers National Science Foundation (NSF) fellowships by states relative to population and awarded solely on the basis of merit, six states have a disproportionately high number. Forty-two of the remaining forty-four are low. Obviously, the six are relatively very high. They are: Massachusetts, Connecticut, New Jersey, Illinois, Wisconsin and California. For the six high states, NSF research grants are *low* relative to fellows. But for all forty-two low states, grants are *high* relative to fellows. This clearly indicates the leveling trend that tends to make all universities equally good. Or, if one prefers to state it differently, it is a factor that tends to make them equally undistinguished.

If we consider the distribution of the top twelve universities, according to the 1965 American Council on Education ratings,

58

ten are in the six states I have named. Seven of the ten are private. The University of Chicago is the only one of these seven private universities between the Appalachians and the Rocky Mountains. Can we continue to play this kind of leadership role? It is a role which, I should add, is equally evident in areas other than science. There is wide consensus that we must—that any less than leadership in quality and independence is untenable in our context.

State of the University, 7 November 1967

LEVI

It is difficult to describe the modern university. It is apt to be large and complicated. It is hard, in any event, to be objective about one's environment and companions. Generalized descriptions may miss the mark. The balance within one institution between undergraduate and graduate teaching, research, the carrying on of the liberal arts tradition at all levels, including the graduate and the professional, and the assumption of responsibilities and service functions may be quite different from that at another. But certain points can be made, if not for all, at least for this one.

To begin with, the range of activities is enormous. It should not be necessary to make this point about the institution which had the first self-sustaining atomic pile, which manages the Argonne National Laboratory, and which has, as an integral part of its concern, hospitals where decisions of life are made every day. The range goes from nursery schools to postdoctoral training and guidance for the professions, the development of the most intricate of laboratories, the operation of educational enterprises in Asia and Latin America, the creation of some of the most significant centers in the world for the study of non-Western cultures. There still may be some popular belief that a university is mainly an institution to which the young are sent with the hope that they will not be too visible while they are growing up. But in general the community at large knows, and perhaps knows too well, that the research and actions of the universities are often pivotal to national security, public health and order, economic and industrial development, and that the understanding of other societies which may be achieved here may determine our ability to shape a peaceful world with them.

Usefulness has invited burdens. Necessity has compelled their acceptance. We are an urban university. Because the cities, states, and federal government have not solved the problems of urban blight and urban living, the universities within the cities have become instrumentalities for redevelopment. Our campus plan becomes the means for achieving a community plan. Our conception of the university has undergone a radical change. The university is no longer an island separated from a community. There is a sense in which the community has become part of the university, imposing upon the institution the requirements that in this new relationship it avoid officiousness and the assumption of powers which it does not have, on the one hand, and on the other, that as lines of autonomy fade the institution preserve its own identity.

The range of activities and the assumption of new responsibilities impose great burdens upon the institution. Even without these burdens a university would not meet the tests imposed by a moderately responsible management expert. Most universities are not planned in the sense necessary either for a business venture or a centrally controlled eleemosynary institution. And this university is planned less than most. The management of the University of Chicago, while ultimately in the hands of the Board of Trustees, in large part resides within the faculty, organized into a federal system of ruling bodies of divisions, schools, and the college, with subruling bodies of departments, collegiate divisions, institutes, centers and committees, and an overall council. But the most important ruling body in this structure, with the greatest power and freedom, and upon whom everything else depends, is the individual professor. The gentlemen who invented the phrase "administration," or, worse still, "central administration," as applied to the University of Chicago, were either unfamiliar with the university, or possessors of a great sense of humor. Yet somehow there is sufficient coherence to marshal and still not interfere with energy and creativity. This fact is recognized by industrial firms when they praise their own laboratories as having the freedom of a university. Three factors are involved. The first is the self-selection of the faculty, whose standards and abilities derive in part from the kind of education you are receiving. The second is the impetus of the character of the institution itself, including a recognition that the system will work only with a minimum of rules and regulations. And third, through discussions more or less rational at many levels, and through ceremonies of many different kinds, the institution each day rediscovers and informally redirects its aims. This kind of self-planning, which is so important to the spirit of this institution, is not easy to achieve, but is much more compelling than may be at first recognized, and it is a priceless asset worth preserving. In these matters Chicago is aided by its comparative smallness in numbers and by its location in a living as well as a working community. In a sense there is no such thing as "after hours" at this university.

"The Role of a Liberal Arts College within a University"
Liberal Arts Conference (Chicago), 4 February 1966

PATIENCE AND ZEAL

LEVI

There are certain characteristics which ought to distinguish a university from other institutions. There are additional characteristics which distinguish the University of Chicago. A university is old. It reflects the wisdom of man's knowledge and the error of his ways. A university is young. It reflects the excitement of discovery and understanding. A university is complex. It mirrors the search to comprehend man's nature, the social order, the very universe. A university is unified. It has a purpose. It treasures the cultural traditions of many societies so different and yet so much the same. One does not get to know a university or its work in an evening, in an orientation week, or for that matter in a lifetime. Just as a viable university must always try to know itself, so you will find your understanding of this place will grow and change, reflecting in part the change and growth which is in you. This process has already begun. It demands a mixture of zeal and patience, a mixture not easy to carry. . . .

There is a sense in which a university has a variety of purposes. It is an institution in the community and shares responsibilities with other institutions. There are a variety of housekeeping functions. If they are performed well, they can make life more pleasant. The university runs hospitals, legal clinics, offers psychiatric and psychological help within the public schools, and performs social service work. This is not just research, but service of the highest order. The friendship and concerns of those who live in the university community add dimensions to university life. Nevertheless, a university over a period of time acquires a dominant purpose and measure. This university from its very beginning has been highly articulate and conscious of its dominant purpose and its reason for being.

The University of Chicago exists for the life of the mind. Its primary purpose is intellectual. It exists to increase the intellectual understanding and powers of mankind. The commitment is to the powers of reason. Reason is the way, the means to an end, the indispensable tool. The life of reason is a difficult life. It requires clarity, intellectual rigor, humility, and honesty. It requires commitment and considerable energy. It requires that we ask questions not only of others but of ourselves. It requires that we examine not only the beliefs of others, but those newly acquired doctrines which all are prone to believe because they are held by the group we favor, or are the cherished inspirations which come to us in the middle of the night and which we are certain cannot be wrong. One does not proceed on this path through an act of faith alone; prior innocence is no protection. Habits of thought and searching intellectual honesty must be acquired and forever renewed. The standards of excellence are demanding, and excellence is required. To comprehend our cultural traditions, to appreciate the works of the mind, to see as well as others have seen, to know and express beyond the present limits of knowledge, to preserve and open the way of reason for others—these are the goals. The path is not an easy one.

Nor is it the only path. There are many ways to the good things in life. The university is only one institution among many. We cannot be all things. We must resist the temptation to demand all pleasant things for ourselves because we would enjoy them. As the great professor Robert Redfield said some years ago: "A university that represents itself as just like other agreeable places to spend time either is no university or is deceitful. A true university cannot reflect the total society in its tastes and interests. It has made a somewhat different emphasis in choosing among the many goods open to man." We must resist also the well-intentioned demands which are made upon us which would make us just another social or governmental agency. We must acknowledge that there are doubters—possibly some among you—and all of us at times are afflicted with these same doubts, concerning the life of reason and the life of action in these troubled times. Universities have often existed in troubled times, and often, including in this half century, when faith in reason has been lost. But the faith of a university and its inner integrity are never more important than in such periods of doubt.

I join with others in welcoming you to what we trust will be an exciting period of discovery and to that growth which will win for you the highest powers of man.

> "The Shape, Process, and Purpose of the
> University of Chicago." Class of 1971 Assembly
> 24 September 1967

LEVI

There are two other qualities of the University of Chicago. First, the university conceives of itself as dedicated to the power of the intellect. Its commitment is to the way of reason. It stands, as Robert Hutchins said, in perpetual agreement with Cardinal Newman that the object of a university is intellectual, not moral. This is not to say that adherence to reason, the self-criticism and discipline which this imposes, does not itself partake, indeed it requires, the highest morality. Second, it must be admitted the university has a mixture of traits, lovely and unlovely, arising out of the sense of its own importance and of its uniqueness. Perhaps this is the free-swinging enthusiasm of the Middle West —a response to those who thought this was an unlikely place for a university. Perhaps this arises because the university knows that its reason for existence is to be a model of excellence. Perhaps it arises out of the confidence that those who founded the university had in the overwhelming importance of knowledge. However objectionable these traits at times may be, they have given the university its willingness to innovate, to stand alone, and to endure. . . .

Perhaps, then, one should ask, "What is the service of this university?" The answer is traditional and old-fashioned. Its greatest service is in its commitment to reason, in its search for basic knowledge, in its mission to preserve and to give continuity to the values of mankind's many cultures. In a time when the intellectual values are denigrated, this service was never more required. I realize, of course, that in all this there appears to be a paradox. It is highly probable, although the subject is not a simple one, that given their choice of profession, training at the University of Chicago has increased the earning power of our students. Basic scientific work at the university could not help but have its impact upon industry. Our graduates do hold a variety of important positions in industry, in the professions, in teaching and in national laboratories. The university has been a center of self-criticism for our society. We did in fact play a major role in restoring and maintaining an integrated community, and the university's work has given leadership through example as well as study in urban affairs. And while our college is surely not free from the pressure of the discipline of learning, the combination of a research-oriented institution with a small undergraduate college has given us the opportunity for many of the qualities sought—and frequently sought in vain —by the small liberal arts institution. But these results are in fact dependent upon the university's self-limiting goals; its recognition that its only uniqueness ultimately arises from the power of thought, the dedication to basic inquiry, the discipline of intellectual training. Even the university's role with other citizens and institutions in reestablishing its community—an emergency response, which might be thought to be an exception—would have been impossible without the recognition by the faculty who lived in the area that the continuation of the community was important because of the intellectual interdisciplinary values this proximity helped to support. That was basically why they wanted to live there. It would have been impossible also without the background of training, recognition of problems, and creativity which followed from the university's pioneering role of many years in the study of urban society. It is perhaps pardonable to say that a different kind of university could not have saved the community. The university's role is not based upon a conception of neutrality or indifference to society's problems, but an approach to the problems through the only strength which a university is entitled to assert. It is a conservative role because it values cultures and ideas, and reaffirms the basic commitment to reason. It is revolutionary because of its compulsion to discover and to know. It is modest because it recognizes that the difficulties are great and the standards demanding.

The assertion and existence of these values within the university has given the institution a considerable amount of freedom and a certain magic of wholeness. One does not direct the University of Chicago to the kinds of inquiry it should pursue, or the point of view its professors should have. I assume there has been no point of time when some professors' views were not irritating to some segment of the community. In a day when it is demanded by some groups that the university as an institution take an official position on social or political action, or close its campus to those whose presence carries an unacceptable symbol, this insistence upon freedom within the university may appear either as outmoded or as a test of whether the university really has meant what it has always said. I think we have shown, and I trust we will show, that we do mean this commitment to freedom—to inquiry, to know and to speak. For those who regret this conclusion, and believe a university can and should be captured as an instrument for directed social change in the society, there is perhaps this compensation: the world of learning is much too complicated to be directed in this way; the results would be disappointing in any event. I cannot help but think, although I am not sure the point is relevant, of the casual businessman who feels sure that the teaching of economics at Chicago has departed from classical economic truth, and I place him alongside the casual-trained economist who is sure there is something wrong in Chicago's always having had the strongest classical economics department in the country.

The freedom of the university and its scholars to refuse to take on new assignments is extremely important. Universities today are involved in pressures and temptations to respond to calls for all kinds of social engineering and management tasks. Many of these requests parallel similar demands for instant medical cures and instant scientific discoveries. For some of the tasks which the universities would be given they are totally unprepared; neither professional skills nor scholarly disciplines have prepared the way. Institutions which are in fact barely capable of running themselves are now scrambling for the opportunity to tell others what to do. I recall a foundation official who some years ago thought it would be a good idea if schools of education played a greater part in running universities. He was not referring to Chicago's eminent school. But his point was that some schools of education called upon to advise foreign universities after World War II revealed they were totally incompetent. For some reason this made him think they should practice on their own institutions. Schools of education now have many demands placed upon them, and this is true of many other areas of the social sciences. The faculties at Chicago have been selective and careful about accepting these assignments. The result is they have been able to concentrate on research and demonstration projects of far-reaching significance. It is no service to claim there is research where there is none; to assert special skill when none has been acquired. What is at stake is not only the character of American universities, but the very quality of American life. What is at stake also is our ability to develop the knowledge and skills to provide the answers which are sought. These must not be pretend answers.

I have referred to the sense of wholeness and a certain quality of magic. I recall the late Leo Szilard, puckish great scientist, describing the uncertain quality which made for a great laboratory. He could tell, he said, all the danger signals that indicated when things were not going well. But he could not say what made for a good or great laboratory. He only knew, he said, there was a sense of wholeness when this occurred. It was, he said in the most matter of fact way, a kind of magic. The University of Chicago in all probability could not be created today. The task would be too great and beyond reach. But the university can be refounded and recreated, as is the necessity for all institutions if they are to endure. The challenge to the university and its friends is to carry forward for our time this extraordinary tradition and instrument, which began all at once, assumed a unique combination of research, teaching, and professional training, and over its history has departed very little from the values it seeks. Perhaps this is why it carries also that magical sense of wholeness.

University of Chicago Citizens Board
16 November 1967

LEVI

One has to ask again what is the greatest service of the university. Its greatest service is the preservation of an intellectual tradition. The university is the home of ideas. Many of these ideas are incorrect and foolish. Many are persuasive, dangerous, and devastatingly impractical. Faculties are not selected for a general ability to be prudent and practical. If the desire is to make of universities one more governmental agency, then of course all that will result is one more governmental agency. The vision of the university does not come from Health, Education, and Welfare. It does not come from the professional education-ist. It comes from a tradition where knowledge is really sought for itself. And it is on this basis that universities are worth sup-porting, for therein lies their difference.

We live in a curious time. There never has been in the history of the world as much conversation broadcast on a widespread basis by the mass media reflecting the thoughts of almost everyone on almost every conceivable subject. That conversa-tion reveals what every study of opinion has shown—that people have strange ideas, that commonplace views are really not the glory of a civilization. They never have been. This is one reason we have a bill of rights and a constitution in order to force a sober second thought. There is an enormous job of education to do. And there is a task of leadership. But the continuing task of education and leadership requires, if the continuity of civ-ilizations is to be maintained and understood, places of deliber-ate and structured thought. It requires the examination of problems of our time free from the necessity of appearing to be relevant or popular, or even, finally, correct. From this kind of pursuit will come the few ideas which will change the world. If universities, or at least a remaining few universities, cannot fulfill this function, then we had better create institutions of higher learning, free from the demands of mass culture and service, to perform this function.

. . . Beyond this, a university must know its own character. It is not enough to say it is dedicated to education and to the cul-tivation of intellectual pursuits. It must be able to see itself as a whole in spite of diversity. To see itself as a whole requires a recognition throughout the entire enterprise of the primacy of the commitment to teach and thus preserve the cultures of many civilizations—of the primacy of the commitment to basic inquiry and to the candor and discipline of reason. Perhaps the answer is that the limits of the institution's growth must be compatible with these commitments. The continuing strength and unity within will measure that growth. Perhaps all this means is that one must work harder to build up the central strength if there is to be growth at the periphery.

University of Chicago Club (Washington, D.C.)
3 May 1968

COMMITTED TO A WAY OF REASON

LEVI

I trust I will be forgiven a personal word. I approach this un-
likely moment with many memories. I come to it also with
understandable concern. I do not misconceive the importance
of this office which has changed through the years. Rather, the
goals, achievement, and tradition of this university are dis-
turbingly impressive. Our university has had a standard of ex-
traordinary leadership, difficult to maintain. I am grateful to
Chancellor Hutchins, Chancellor Kimpton, and President Beadle
for their presence today. They will understand my anxiety. It
is not that we fear mistakes. Perhaps we should fear not to
make them. President Hutchins in his address—given forty
years ago—spoke of the university's experimental attitude, its
willingness to try out ideas, to undertake new ventures, to pio-
neer. In some cases, he said, the contribution was to show other
universities what not to do. Let me say, with rueful pride, since
that time we have made many similar contributions. I hope we
always will.

. . . The very idea that centers of education are for thoughtful,
and therefore personal, consideration of values, and for in-
creased understanding, is lost by those who insist that uni-
versities are mechanisms of service to be used in a variety of
ways for the interests of the larger community.

There are many institutions for service in our society. Centers
of learning and instruction have considerable difficulty in per-
forming their central tasks; one may question the wisdom of
assigning to them additional duties. In any event, among col-
leges, schools, and universities there are important differences.
Our history, capacity, and objectives are not all the same. Each
institution must find its own mission.

The mission of the University of Chicago is primarily the in-
tellectual search for truth and the transmission of intellectual
values. The emphasis must be on the achievement of that under-
standing which can be called discovery. President Beadle has
spoken, as is his special right to do, of "the incomparable thrill
of original discovery." He has referred to the importance of
having students participate in the process through which knowl-

edge is reaffirmed and additions to knowledge are made. This, of course, is the process of education, whatever the means used, and it applies to the dialogue as well as to the experiment. We should reaffirm the close connection between the creativity of teaching and the creativity of research. And we should reaffirm also our commitment to the way of reason, without which a university becomes a menace and a caricature. . . .

The issue raised is central to what a university should be and what it should stand for. It is of course quite true that the ideas of individual scholars in universities are not likely to immediately sway the world, although some have had considerable effect. The tasks which university faculty have undertaken, sometimes within, sometimes without the universities, should not obscure the fact that universities exist for the long run. They are the custodians not only of the many cultures of man, but of the rational process itself. Universities are not neutral. They do exist for the propagation of a special point of view: namely, the worthwhileness of the intellectual pursuit of truth —using man's highest powers, struggling against the irrelevancies which corrupt thought, and now standing against the impatience of those who have lost faith in reason. This view does not remove universities from the problems of society. It does not diminish, indeed it increases, the pressure for the creation and exchange of ideas, popular or unpopular, which remake the world. It does suggest that the greatest contribution of universities will be in that liberation of the mind which makes possible what Kenneth Clark has called the strategy of truth. "For," as he says, "the search for truth, while impotent without implementation in action, undergirds every other strategy in behalf of constructive social change." One would hope that this liberation of the mind would result from a liberal education at Chicago at both the undergraduate and graduate level.

Inaugural Address, 14 November 1968

PRIVILEGED AND PRECARIOUS

LEVI

In a modern university, where many of the oracles, if not demons, live, much is routinely carried on for its own sake, as part of prescribed exercises, or as part of the ongoing enterprise—a position we share with management consultant firms, to put the matter in not too glorious a way. And yet a university must be concerned with fate, for what is involved is knowledge and understanding, and the uses of knowledge and understanding in changing behavior and enriching life.

The concern for man's fate thus is central to our work. The tragedy or comedy of universities occurs when either this is not recognized or when the manner of recognition is such as to obliterate or seriously impair the basic values for which we exist.

For higher education, our period is marked by the enormous rapid increase which has taken place in the national student population, proliferation in the number of institutions described as universities, and strong pressures for leveling. One consequence has been an outpouring of popular criticisms about formal education, descending into apocalyptic talk and not distinguishing among the levels of education. . . .

We are one university, not in order to be all things to all people, but because there are special values and strengths arising out of the common endeavor. One of these values is the recognition that no discipline, by itself, can set a final judgment on the uses and meaning of knowledge. Of course, specialization and different professional missions divide us, but they also are forces for coalescence. We do not claim this unity is ever simple, easily achieved, or approaches completeness. If this were so, the idea of a university would be less important. Frequently the unity has been greatly impaired by burdens—necessary or unnecessary—placed upon us.

Nevertheless, the force of the effort has its impact. It sets standards, reminds us of our aims, helps us achieve a centrality and versatility in instruction and research, commonly considered, not otherwise possible. This is what has shaped our College, provided the theory for our Divisions, set its mark upon our professional schools. And this is what has provided a guiding inquiry for the University's response to changing responsibilities, not causing us to retreat from the world, but asking of us what kind of contribution we can make consistent with this unity.

The concern of the University is the fate of mankind. The faith of the University is that our contribution is to be made through the advancement of knowledge and understanding. We

70

have never known how this could be done with less than intellectual excellence—of the individual mind. What a strange fixation! What a curious pattern! But this is what we have been doing, and are doing, between the spring and the downfall.

Trustee-Faculty Dinner, 12 January 1972

LEVI

This annual feast for all faculty and with all Trustees reflects the character of our institution. Perhaps the event is contrived to ease the melancholies of winter scholarship and heavy responsibility. But it shows a unity not found in many universities. Looking at this gathering one is conscious of extraordinary individuals present. You carry the burdens and, one hopes, the glory, of "a college made to order . . . a university by enchantment." I salute the patrons and scholars among you: the "well deserving patrons . . . whose worth, bounty, learning, forwardness, true zeal . . . and good esteem" continue to make this University possible—advocators, defenders, and vindicators of a precious realm which has your guardianship, your trusteeship; and the men and women who as scholars persevered, achieving that which not one in the many can attain, despite the weakening of the body, the dulling of the spirit, the abating of strength and courage which comes from study, despite "such hazards and inconveniences, as . . . madness and simplicity," to say nothing of the loss of wits, and the knowledge that "after all their pains, in the world's esteem, they may be accounted ridiculous and silly fools, idiots, asses and (as oft they are) rejected, contemned, derided, doting, and mad." It is with you the hope or realization depends that this University will be, as was predicted, "the greatest seat of learning in the modern world." . . .

I doubt if in our society education can or should want to escape the burden of the modern counterpart which seeks to infuse into the morality it transmits a better understanding of the good society and of the potential of the individual. A university has always been a privileged and precarious place. We are of the society, but we have been assigned also—or we have taken—that in-between role, in which we question whether the society, as it is, best serves the aspirations of the community of mankind. We are also teachers of morality through our disciplines and beyond them. And we have given to our society, although

71

not we alone, more effective power than chants or spells. But in their own way these powers may become chants or spells. We fall victims to them. We encourage others to do the same.

Then we must find new insights from that unity which joins us—a unity which goes beyond the compartmentalization of craft, the mindlessness of technique, and reminds us that the dialogue among us must help us find our way back.

Trustee-Faculty Dinner, 10 January 1973

LEVI

Any serious discussion of the values and purposes of higher education must take into account John Henry Newman's *The Idea of a University*, given in 1852 as Rector-Elect of the new Catholic University of Dublin. Newman argued eloquently that the purpose of a university was not to achieve social or political objectives, not to inculcate religion, or to provide training for material advancement, but rather to teach general knowledge—the acquisition of which would be an acquired illumination, a personal possession, an inward endowment. The aim was not a modest one. It was to bring students to an understanding of those ideas, embodying scientific and philosophical process, which could be representative, at least, of mankind's achieved perception of the nature of the universe. To accomplish this would require of the student exercises of mind, reason, and reflection—a cultivation of mind worth seeking for its own sake. It also required for the institution a vision of unity, where the major disciplines, including theology, were represented in the circle of learning, and through competition and interaction, would complete, correct, and balance each other.

It is sometimes forgotten that Newman, himself, having taken this position, was careful to point out persuasively that the rigorous paths he was advocating would bring major benefits of value to the individual and to society. Citizens would be better able to see things as they are and to discard what was irrelevant; the national taste would be elevated; the conditions of private life improved. But these were attendant results, although he was willing to call them the practical aims of education, dependent upon the goals he envisaged. It is ironic that this most powerful statement of the evils of specialization, compartmentalization, and intellectual carelessness, reflected in the modern university, should have come from Newman who, for strategic reasons, removed from his ideal of a university the advancement of knowledge through scientific and philosophical research, placing this work instead in separate academies and institutes. But we have not followed this exception. Rather, shrinking from any conception of unity, we have made our universities vulnerable to all the pressures of the moment.

To ward against the pressures of the moment, Newman continually stressed the weakness of a university in areas outside its domain. He decried the pretentiousness of disciplines and scholars, promising more than can be accomplished. To his critics who wanted education to be a machine of change mounted on wheels of zeal, he replied: "Quarry the granite rock with razors, or moor the vessel with a thread of silk; then you may hope with such keen and delicate instruments as human knowledge and human reason to contend against those giants, the passion and the pride of man." Perhaps we have more excuse, if one is needed, to be pretentious today. The work of discovery, which has importantly changed many of the aspects of the world, does go on in our universities. We no longer think, as Newman did, that the natural home for experiment and speculation is retirement. But surely we must have learned to our sorrow that with the advance of scientific knowledge, the threat of hubris increases. There is a special arrogance in a society which believes that basic research is no longer important because it already knows enough to accomplish anything it pleases, and a special danger when the devices of influence and manipulation we have concocted are no longer subjected to the scrutiny of the hard-won wisdom of the past. Having no sufficient countervailing values of their own, our universities have been made vulnerable to all the ambitions of society. The result may be a very impressive uproar and a great churning, but it cannot be called education. We are in the greatest danger of becoming a people who are eager to chop off pieces of our minds just for the fun of it.

It is not as though we were in a period when there is less need for education. The attempt to reach more minds than ever before is a great and worthy task. But it will not be accomplished by deciding that the needs and appetites and distractions of our day give us some license to step aside from the dialogue of values and understanding which has given the human adventure its excellence. If we are to continue this dialogue, not only for ourselves, but for our children and their children, we need an ancient faith in mankind and its mission, in the ability of man to know, and in the worth-whileness of knowing. We must become again defenders of this faith.

Twentieth Anniversary Celebration of
Hebrew Union College, Los Angeles
12 February 1974

A SPECIAL UNITY

LEVI

In my own view, tiresomely repeated, the special quality of Chicago is to be found in the unusual unity and interrelationships which exist, despite separatism and diversity, in the shared sense of intellectual purpose, and in the insistence, which we have inherited and furthered: that teaching and discovery are properly part of the same venture. . . .

I have continually stressed as one of the characteristics of our institution the close relationship between investigation and teaching. By this we mean to insist upon a special quality in both; investigation is teaching, and teaching, as we would wish it to be, must have the creativity of finding out, of seeing something new, of learning one was wrong. We do not regard the learning process as having ended for anyone, and this is one of the reasons, regarding faculty and students as involved in the same search for understanding, where the joint reformulation of questions is so important, we have tended to emphasize small classes where a continuing dialogue or the doing of experiments —not just the redoing of them—is possible. We continue to emphasize small classes, and the individual involvement of the faculty member, not as a captain of a team where the cohorts do the work, as extremely important.

The result of this kind of emphasis has given the University from the beginning a conception of its own unity, and this has given the institution a way of protecting the diversity within itself at the same time that one area has been able to profit from the efforts of another, even though the approaches may be entirely different. This unity of diverse approaches has created for the University a liveliness which has made it possible for an institution committed to basic research to stimulate continually ideas which may have practical importance in areas remote from where the original investigation was made. "What," I was asked recently by the nephews of George Babbitt, "has the University been doing to solve the energy crisis?" If I had been bright, I would have said, "Some scientists have been working on the light-collecting properties of the horseshoe crab."

State of the University, 8 April 1974

LEVI

The origin and history of the University is responsible for the emphasis which it has on quality, discovery, and the worth of the exceptional mind. From the first President and my predecessors, from all the Chairmen and Trustees of the Board, from the first founder and the friends of the University, there has come an understanding of an unusual mission—a willingness to insist upon the ideal despite our imperfection. It is this setting which has made possible the work, collaboration, and self-direction of an inspired faculty.

Campaign for Chicago Dinner (Chicago)
14 November 1974

LEVI

Moreover, the role which Kate [Mrs. Levi] and I had was an easy one—even though there were difficult times, I suppose—because it was from the University itself that the right answers came. All one really had to do, was to take the time to think about what the University meant and what its role was and therefore what its future should be.

Now I do have some anxiety, as I had every day when I was President, about the future of the University, because it has always seemed to me to have that fragility that exceptionally good things always have. I suppose it is a truth, that exceptionally good things really are accompanied by that fragility. The kind of wholeness which this University has, has to come from each one of you, a kind of inner responsiveness to the institution which does not exist elsewhere and which could be lost. But

75

then I say to myself: this University has lived with that fragility and that strength through all these years, and the inner resources have always been there to respond to the needs of the time and to the future, and I know that its future is strong.

Farewell. Faculty Reception, 8 February 1975

2

THESE THOUSAND-ODD KINGS
"The Faculty Takes Precedence Over Everything Else"

It cannot too often be repeated that is it men and nothing but
men that make education. If the first Faculty of the University
of Chicago had met in a tent, this would still have been a great
University.

HUTCHINS

A SPIRIT OF COOPERATION

HARPER

. . . for with money and with men the highest ideals may be
realized.

Quinquennial Statement, 1 July 1896

HARPER

Some interest was excited in the first years of the organization
of the University in view of the larger salaries paid to Heads of
Departments. The position taken by the Trustees in this matter
has never been challenged, nor does anyone today regret the
action. In my opinion this action was one of utmost importance.
I do not mean to suggest that men of prominence in the field of
letters and science are mercenary, but this action was taken as
an expression of the serious interest of the Trustees in the work
which they had proposed for themselves. Two policies were open
for the organization of the staff of instruction. The first, strongly
urged by many educators, was that of selecting a few younger
instructors and allowing the work to grow more gradually under
the domination of a single spirit. The other policy, which was re-
garded as impracticable by many, was the one adopted, namely,
to bring together the largest possible number of men who had
already shown their strength in their several departments, each
one of whom, representing a different training and a different
set of ideas, would contribute much to the ultimate constituton

of the University. Considerable risk attended the adoption of the second policy, for it was an open question whether with so large a number of eminent men, each maintaining his own ideas, there could be secured even in a long time that unity of spirit without which an institution could not prosper. During the first year there were times when to some it seemed doubtful if the experiment of bringing together so large a number of strong men would prove successful; but during the middle of the second year certain events occurred which led up to the birth, as it were, of the spirit of unity which had not been hoped for. The Saturday morning on which this new spirit first manifested itself in its fullness may well be regarded as the date of the spiritual birth of the institution. From that time to the present there has never been the slightest question in the mind of any student of the situation that there existed a strong and powerful influence outside of any personal agency which made for unity of spirit. That this should have come so early in our history was the occasion at the same time of surprise and satisfaction.

The organization in Departments with recognized Heads was effected more rigidly than in any other institution. This organization secured to each Department a separateness and an independence which exhibited both advantages and disadvantages. It was advantageous in that it located responsibility, drew sharp lines, and made more evident points of strength and weakness. It was disadvantageous in that for a time it prevented a much-needed correlation of work between closely related Departments, and laid perhaps too great emphasis upon the difference in rank of officers. Both of these difficulties, however, soon took care of themselves. After a period of three or four years, the process of synthesizing began, and of their own accord Departments, without losing their independence, began to come together for conference on all questions of common interest. Out of this voluntary association there grew up at first Conferences, and very recently by legislative enactment the Group Faculties. I shall refer to these in another connection, and mention them here merely to show the evolution which gradually took place. The other difficulty was also largely removed. It soon became apparent that those Departments in which all the members of the staff came together in democratic fashion and worked out the plans of the Department were best organized for securing

78

good results. Despotism on the part of a Head of Department was short-lived, and while some Heads of Departments reserved larger authority than others, the general relationship of the members of the staff in almost every Department was adjusted to the characteristics of those concerned. The organizing spirit in not a few Departments became that of some other officer than the Head, who perhaps gave himself more exclusively to the work of research instead of to that of administration. Upon the whole, therefore, the plan has probably developed as few difficulties as any other plan which might have been followed. It has the supreme advantage of being exceedingly flexible, and the administration of the different Departments is today almost as varied as the number of the different Departments. This is as it should be. The machinery is a secondary matter, and should be as far as possible that which the men most closely interested themselves prefer.

Only after the first year were the Departments of Botany and Physics organized. It is also to be noted that during the first years the Departments of the Germanic and Romance Languages were to some extent slighted, especially in the field of higher work. This discrimination, however, is a thing of the past, and these Departments are now fully organized. At the close of the second year the so-called Department of Biology was divided into five Departments, namely, Zoology, Botany, Anatomy, Physiology, and Neurology, and still later the Department of Paleontology was set apart. Here again the question may be raised as to the more minute division of Departments. It is generally believed that the lines of departmental organization may not be strictly drawn. From a more scientific point of view, it is quite certain that the study of special problems will carry the student into two or more of the different Departments as they are now constituted. In general little difficulty has arisen from the divisions. There have been times when the line between Political Economy and the Social Science was not satisfactory; as also that between Geology and Zoology. The relationship of Paleontology on the one hand to the geological work, and on the other to that of Zoology, has been disputed, but the departmental organization as originally adopted, with the slight modifications which have been made, seems upon the whole the one best adapted to the interests of all concerned.

A spirit of cooperation has grown up which has shown itself in many ways, and from the more developed growth of which much good may be expected. The staff has been singularly free from cliques. A caucus is something practically unknown. Debate is always free and outspoken. The division of the Faculties varies with almost every question which comes forward. Men who oppose each other vigorously on one subject work together most harmoniously when another subject comes forward for consideration. At two or three times within the ten years there has been more or less excitement. This has demonstrated the sincerity of men in the expression of their convictions, and, as stated above, men who on one of these cases were vigorous opponents, on another clasped hands as allies. Upon the whole, it is perhaps strange that such periods when feeling has become, perhaps, too intense, have not been more frequent. In no community in the world has there been shown a greater readiness to permit the rule of the majority.

It seems evident that a closer bond of union will exist between the Professional Faculties and the staff of the Faculties of Arts, Literature, and Science than is ordinarily found in institutions of learning. No sharp line has yet been drawn between the members of the Professional Faculties and those of the other Faculties. It is my most earnest hope that the tendency which has already shown itself in this matter may continue, and that as other Professional Faculties shall be organized they shall not be isolated from the University at large or from any portion of it, but rather that they shall take their full share in the discussion and disposition of all questions which concern the University life and policy. The future of professional work in this country is largely dependent, in my opinion, upon the closeness of its relationship to the University.

Concerning the individual work of the members of the staff I cannot speak too strongly, but this work is represented in the large number of men and women who have received degrees from the University, and in the remarkable number and notable character of the publications which have been put forth by members of the staff. For a record of this splendid service I refer you to the special volume of this Report, entitled *Publications of Members of the University, 1892–1902*. The honors conferred on the various members of the staff by governments and by institutions of learning are more numerous than can here be recited. . . .

COMPLETE FREEDOM OF SPEECH

There are two points in connection with the work of the members of the staff mention of which I cannot omit. The charge of sensationalism has been made by some unthinking persons against certain instructors in the University. This has had its origin in the misrepresentations of professorial utterances which have appeared in the public press, having come from the pens of irresponsible reporters. An effort has been made in most of these cases to discover the basis of the newspaper statements, and it has generally been found that a remark, entirely innocent, has been twisted either by the reporter or by the editor to subserve a humorous purpose. I take the liberty of repeating here a statement made at a recent Convocation:

"I am moved to make a statement of fact and opinion concerning two related subjects which quite recently have attracted some attention in the public mind. The first of these is the freedom of opinion enjoyed in these days by members of the University. The second is the use and abuse of this right by professors of the University Faculty. Concerning the first, I may be permitted to present a statement adopted unanimously by the members of the Congregation of the University on June 30, 1899:

Resolved, 1. That the principle of complete freedom of speech on all subjects has from the beginning been regarded as fundamental in the University of Chicago, as has been shown both by the attitude of the President and the Board of Trustees and by the actual practice of the President and the professors.

2. That this principle can neither now nor at any future time be called in question.

3. That it is desirable to have it clearly understood that the University, as such, does not appear as a disputant on either side upon any public question; and that the utterances which any professor may make in public are to be regarded as representing his opinions only.

"To this statement of the Congregation I wish to add, first, that whatever may or may not have happened in other universities, in the University of Chicago neither the Trustees, nor the President, nor anyone in official position has at any time called an instructor to account for any public utterances which he may have made. Still further, in no single case has a donor to the University called the attention of the Trustees to the teaching of any officer of the University as being distasteful or objectionable. Still further, it is my opinion that no donor of money to a university, whether that donor be an individual or the state, has any right, before God or man, to interfere with the teaching of officers appointed to give instruction in a university. When for any reason, in a university on private foundation, or in a university supported by public money, the administration of the institution or the instruction in any of its departments is changed by an influence from without; when an effort is made to dislodge an officer or a professor because the political sentiment or the religious sentiment of the majority has undergone a change, at that moment the institution has ceased to be a university, and it cannot again take its place in the rank of universities so long as there continues to exist to any appreciable extent the factor of coercion. Neither an individual, nor the state, nor the church has the right to interfere with the search for truth, or with its promulgation when found. Individuals or the state or the church may found schools for propagating certain special kinds of instruction, but such schools are not universities, and may not be so denominated. A donor has the privilege of ceasing to make his gifts to an institution if, in his opinion, for any reason, the work of the institution is not satisfactory; but *as donor* he has no right to interfere with the administration or the instruction of the university. The trustees in an institution in which such interference has taken place may not maintain their self-respect and remain trustees. They owe it to themselves and to the cause of liberty of thought to resign their places rather than to yield a principle the significance of which rises above all else in comparison. In order to be specific, and in order not to be misunderstood, I wish to say again that no donor of funds to the University—and I include in the number of donors the founder of the University, Mr. Rockefeller—has ever by a single word or act indicated his dissatisfaction with the instruction given to students in the University, or with the public expression of opinion made by an officer of the University. I vouch for the truth of this statement, and I trust that it may have the largest possible publicity.

"Concerning the second subject, the use and abuse of the right of free expression by officers of the University staff: As I have said, an instructor in the University has an absolute right to express his opinion. If such an instructor is on an appointment for two or three or four years, and if during these years he exercises this right in such a way as to do himself and the institution serious injury, it is, of course, the privilege of the University to allow his appointment to lapse at the end of the term for which it was originally made. If an officer on permanent appointment abuses his privilege as a professor, the University must suffer and it is proper that it should suffer. This is only the direct and inevitable consequence of the lack of foresight and wisdom involved in the original appointment. The injury thus accruing to the University is, moreover, far less serious than would follow if, for an expression of opinion differing from that of the majority of the Faculty, or from that of the Board of Trustees, or from that of the President of the University, a permanent officer were asked to present his resignation. The greatest single element necessary for the cultivation of the academic spirit is the feeling of security from interference. It is only those who have this feeling that are able to do work which in the highest sense will be beneficial to humanity. Freedom of expression must be given the members of a university faculty, even though it be abused; for, as has been said, the abuse of it is not so great an evil as the restriction of such liberty. But it may be asked: In what way may the professor abuse his privilege of freedom of expression? Or, to put the question more largely: In what way does a professor bring reproach and injury to himself and to his institution? I answer: A professor is guilty of an abuse of his privilege who promulgates as truth ideas or opinions which have not been tested scientifically by his colleagues in the same department of research or investigation. A professor has no right to proclaim to the public a truth discovered which is yet unsettled and uncertain. A professor abuses his privilege who takes advantage of a classroom exercise to propagate the partisan views of one or another of the political parties. The university is no place for partisanship. From the teacher's desk should emanate the discussion of principles, the judicial statement of arguments from various points of view, and not the one-sided representations of a partisan character. A professor abuses his privilege who in any way seeks to influence his pupils or the public by sensational methods. A professor abuses his privilege of expression of opinion when, although a student and perhaps an authority in one department or group of departments, he undertakes to speak authoritatively on subjects which have no relationship to the department in which he was appointed to give instruction. A professor abuses his privilege in many cases when, although shut off in large measure from the world, and engaged within a narrow field of investigation, he undertakes to instruct his colleagues or the public concerning matters in the world at large in connection with which he has had little or no experience. A professor abuses his privilege of freedom of expression when he fails to exercise that quality ordinarily called common sense, which, it must be confessed, in some cases the professor lacks. A professor ought not to make such an exhibition of his weakness, or to make an exhibition of his weakness so many times, that the attention of the public at large is called to the fact. In this respect he has no larger liberty than other men.

"But may a professor do all of these things and yet remain an officer in the University? Yes. The professor in most cases is only an ordinary man. Perfection is not to be expected of him. Like men in other professions, professors have their weaknesses. But will a professor under any circumstances be asked to withdraw from the University? Yes. His resignation will be demanded, and will be accepted, when, in the opinion of those in authority, he has been guilty of immorality, or when for any reason he has proved himself to be incompetent to perform the service called for. The public should be on its guard in two particulars: The utterance of a professor, however wise or foolish, is not the utterance of the University. No individual, no group of individuals, can speak for the University. A statement, by whomsoever made, is the statement of an individual.

"And further, in passing judgment, care should be taken that the facts are known. It is a habit of modern journalists, and especially of the average student reporter for the newspapers, so to supply facts, so to dress up the real facts, so to magnify and exaggerate, so to belittle and ridicule universities and university men, that serious injury is wrought, where perhaps so such injury was intended. It is the fashion to do this sort of thing, and it is done regardless of the consequences. Real regard for the interests of higher education would lead to the adoption of a different policy; but, as matters stand, the professor is often charged with acts and utterances implying an imbecility which is not characteristic of him, and to him there are frequently ascribed startling and revolutionary sentiments and statements of which he is wholly innocent. I may sum up the point in three sentences: (1) college and university professors do make mistakes, and sometimes serious ones; but (2) these are to be attributed to the professor and not to the university; and (3) in a large majority of instances the mistake, as published to the world, is misrepresented, exaggerated, or, at least, presented in such a form as to do the professor, the university, and the cause of truth itself, gross injustice."

LIFT YOUR GAZES—AND CARRY YOUR OWN WEIGHT

I take the liberty of presenting the following suggestions:

Those who are Heads of Departments and clothed with the responsibility of such Headship should consider carefully what is involved in this responsibility, and the manner in which it affects the relations of the Head to the other members of Departments. The Head should be something more than a mere chairman of the Departmental Faculty. It is quite certain that the Head should not regard himself as the autocratic ruler of the Department. In some cases the Head has gone to one extreme, and the result has been lack of proper organization and effective service. In other cases the Head has gone to the other extreme, and the result has been friction and estrangement on the part of members of the Department. It is possible that in some Departments there are officers who because of natural temperament are better able to administer the affairs of the Department than the Head himself. It is not an altogether unfortunate thing that this fact should be recognized and the younger officer be given permission to do that work because he can do it with less effort. The distribution of the work of the Department is perhaps the most important single factor in its ultimate success, and this must in large measure rest with the Head after consultation with the other members. It seems inconceivable that a Head will ever allow himself to break the close personal relationship which ought to exist between himself and his colleagues. Yet this sometimes happens to the great detriment of the Department.

The University has been accustomed in the case of some Departments of Science to make provision for a Laboratory Assistant or Research Assistant whose services shall be at the disposal of the Head of the Department. The actual outcome of this plan is much greater than might at first be supposed. It really means that the Head, notwithstanding administrative duties, is thus enabled to carry on his research work, because to the Assistant he may assign work which under his supervision is as well performed by the Assistant as by the Professor. I can easily see how the employment of such an Assistant upon a small salary would actually double the productive power of the Professor, while the training thus secured by the Assistant would be of more service than any course of study which could be prescribed. The question is therefore whether the time has not come for the appointment in every Department of such a Research Assistant, one who can be asked to collect material, arrange bibliography, and perform that ordinary service which requires so large an amount of time and which another may perform with as great satisfaction as the high-salaried officer.

It is probable that too large a portion of the time of instructors is given to the preparation of ordinary textbooks. It cannot be argued, however, that the preparation of college textbooks, as well as that of textbooks for secondary schools, does not fall within the legitimate province of the university professor. It is not so much a question of the thing itself, but rather the proportion of time thus employed. It is important to recognize the fact that, while there is a demand for restatement of truth already secured, such demand should not lay too heavy a burden upon any one man or upon the men in any single institution.

There should be established Research Professorships, the occupants of which might lecture or not according to the best interests of the work in which they are engaged. This is practically the character of the Professorships in the Observatory. There should be chairs in other Departments, perhaps a chair in every Department, to which there might be made a permanent appointment, or which might be occupied for a longer or shorter period by the various members of the Department capable of doing research work.

Another step forward should be taken in the matter of salaries. The sum of $3,000 is not a sufficient income for one who holds the full professional rank. This salary should be at least $4,000, while that of the Associate Professor should be made $3,000. With the salaries thus arranged, the Assistant Professor receiving $2,000, the Associate Professor receiving $3,000, and the full Professor who is not a Head of a Department receiving $4,000, the situation would be greatly improved. While it may not be said that there is too large a difference between the highest salaries and the lowest, it may be said truly that not enough men receive the higher salaries. The difficulty of carrying out such a policy with the continually diminishing rate of interest received on endowments is self-evident, but this means simply that a larger endowment is needed for the satisfactory support of the work undertaken.

Arrangements should be made to encourage a larger number of men to devote six months of the twelve to research and investigation, their lecture work and teaching being confined to the other six months. This plan has already been adopted in several individual cases. It is very desirable to place the advantages of this arrangement at the command of others. With the privilege thus secured of living a year abroad and a year at home, the highest results may be achieved.

The University should plan and execute at the earliest possible season a pension system which should make ample provision for those who have been connected with the University for a definite period. Such a system goes far to make the calling of the professor an attractive one, and to relieve his mind from anxiety concerning his old age. The man who at twenty-five or twenty-seven takes up his work in the University on a salary of $1,200 or $1,500, whose expenses increase more rapidly in proportion than his income, with only a meager salary at the best before him, will be greatly helped by the knowledge that provision has been made for him in case of illness or old age. Such a system has already been introduced in one or more of our institutions in America, and no institution can be regarded as thoroughly established of which such a provision does not form a part.

There are certain obligations which members of the staff sometimes fail to observe. Among these may be mentioned:

A. Promptness at the beginning of the Quarter's work. It is a wrong to the institution and an injustice to the students for a Professor to fail to make his appearance at the first exercise for which he is announced in the University schedule.

B. The continuation of lectures and recitations to the end of the time for which he has been announced. It has sometimes seemed that the final date of an official term of residence was

87

but slightly regarded by those who had some occasion to leave at an earlier period.

C. Access to instructors is a right which students may demand, and a reasonable amount of time should be set apart for such work. The office hour should be kept as regularly by a Professor as by a Dean.

That custom which seems to forbid one officer visiting the classroom of another, or to make such visits questionable, is an unfortunate one. Much good would follow from the intervisitation of classes by the different officers. The failure of instructors to observe the teaching of other instructors is at least in part responsible for the failure of many to make use in their work of the most common pedagogical principles. It is the purpose of the President to take occasion to visit the classrooms of instructors as frequently as his other duties will permit. It is hoped that the other officers of the University may think it wise to adopt this custom. . . .

The place of the Congregation Dinner should be more permanently fixed. This dinner has been changed from time to time, and for this reason has not become as permanent an institution as might be desired. It has, however, an important function to perform: (*a*) in bringing together the members of the Congregation, including representatives of the alumni as well as of the Faculties; (*b*) in affording members of the Congregation an opportunity to bring their friends into closer touch with the University; (*c*) in affording an opportunity for showing proper courtesy to the Convocation orator and special guests of the University; and (*d*) in giving the President an opportunity to speak confidentially to the members of the University on subjects of special importance and interest—an opportunity which is not otherwise afforded, unless the time of the regular meeting of the Congregation is taken.

It will be necessary within a short time to take up the consideration anew of the constitution of the Senate. This body, consisting originally of ten or twelve persons, now has a membership of thirty or more. The close and confidential assistance which the smaller body furnished the President cannot be rendered by the larger body. Is it probable that the Senate should ultimately become a representative body, its members to be selected by the Board of Trustees, or to be elected by the various Faculties?

In the recent reorganization of the United Faculties, certain group committees were established consisting of the officers of instruction belonging to closely related Departments. The chairman of each group, in accordance with the regulation, is to be elected by the members of the group. Experience has already shown that the chairman is not always selected with a view to his executive ability. It would seem necessary, therefore, that, as in an important eastern institution, the chairmen of these committees be appointed, like the Deans, by the Board of Trustees.

In the future differentiation of the work in each case the Dean of a Faculty should be that officer who is the chief administrative officer of the Faculty, and upon him should be placed the particular responsibility for the administration of its work. The Dean or Deans in such a Faculty should have for their function the more restricted work of dealing with students. The time has come, for example, when the Dean of the Junior Colleges and the Dean of the United Faculties should be relieved from the responsibility of dealing with particular students. The administrative work of the Faculties themselves in connection with the curricula and outside relationships is sufficient to engross their time.

. . . Contracts with members of the teaching staff are not treated like contracts with the officers of the university conducting the business side of the institution or like contracts made in ordinary business affairs. A large university is accustomed to accept the resignation of a professor or instructor whenever it may be proffered, whatever may have been the time for which the professor or instructor was appointed. Resignations are thus accepted in the case of men who have been appointed to do a certain service, and before even beginning to do that service desire to connect themselves with another institution. It is not considered out of place for one institution to make assiduous effort to draw away a member of the staff of another institution. The feeling prevails everywhere in the large universities that whatever is for the best interests of the individual will in the end prove to be for the best interests of education; and the university can in no case afford to deprive an individual officer of an opportunity to accept a position of greater possibility and influence. It is only in the smaller institutions of learning that this principle is not recognized.

Decennial Report, 1 July 1902

TO RESEARCH AND TEACH TOGETHER

HARPER

In order to secure the efficient administration of those departments of work in which the university as a whole is interested, the trustees have established certain University Boards, one for the administration of the University Press, one for the administration of the libraries, laboratories and museums, one for the administration of the work in Physical Culture and Athletics, and one for the administration of the affiliated work of the University. Each of these Boards consists of five or more members selected from the faculties. The work of each board will be supervised, in general, by the Council and the Senate.

Convocation, 1 April 1893

JUDSON

It was another thought at the outset that opportunity should be afforded to do real university work in the line of investigation and the attempt at the discovery of new truth. In other words, the University as founded was not to be a mere teaching institution. It was to be also an investigating institution. It was to this end that provision was made that the faculty should not be so overloaded with teaching duties, as has unfortunately been the case in many institutions. It was to this end in part, as has been said, that the plan of four quarters and of excess work for vacation credit was devised. It was to this end that provision was made at the outset for the publication of results of investigation. All these things seem essential to a modern university of the highest type.

Convocation, 12 June 1906

JUDSON

Research and publication have aways been an essential feature in our Faculty life. The *President's Report* from year to year contains lists of publications. The time here is so short as to make it impossible to discuss this subject adequately. I may say merely that nearly every member of the staff is engaged in the active prosecution of his field, and the number of articles in scientific periodicals and of books annually produced is very large. The twelve departmental journals afford one avenue of publication, and I can only add that the lack is not of active productivity on the part of the Faculty, but of the means of putting the results before the learned world in proper form.

Convocation, 6 June 1916

JUDSON

On pp. 203 and 151 of this report will be found a detailed statement, (1) of publications by members of the Faculties within the last year, and (2) of investigations still in progress.

Attention is called by the Dean of the Graduate School of Arts and Literature to the advisability of cooperation in research by members of closely related departments. It is hoped that an adjustment may be reached whereby the efforts put forth by different members of the Faculties in this way may produce larger results. . . .

The Dean of the Faculties of Arts, Literature, and Science discusses briefly the question of efficiency on the part of the members of the Faculties. The conditions of college and university teaching are in some respects different from those attending employment in commercial organization. Some things can be measured definitely, but to other things it is very difficult to apply any common unit. Business efficiency may easily be estimated in terms of results which can be measured rather precisely. It is of course quite possible to know whether classrooms and laboratories are used to the best advantage, and to know how much time of a given member of the faculty is devoted to instruction, and how much to research. It is possible to measure the amount of instruction in terms of number of students and time spent. It is also possible to estimate the amount of laboratory service given to members of the Faculty and the cost of such service, as also the amount and cost of laboratory material consumed. It is, however, more difficult to estimate in any exact way the real efficiency of the instructor in producing results with his students. It is true that those who come under the instruction of a given person have as a rule rather a definite opinion on the subject, and that the opinion of intelligent students for a series of years is seldom far from right. There is, however, no other adequate standard which can be applied to what after all is not a material but a spiritual quality. Teachers of a high order are difficult to find, and are exceedingly valuable when found. This at all events is clear, that teaching of unusual excellence should be recognized by the University as one distinct ground for advancement. It is not all members of a faculty who are qualified to pursue original research so as to secure results of any great moment. Certainly mediocre powers of investigation cannot compare in value to an institution of learning with strong abilities in the line of teaching. Even in dealing with graduate students the same qualities appear. Indeed, it is questionable whether in many cases an investigator of unusual power is not stimulated and benefited by contact with a group of students whom he can lead along the lines of discovery. At all events, in all classes good teaching should be demanded, and unusually good teaching should be rewarded. The teaching function of the University is not inferior in importance to its other functions of specialization and research.

The President's Report 1909–10

JUDSON

And this effort for mastery may largely consist of investigation along new lines—what we call in our scholastic cant "original work." And this implies literary or scientific production. After all, what greater delight is there than the acquisition of new truth? A healthy mind is as eager for discovery as a healthy body is for its food. The incurious mind is merely out of place. It should be the soul of a cabbage, not of a man.

But the final test of university work is after all no one of them. The test is not even *specialization*, although this in some shape is the form which the graduate's labor usually assumes. But specialization is also common in quite other places. Unclassified students specialize—they delight to call themselves "specialists." Young misses in training like the apostles to become fishers (of men) also specialize in literature, in music. And so in many lines.

The final test is not *production*. We expect our budding doctors to make theses which are printed and deposited in the library. And if the process goes on before many years we shall have several miles of such valuable literature gathering dust on the shelves. Indeed when one is threatening to inflict another book on a book-burdened world it is, I suspect, perhaps time

to heed Punch's advice to young people about to be married—
"Don't." The burden of proof is always on the book. It *must*
prove its right to be—if it can.

No doubt there can hardly be a higher ambition than to add
to the stock of human knowledge. But it is no low form of am-
bition to seek to know in order to impart. "A mere teacher," we
say. It would be well for us all if we have more men and women
who are "mere teachers"—who aim at the highest excellence in
a profession which is over-run with a multitude of mediocrities.

"University Ideals." Date and Occasion Unrecorded
From the H. P. Judson Papers in the
Joseph Regenstein Library

BURTON

We need food, of course. We need houses, of course. We need
railroads, of course. We need all the material things of life, but
for what purpose? Is it not that the life of man which ultimately
is—I am not speaking in terms philosophical—the life of his
soul, his relationship with other souls—shall be upon a higher
level? In all these things scholars and men of business are
equally concerned. Scholars and men of business are concerned
with the conditions which make that life, or the higher life of
the human race, possible to go on.

After all, what is the difference, ultimately, between research
and the lack of it? Is it not this, simply, that without it we must,
in all of the great concerns of life, guess, and as we are able to
make progress in research we are able to substitute—not full
knowledge; that will never come to the human race—an enlarg-
ing knowledge, an ever enlarging knowledge, for our mere con-
jecture or impressions or prejudices?

So, I am pleading for two things at once: First, that we shall
recognize the value to us of all this which I have called research,
and, second, that we shall recognize that together we must work
to accomplish results, you making your contribution and we
making our contribution, if for a moment I may speak as the
representative of Scholarship, addressing you as the represen-
tatives of Business.

What, then, are some of the consequences of this that I have
been saying, that these two groups of men ought to be more
deeply interested in one another's work? We, if there have been,

on the part of the University, prejudices towards Business as something that was on a different level from our own task, should abandon that prejudice; and, if it has been true that you of Business have looked at the University as a thing apart from life, that had no contribution to make to it, then either we should change our ways so you may have a different opinion of ours or you should come better to understand us and, thus, come to have a different attitude towards us.

The university, as the representative of research, must in my conviction come ever closer to the things of practical life, by which I do not for a moment mean that we shall abandon those studies that are remote from altogether practical objectives, that we shall cease to look into matters of science or history, that we shall cease to be concerned with languages, literature and philosophy, but that we will do that, and then we shall also come into contact with practical life.

The Institute of Meat Packers applied to the University of Chicago something over a year ago, inquiring as to whether the University was willing to co-operate with them, partly in the field of instruction and partly in the field of research. I can imagine the shiver that would have gone down the back of the president of a medieval university when he was asked to co-operate with the Institute of Meat Packers. I want to assure you no shiver went down the back of the president of the University of Chicago. He recognized at once that the justice of Meat Packers dealt with one of the practical things of life, that the university was concerned with those practical things, and if there was any possibility of co-operation, that co-operation ought to be entered into, and it was. We are now working with them, both in the field of research and the field of instruction. Not only that, but to the best of my remembrance for the moment there are fifteen other cases of such co-operation between the University and bodies which are engaged in practical affairs of manufacture or of similar industries, having to do with the world of Business. All this must go on not, as I have said, to the sacrifice of those other things that dwell in the clouds, under suns, and come down to earth in rain, but to the expansion of the field of university life.

"Business and Scholarship—What Have They to Do with One Another?" Executives' Club of Chicago, 27 February 1925

BURTON

Able men are the one indispensible element in a strong school. Buildings are necessary—good ones are desirable—but they are useless without men, while strong men even in very poor buildings will make a great institution.

It is matter of great gratification to me that the alumni have seen this fact and have directed their effort especially to the raising of the six million dollars that is to be devoted specifically to that increase of salaries which will enable us to hold our strongest men, to fill vacancies as they arise with the ablest men in the world, and to add to departments that are undermanned men of this kind and no other. This we are determined to do.

I had the pleasure a little while ago of approving the nomination of a man to a chair in English who is said to be the ablest man in his particular field in the world—and if there were an abler man—You have heard perhaps of the German pastor who was asked why he always traveled third class. "Why," he said, "there isn't any fourth, is there?" Cheapness was his ideal, and he wanted to go the limit. Well, quality is our ideal, and we want to go the limit.

I have had the pleasure today of approving the calling of a man to be assistant professor in the medical school who has had practically fifteen years of preparation for this work, but of whom we are asking that he shall spend two more years in order to be ready for his work—a man of character, ability, culture, and extraordinary preparation.

This is the kind of men we want and no others.

Alumni Dinner, 26 February 1925

A BROAD HORIZON, A SOCIAL SENSE, HIGH IDEALS

BURTON

We have, at the University, what is called the Quadrangle Club, and one of my colleagues remarked to me a few days ago that this social club was the most valuable asset the University had from a scientific point of view. At noontime, the physicist, the chemist, the botanist, the historian, and the astronomer sit down

95

around the same lunch table and there is no constraint and no program. A chance remark of the historian brings the botanist and the chemist into the discussion and perhaps before they have finished their luncheon each one has gathered from his colleagues something which has helped to correct the one-sidedness of his thinking or to suggest an entirely new line of thought. The mere fact that one can, with little effort or none, learn the latest thought of investigators in remote or similar lines of thought, serves to broaden our horizon, increase our points of contact, and stimulate our thinking.

This, then, is what I am trying to affirm: that in this age of the world, characterized as none other has ever been by research, an age which by virtue of that fact has made greater progress in acquiring knowledge of the world and of how to live in the world than was made in twenty centuries before—in this age of the world in which commercial enterprises have the far-sightedness and breadth of mind to establish institutions of research, there is a place for the university and a duty to be discharged, which neither the college, nor the professional school of science or medicine or technology, nor the specialized research laboratory, can achieve. And this task is, as I have said, to deal with the fundamental and the seemingly useless, which often proves ultimately to be the most useful, to broaden men's horizons, to facilitate contacts and relationships, to secure that symmetry of investigation without which research itself is in danger of being so one-sided as to lead to disaster.

I have left myself very little time in which to pay any attention to the other three parts of the business of the university, dissemination of truth, training of men for practical service, and the development of personalities. Let me just say, in a few words, respecting dissemination, that the university recognizes that its duty is not only to find out truth, but to give to whatever it discovers the widest possible publicity. No university professor patents his discovery. From the foundation of the University, there was incorporated, as an essential part of it, the University Press, and from the beginning honor has been given to the man who publishes the results of his work, in other words, to the man who, having discovered something which can be of use to the scholars of the world, puts it on the printed page and sends it out to the world. I am happy to be able to say that the University Press, which for many years had a hard struggle for existence, is now on a firm foundation and that its purpose is, and always will be, not to make money, but to send out in the most accessible form the thinking of the members of the faculty and of the other men connected with it.

I must be equally brief in speaking of the third and fourth purposes of the University—to train men for service and to develop high-minded personalities. But I do want to take time enough to say that we regard these as indispensable parts of our task, both because of their intrinsic importance and because research itself cannot be most successfully prosecuted when divorced from them. The real values of life are in people, and this fact needs always to be in the back of the mind, at least, of the investigator. If ever we imagined, as I think a generation ago many of us in America did, that knowledge is of itself sufficient to make democracy safe for the world and the world safe for democracy, we surely have been disillusioned by the experiences of the last decade. To know is not enough. It has in it a fatal defect. Precisely those to whom we intrust knowledge it is most important should also possess character, a broad horizon, a social sense, high ideals not for themselves only but for society, and a will trained to refuse the worse and choose the better and to prefer a contribution to the welfare of the race to any possible personal gain for themselves.

Chicago Association of Commerce and
The University Club of Chicago, 1923

BURTON

In all the Divisions of the University enumerated above, and in the professional schools named below it must be remembered that the emphasis will always be on the quality of the work, on its thoroughness and acuteness. What the world needs is by no means more products of study which are fairly good, or more men fairly well educated but work which is of the highest quality for accuracy of observation, keenness of interpretation, perfection of expression. . . .

Even this brief statement of the matter is sufficient to make it clear that the colleges of a University which is made up in no small part of graduate and professional schools call for constant attention and constant study, lest their requirements and possibilities be overlooked, and for treatment in important respects different from that which is given to the other divisions of the University. Some men can do good work both for college students and for graduates. But the practical exigencies of the situation will usually require most members of the faculty to devote themselves to one class and largely to give up work in the other field. Good college work is the essential basis of good graduate work. Neither must cut the nerve of the other. Research must not be sacrificed to large college classes, but neither must college teaching be entrusted to men whose only interest is in scientific problems and to whom undergraduate teaching is a perpetual bore. College teaching is a highly dignified and important service worthy to stand on its own merits, and to be conducted in the best possible way, not as an incident of work supposedly or really more important.

On the other hand, there are undoubted advantages in conducting college work in close relationship with graduate work. It broadens the horizon and vision of the student. It keeps him from thinking that four years will give him a complete education. It injects into the college the spirit of research, which, though it cannot be cultivated in college for its additions to human knowledge, is essential to the best atmosphere of the college.

"The University of Chicago As It Should Be in 1940:
A Confidential Statement by the President," 1925

EDUCATION BY COOPERATING IN RESEARCH

MASON

The expanding interests and increasing calls for assistance are excellent proof of departmental activity in new and specialized studies. This is as it should be. At the same time there is always a danger that a wish to increase the range of our service will cause a loss of significance in all that is actually accomplished. Research work having a quality that gains general recognition is the true objective of the University of Chicago. A high standard of performance in every research effort of our own staff is the only means to establish the scholarly aims of those working under their direction. The indication, therefore, is toward greater freedom from routine duties caused by an unusually large body of advanced students working with any professor who is trying to do creative investigation. The groups under guidance should help rather than hinder, and consequently the student members of any group should be selected with that particular end in mind.

The human element is, therefore, to be considered in protecting the values of our research programs much more than the simple mechanical ones of general equipment, buildings, and library facilities. Every step toward better application of human energies is an advance of importance. Freeing from departmental routine, obviously, must mean better control of admissions to graduate study under our research professors; it must mean greater attention to the continuous pressure upon our staff in order to prevent waste of power, that we may do better research instead of more.

All undergraduate problems are closely related to those in the graduate school, and in part they will be solved simultaneously. We have a program of research, of graduate work, and of undergraduate work. One of the greatest duties that we have to perform is to create in the University of Chicago a university in which participation in scholarship is pleasant, looked for, and appreciated by the undergraduate body. I do not believe that that is an impossible ideal. We are closer to it than any institution I have known before. We are not there. But with the research background of this institution there seems to be clearly indicated a type of performance in education which it is our specific duty to try—education by participation in research. We cannot drive that to the limit. There must be, in addition to participation in research by students, a training in the technique for that participation, and there must be means for obtaining general information. It seems clear that the last two can be left to the individual students without nearly so much detailed supervision as in the past, if they are stimulated to real interest by contact with our creative scholars.

The President's Report 1925–26

MASON

In conclusion, I may refer to an action of the Board of Trustees that should broaden our way to better research and to more effective teaching. The Faculties of the University have been held hitherto within a somewhat rigid plan of service that called for definite amounts of teaching without recognition of equally pressing demands for administrative and research effort. It was recognized that a better balance of work would be made possible through individual study of department needs and personal abilities, with the result that hereafter our Faculties will be less rigidly held to a specific program of work. It is expected that better results will be secured through this approach to our many duties, and we confidently look to the future under this more liberal interpretation.

Convocation, 20 December 1927

MASON

The time is ripe to work intensively in the gaps that lie between the salients that have been established by the advance of knowledge in the special fields. After all, it is the problem that is of supreme importance; not the reputation of a department or of an individual scientific worker, but the problem as it relates to our understanding of the laws of nature and the behavior of man. As the different departments derive new knowledge, it will be found that in the gaps between departments lie many vital problems. Through co-operative work by men brought to occupy these fields, I believe we may hope to accomplish great things, particularly in this University, a university, as I see it, unique in its frankness of expression and internal friendships and confidences, and unique in internal understanding.

Co-operative research need not be formal. There are some individuals who must be left alone, to push forward unhampered by the attempt to attach their minds to others. But others work well in close co-operation. Yet all work best when there is at least an informal understanding of one another's problems. In formal and informal co-operation lie great hopes for our future, especially in these borderland fields.

Recent support for the University has been largely support for the work on the graduate level and for the research work of the institution. We have thought much of the undergraduate problem, but we have gained new support mostly for the graduate work and research.

You know how the humanities have been stimulated by a grant through which great acceleration in speed of production will be provided. The social sciences have a program. Are they going to be equal to it? That is their own question; they have a unique opportunity through the stimulation obtained from recent support. A social science building is partially assured for the future. Support is already obtained for new men, new assistance, new supplies; and the effort that is to be made at Chicago in bringing together men trained in different techniques in a co-operative endeavor on the problems of living is something which has never been seen before in America or in any other country. A great responsibility and a great opportunity lie before us. Natural science has been stimulated as well, and in all major divisions of the University increased effort is to be the rule.

We shall not forget education. We all believe that in the combination of research, education, and service to the community there really does lie the basis of a wholesome existence of the University.

We in Chicago believe that the skeleton of it all is productive scholarship, and that as that skeleton is clothed with flesh it takes the outlines of a real education, a human education, an education in which through the solution of problems there comes the ability to meet the problems of life. We are not primarily an institution to perform civic service in the community, but that we must perform civic service to a certain degree is evident if we are to keep our contacts fresh, to keep our work in touch with real life, and to prevent ourselves from promoting a scholarship which is dead.

The undergraduate problem may be treated in two ways by an institution of higher learning: it may be abandoned or it may be solved. We are hoping to solve it. We are hoping and believing that increasingly there is greater sympathy within the faculty with the problems of undergraduate education, greater interest in the utilization of the research forces of this institution for the stimulation of effort in the proper way in undergraduate education. The administration and Trustees expect from each department an understanding and sympathy with the problem of the undergraduate, the problem of the graduate student, and with the right performance of intensive work in the discovery of new knowledge.

101

Each man in a department need not combine these functions; but each department, through whatever medium it may choose, and in whatever administrative way it may think best, is responsible for all three. It is a great pleasure to see the interest that many of the departments are showing by allocating the different types of work administratively to different members of their groups.

About undergraduate education we could talk a long time. I will merely cite the case of the professor who dreamed he was lecturing to undergraduate students and woke up and found that it was true!

We demand quality of output, and not quantity. We shall have the courage to cut down in size and in numbers if it makes for the performance of our duty in a higher way. It is not a matter of complacent conceit to us that Chicago's duty is to lead; not to furnish more output of the same type, but to show the way, as it always has shown the way in this part of the country.

We must remember that every man performing within the University his duties of education or his duties in productive scholarship in a perfunctory manner only is a liability to the institution. It means that every graduate student of hopeless mediocrity—and there are some such admitted and allowed to remain, and allowed occasionally to take a degree from this institution—every such graduate student is a liability, not an asset; and every undergraduate who leaves this institution not even knowing what scholarship is, never having caught the fire of intellectual interest to stimulate him through his life, but carrying with him a diploma from the University of Chicago, is a liability and not an asset. Our duty in the future, even more than in the past, rests in quality of scholarship and character in performance.

Trustee-Faculty Dinner, 12 January 1928

MASON

I . . . cordially welcome any suggestion—and I am sure the Faculty will—tending to keep from insulation the different groups that constitute this remarkable family. We are so frank, so friendly, so entirely in accord, that any lack of complete understanding is due to one thing only: to the fact that we are all so busy that we sometimes do not take the pains to see that we are in contact one with another as much as we should like to be. Certainly the Faculty-Trustee contact is one to be promoted. . . . Within the Faculty we have divisions, and we must think of some means by which we may keep the contacts fresh and stop the insulation which results from our absorption in our own fields. One thing we need is a centralization of offices of administration. Another thing I would suggest is an annual meeting of each department or of each group of departments which now meet together. We have the monthly meetings, the journal clubs, those groups in which scientific discussion is carried on throughout the academic year. I am wondering if it would not be a wholesome thing if one of these meetings a year were turned into an annual meeting, and within that group it should be a stock-taking meeting. The work of the past year would be surveyed and the work of the year to come would be outlined as far as that is possible. I know with what eagerness I should welcome—and I am sure all of the administrative officers of the University would welcome—an opportunity to attend such a group meeting as that. I feel that it would satisfy a sound and wholesome internal need, the need of self-direction. Even in so small a group as a department, once a year is none too often to survey what has been done and to plan for the future. We have a great group of productive scholars within the University, and they must direct their own efforts. They cannot be directed, but they must direct their efforts in such a way that the maximum advance of knowledge will come from their activity. Chicago always has been, and always must remain, a pioneer, a pathfinder. That is the reason for its existence, and we can see more clearly into the wilderness by group co-operation. . . .

Education by participation in research. It is not too much to hope for. It is not too much to study to see how far we can go, and as I have talked with some members of the Faculty I have been startled to find to what an extent that is already in existence in various departments of the University. Our true program, it seems to me, is an intensification of the program we have always had: the research work of the Faculty centered in the most vital problems which they can find. We must cut the lines of departments when necessary, in centering groups of men in common effort on a problem—for the problem is the real thing, the department the artificial thing. We need a set of problems of vital importance under solution co-operatively by this

103

great group of men, with graduate students as many in number as can well, enthusiastically, and ably co-operate in that problem of research performance, far less course-giving and course-taking than is at present the habit. The curse of the American student is taking courses, and the difficulty for the Faculty is giving courses. I speak, naturally, in exaggeration and very extremely when I say that I believe half of the energy of the Faculty can be saved from course-giving if we allow participation, but I believe that is not very wild as a guess—not for tomorrow, but when we learn this game a little better—and I believe that the students will profit from it.

Trustee-Faculty Dinner, 12 January 1927

THE GREAT SCHOLAR IN THE GREAT PLACE

HUTCHINS

The future of the University, financially and educationally, will depend on the excellence of the faculty.

"Report of the President 1934–35" (Unpublished)

HUTCHINS

No man can come to the presidency of the University of Chicago without being awed by the University and its past. From the moment of its founding it took its place among the notable institutions of the earth. Through four administrations it has held its course, striving to attain the ideals established at the beginning and coming closer toward its goal each year. Favored at the outset by unprecedented generosity and a strategic location, it has made the most of what God and man have given it. Its present position it owes even more to the devotion and ability of its Faculty than it does to the advantages, geographical and financial, with which it began. The guaranty of its future is the devotion and ability of these men and women, who have set their mark upon the University, so that whatever changes in organization may come, its spirit will be the same.

That spirit has been characterized by emphasis on productive scholarship, by emphasis on men before everything else, on work with and for Chicago, and on an experimental attitude. And these four characteristics will, I think, be the insignia of the University's spirit to the end. At a time when most educators were chiefly concerned with undergraduate teaching, President Harper assembled in the Middle West a community of scholars. Resisting all suggestions that the sole obligation of education was the training of the youth, he selected his Faculty for its eminence or promise in research. And so the University established itself in a decade as a significant and distinctively American achievement, giving new life to scientific investigation throughout the country, stimulating support and encouragement to scholars everywhere, and bringing the research worker for the moment into his own.

At Chicago he came into his own in the opportunities he received to prosecute his investigations in his own way, without interference, with adequate compensation, and with the sympathy of the administration. He did not so quickly secure the buildings and equipment that would have saved hours of toil and inconvenience. The University, administration and Faculty, took the view that men were the first consideration, and that facilities for them must sooner or later appear. These Quadrangles are the justification of that faith. But before one of them had arisen the University had made one of the great advances in the history of American education: it had established a maximum professorial salary more than double that prevailing in the United States. This action demonstrated the University's emphasis on men first of all; it announced to the public that professors might be worth more than a bare living wage; and it shocked the friends of other universities into helping them to provide their faculties with reasonable incomes. These salaries were not only higher than any then paid in education, but they were also comparable to those paid in business and the professions. They enabled the scholar of that day to take his place in society with confidence and self-respect. The group that came together here under these conditions has been the glory of the University for thirty-seven years. The presence of that group has drawn other men to it. During long periods of necessary retrenchment their spirit has kept men here. They have transmitted their spirit to their successors.

From the beginning they hoped to make their work count beyond the borders of the University. Through extension and home study they attempted to affect the life of the people, particularly in and about Chicago. To them they brought a consciousness that the University wished to be their university, dedicated to the proposition that all men are entitled to whatever education they can effectively utilize. Through affiliation with schools and colleges in the surrounding territory, the University assisted in the improvement of education at all levels. Although this contribution was perhaps not epoch-making, it illustrated the University's attitude toward its environment.

That attitude in this and all other particulars was experimental. When, for example, the program of affiliation lost its usefulness, it was abandoned. In education it is too often forgotten that the essence of experimentation is that final decision is reserved until the experiment is complete. Policies adopted as experiments have a tendency to change into vested rights. At the University of Chicago, where the principal tradition has been that of freedom, it was natural that the true experimental attitude should flower. No one has been so sure that his work was perfect as to decline suggestions as to its improvement. No one has been so convinced that his work was important as to refuse the co-operation of others. In co-operation experiment after experiment has gone forward. Where one has succeeded the faculty has been gratified and sometimes surprised. Where one has failed they have tried something else.

It is in this fashion that the University of Chicago has been most useful to American education. The University's value in the Middle West has been to try out ideas, to undertake new ventures, to pioneer. Partly because of its geographical position and partly because of the number of teachers it has distributed up and down the country, its pioneering has been remarkably influential. In some cases the experience at Chicago has shown other universities what not to do; in more it has opened new roads to better education and set new standards for the West. And that, I venture to think, is the chief function of the University of Chicago. That function is as important today as it was in 1891.

In considering the performance of that function today, we think first of the work in which the University has been most eminent, that of research. Here we find that one thing that has bothered the layman about research, particularly in the field with which I am most familiar, that of social problems, is its

106

remoteness from reality. He has assumed that the scholar was trying to understand the world about him; he could not observe that he often went into it. And it is true that the unfortunate circumstance that universities were founded by people who could read and were proud of it has tended to emphasize the importance of that exercise and to make the library the great center of scientific inquiry. In the law, for instance, scholars have for generations thought that their only material was the reported opinions of courts of last resort. And students of the law of family relations who could not regulate their own would often reach conclusions as to the proper rules governing those of other people from an analysis of decisions handed down by judges whose domestic situation frequently left much to be desired. Today, on the other hand, students of social problems have learned from students of the natural sciences that only by keeping in touch with reality can real life be understood. Students of government are studying the people who do the governing and those they govern. Students of business are studying it as it works instead of speculating about it; and legal scholars are examining the actual operation and results of the legal system instead of confining themselves to the history of phrases coined by judges and legislators long since dead. In this movement the University of Chicago has played an important part and must continue to do so. And naturally enough its work has been centered on this city and its surroundings. Through the co-operation of the Chicago superintendent of schools, the Department of Education is working with teachers from three hundred public schools and conducting studies in seven of them. The School of Commerce and Administration is carrying on research in fifteen or twenty local industries. The School of Social Service Administration has revolutionized the treatment of the orphan in the city of Chicago. The Department of Hygiene and Bacteriology is in co-operation with the city health office. The Local Community Research Committee, representing the social science departments, is managing fifty studies of the community. If the focus of research is the world about us, the focus of research at this University should be primarily that part of the world about us called Chicago and the Chicago area. Research so focused is bringing up-to-date and giving a somewhat new accent to the University's traditional interest in its environment; it is going far toward bringing scholarship in touch with life as it is being lived today; and it may eventually lead to some slight advance in the life that is to be lived here tomorrow.

With research so focused, the necessity of co-operation within the University becomes increasingly clear. We are studying and proposing to study problems that do not fit readily into the traditional departmental pattern of a University. The rounded study of such a question as the family, for instance, would involve here the co-operation of eleven departments, from art to zoology, and of seven professional schools, from divinity to medicine. And so much has our attitude changed since departmental lines were laid down that a much narrower phenomenon, like radioactivity, would require a scarcely less representative attack. What co-operative research will mean to the organization of this University is not yet clear. Much has been accomplished here by informal committees like that on local community research; other universities have established formal institutes with the same aim. What is clear is that we must proceed to give opportunities for co-operation to those who have felt the need of them, without in any way coercing the lone research worker into co-operation. What is clear, too, is that we must regard the University as a whole, and consider the formulation of University programs rather than departmental or school policies. We shall shortly make important appointments in economics, education, psychiatry, home economics, pediatrics, the Graduate Library School, and the Law School. If those appointments are made with reference only to the specific needs of the specific departments, we shall doubtless secure a splendid series of individuals. If they can be made with reference to University projects in the study of human problems, in which all these departments are interested, we shall have a splendid group, each of whom will contribute his special abilities to the common enterprise. To such common enterprises the architectural plan of the University is admirably adapted. And its organization, with the Medical School on the South Side in the Ogden Graduate School of Science and the Department of Education in the Graduate School of Arts and Literature, avoids some difficulties confronted elsewhere. We have therefore many advantages, not the least of which is the temper of the Faculty as revealed in the admirable co-operative work now under way. We should make the most of them by careful and continued attention to the possibilities of extending this type of effort into other fields.

Inaugural Address, 19 November 1929

HUTCHINS

Co-operative planning and even co-operative work certainly do not mean the suppression of the individual. The great glory of universities will always be their great individuals. Although I should be glad to face the complexities of dealing with a faculty composed entirely of geniuses, the chance that I shall ever have to do so is slight. Great individuals are rare. We should get all we can. They should work in their own way. The rest of us, who will constitute the majority, should fit in with and contribute to the university scheme of things. But there must be a university scheme of things, and it cannot be concocted, much less made effective, by the President's Office alone.

Any university scheme of things must take account of education as well as research, and on this topic the authors of the inaugural address expressed themselves in general, not to say equivocal terms.* They had a good deal to say about the education of teachers, when everybody knows that teachers are born, not made; they took a side-swipe at the methods of admission to the graduate schools, when it is common knowledge that nobody can tell in advance what a graduate student will amount to; and they hinted that it might be wise to award different forms of public recognition to students prepared to be teachers and students prepared to be research workers. Admitting that the born teacher is a gift from heaven that every university should cherish, it would seem that even he might be assisted somewhat if he could learn something before he began to teach of the major difficulties that will confront him. On the other hand the research man will doubtless derive benefit from a program that frees him from everything that does not develop him as an independent research worker. On both these points large numbers of people, particularly people running colleges, are now agreed. . . .

---

*Mr. Hutchins had begun his remarks by explaining the origin of his inaugural address this way, "It was the product of the joint efforts of our toastmaster, the Vice-President and Dean of Faculties, the Associate Dean of Faculties, Weber Linn, Westbrook Pegler, and the operator of the University telephone exchange. Her contribution was that element of confusion which runs through the speech and is perhaps its most prominent characteristic."—ED.

NOT THE BIGGEST FACULTY, BUT THE BEST

The claim to existence and public support that this University can make above all others is that it will be pre-eminent in research and pre-eminent as a pacemaker in education. It follows, therefore, that in the selection and promotion of our own staff men who assist in bringing us to, or keeping us in, either of these positions deserve equal consideration at our hands. The man who does both is rare and deserves special consideration. But it is clear that a contribution of some sort is a prerequisite to consideration of any sort. Routine teaching, even excellent and entertaining routine teaching, however valuable it may be in the small college or the state university, is not enough at the University of Chicago. Neither is routine productivity, and we all know that there is such a thing. We should have no more desire merely to add to the number of books in the world than we have to add to the number of college graduates in the world. Our aim should be to secure men if possible who are both distinguished scholars and creative educators. If this is impossible and it is, on a large scale, let them be one or the other. But let us be sure that they are one or the other—men who are inventive and creative in research or men who are inventive and creative in education. And let us reward invention and imagination when we find them in education as highly as we reward them when we find them in research.

These rewards we are constantly increasing and have pledged ourselves to increase still further at the earliest possible moment. We are resisting expansion with all the strength we can muster and directing the attention of the public at every opportunity to the necessity of first raising the standard of living of the existing staff. This matter involves more than salaries. It involves also faculty housing, the education of faculty children, faculty clubs, and perhaps even investment facilities for the faculty. It involves, in short, keeping constantly in mind that the faculty takes precedence over everything else, including the students. The primary responsibility of any university is to see to it that its faculty is the best it can afford. This requires the cooperation of the faculty to an extent not always appreciated. I see nothing fatal about abandoning certain work or omitting it temporarily if a first-class man is not available to do it. A few graduate students might go elsewhere, but it is better that they

110

should than that inferior men should be members of our staff. It does not seem to me indispensable that we cover every section of every field all the time. Until we can say that all our present work is worth doing and is being well done, until we can say that the people doing it are receiving salaries of which we need not be ashamed, we can derive little satisfaction from the thought that our faculty is getting larger every year. The university with the longest list of courses is not necessarily the greatest. I commend to your imagination the picture of a university with a faculty of one hundred men and women all getting, and deserving, $50,000 a year. In the absence of additional endowments specifically for additional work, suggestions that additional work be done amount to suggestions that the salaries of the present staff remain as nearly constant as possible. If we can restrain our enthusiasm for a larger faculty until we are sure that all the men and women we have are worthy of their compensation and have compensation worthy of them, we shall secure, not perhaps the biggest group of scholars in America, but certainly the best. . . .

But no matter when higher salaries come and from what source, they are likely to have consequences that we must face sooner or later. The first of these is the adoption of full time in the medical sense throughout the University. Under that plan, as is well known, fees for the services of the medical staff are collected by the University and become part of its funds. We know that the majority of the faculty of any university are today actually part-time men. Many of them are doing hackwork at pitiable remuneration in order to keep alive. The effect on their teaching, their research, and their morale is harmful and sometimes ruinous. As long as university salaries in America are at their present level there is nothing that can be done about this situation except to lament it. As salaries are increased beyond the existing maximum at this University, we can and should demand that the faculty become full-time men. Not that I should ever wish to remove scholars from relations with the outside world. On the contrary, I hope we may encourage these relations. A scholar should do whatever develops him as a scholar. But I submit that the only way to determine whether he does outside work for its own sake or for the money that is in it is to have the money turned over to the university.

111

And I think, too, that with adequate salaries, if we ever get them, may come the question whether new appointments above the grade of Assistant Professor ought not to be made for periods of three years. Permanent tenure has doubtless done something to keep faculties poor in more ways than one. Many boards of trustees, consciously or unconsciously, have regarded it as a substitute for cash. Some have hesitated to pay high salaries when they knew they must continue to pay them whatever happened to the effectiveness of the recipients. Deans, departmental chairmen, and presidents have been able to excuse or defend weakness by saying that permanent tenure tied their hands. I have few illusions as to the effects of abolishing permanent tenure. Business men who scoff at the professor's insistence on a life-job will admit to you that in effect they have permanent tenure in their own business for men who have served faithfully for a long period. The effects of abolishing it in university work would not be nearly as revolutionary as its enemies or friends seem to think. And since its abolition would have to be accompanied by higher salaries, a university might find itself embracing an expensive shadow. Permanent tenure has performed, too, one significant service: it has preserved, in so far as anything has preserved it, freedom of speech in the universities. But even in important institutions it has failed here in serious crises. A faculty-devised and faculty-managed system of protecting the professor against the social, religious, or political prejudices of the administration and the community is likely to be more effective in preserving academic freedom than the vulnerable armor of permanent tenure. About all we can say with certainty on this matter is what a professor of mine used to say whenever anyone asked him a question: "It is a very difficult problem." It is so difficult that I mention it now, though we may meet it only after many years or not at all.

Trustee-Faculty Dinner, 8 January 1930

HUTCHINS

We are trying to improve the teaching work in the colleges. There is no use to deny that in the past teaching has suffered because emphasis has been on research, since the Chairmen of Departments, who have had practically all the policy-making, other than that power which rests with the President's Office, have been interested primarily in research. We must remember that this is a policy which has given us a situation in which nine of our departments are the best in the country. Of no other University, with the possible exception of Harvard, can this be said. But this has led to the appointment of men with ability in research rather than with ability in teaching and has hurt the undergraduate. Our problem now is to bring in productive educators, men who will do on problems of teaching the same constructive work which has been done on problems of research.

Alumni Dinner (Chicago), 22 January 1930

HUTCHINS

In a university, therefore, we should have students interested in study and prepared for it. If the ideal of the country and of the educational system is the common good as determined in the light of reason, vocational instruction will disappear from the university. Courses designed solely to transmit information about current affairs will disappear as well. Such research as merely counting telephone poles will also vanish. Professors whose only interest is in dealing with immediate practical questions will vanish too. These excisions would leave us with a group of professors studying fundamental intellectual problems with students equipped to face them.

New England Church of Chicago and
Fortnightly Club of Chicago
3 March 1937

A CONTINUING WORK OF CREATION

HUTCHINS

What the University has been trying to do may be briefly stated: it has been trying to become a university. Of the changes that have taken place those popularly known as the New Plan have been the least important. They have attracted most attention because they are most easily understood and are of the greatest interest to the general public. But they were superficial symptoms of a more significant development, the development of a university. To free students from compulsory attendance at classes, from the deadening influence of the credit system, from grades, from course examinations, from arbitrary time requirements—all these things are nice things to do and have proved successful things to do as well. But they cannot compare with the performance of the task upon which the University has been engaged, which is the task of clarification.

The first step was taken in 1930, when the five divisions were established. This made it clear that we thought there was a distinction between general education and advanced study. General education was to be the function of the college, advanced study of the upper divisions and professional schools. This action defined a college, and a university, and by implication a college in a university. A college is an institution devoted to general education. A university is an institution devoted to the advancement of knowledge. A college in a university is an institution devoted to discovering what a general education ought to be.

Now I am very far from saying that such definitions as these will solve all the problems of the higher learning. Even after they have been agreed upon an institution cannot rise to excellence without an excellent faculty, libraries, and laboratories. But I do venture to assert that unless these definitions are made, an institution cannot be a university. It may have an excellent faculty, libraries, and laboratories; if it does not know what it is doing it will have them only by accident, and it will not have them long. . . .

With good students, good teachers, and good scholars we have not been doing a good job. What the University of Chicago has done is to release students, teachers, and scholars so that they can be as good as they are. What we accomplish here in the future will depend on our selection of students, our selection of professors, and the state of our finances. We shall no longer be in a position where no matter how good all these things are we are nevertheless unable to make good use of them. We have set ourselves free.

Convocation, 13 June 1933

HUTCHINS

The research work of the University has been so excellent and has brought the institution so great a reputation that it must be clear that the reorganization was not designed to alter its present course but merely to facilitate what was already going on. The major task of the University of Chicago is and always will be the advancement of knowledge. In the process of advancing knowledge co-operation in investigation has developed here to a remarkable degree. In the social sciences there was a permanent organization devoted to the fostering of such investigation expending some $200,000 a year. In the biological sciences and the humanities faculty committees were directing the expenditure of similar though smaller funds. In the physical sciences a long-time program for the exploitation of the whole field had been drawn up in the last administration and partly financed at that time. The investigations of the faculty were falling naturally into groupings and men were being added every year because they could contribute to the joint effort of one group or another. The formal changes that have ensued have merely legalized the extra-marital relationships that had already been formed. Indeed it was the existence of these relationships that suggested the creation of divisions of the Humanities, the Social Sciences, the Physical Sciences, and the Biological Sciences.

Convocation, 23 December 1930

Hutchins

Cooperative research, too, is facilitated though not made compulsory, by the divisional scheme. Any program that attempts to coerce investigators into such research will fail. Any program that does not provide the fullest opportunity for such research is reactionary. The divisional organization at Chicago originated in the research committees that were directing investigations of a more or less cooperative type in the Social Sciences, the Humanities, and the Biological Sciences. Since faculty members with common interests from the different departments are now brought together in the divisions as parts of working and planning units, we expect the divisions to give impetus to cooperation in investigation. We do not expect any division to insist upon it as the criterion of professional excellence.

The reorganization of the University, then, should contribute to the advancement of knowledge through attracting, training, and stimulating people who can advance it or train others to do it. The whole plan should revitalize the research activities of the University. What else is necessary? A committee of the University Senate studied this matter for a year, and came to the conclusion that, "In the future, as in the successful past, the quality of the staff will largely determine the quality of graduate instruction." We do not suppose that any changes in our machinery will turn stupid students into brilliant ones, poor teachers into great ones, or indifferent investigators into Nobel Prize winners. We do feel, however, that the changes in our organization will make teaching and research more attractive and more effective, and will at the same time adjust the University to the needs of the individual student.

Association of American Universities
(Chapel Hill, North Carolina),
13 November 1931

Hutchins

At any time under any conditions there is only one way to get a distinguished university. That is to get a distinguished faculty. Whatever we may say about our deplorably small scholarship and fellowship funds, for example, we must grant that the chief attraction to good students is good professors and that if the professors are good enough the students will come to study under them even if they have to spend their own money to do it. If the distinction of this university is to endure it must continue to have a distinguished faculty.

FREEDOM, MEN, AND WHAT MONEY THERE IS

. . . Perhaps I am hysterical on this subject, but it sometimes seems to me that the whole question of the excellence of a university turns on the nature of its appointments and promotions. In the President's Office of this university we are quite aware of our stupendous ignorance of almost all the fields of knowledge. We know too that the Divisions and Schools contain some of the greatest experts in the world in the fields of which we are most ignorant. But we are so obsessed with the notion of our responsibility that we have sometimes, with the utmost trepidation and reluctance, declined to approve the recommendation.

There are several reasons for this. Although I am in favor of a congenial faculty, congeniality sometimes suggests appointments which will be restful rather than inspiring. I have no doubt that the desire for friendliness has something to do with the fact that in 1929 fifty-two percent of the entire faculty had received their highest degrees at the University of Chicago. For so young a university that is a very large, perhaps a too large proportion.

I am also in favor of a humane administration. Under present conditions I should be opposed to dropping any member of the faculty who had been here more than a year or two unless he had another job or unless he was grossly and admittedly incompetent. But I am not in favor of a sentimental policy, which would dictate the promotion of members of the staff merely because they had been in residence a long time. Such a policy must result in the deterioration of the University.

Still less do I favor the view that the eminence of a department depends on the ground that it covers. This indeed seems to me the most fruitful source of pedestrianism in universities. It cannot be said too often that the eminence of a department depends on the eminence of the men in it. If all our departments were made up of men who were eminent or who gave promise of becoming so, we should not need to worry very much about what fields they occupied or what courses they taught. Especially in the present state of our finances it is folly for us to appoint a mediocre individual merely because we think the University should have somebody in a given field. In this connection I suggest to you the significance of the actual increase in registrations in some departments where many courses have been abandoned but the important men are still active.

And so I cannot become interested in the restoration of the Divisions and Schools to their pre-depression numerical strength. I am on the other hand interested in very little else than their restoration to their pre-depression distinction. This means that as we get the money we should find the men and women who will succeed not to the subjects studied or the courses taught by those who have retired, but to their high rank in the scholarly world.

These are, then, two prerequisites to a great university—a certain amount of money and a vast amount of care in the selection of the faculty. Of course there are at least two more: academic freedom and an intelligible organization. This is one of the few universities in America where academic freedom pure and undefiled may be said to exist. This we owe to the intelligence and vision of the Board of Trustees. Although our organization is not yet perfect, we have a scheme that interferes less with the

117

scholarly and educational work of the University than that of any other institution. Henry James in the preface to *What Maise Knew* discussed at length what he called the constant force that makes for muddlement. He pointed out that the constant force that makes for muddlement afflicts all activity all the time. We cannot hope that this University will escape its influence. All we can do is to resist it to the end. Some steps we have taken have served to clarify the purposes we have in view. Gradually I hope we may take others that will drive muddlement as far from the University as we can ever expect to keep it.

But if I were asked to say which of these four prerequisites were most important, I should vote for academic freedom and the discriminating choice of professors. With a reduced income and a confused organization a university may still struggle to greatness. Without freedom a university is gone, just as the German universities have now disappeared. With a mediocre faculty a university might as well be gone. We who are the inheritors of the great tradition of this university, who breathe the freest air on this continent, must see to it that as the years go by the standard of the University of Chicago does not falter.

Trustee-Faculty Dinner, 10 January 1935

HUTCHINS

When we look at the state of professional education and of scholarship in professional fields we are forced to doubt whether training and research can receive equal emphasis from the same faculty. Where this effort has been made it has not been uniformly successful. The course of study and the personnel seem to tend in one direction or the other, and that direction is usually toward professional training. The pressure of the profession, of the students, and of the public has forced many professional schools to confess and finally to boast that their primary object is to train men for the profession. Scholarship under such conditions sometimes tends to be an incident of such training and is frequently investigation of a very practical type designed to promote the professional work of the student and the teacher. Undoubtedly the universities in the United States must assume the obligation of professional training. Investigation may show, however, that scholarship in professional fields has suffered because it was remitted to men who have felt that they must de-

118

vote themselves to preparing people to be doctors, lawyers, preachers, teachers, and business men.

Undergraduate Assembly, 12 December 1933

HUTCHINS

One of the ways in which we have kept up our teaching and research in the past five years is by engaging retired professors for part-time work. They have drawn their retiring allowances (not to exceed $3,000) and have taught necessary courses for a small additional stipend. Twelve of them are to teach next year. Although this arrangement has been compulsory during the depression, it has been embarrassing in dealing with retired professors who have not been engaged and has postponed or disturbed permanent adjustments in the departments. The practice should be terminated at the earliest possible moment.

Another practice that we should terminate as soon as the budget is balanced is that of appointing full professors on temporary tenure and others above the grade of instructor for one year. There are now 787 members of the faculty on temporary appointment, 29 of whom are full professors.[1] Assistant and associate professors should be appointed for three years and full professors permanently. We shall find our competitive position in securing new men difficult if we are limited to one-year appointments. Moreover, an assistant or associate professor should have three years at least in which to demonstrate his qualifications for promotion. The sense of insecurity generated by the annual consideration of his name is not conducive to the best work.

On permanent tenure for full professors I have changed my mind. I used to be against it because I thought it was an invitation to mediocrity and had a debasing effect on salaries. These things are probably true; but I regard them as less unfortunate than the possible consequences to a temporary faculty of a wave of hysteria like the one we have been passing through. By careful selection of full professors the Administration can obviate some of the difficulties associated with appointments for life. I recommend that when the budget is in balance we put full

---

[1]This does not include 25 clinical professors on the faculty of the medical schools.

119

professors on permanent tenure and appoint associate and assistant professors for three years.

"Report of the President 1934–35" (Unpublished)

TRUSTEES AS SOLDIERS OF FREEDOM

HUTCHINS

But the Board of Trustees has done something even more important than impressing benefactors with its financial skill. It has seen to it that the members of the faculty breathe the freest air on this continent. No group has done more to establish the great principle of academic freedom than the Board of Trustees of the University of Chicago. No man of that group or anywhere else has a clearer notion of the value of that principle than Mr. Swift, and no man has fought harder for it than he. The commanding position of this city and its university means that the whole structure of education in the Middle West is built on the University of Chicago. If it had ever wavered in its adherence to the principle of academic freedom, that doctrine would have suffered a blow from which it might never have recovered.

It takes brave and far-sighted men to resist the clamors of the moment and to stand on a principle which compels them to seem to sponsor opinions which they may despise. Only a few feeble voices, and academic ones at that, would have been raised against the Board if it had suppressed the so-called heterodox views of its earlier professors and the so-called radical views of more recent days. The fact that the views were neither heterodox nor radical, the fact that they were in each case the views of a small fraction of the faculty does not diminish the glory of the men who defended them. The Board has taken the position that the interests of society will be best served if men who are chosen because of their intelligence and their devotion to the truth are permitted to seek it no matter where it leads. The professors of the country are set apart for this purpose—the purpose of seeking and telling the truth, though the recital may be disagreeable and sometimes offensive. The independence and courage of the faculty result from the independence and courage of the Board.

University of Chicago Citizens Dinner
26 September 1941

ACADEMIC FREEDOM

HUTCHINS

When we examine what the aims of the modern university are and what the community's legitimate interest in it is, we see the various relationships in a university in a different and, I think, a clearer light. The modern university aims to develop education and to advance knowledge. It is obvious that the freer it is the more likely it is to achieve these purposes. All the history of education shows the dangers of permitting public opinion to determine the content of the course of study. In Europe until the current dictatorships the state has recognized this fact by granting the most complete freedom to the universities. All the history of science shows the fatal consequences of allowing popular prejudices to inhibit the search for truth. Although no modern university would decline to abide by the law, as many medieval ones did, they would contend that they will perform their greatest service to the community if they are left free to determine for themselves the content of education and the direction of research.

I should argue that society has thought it worthwhile to set apart men who are to search for knowledge impartially and to communicate it in the same spirit. It has thought it worthwhile to provide a haven for the individual specially qualified to pursue the truth and to protect him from the community, from influential citizens, and even from his colleagues. In this view a university is first of all a group of professors. . . .

The president of a university represents both the trustees and the faculty. At Chicago this is made explicit by the practice of having the President nominated by a joint committee. One of the president's duties to both the faculty and the board is to act as chief interpreter of the University. One of his duties to the trustees is to see to it that they have all the information about the University they will consume. Another is to prevent the faculty from wasting the university's funds. One of the president's duties to the faculty is to help the trustees so to understand the university that they will not be tempted to use their financial control to control the educational and scientific work of the university.

121

How may the legitimate interest of the public be protected if the trustees are not to regulate education? Professors are citizens and are affected by the customary influences brought to bear by the community on members of it. They are, of course, subject to law. The president is in a position to communicate to the faculty the state of public opinion, which in turn the trustees are in a position to communicate to him. But it must be clear that if professors are to be guided by the prejudices of editors, bankers, lawyers, ministers, industrialists, politicians, or any other groups they cannot hope to be professors or constitute a university in any real sense of those words. We must hold that the community wants real professors in real universities and that it has conferred upon them such privileges as are required to make its wishes effective.[1]

It follows that a professor on permanent tenure should not be removed unless he is incompetent or commits some illegal act. Whether he is competent is not a question the trustees or any other group of laymen would wish to decide. Aside from their lack of acquaintance with many of the fields studied in the university, the trustees would not wish to establish a precedent which in the hands of their successors might be an instrument of destroying that freedom of teaching and inquiry which is indispensable to a university. Only a group of qualified scholars can determine whether a professor is competent.

When the issue is the renewal of a temporary appointment it would be unfortunate if the teacher's political, social, economic, or religious views played any decisive role. In the past few years the Board has adopted a policy of making all new appointments temporary. This was done as a matter of financial discretion, to protect the University from the possible consequences of the depression. If the University permits considerations other than competence to affect the continuation of temporary appointees, the dangers of this policy are obvious. A professor on temporary tenure may fail of reappointment because he does not meet the requirements of the President of the University, the Dean of his Division or School, or the Chairman of his Department. These officers should, however, limit their investigation to the professor's scholarly and teaching abilities and his personality as it

[1]It will be noted that the Catholic parochial schools are wholly independent of public control.

122

affects their exercise, to his desirability in comparison with others qualified for the post, and to the funds available for carrying on the work in his field.

This amounts to saying that a professor on permanent or temporary tenure should not be removed or fail of reappointment because of outside activities, assuming they are not illegal and do not consume so much of his time as to render him incompetent to do his university work. Outside activities are as much protected by academic freedom as the actual business of teaching and research. If this were not so members of the faculty could be removed because a board of Protestants did not like Catholics, or a board of Baptists did not like Christian Scientists, or one of Democrats did not care for Republicans.

I do not deny that professors under these circumstances may "embarrass" the University. Even if they say, as they should, that they do not represent the University, the headlines they get usually originate in the fact that they are professors at The University of Chicago, and their title is never missing from newspaper accounts of their doings. This occasional "embarrassment" is part of the price that must be paid if the University is to be a great university, or indeed a university at all. . . .

But assuming a case where the President, the Trustees, and the Faculty all agreed that a professor had embarrassed the University, what then? If he were a competent teacher and scholar on permanent tenure, he should not be removed. If he were a competent teacher and scholar, on temporary appointment, if the funds were available for his work, if there were no better man ready to take his position, he should not fail of reappointment.

Although a professor in the case assumed should not be removed, it does not follow that he would not feel the consequences of his actions. He would be admonished by the chairman of his department. He would be subjected to the criticism of his colleagues. His professional standing and professional future would be seriously affected. These pressures a group of professors know very well how to apply, and they apply them constantly.

These are the consequences of regarding a university as a group of professors rather than a legal person, a public utility, or a business corporation. I have no hesitation in saying that the more a university approaches this definition the greater it will be. In a state university the exigencies of politics make the attainment of this ideal difficult, if not impossible. The University of Chicago suffers under no such handicaps. It is admirably situated to continue the demonstration that began with its foundation, the demonstration of what a university should be.

If we examine the recent charges against the University in the light of these principles we see that if they had been proved they might have gone far to convince a group of qualified scholars that some of our professors were incompetent. The allegation was that we were conducting propaganda in the classroom. Propaganda is not teaching, and we should certainly feel that a professor who indulged in it had given evidence that he did not belong in the University.

"Report of the President 1934–35" (Unpublished)

HUTCHINS

Academic freedom is reluctantly conceded by some non-academic people as a regrettable but inescapable incident of the management of universities. One sometimes hears that it results from the unionization of teachers into the Association of University Professors. The impression is that through some bad old custom or some bad new pressure professors have acquired a special privilege which they do not need and should not have. On the contrary, academic freedom is indispensable to the central function of the university. The main task of the university is candid and courageous thinking about important issues. An institution may do many other useful and valuable things: it may train men and women in their vocations; it may house and feed the young until they can go to work; it may play football and play it very well. But it will not be a university unless it engages, as its principal obligation, in candid and courageous thinking about important issues. The better the thinking, the more candid and courageous it is, the greater the university. Mr. Rockefeller, Mr. Harper, and the Board of Trustees of the University of Chicago determined at the outset to make a great university rise out of the swamp on the Midway. They were therefore compelled to set an example of academic freedom that has never been surpassed and seldom equaled anywhere in the world.

It would be folly to expect the thinking of 600 professors to lead them to identical conclusions on every important issue. If it did it would suggest that the thinking was not very good, or that it was somewhat less than candid and courageous. The University as such adopts no positions: it sponsors the search for truth. The members of the faculty may take any position within the law. As teachers they may not indulge in propaganda and may pose as experts only in fields in which they are expert. As citizens they may say what they like. When they speak as citizens outside their own fields they are expected to emphasize what everybody should know anyway, that they do not speak for the University.

What is it that makes the University of Chicago a great educational institution? It is the intense, strenuous, and constant intellectual activity of the place. It is this activity which makes the life of the student an educational experience. Presented with many points of view which are the results of the candid and courageous thinking of his different instructors, he is compelled to think for himself. We like to think that the air is electric, and that from it the student derives an intellectual stimulation that lasts the rest of his life. This is education. It is education for freedom. As long as this kind of education continues, we may have good hope for the liberties of our country, for such education is both the cause and the effect of liberty.

University of Chicago Citizens Dinner
26 September 1941

ANIMATED BY A COMMON PURPOSE

HUTCHINS

I sometimes doubt whether we have achieved a university in America. But I do know that if there is one, the University of Chicago is it; and if there is not one, the University of Chicago is the place that has the best chance of becoming one. A university is not a series of individuals, however great, or of departments or schools, however strong. A university is a unified organization, animated by a common purpose, and that purpose, oddly enough, is education and research. By education I mean

125

the cultivation of the intellect. By research I mean the pursuit of truth. This institution is the most effective engine of education and research in the United States. The University of Chicago comes closer to understanding what education and research are than any other in the United States.

. . . The unsung hero who laid out the architectural plan of the University made it possible for individuals, departments, and schools to work together, if they wanted to, in a degree that is unattainable elsewhere. The divisional organization, which brings isolated departments out of their isolation into large groupings, gives still further impetus to that community of purpose and community of effort which make Chicago either a university or the closest thing to one that we know. . . .

Finally, the University as we conceive it, dedicated to the cultivation of the mind and the search for truth, is the symbol of all that this country has to defend. We say we will defend our freedom. But what is freedom but the freedom to cultivate the mind and follow truth, with all the corollary freedoms which these imply? We say we will defend democracy. But what is democracy but a form of government that recognizes these freedoms —a form of government that demands, in the public interest, that every citizen develop his intelligence and gain such knowledge as he can? The kind of university the University of Chicago is striving to be is a symbol of the hopes of suffering humanity throughout the world. Our task is to make the University of Chicago stand in fact for what it stands in theory—to make it the perfect symbol of the highest aspirations of men. We must renew our devotion to the cultivation of the mind and the search for truth. If we enter upon total defense, we must keep this spark alight. If we go to war, we must tend it carefully still. So shall we keep the fires of freedom burning and serve our country and all mankind.

Chicago Association of Commerce, 29 January 1941

HUTCHINS

. . . for the University will do most for the world if it centers its attention on fundamental problems. The University must be free to determine what those problems are and what is the best method of attacking them. The institutes should be financed to a sufficient extent from the University's own funds, so that they can reject contributions from outside sources which are conditioned on the pursuit of research which the University should not undertake.

DECISIVE DEMOCRACY
THE COMMITTEE OF THE COUNCIL

Although the statutes did not require it, the practice of the administration had been to make appointments to the faculty only with the approval of the department concerned. The new constitution gives the Chancellor the privilege of recommending appointments to the Board after consulting the department involved, even though the department does not approve.

The effect of the new constitution is to give the supreme academic body, the Council, a very democratic base, but to make it, at the same time, small enough to be efficient. The executive veto power enables the Board to prevent divagations from established or desirable University policy; the Council's power of disapproving proposals of the executive is a safeguard against autocracy. The change in the practice in regard to appointments makes it possible to improve a department which does not want to be improved.

The constitution places responsibilities on the Board of Trustees which it has not been willing to assume in the past. The Board may now be called on to decide purely educational questions, including the question whether a proposed appointee has the academic qualifications demanded of a member of the faculty of the University of Chicago. In the past such issues have, in effect, been decided by the faculty, since the executive has had no veto power and has not made faculty appointments without faculty consent.

Some dangers undoubtedly lurk in a plan which may require a lay group to decide educational questions. On the other hand, I am inclined to think that the greatest danger in American universities is that which comes from the inertia of academic vested interests—a danger far greater in endowed universities than the danger of ill-considered action by a disinterested group of laymen. In our own case the Board has a long tradition of self-restraint in academic matters, which means that it will decide only those educational questions which cannot be amicably settled by the faculty and the administration. The number of those questions should be small; for the communication between the faculty and the administration is greatly improved by having a small council representing the faculty and a small committee representing the Council meet frequently with the principal officers of the University.

State of the University, 25 September 1945

CRESCAT SCIENTIA

HUTCHINS

Research is the characteristic activity of the University of Chicago.

... Research with us is a serious undertaking, and not an occupational disease.

Assembled Faculties, 7 January 1942

HUTCHINS

This University is devoted to basic research. It has the facilities, the organization, and the staff that make basic research possible. Its accomplishments over the years have won for it a leading place among the research institutions of the world. Fundamental to the progress it has made is the belief that free and independent research is essential to the advancement of knowledge. The best judge of the direction which research should take is the man who is doing the job. If his interests and the projects in which he engages are defined and limited by preconceived ends, or if they are solely directed towards specific, practical, marketable and speedily achieved results, his research is not free and has no place in a university. There is too much to do, too much yet to be discovered, to use the talents and the time of research scientists in a university for purposes other than those indicated by the development of their work itself. The ultimate practical value of such free research to industry, medicine and government has been shown time and time again. Such research has continually resulted in the enrichment of life and the improvement of health for all mankind. Without the basic research which is the business of university scientists,

128

there can be no steady progress in the laboratories of industry.

Business is usually not able to carry out basic research. The interdependence of knowledge demands the cooperative efforts of scientists in many different fields, and the costly equipment that is essential to basic research is far too elaborate for most businesses. Basic research requires an expenditure of time and a specialization of temperament that are sometimes not in harmony with the purposes of business. Great strides have been made in your industry through the research carried out in the private laboratories which you maintain. In very recent years some of the most dramatic and important developments in medicine have come from the research laboratories of the meat packing industry. Your research departments have found ways of using by-products and waste products for the good of all mankind. But this research is only possible because it has as its foundation the basic work to which this University is devoted.

Look at the location of the new laboratory. It is not only on the University of Chicago's campus; it is part of the University. It participates in the high scholarly standards and the devotion of purpose for which the scientists of this institution are known. The Director of your Institute and the members of his staff meet and confer about their problems with the members of the faculty in their laboratories, in their offices and at the luncheon table. The interchange of ideas that takes place is characteristic of universities, and in particular of this one.

> "About Research at the University of Chicago"
> Dedication of American Meat Institute
> 3 October 1950

THEIR ONLY DUTY IS TO THINK

HUTCHINS

How do we determine whether a professor can think? The competence of a professor in his chosen field should be determined by those who are qualified to have an opinion. If a professor is held to be incompetent by those admittedly expert in the field, he cannot complain that it is unjust to relieve him of his post. The activities of a professor as a citizen, however unpopular they may make him or the university, can be called in question, like those of other citizens, only by the duly constituted public authorities, and they can act only under the law. Education and research require the best men. They will not enter academic life if it carries special disabilities with it.

Even when a professor's peers believe that he is incompetent and recommend his dismissal, great care must be taken to see to it that he is not a victim of the prejudices of his colleagues. Professors do not like unconventional people any better than the rest of the population does. I have no doubt that the majority of the professors of the country voted for Landon. A professor has, or is likely to have, a vested interest in his subject, or even in his point of view about his subject. The man who is breaking new ground, and who consequently thinks that most of his colleagues are wrong in their points of view, will hardly be the most popular member of the faculty. Geniuses have had a hard time as professors in America. Every effort must be made to protect the originality as well as the independence of the thinking in a university.

Like most other chancellors and presidents, I have spent a considerable part of my life defending professors with whom I did not agree. A principle is no good unless it is good in a crisis and unless it applies to those who hold views opposite to yours as well as to those who share your opinions. It makes no difference, therefore, whether or not the chief executive of a university likes and agrees with a professor; he must defend his independence because the life of the university is at stake. Professors are not employees, either of the chief executive or of the board of trustees. They are members of an academic community. The aim of the community is independent thought. This requires the defense of the independence of its members.

I know, too, that by my standard no perfect university exists in the United States. This is merely saying that, human institutions being what they are, they must always fall short of the ideal. What I am seeking is the definition of the ideal, which is the criterion by which universities must be measured. If we know where we ought to be going, we can tell whether we are on the right path. The perfect university cannot arise unless we know what a perfect one would be. The indispensable condition to the rise of the perfect university is the guaranty of the independence of the university and its members. The infringement of the independence of the universities and professors that we have today means that we can never get the kind of universities and professors we should have.

I do not claim that professors are the only people who can think or the only people who do. I merely say that unless a man can and will think he should not be a professor, and that professors are the only people in the world whose sole duty is to think. To require them to stop thinking, or to think like everybody else, is to defeat the purpose of their lives and of their institution.

I recognize, too, that these are dangerous times and that the state must take precautions against those who would subvert it. I do not suggest that those who want to force conformity upon academic bodies do so from any but the most patriotic motives. I do say that they are misguided. The methods they have chosen cannot achieve the result they seek. They will, on the contrary, imperil the liberties we are fighting for, the most important of which are freedom of thought, speech, and association. If we cannot ourselves understand and apply our own principles, we cannot expect the rest of the world to rally to them. Since the struggle in which we are engaged is one for the loyalty and adherence of mankind, the clarity and conviction with which we hold our own principles are at least as important as our military strength. The question of freedom of thought, speech, and association is much more than an academic question.

Parents' Association of the University of Chicago
Lab School, 1 November 1950
Hillman Lecture (Columbia University)
21 November 1950

HUTCHINS

The preoccupation of the Board of Trustees with money is natural and necessary, for the principal function of the Board is to preserve and develop the University's funds. But the faculty is preoccupied with money, too, which suggests that, whether or not we have a community, we have not a dedicated one. I do not attribute this to sordid interests on the part of the faculty. I ascribe it to the failure of the leadership of the University to direct the attention of the faculty to objects worthy of it and to the resulting absence of any other common concern when it assembles. I must also allot a large share of the blame to my failure to insist upon sacrifice as an element in dedication. While attacking the materialism of the age, I have succumbed to it and have led the faculty to suppose that all the legitimate ambitions of the University would be achieved if the faculty had higher salaries and better living conditions. I do believe that the faculty should have higher salaries and better living conditions. But these things have little to do with dedication, and undue emphasis upon these things may tend to thwart the creation of a dedicated community. I should have held before the University the vision of a cause. Instead I offered bread, and I promised cake.

What this university could offer, and what it does offer to a greater extent than any other, is fulfilment through participation. What other universities offer, even the best of them, is fulfilment through being left alone. This is, in fact, what academic freedom in the conventional view of it seems to mean. But being left alone is a very poor and primitive definition of freedom of any kind, and, as applied to academic freedom, will be found quite inadequate to protect the University in the grim struggle to maintain its independence that the coming years will bring. Our problem is not merely to work out an adequate definition of academic freedom, but to induce people to care about it.

This is an undertaking of the first magnitude. We do not need to look beyond the regents and trustees of great universities to see that the notion of academic freedom as a right that a professor has to be left alone because he is a professor makes little appeal to the imagination of our people. But the conception of a dedicated community, which must be free because its purpose is independent thought, and the members of which reach fulfilment through participation in it—this conception can be made intelligible, and because it can be made intelligible it can be defended. Its value can eventually be conceded even by people who have no conscious desire to think independently or to reach fulfilment of any sort.

Farewell Address. Trustee-Faculty Dinner
10 January 1951

UNDERSTANDING THE COST OF IT

KIMPTON

It is the purpose of a university to seek the truth, and to disseminate it, when found, freely throughout the world. The first part of this purpose is concerned with research and the second with teaching, broadly conceived. It is out of basic research, the extension of human knowledge, that progress in the practical affairs of life becomes possible. It will be out of a basic study of growth that cancer will become understood and solved as a medical problem. It was out of pure research in mathematics and theoretical physics that the composition of matter became sufficiently understood so that the power of the chain reaction became an actuality. I believe we all understand research when it is concerned with such things as a cure for cancer or an inquiry into the nature and structure of the nucleus of the atom. We understand these things because new techniques result for the treatment of disease and more violent explosions can be made to occur under controlled conditions. But a university has a higher dedication than explosions or even the relief of human suffering. It believes that knowledge ought to be acquired for its own sake, that the search for truth has no particular end beyond itself. Thus we study the beginnings of our civilization in ancient Babylonia, the movement of the stars in the Southern Hemisphere, the origins of American words, the philosophical viewpoint of the Greeks—none of which has a practical application to much of anything. If you ask why we do this and whether it it worth doing, I can only answer that man is so constituted that he desires to know the true, the good, and the beautiful, and one of the primary purposes of a university is to satisfy this deep human craving for knowledge. If a university is really and seriously to pursue this high purpose, its scholars must be free to follow wherever the path of discovery may lead them, and brave enough to announce to the world what they have seen along the way.

But knowledge of truth, of good and evil, are not easily come by, for, to mere humans, truth is seldom the result of pure inspiration or revelation. It most often comes about as an evolu-

133

tion in the exchange of ideas. Thus, a university's staff will and must dispute with one another and with those outside the university, and it is part of the policy of a great university to tolerate, indeed to promote, the discussion of issues no matter how controversial they may be. And this holds in the fields of American foreign policy and economics quite as much as it does in astronomy and zoology. A good university must not be, it cannot be, dedicated to any special doctrine. In the very best sense, therefore, a good university is both conservative and liberal. It is conservative in holding to the fundamental values of our civilization. It is liberal in providing freedom and security for the growth and experimentation of ideas. Thus it is that conservatism and liberalism meet at this high level in a university. There is also a meeting, a very unfortunate meeting, when conservatism becomes reaction and liberalism becomes leftism. So it is that the reactionaries and the extreme left wing unwittingly join together in a Nazi Germany and a Communist Russia —both as far as possible from the fundamental values for which we as a Christian civilization stand.

Inauguration Banquet, 18 October 1951

NOTHING BEYOND A SATISFACTION OF THEIR OWN CURIOSITY

KIMPTON

We were the ones to announce in the heartland of American practicality that the distinguishing mark of a university is research. We went further than this. We said that no matter how others might come to use or abuse the word, by "research" we meant the pursuit of fundamental knowledge. And we said, secondly, that we at least should be concerned with the search for new knowledge for its own sake. From the beginning, we were fully aware that the essence of university research is to be completely free and uncommitted to practical results. What has since happened makes unmistakably clear that we were aware of the course of history, for when investigation ceases to proceed for its own sake and when it ceases to be concerned with fundamental principles, basic research also ceases, and the roofs which house it no longer cover a university. Now nothing is more important in planning our future than to note carefully which of our many past actions and ideas have been continuously underlined by the course of history. In the future, therefore, as in the beginning, the essence of a university, so far as we are concerned, is the search for fundamental knowledge freely pursued for its own sake.

It is perhaps more difficult to sense the part of history that is not continuous. The scene is always full of changes. The question is which of these variations will have their little day and which of them are premonitions of the future. How can we capitalize upon those changes we must continue to reckon with, and capitalize even upon aspects of them that first appear to be liabilities? How can we choose and assimilate and relate all of them to what we believe are our permanent aspirations? Here I say again that we must have the big picture. Without it, we can expect only that reward that comes to those who, without vision but with energy and conscience, do the work of the world. And, if the picture is to be some approximation of a future possible and worthy of realization, it must be part realism and part fantasy. Let us begin, though, with the realistic, and with certain visible changes that I believe will long be effective.

Anyone who has to concern himself with something as mundane as making an annual university budget knows that basic research has become increasingly expensive. This is true, even though, in the intervals between submitting their budgets, the scientists talk blithely about the good old days of Bunsen-burner chemistry and apple-orchard physics. The great causes, however, for this increase are basic to our modern economy, which continues to spiral all costs upward, and to modern research, which for the most part has entered realms of truth that can be penetrated only by teams of workers manipulating complex machinery. Modern research is more often than not big enterprise, and big business is no longer something outside a university. How, then, is a university, which is big business, to support itself without looking to the practical results which big business depends upon but which are alien to our permanent aspirations?

This change has been accompanied by another and we are among the first to feel its impact. More and more, enlightened industry, far-seeing government bureaus, and intelligent associations of professional men are realizing that basic research must go on, however great the cost. It must go on if, in the long run, government, industry, and the professions are to make continuous progress; and it must go on in a university because only there exists the freedom to pursue it. Important new developments will occur in the world of practical affairs only to the extent that new basic knowledge is developed, and, paradoxically, the search for basic knowledge can be carried on best by men who are seeking nothing beyond a satisfaction of their own curiosity. Now, the danger involved in this new interest on the part of industry, government, and the professions is apparent. These are not philanthropic groups; they have a job to do and money to make. It is not surprising, therefore, that fast money has been slowly and with reluctance reinvested in the search for basic knowledge, nor is it to them a hope of immediate and practical rewards. These offers to solve the problem of the moment we must decline. Yet I wish to say in fairness that I have seen a great change among the men of practical affairs in the last several years as they increasingly recognize that one generation lives upon the remote speculations of its predecessor. And as they have changed, we also have changed. We have come to recognize that the relationship between a university and the world beyond its walls is not so simple as we once thought it to be. This relationship is complicated in part, because knowledge is complicated, and in part because the objectives of a university are complex. It is easy with words to oppose the pure and the practical, the general and the specialized, the cultural and the vocational, but the neat compartmentalization of words should not blind us to the facts. These two worlds that we too casually set in opposition are connected by a broad highroad that runs both ways, and the traffic is heavy in both directions. Furthermore, the processes by which we gain knowledge are usually not compartmentalized, or if they are, knowledge suffers, pure as well as applied. Very often speculation of the remotest sort is set in motion by the practical needs of men. And finally, a university does not have, and never has had, any single aim. It has a primary aim, and it always must keep this aim primary—to enlarge our fundamental understanding of the universe—but it has the secondary aim of making this knowledge available to all parts of the world that can be entrusted with it. These I take to be facts that must give structural design to any picture we make of the future of our University.

Events have occurred in our community which furnish a concrete verification of these propositions. At first slowly and by mere natural affinity, translation centers have been built around the University to bridge the world of speculation and the world of action. Competent people drawn from applied fields have been placed close to those who are doing basic research. In recent years this trend has been quickened by its own momentum and by design. The Public Administration Clearing House, the Executive Program, the Cowles Commission, the national headquarters of the American Bar Association, The National Opinion Research Center, the Industrial Relations Center, and the relationships with hospital administrators and the food industry translate the social sciences into enlightened economic and social action. The Argonne Laboratory, our hospitals and clinics, the industrial sponsorship of the Nuclear Institutes, the Food Research Institute, the Institute of Meat Packing, and the United States Weather Bureau Headquarters seek for practical applications of our research in the natural sciences. The University Press, the Midwest Inter-Library Center, and the Round Table concern themselves with the entire University. This is the direction of our modern history, but where does it lead us? Where are we being projected by all these modern historical forces that combine great danger with great power? The danger is that we can become merely a service and repair station, but it is within our power to become The American Research Center.

Trustee-Faculty Dinner, 7 January 1953

TO TEACH, AND TO TEACH ONE ANOTHER

KIMPTON

We do not gladly teach, and certainly not in the evening. Even in the College where teaching, in theory at least, receives the total emphasis, escape into the divisions is the dream of many. Those who teach develop a sense of inferiority, and no wonder, since the general judgment is that they really are inferior. Even our 4E contract is based upon the principle, however poorly implemented, that no one shall be lured into responsibilities within or without the institution that he does not freely choose, and he always chooses research. This atmosphere pervades the institution. The student in the College who states that he has no intention of going on to the Ph.D. is looked at with shocked surprise, and it is no wonder that we rank among the first two or three institutions in the country in turning out undergraduates who go on to scholarship and research.

Trustee-Faculty Dinner, 13 January 1954

KIMPTON

And then there has been this knotty problem in the universities of teaching versus research. A faculty member is not advanced, it was lamented in most universities, if he is a good teacher; and if he devotes his time to research he neglects his students. Why isn't the answer to this, said we at Chicago, to have an undergraduate teaching faculty who are advanced because they are good teachers, and why not have a graduate faculty who teach in conjunction with their research? Since graduate training is in the techniques of research, teaching and research at this level go hand in hand. Here, once again, a fairly obvious idea, but it took the University of Chicago to face up to it and implement it.

Student Assembly, 28 January 1952

KIMPTON

We began, in the thirties, a new program in undergraduate teaching which has caused more discussion and serious thinking in the educational world than any other single thing in the last twenty years. We said that a good teacher was important in his own right, and should not be expected to do research and publish.

Mid-Continent Trust Conference, 9 November 1951

KIMPTON

As Hutchins took a look at American undergraduate education, particularly in the university, he found that he had three criticisms.

138

The first could be described in this way. While the great schol-
ars of the university gave the chief luster to the university, upon
the whole, they were not very good undergraduate teachers.
There are many exceptions and all of you know them in terms
of your own college experience. On the whole, a man of high
stature is somewhat bored to say the least in lecturing in phys-
ics to a freshman. That is a fact and we should all face it. It is
just as true that our greatest men in the field of research and
scholarship are by no means necessarily our greatest teachers.
This then was his first problem—to set up a teaching faculty
which shall be separate from the research faculty of the univer-
sity and this teaching faculty shall be exclusively concerned
about undergraduate education. . . .

One of the problems which I have not discussed yet but let
me discuss now is that [by] completely screening the faculty
from the rest of the university we began to lose the easy com-
munication of ideas among faculty members which has always
been a great source of pride at the University of Chicago. We
try to have men, no matter how diverse their backgrounds, ex-
change ideas with their colleagues. It so happens that this
separate faculty that we had—that they began to lose communi-
cation with the graduate faculty. This was a genuine source of
concern to us. This faculty, which had provided a marvelous
course in general education, was beginning to lose touch with
the faculty that did the graduate work and research work of
the university. A man like Fermi had something really great to
contribute to a course in general education at this level. There-
fore, how do we begin to put these faculties back together
again?

University of Chicago Citizens Board, 25 June 1953

A PERFECTLY SIMPLE COMPLEXITY OF ORGANIZATION

KIMPTON

It is the duty of the administration, with the support and coop-
eration of the Board of Trustees who legally own and control the
University, to provide this faculty competent to operate within
this framework. But even the administration, I can assure you,
does not have complete jurisdiction with regard to the appoint-

ment of a faculty member. In the normal course of events, it must await the recommendation of the appropriate department and dean before appointing a professor, and it would be unthinkable to demand the resignation of a professor, even though requested by students, the public, or the trustees, without a similar recommendation. This is because of the existence of academic freedom, an institution in which great trust is properly placed at the University of Chicago. It applies only to the faculty of the University, and it means that that faculty has the right to do its teaching and research in complete freedom from the restraints the administration or the public might seek to impose. Within this general structure as described, the individual faculties of the College, divisions and schools are autonomous. The Council of the University Senate is empowered to rule on issues that affect more than one academic unit, but each faculty may decide on what basis its degrees are granted and the steps to be taken for the award of these degrees. Thus, when our College faculty votes to substitute quarterly examinations for "R" grades, to add a history course to the curriculum, to require that fourteen comprehensive examinations constitute the program for the bachelor's degree, it is operating within its rights. The College faculty is made up of specialists who are entitled to final responsibility in these matters, and their decisions are not subject to the vote of the administration, another faculty, or a group of students.

Student Assembly, 28 January 1952

KIMPTON

Perhaps I have said enough to indicate that the University is a complicated affair. Its administration is complex, its accounting is almost incomprehensible, and its organization fits no known chart. But, in addition to this, there is the fact that most of the faculty members are among the outstanding men in their specialties in the world. These people cannot be dealt with as though they were employees. They cannot be ordered to do anything or to stop doing anything.

Moreover, you have often heard, I suppose, that the head of any important university has unlimited responsibility and almost no power. As a practical matter he cannot hire a faculty member. Admission to the faculty is like admission to an exclusive club. If the members of a particular faculty don't want

someone in, he probably won't get in. Certainly he would be un-
comfortable if the head of the institution tried to put him in.
Nor can the head of an institution fire people. The associate pro-
fessors and the professors, like federal judges, are appointed for
life or until retirement and for the same reasons. The head of
an institution, therefore, must work almost entirely by persua-
sion. And in the event of disagreement, the persuasion of very
bright and learned people is not a simple matter.

Commonwealth Club of Chicago, 17 May 1951

Kimpton

First of all, it is thought to be a great faculty, thereby participat-
ing in the magic with which the University is surrounded. Some,
of course, are inclined to say that it was better in the past than
it is today, but this is merely to share the common belief that
the only great professor is a dead one. It is admitted to be a
great faculty, but it is an odd one, judged even by the high stan-
dard of oddity generally associated with higher education. The
faculty member of the University of Chicago is thought to repre-
sent a cause, to be a posturing special pleader upon an issue that
must be unpopular or disassociated with reality or both. It is
even suggested that the University has drawn to it for aid and
comfort those who have been unable to fit into any previous en-
vironment but assemble here in happy and irresponsible eccen-
tricity. By way of reply, we point out that we are a pioneering
and innovating institution, that we really believe in and practice
academic freedom, and that human and scientific progress
comes only through advocating causes that, *de novo*, at least,
are usually unreal and unpopular. This has been our genius and
the spring from which our leadership has flowed. Conversely we
point out that if a university is too popular, if its grasp is firm
only upon immediate reality, it is merely advocating the *status
quo* and is not living up to what in long run terms at least must
be expected of it if it is to justify its existence.

Trustee-Faculty Dinner, 13 January 1954

Kimpton

It would be impossible to touch on matters of concern to the
entire University without mentioning the 4E contract. It is
finally peeping out from behind the cloud of politics, principles,

tuxedos, and *New Yorker* stories so that we can begin to get a partial look at it. The general ideas behind it are not bad. A professor should not neglect his students, his teaching, and his research through employment outside the University. Nobody would be inclined to doubt that premise, I venture to say. It is the converse of this which begins to get us into difficulties: A professor is entitled to have any outside employment he chooses, so long as he does not neglect his students, teaching and research. Here some of us at least begin to bog down a bit. The University has placed a man upon its faculty because of competence in a certain field of knowledge. If such competence is directly sold outside the University to the individual's profit, is not the University cheated in its contract and does not the man run a risk of being corrupted in the process? Is it possible, however, that there is such a thing as the indirect sale of competence in which the University can have no legitimate interest and the man cannot become corrupted? I think of such things as the making of a speech, the sale of a book, in which the professor is doing what he should be doing to advance his own and the university's interest. It is a fact that even this late in the history of the University we have not arrived at a complete answer to the basic question of the relation of our faculty to our university. A still more important fact is that if we continue to work together upon our common problem, we shall arrive at a workable solution, because it will be obtained without acrimony and bitterness.

Trustee-Faculty Dinner, 9 January 1952

SPIRIT—AND MUSCLE

KIMPTON

It may or may not be true that every great university has a kind of *Geist*, or character, or unity; I only know that this one has. As I read our history, we had it the day our doors opened, and there has been no significant change since then. All sorts of people, including me, have tried to monkey with it, but nobody can win. One may like or dislike it, but there it is. It is not too easy to put into words, but its essence is a passionate dedication to pure research and scholarship. Everything else is secondary and derivative. This is the *Geist*, the character, the unifying principle of the institution. Most of our mistakes—if one chooses to call them that—have been the result of trying to make some other objective, however worthy, superior or even equal to this. The old college is an example. It was a superbly conceived and executed enterprise. One can only say in sorrow that it did not suit the nature of the beast. To teach as a part of the quest for new knowledge has its dignity; only to teach has none at this University. And our current difficulties at Downtown College are again related to this problem. Since the turn of the century, we have instructed adults in a Loop location, and most would agree that this activity is important, both in itself and as a part of our service to the community. But, here again, this teaching has not in recent years reflected the *Geist* of the institution; it is not the University of Chicago.

If this is our genius, so be it. It is a mark of maturity to accept one's fundamental character for what it is and proceed to solve life's problems within its context. . . .

If we are to remain a small university of the highest excellence, more attention must be given, as the Harris Report correctly points out, to promotions to tenure. It simply is the truth that we have promoted too many too easily, too often from our own graduates, and too frequently from those who have served time without particular distinction in our own lower ranks. The awfully nice fellow with a charming wife and family is a dangerous man, more subversive than the Communist. He is not the stuff from which great universities are made. There is too much nonsense talked about the hardship created by letting a man go who has passed through the apprentice ranks, and it is darkly hinted that we shall not be thought a good place to start if we do not promote to tenure the great majority of those who begin their career with us. This is pure balderdash. Chicago will remain a great place to begin one's teaching and research as long as it remains a great place, and not a day longer, and it will cease to be a great place if we promote all the nice young fellows around. We all know at least one great university of this country which almost never promotes to tenure from its own lower ranks, and it remains a superlatively good place to go to and be from. The same university, after some three hundred years of disillusioning experience with the cussedness of academic human nature, instituted a system of outside, *ad hoc* committees, presumably to shame the local faculty into making recommendations to tenure of real stature. I for one would be sorry to see us resort to such a system. It is cumbersome, expensive, time-consuming, and, however much it is glossed over with academic genteelisms, it indicates an administrative distrust of local motivations and standards. Anyway, I have read too many glowing letters—some even about me—and I have had too much bad outside advice, to give much credence to foreign counselors who, after all, have nothing to lose. It is our University, and no system involving outsiders is going to save it; we must rely finally upon our own sound and honest judgment.

There is no particular problem with the really first-rate department. It, of course, is always an administrative headache; it always demands more than its share of money and endless special privilege. But it recommends good people for promotion, and it is ruthless in weeding out the unfit. Occasionally—and here the storm warnings should be unfurled—a department has been so good for so long that in its sublime arrogance it decides that only its own products can succeed the masters. A few such appointments, a few deaths, and a couple of retirements, and the great department is no longer great. But it is the weak department that is the real problem. There seems to be no force on earth that can induce a weak department to recommend good appointments. Whether it is a fear of being eclipsed by abler young people, or whether its members simply are not acquainted with any competent scholars in the field, I do not know. Industry, when faced with this predicament, can "kick upstairs," bring about early retirement, or even occasionally fire somebody; but, in the academic, the administration can only sigh and pass on, awaiting through retirement or death the opportunity of appointing a new chairman of the department.

. . . In what I have to say I do not wish to seem to malign the deans; a good dean is a very pleasant thing to have around, but he shares the weakness of the head of the institution—he rarely knows what is going on. The department chairman and the dean of a professional school to a slightly less extent are directly confronted by the faculty, and a good or a bad chairman can make or break a department. A great deal can be said, incidentally, for the old *head* of a department, a system which we inherited from our European ancestors and which we in the American universities have now largely abandoned. He was appointed for life, it was his department, and he ran it. And I mean he really ran it. The running of a department was a career, as important to the head as his own research and teaching, and sometimes' far more so. All decisions were his after whatever consultation he chose to engage in; but he knew that the stature of his department was his own stature in the university and in the academic world in general. There were some great department heads in those days, and, more important, there were some great departments. I still share enough of the faculty resentment for the administrator to realize that the old system had to go, but there are some lessons here for us. What is everybody's responsibility is nobody's responsibility, and a present-day chairman must have more of a function than presiding at meetings. He must be selected with great care by the faculty and administration, and he must be armed with real power. Of course, he should consult with his senior colleagues before any major moves, but he can become immobilized by too much democratic razzle-dazzle. Above all else, the department must be his real responsibility, rather than a rotating chore that he reluctantly assumes for his allotted term. The chairman of the department is the one the administration of the university can trust in the all-important business of promotions, and it is on him that the future quality of the university rests.

. . . the future of the great private university primarily dedicated to pure research [is] touch and go. The excellence of our people is the only thing that matters, and the Harris Committee reminds us that 66 per cent of our staff has been appointed in the last ten years. It is a terrifying thought, but, almost literally speaking, a university can be made or broken in a decade.

State of the University, 3 November 1959

WE CANNOT DO EVERYTHING

KIMPTON

You have received better specialized training here than I, for you have been taught by some of the great teachers and investigators of our time. My role in the University has cast me as a glib generalist, posing upon occasion as an authority on matters about which I am relatively ill-informed. On the other hand, there are a few things that I have had to learn and learn thoroughly. A faculty, for example, demands candor and truthfulness in its relations with the head of the university. It may not always reciprocate, mind you, but it wants and deserves the truth. And another research discovery I have made is that a faculty works best with a minimum of administrative meddling. "Get good people and let them alone" is my lowly contribution to the advancement of higher knowledge. Our University treated us well in giving us both the breadth of knowledge and intensity of concentration that together make up the essentials of an education. . . .

For some strange reason, to be well-educated by one's alma mater also gives one the right and indeed the obligation to comment upon its future. I hope you will agree with me that the University of Chicago should remain small. I state this as my first requirement because in my opinion, which I hope you will share, so many things follow from it. If we grow much larger we are going to have to accept money which could well lose us our precious freedom. It is an ancient adage but still a true one that the payer of the fiddler calls the academic tune. And we can accept money for our growth which will forever commit us to enterprises and associations of which we should have no part. The temptations in the future will be tremendous. We could build a school of agriculture through the liberality of some bucolic-minded philanthropist, and we could fabricate a rocket that would reach the moon and might come back. It will be tempting to do such things in the days ahead; money will be freely offered. I hope we resist these temptations, for we would be departing from our natural genius. This faculty cannot become much larger without losing its warmth, its informality, and its easy communication. Nor can the student body grow much larger, except at the undergraduate level, without becoming unwieldly and unacquainted. Let us leave these things for the state institutions which have to do them and ourselves remain small in numbers and high in quality. We need enough facilities to house our students and office our faculty, but very little beyond this. It was said in the old days of German scholarship that the end of a great professor occurred when he offered to show you his new institute. There will never be enough good professors or indeed good students for us to double our population and retain our quality.

Farewell. Convocation, 10, 11 June 1960

KIMPTON

And I confess to a growing uneasiness also about the increasing involvement of our university communities in the problems of the city, state, nation, and the world, though I have always been an advocate of it both by precept and example. The scholar has traditionally enjoyed the respect of the world just because he was a scholar—a man of learning of detached and balanced judgment. He was a dispassionate critic, an informed observer —an unbiased spectator. The university was venerated because it was the community of such scholars, guaranteeing them complete freedom to pursue their research and scholarship wherever the unbiased search for truth might lead them. This was the tradition of the university and it enjoyed great prestige and, indirectly, great power. Is it consistent with advocacy, with involvement, with participation?

Convocation, 16 December 1966

BEADLE

The almost frantic competition for the relatively small number of top scholars who remain in academic work accentuates the problem, for, to increase the attractiveness of positions, teaching loads—especially at the undergraduate level—are reduced virtually to the vanishing point. I recently asked the dean of a major university what he had done about his teaching requirement when he appointed a certain young scientist whom I knew to be an excellent teacher as well as a brilliant scholar. Had he waived the teaching requirement? "No," he replied, "I postponed it."

The difficulties that arise by tempting scholars away from teaching are being increasingly recognized nationally. Hopefully, corrective measures are in the offing. In the meantime, I believe that the University of Chicago College has come closer to a satisfactory solution than has any other major university in the country. The College seeks as faculty members mature, competent scholars with a high degree of skill in teaching and a real desire to spend a substantial fraction of their time doing so. Division members who wish also to participate in general education courses may be given the opportunity to do so. Although there remain problems to be solved, I am convinced that the present University of Chicago College plan belongs in the University of X—because it provides for teaching by faculty members who find it a rewarding experience, not an onerous duty.

"The University of X: An Academic Equation"
Inaugural Address, 5 May 1961

BEADLE

The University has from its beginning steadfastly defended the principle of freedom of thought and speech. In 1899 the "Congregation" of the University unanimously resolved as follows:

First: That the principle of complete freedom of speech on all subjects has from the beginning been regarded as fundamental in The University of Chicago, as has been shown both by the attitude of the President and the Board of Trustees and by the actual practice of the President and the professors;

Second: That this principle can neither now nor at any future time be called in question; and

Third: That it is desirable to have it clearly understood that the University, as such, does not appear as a disputant on either side upon any public question; and that the utterances which any professor may make in public are to be regarded as representing his opinions only.

It is easy to declare high principle. Often it is far more difficult to defend it and live by it. The University of Chicago has a remarkable record of doing both. For example, when the National Defense Education Act was made law, it contained a disclaimer affidavit required of all recipients of its loan funds. This disclaimer affidavit began with the words "I do not believe in . . ." I do not go on, for what follows is not important to the principle involved. Saying "I do not believe in . . ." is a way of saying "I hereby close my mind on whatever follows, for I cannot think about it without running the risk of believing in it." Many universities objected in principle, but took the funds in fact. The University of Chicago faculty, officers and trustees refused to compromise.

Convocation, 7, 8 June 1968

A REAL COMMUNITY OF LEARNING

BEADLE

It is important that all of us understand our goals and our plans and take cognizance of them. In doing this, I do not mean that we must be one big happy family with no differences of opinion. God forbid that we should be so dull. Remember, it was recently pointed out by the Provost at Princeton University that, as a matter of fact, some tension between faculty and administration is actually desirable. I agree but there must be some effective communication and at least some mutual understanding.

. . . As far as I know, we are the only major urban university with as many faculty living in the immediate neighborhood as do here. Charles O'Connell, awhile back, checked this and found, in fact, that 70% of the faculty members of the university live within a mile radius of the quadrangle. Therefore, unless you have seen situations in other urban universities, for example, Harvard, Columbia, Berkeley, UCLA or NYU, it is easy to underestimate the importance of this factor toward promoting constant and rewarding interdisciplinary dialogue that is so much a part of our tradition here at the university.

I am glad to say that I have just recently heard that there are now very definite plans for some twenty new homes for faculty members in Hyde Park. Of course, we need many more than that. We have hopes that there will soon be many more. . . .

I believe it is useful, yes, even a responsibility, for all of us to review our activities from time to time, our activities as individual faculty members, members of an academic university and members of the university as a whole. The latter is our main purpose today.

You, as faculty members, are the heart and life blood of the university. What you are and what you do determines in large part what the university is and what students it will attract. Trustees and administrators are not without their roles, their judgments and their actions cannot help but influence for better or worse the quality of the faculty and its collective morale.

Therefore, let me first talk about the faculty. You are now some nine hundred. Twenty-two years ago you were five hundred. . . .

First, and I am sure in the minds of all of you, most important is faculty salaries. Obviously, if we are to hold and strengthen a superior faculty we must keep our salaries competitive, taking into account a climate that does not appeal to everyone, the high cost of living in our area and other factors. It is clear, therefore, that our faculty salaries must be near the top for major academic institutions in the nation. They are, in fact, that now. However, they will have to be increased in order to maintain that position and, at the same time, be brought into a more equitable balance as among academic areas of the university.

With ever-increasing government and foundation support in the form of grants and contracts, supplementation of nine-month salaries for two or three months has become common in some academic fields. This opportunity is much more widely available in the sciences, mathematics and social sciences, than it is in some other areas.

It is my personal belief that the traditional nine-month academic appointment no longer makes good sense. The California Institute of Technology has abandoned it. MIT did likewise but under financial pressure reverted and, as all of you know, Chicago experimented with the controversial 4-E contract but gave it up. Again, this was done at least in part for financial reasons.

It is painfully evident that we here cannot hope in the foreseeable future at any one single moment to offer every faculty member a 4-Q appointment but I do believe we should consider a plan whereby we gradually work toward this as an objective in all academic areas, as we have already moved to some extent in the divisions of biological and physical sciences.

State of the University, 6 November 1962

STRENGTHENING THE FACULTY AGAIN

BEADLE

Let me therefore discuss the faculty in general, for in a real sense the faculty is the University. Unless we attract and keep the best, all else will be in vain. On the other hand, if we succeed in this, the rest will be easy—students, physical facilities, libraries, administration, and financial support.

During the past two years we have made a special effort to continue the tradition exemplified in Rockefeller's simple dictum, "The best men must be had."

A review of the new faculty members who have been appointed, effective since July 1, 1962, that is, during a sixteen-month period, shows that their number is 271. The majority of these, some 240, are replacements. I estimate the net increase to be about thirty-five. Of those who have accepted appointments or taken up residence during the academic year 1962–63 and the first four months of the present academic year, thirty-five are full professors. . . .

These and other appointments have added significant strength to several Departments and Schools of the University. A number of factors have helped to make this possible. The most important of these is the fact that an eminent faculty attracts additional outstanding scholars. But without the special Trustee Fund for strengthening the faculty, no such progress could have been made. A salary structure that places the University above most other academic institutions in the nation is also most important in the present highly competitive search for the best. Finally, I want to say that the efforts of Provost Levi have been most effective, both in urging academic units of the University to search for outstanding scholars in their areas and also in helping persuade such candidates to accept appointment at the University. . . .

We intend to continue these efforts to build faculty strength.

State of the University, 5 November 1963

BEADLE

The Trustees of the University clearly recognized its many other problems and determined to solve them. As tangible evidence, they were personally and anonymously creating a fund of 3.5 million dollars to be used by the officers, over and above the regular budget, to rebuild faculty strength. . . .

First in importance in any university is faculty quality. Without a superb faculty, no university can be great; with one, it is difficult not to be. To insure such strength, dedicated, persuasive leadership with discriminating judgment is essential. That was found in Edward Levi and achieved by persuading him to become Provost. It is fortunate that he proved vulnerable to his own technics.

I shall not forget one of his first efforts. A major department of the University was in despair. In attempts to regain lost strength, it had made eleven offers to top scholars and had had as many turndowns. Morale was low. Mr. Levi said to the Chairman: "Your salaries are too low. Raise them. The Trustee Fund will pick up the increase." His persuasive powers, plus top salaries, brought rapid success. That department is now one of the best in the nation.

It became progressively easier to repeat the process in other areas. The result: In seven years some 1200 new faculty members have been brought to the University from many parts of the nation and the world. With normal turnover this has resulted in a net increase of 250 in the total faculty, now about 1125. The faculty salary average has nearly doubled.

Farewell. Convocation, 7, 8 June 1968

RESEARCH, THE HIGHEST FORM OF EDUCATION

LEVI

Foremost among the beliefs which have given this University its style and viability is our confidence in the individual scholar.

Class of 1975 Assembly, 26 September 1971

LEVI

Much has been written of the financial arrangements of those days, the creative use of material resources generously given. But the basic faith was not in material resources. The faith was in the intellectual powers of the mind. It was considered important, more important than anything else in the world, to uncover and understand the cultures of the past, to appreciate the works of the mind, to penetrate the mysteries of the universe, to know more about the environment, the societies, and the nature of man. The university's seriousness of purpose was proven from the first by its insistence upon freedom of inquiry and discussion. Intellectual tests for truth made other standards irrelevant. Schools for the propagation of special points of view might exist, Harper wrote, but they could not be called universities. The emphasis on the need to question and reexamine, both as part of the inquiry of research and the inquiry of teaching, established a basic unity for all of the university. The basis of that unity underscored the relationship between teaching and research. That unity encouraged discussion among disciplines. It supported the individual scholar as he crossed accepted boundaries of knowledge. It made possible—even compelled— continuing debate concerning the place of professional, specialized, general, and liberal education within the university. It made the university self-critical.

Inaugural Address, 14 November 1968

LEVI

Certain characteristics of the present institution are at once evident. We believe in research. Possibly the most extreme form of our faith in research was stated by Robert Hutchins when he said: "A university may be a university without doing any teaching. It cannot be one without doing any research." Mr. Hutchins was pointing to the inevitable stresses and conflicts which arise in an institution dedicated as we are to both research and teaching. If we had to choose, we would take research. Perhaps it is important to restate this faith at a time when some fear the consequences of knowledge and when others think of research as trifling fact gathering. We believe in the search to know and in its preeminence.

Class of 1971 Assembly, 24 September 1967

LEVI

A great deal of the research has been trivial. Some of it, as for example the creation of the first self-sustaining nuclear pile, has been frightening. A large part, witness the work of Dr. Charles Huggins, has been lifesaving. Much of it has rediscovered for our own time the conditions of older cultures and given us a greater awareness of our own. To the work of the scholars of our university, we owe a considerable amount of mankind's knowledge of the nature of matter, the earth, the planets, and the stars, and much of what we know—although we know too little—about the forces within our society. The first basic work in urban sociology, the widely known Chicago school in economics, the Chicago school in literary criticism, the seminal work in the learning process itself are illustrations from the humanities and the social sciences.

The decision to emphasize research was made more than seventy-five years ago. William Rainey Harper was opposed to the original idea to build only a college. "It is not a college, but a university that is wanted," he wrote. Harper wanted a college as part of a university and in the Middle West. He faced the opposition of many who felt that to combine a university with a college would be to create a "mongrel institution" which was "neither fish, flesh, nor fowl," and who thought that in any event the city of Chicago in the uneducated Middle West was decidedly not the place to put a university. Harper himself was that kind of researcher who was for that very reason an enthusiastic teacher. His plans provided at the outset "to make the work of investigation primary, the work of giving instruction secondary." This was to be implemented by making promotion of younger men "depend more largely upon the results of their work as investigators than upon the efficiency of their teaching, although the latter will be by no means overlooked." Beginning with this early statement of what is now often erroneously reduced to the label "publish or perish," Chicago has welcomed the opportunity and the strains inherent in an institution dedicated to both research and teaching.

University of Chicago Citizens Board
16 November 1967

LEVI

But research properly conceived is the highest form of education. Without new insights and a new vision, no one can recreate for himself or for others the great traditions of the past, understand the cultures of today, or work with theory as a living structure.

"The Choices for a University." University of Tulsa
Presidential Inauguration, 10 November 1967

LEVI

Today, with the growth of specialization and freedom, we ask of the individual scholar only that he formulate his views so that

154

they may enter into some kind of a marketplace for rational discussion.

University of California, Legal Center Dedication (Berkeley), 2 January 1968

LEVI

The mission of the University of Chicago is primarily the intellectual search for truth and the transmission of intellectual values. The emphasis must be on the achievement of that understanding which can be called discovery. President Beadle has spoken, as is his special right to do, of "the incomparable thrill of original discovery." He has referred to the importance of having students participate in the process through which knowledge is reaffirmed and additions to knowledge are made. This, of course, is the process of education, whatever the means used, and it applies to the dialogue as well as to the experiment. We should reaffirm the close connection between the creativity of teaching and the creativity of research. And we should reaffirm also our commitment to the way of reason, without which a university becomes a menace and a caricature.

It is of course easy to be in favor of reason. But the commitment is somewhat more demanding and difficult. President Harper in his decennial report took occasion to emphasize "that the principle of complete freedom of speech on all subjects has from the beginning been regarded as fundamental to the University of Chicago." At the same time he repeated the policy that "the University, as such, does not appear as a disputant on either side upon any public question, and . . . utterances which any professor may make in public are to be regarded as representing his opinion only." Academic freedom is stronger now than it was then. But the propriety of the corporate neutrality of the university on public policy issues having moral aspects has been seriously challenged. The position questions the power or persuasiveness of ideas in themselves, recognizes the superior authority of official certification, or places reliance on other forms of power. Perhaps the position reflects the kind of frustration described by Louis Wirth in 1936. Professor Wirth wrote: "At a time in human history like our own, when all over the world people are not merely ill at ease but are questioning the bases of social existence, the validity of their truths, and the

155

tenability of their norms, it should become clear that there is no value apart from interest and no objectivity apart from agreement. Under such circumstances it is difficult to hold tenaciously to what one believes to be the truth in the face of dissent, and one is inclined to question the very possibility of an intellectual life. Despite the fact that the Western world has been nourished by a tradition of hard-won intellectual freedom and integrity for over two thousand years, men are beginning to ask whether the struggle to achieve these was worth the cost if so many today accept complacently the threat to exterminate what rationality and objectivity have been won in human affairs. The widespread depreciation of the value of thought, on the one hand, and its repression, on the other, are ominous signs of the deepening twilight of modern culture."

Inaugural Address, 14 November 1968

LEVI

I regret to report that a few weeks ago a noted social scientist, an alumnus of this University and a former member of our faculty, who was invited by the University to give an address, was prevented from doing so, and those who had invited him were prevented from hearing him, because of intentional acts of disruption by those who did not agree with his views, as they understood them, from some of his prior publications. The speaker actually gave his prepared talk the next day before a small group of faculty and invited guests, but this does not change the seriousness with which acts of disruption of this kind must be regarded. Throughout history, those who have tried to prevent, and sometimes have succeeded in preventing the presentation of scholarly discourse, whether of the written or spoken word, have often been well motivated. The arguments for this kind of censorship are not new, and they can always be made. Undoubtedly these arguments must and should be continually debated. This is a necessary act of education. What is involved is the question of the purpose of the University, and the number and kinds of restrictions on speech, or writing, or upon reading and listening, which are compatible with that purpose. Censorship upon speech within the universities often comes from the outside. This seems to have been mainly the case in this instance.

State of the University, 8 April 1974

LEVI

In 1902 President Harper referred to the firmly established policy of the trustees "that to the faculties belongs to the fullest extent the care of educational administration." "The responsibility," he said, "for the settlement of educational questions rests with the faculty." On this policy the initial greatness of the university was built. The trustees, whether they agreed or not with particular decisions, have been the strongest advocates of this policy. And the faculty have fulfilled this responsibility, protecting on the one hand the freedom of the individual scholar, and shepherding at the same time, although not without some pain, some of the most interesting programs for both undergraduate and graduate instruction attempted in this country. I stress the position of the faculty because obviously the quality of this university rests upon them and is created by them. And the burdens upon them have increased because the conditions of education have changed.

Inaugural Address, 14 November 1968

LEVI

I need hardly say that the quality and influence of a university are not easy to measure, although one may believe one has an informed opinion on the subject. Obviously, no one measure is complete, and the subject invites meretricious tests. In my own view, tiresomely repeated, the special quality of Chicago is to be found in the unusual unity and interrelationships which exist, despite separatism and diversity, in the shared sense of intellectual purpose, and in the insistence, which we have inherited and furthered, that teaching and discovery are properly part of the same venture. Nevertheless, the periodic surveys made of the rankings of graduate departments are suggestive of our recent history, and along with the selection of faculty for membership in various learned societies, give some indication of present standing.

President Harper, although he believed he was founding a new kind of university, knew that institutional ranking had some importance. He came to speak of Chicago as being among the top five. A survey of graduate departments in 1925 placed The University of Chicago first. It is of that period, Robert Nisbet has written, that for two decades The University of Chicago was once "unquestionably the greatest single University, department for department, school for school, that this country had seen." But the Keniston survey in 1957 placed the University on a point system as sixth among institutions, and also ranked the University as sixth in the number of its departments found among the first ten. This downward trend, and there is always a time lag, was further reflected in the American Council of Education 1964 survey which, while on one interpretation continued to place the University as sixth, found the University only ninth among institutions in the number of departments ranked among the first ten. Then in the last survey of graduate departments made under the auspices of the American Council of Education in 1969, the University's return to academic strength was signaled by a ranking of third, fourth, or fifth in the nation, depending on which method of calculation one uses. Taking the number of departments ranked in the top five, Chicago was third; it was third also in the number of departments ranked in the top ten, but tied with Yale, and after Berkeley and Harvard. My understanding is that if one uses as the measure the number of departments ranked in the top seven—and I am not sure why one would do this—Chicago ranked fifth.

The present membership of our faculty in three learned societies appears to show that Chicago is third in the nation in the number who are members of the American Academy of Arts and Sciences, following Harvard and the Massachusetts Institute of Technology; fifth in the number in the National Academy of Sciences, after Harvard, Berkeley, the Massachusetts Institute of Technology, and the California Institute of Technology, and fifth also in the number in the American Philosophical Society, after Harvard, Princeton, Berkeley, and Columbia. If our figures are correct, Chicago was fourth in the National Academy memberships in 1956, and third in 1963. . . .

Five long-term characteristics of the University persist. The first of these is the responsiveness of Departments and faculty generally given additional support. This may seem obvious, but it is not; it is, in fact, the mark of a strong institution. I do not say it always happens, but I think of examples in prior times, such as History, Anthropology, English or the professional Schools, such as Law or the Graduate School of Business, or more recently the creation of one of the strongest Psychiatry Departments in the country, and the renewed strength today of

Surgery. Connected with the first is the value which the University has always placed on the individual scholar, and its refusal to adopt a system which assumes that only a proportion of the faculty can have scholarly excellence. Because this continues to be the environment which individual faculty are invited to join, the University, despite the policy of careful budget constraints, appears to be having less difficulty in making appointments this year than in prior times. It is this environment also which has made so important the University Professors made possible by the special Trustees Fund. The University Professors help renew the University's strength from outside, but because of the overall quality of our faculty, these appointments do not have the weakness of the star system which has so seriously injured many other institutions. This year Professor James Coleman rejoined our faculty as a University Professor, confirming by his presence, I would judge, the extraordinary status of our Sociology Department. He is the ninth University Professor, and we are authorized to have ten. The tenth has been appointed and will be announced soon.

I have continually stressed as one of the characteristics of our institution the close relationship between investigation and teaching. By this we mean to insist upon a special quality in both; investigation is teaching, and teaching, as we would wish it to be, must have the creativity of finding out, of seeing something new, of learning one was wrong. We do not regard the learning process as having ended for anyone, and this is one of the reasons, regarding faculty and students as involved in the same search for understanding, where the joint reformulation of questions is so important, we have tended to emphasize small classes where a continuing dialogue or the doing of experiments —not just the redoing of them—is possible. We continue to emphasize small classes, and the individual involvement of the faculty member, not as a captain of a team where the cohorts do the work, as extremely important.

The result of this kind of emphasis has given the University from the beginning a conception of its own unity, and this has given the institution a way of protecting the diversity within itself at the same time that one area has been able to profit from the efforts of another, even though the approaches may be entirely different. This unity of diverse approaches has created for the University a liveliness which has made it possible for an

159

institution committed to basic research to stimulate continually ideas which may have practical importance in areas remote from where the original investigation was made.

State of the University, 8 April 1974

WILLIAM RAINEY HARPER

HARRY PRATT JUDSON
(*Moffett*)

ERNEST DeWITT BURTON

CHARLES MAX MASON
(*Moffett*)

ROBERT MAYNARD HUTCHINS
(*DuBois—The Drake*)

LAWRENCE ALPHEUS KIMPTON
(*Fabian Bachrach*)

GEORGE WELLS BEADLE

EDWARD HIRSCH LEVI
(*John A. Groen*)

3

THE STUDENT PRINCES

The student body is a second most important component of a great university. How are we doing in this respect?

BEADLE

I don't mind in the least admitting that I regard you as one of the most important parts of the University, and by far the most interesting part. You are important, because it is our job to help you educate yourselves, and you are interesting because, in spite of certain evidence to the contrary, you are bright.

KIMPTON

STRENGTH, CHARACTER AND ODDITY

HARPER

It has been a subject of general comment that the chief characteristics of the student body have been steadiness, sturdiness, strength, strong individuality, high ideals, and clear purpose. Members of the Faculties of eastern institutions have been struck with the individual strength and character of the student body. The student constituency does not perhaps equal in outward polish that of one of the larger institutions of the East, but in ability to organize work, in skill of adaptation of means to end, in determination of purpose to win, in readiness to make sacrifice for the sake of intellectual advancement, no body of students ever gathered together in this country, or in any other country, has shown itself superior to the student body of the University of Chicago.

Decennial Report, 1 July 1902

HUTCHINS

I beg to express to you my very hearty thanks for your cordial welcome. To become the president of a university with a student body so numerous, so intelligent and I may add so handsome would be gratifying to anybody in education. But I am particularly glad to meet you because of your extreme youth; the fact that I am older than you and shall continue to be affords me infinite satisfaction and pleasure.

Welcome. Student Assembly, 20 November 1929

HUTCHINS

Perhaps the greatest difference between your time in college and my own is the popularization in the intervening years of the works of Freud. Far be it from me to decry the significance of this writer. But I must say that he has had, as it seems to me, an unfortunate effect upon your conversation and upon the standards by which you judge yourselves and others. A graduate student in psychology told me last year that in her opinion 99 per cent of the people of this country were abnormal. In addition to providing an interesting definition of normality, this suggested to me that the ordinary difficulties of growing up and being human, from which the race has suffered for a million years, had taken on a kind of clinical character that I could not help hoping was exaggerated. Whenever I have visited with student groups, I have been impressed by your determined insistence that you were neurotic and your resentment at my suggestion that you looked perfectly all right to me.

On the principle laid down by Gilbert and Sullivan that when everybody is somebody, nobody is anybody: if everybody is abnormal, we don't need to worry about anybody. Nor should I be prepared to admit that a serious interest in being educated, the characteristic that distinguishes the students of the University of Chicago from all others, is necessarily neurotic. It may be in these times in this country somewhat eccentric, but it seems to me an amiable eccentricity, and one that should be encouraged. The whole doctrine that we must adjust ourselves to our environment, which I take to be the prevailing doctrine of American education, seems to me radically erroneous. Our mission here on earth is to change our environment, not to adjust ourselves to it. If we become maladjusted in the process, so much the worse for the environment.

Farewell. Student Assembly, 2 February 1951

KIMPTON

Every high school principal and college counselor knows precisely the kind of student they think we want, and they endeavor conscientiously to urge these students to come to the University of Chicago. The stereotype varies a bit in different parts of the country, but it adds up pretty well into a certain kind of youngster. First of all, he must be odd and not accepted in games and social affairs by the other students. He must be bright, not necessarily in the conventional sense of high I.Q., but in some extravagant and unusual way. He must have read and pondered esoteric things far beyond his years. He draws a sharp breath when reference is made to Aristotle, St. Thomas, John Donne, and James Joyce. He wears glasses, does not dance, deplores sports, and has advanced ideas on labor and the theory of relativity. But he is confident that he would have been happier had he lived in the age of Pericles or during some obscure period of the Middle Ages. The converse of this stereotype is also the case. As one college counselor phrased it to me, "it simply does not occur to any of our normal students to go to the University of Chicago."

Trustee-Faculty Dinner, 13 January 1954

KIMPTON

There was perhaps a tendency for every odd and unusual youngster in high school to be attracted by this system and while it is true that almost all geniuses are odd, it is not true that all odd people are geniuses. We do have a problem of that kind although I do not wish to magnify it. We have also a tremendous group of very healthy and wonderful American youngsters. However, it is true that perhaps we draw more than our fair proportion of the rather unusual youngsters who had not fitted too well into the high school environment. Up to that point it was felt that since the youngster was unusual and that we were unusual, that he would fit. However, did this follow? I should say most certainly not.

University of Chicago Citizens Board, 25 June 1953

KIMPTON

Let me take a look at our students for a moment. Now, I like students, and I have worked closely with them in several major universities. They are pretty much alike, and very like you and me when we were a little younger and had no responsibilities. It is a time of rebellion against authority and tradition for its

163

own sake, and of dreamy-eyed embracing of any current "ism" that might yield a better world. We allow them a great deal of freedom at the University of Chicago to talk, and protest, and organize, and even to shout. And like the young all over the world, they grow up, get a job, raise families, and become the backbone of the community. And twenty-five years hence, they wonder what in the world has gotten into this younger generation that makes them so radical, wayward, and difficult.

Commonwealth Club of Chicago, 17 May 1951

KIMPTON

Students are instinctively conservative. This may strike you as very strange to say, particularly about the University of Chicago. However, they are conservative. If a boy wears a haircut in a certain way, which is not the way that most boys wear it, he worries about ostracism and he is usually ostracized. We had riots when Mr. Hutchins put in his first plan and we have had them when we changed over to the new. The real reason, however, is a combination of Spring and the instinctive conservatism of youth. They like it their way—which is the way that they have known.

University of Chicago Citizens Board, 25 June 1953

GETTING THE BEST

KIMPTON

... there are many students whom we want at Chicago who do not come, because of, or even who are repelled by, the lack of glamour in our athletic program. We get them as graduate students, but we need them as undergraduates so that we will not need to make so many repairs in their education.

Order of the C Dinner, 2 June 1955

KIMPTON

I am completely clear on this point—in the long run, most students who will come to a great urban university for their under-

164

graduate education expect their education to reflect the presence of a great university and all it stands for.

State of the University, 10 November 1953

BEADLE

There are many factors that determine what colleges or universities able students elect to attend. In the long run, faculty quality is the most significant of these.

State of the University, 10 November 1964

KIMPTON

Now it is deep within our tradition that our gates are open wide to all those who share one article of faith—a justified belief in a life of the mind. In all else we encourage heterogeneity.

State of the University, 10 November 1953

HARPER

A great deal of satisfaction has been found in the fact that so many of the class of working-people have found it possible to send their sons and daughters to the University to secure an education. No accurate statement of numbers can be given, but it is quite certain that a large proportion of the students of the University coming from the city of Chicago belong to families ordinarily classified as those of the working-people. Nearly every nationality represented in the city is represented in the University. Not infrequently utterances have been made in the meetings of trades unions which have shown an utter lack of appreciation of the work being done by the University for the sons and daughters of the men gathered in those very unions. We understand that it is lack of acquaintance with the institution and its purposes that explains such utterances. In the near future a better conception will be entertained in these quarters. It is true that the sons and daughters of men of the working classes are unable to pay the fees prescribed by the University, but it is to be remembered that hundreds of students each year are assisted in the payment of their fees by scholarships and student service, and in many cases the Scholars appointed by the faculties of the high schools are young men and women of such parentage.

Decennial Report, 1 July 1902

BEADLE

This fall our total quadrangle students are up about 260 over last year, this despite a tuition increase of $255 per year. Almost all this increase in enrollment is in the graduate division and schools. But first-year students in the College are about 100 more than last year, while maintaining or even improving the very high quality of the entering class. It may signify less concern about neighborhood conditions that the percentage of women in the entering class of the College has increased over the twenty-five per cent of a year earlier to thirty-three per cent.

State of the University, 10 November 1964

BEADLE

A trend of some interest is the increase in proportion of women in the entering class. For several years the proportion has increased several percentage points per year. It is now 45 per cent—as compared with an over-all college percentage of 38 three years ago. The Admissions Office feels that this year's entering class is close to an optimum proportion. I suspect this higher proportion of women is a reflection of an increased tendency nationally for women entering colleges to prefer those in or near urban centers, where they hope to become familiar with urban problems and help solve them.

State of the University, 7 November 1967

BEADLE

During the year the University established a $750,000 program to provide scholarships and extra training for Negro students. The program is aimed at discouraging inner-city youngsters from dropping out of high school and encouraging many to pursue a college education. As part of the program 100 high school students from the surrounding community attended a special summer course on campus. The project also includes a tutoring program for freshmen who entered the College in the fall and whose previous education has made them "risks" under the usual admission standards; and a special recruiting program for freshmen to enter the College in the fall of 1969, 1970 and 1971. Special scholarship assistance has been provided.

State of the University, 5 November 1968

HUTCHINS

It is clear to me that you are very superior and that you come from very superior families. Otherwise you could not have come to or stayed in so independent an institution. Some of you and some of your predecessors have tried to divert the University from its course and make it more like other universities. This I attribute to the contagion of the reforming spirit of the University itself and not to any desire on your part for an easier life. All students should want to reform their university. If the University is already unconventional, the only way to reform it is to make it conventional

Student Assembly, 2 February 1951

BEADLE

At the same time we must constantly strive to improve the quality of our student body, at both the undergraduate and graduate levels.

Trustee-Faculty Dinner, 10 January 1962

BEADLE

Let's have a look at students.

In the five years of the College since the fall of 1957, the number of entering students is up by 20%.

The average College Board scores are up by 40 points in verbal aptitude and 75 in math. The percentage of students with A averages in high school has increased from 46 to 77, the number of class valedictorians from 15 to 63, the number of National Merit and General Motors Scholars is up 50%, and the number of members of the National Honor Society up from 125 to 475. The percentage of entering students who live on campus has increased from 66 to 93.

167

Our undergraduates are more intelligent, more articulate, more vocal and more critical than ever. Unfortunately, this year they have been so busy telling Kennedy how to handle the Cuban situation that they have had no time to advise the University administration.

Trustee-Faculty Dinner, 9 January 1963

BEADLE

College students now number 2,642, sixty-one above last year, and twice that of 1954–55. The quality of the entering class of 729 is judged to be at an all-time high. Scholastic Aptitude Test scores are approximately the same as last year—665–672 in verbal and mathematics tests.

State of the University, 7 November 1967

BEADLE

Student quality has also increased. The total enrollment is now about 8,500, with some 2,500 in the College. Although tuition has increased markedly, this has been more than offset for students with established need by an increase of more than three fold in student aid from general income. This year's students received in scholarships, fellowships, loans and employment, from all sources, more than the $18,000,000 they paid in tuition and fees. I doubt if any other major university in the nation does as well. This means no qualified student willing to earn and borrow modest amounts need deny himself an education at the University of Chicago.

Convocation, 7, 8 June 1968

THE HIGH PRICE OF THE PRIVILEGE

LEVI \

And the costs of education at Chicago are unavoidably high. A rough approximation of the cost per student per year, without including any capital building costs at all, is $4,603. This is, of course, an average, but it understates the cost. The tuition, as you well know, is high, but happily not half that high. Recog-

168

nizing the fact that income disparity among our students' families is probably greater at Chicago than at comparable institutions, Chicago returns in unendowed scholarship aid 32 percent of the tuition it receives.

Class of 1971 Assembly, 24 September 1967

HUTCHINS

More than the co-operation of the faculty is required to make faculty salaries what they ought to be. We must have also the co-operation of the students. No one has ever been able to advance a satisfactory reason why a student perfectly able to pay the full cost of his education should not do so. It would appear that the difficulties of organization resulting from the size of student groups and the fear of inter-university competition have been the principal obstacles to such a policy. We are now strong enough and well enough equipped, it seems to me, for us to consider seriously experiments in this direction. We may watch with interest the progress now being made in our own clinics in charging the patient according to his ability to pay. What difficulties are there except those of organization that I have mentioned in applying such a policy to education? If there are any they do not rest on the moral right of every individual to a free education in a private institution.

Trustee-Faculty Dinner, 8 January 1930

HARPER

Special consideration from the business point of view must be given to the problems connected with the expenses of student life. It is a mistake to encourage luxury, or even to make it possible. However wealthy a young man may be, he cannot spend a large sum of money annually and be a student. For the time being, at all events, he must limit his expenditures, and directly or indirectly the university must see that this is done. On the other hand, it is equally important that provision be made for the assistance of worthy students who find themselves unable to continue their work because of the lack of means. It is possible to make mistakes in assisting students who do not deserve assistance, and in rendering assistance in a manner which will injure the student even if he deserves help. To require that every student who receives help from the university shall make suitable return to the university in the form of service or of repayment of money is a practical business way of treating the whole matter. Help should be rendered only in return for work done or as a loan to be repaid. In the latter case there is no objection from the business point of view, if the loan is arranged on terms especially favorable to the student. Such a student cannot be expected in every case to furnish satisfactory security, but without such security money should not be loaned except to those whose character is personally known to the officers to be above reproach.

Decennial Report, 1 July 1902

HELP AND SELF-HELP

JUDSON

Fellowships have been established and maintained in American institutions of learning in order to encourage students in the pursuit of advanced work. But a single generation ago a bachelor's degree marked the acme of scholastic attainment in our colleges. The few who realized a lack of something beyond a college course were forced to cross the ocean in order to find it. The beginnings of real university instruction in this country had to be fostered by a system of bounties—in effect a sort of protective tariff on domestic learning. Under this stimulus, and doubtless largely on account of it, graduate schools have multiplied and grown luxuriantly. The number of resident graduate students, other than those in professional schools, was 5,612 in 1898–99, which was at the rate of 74 graduate students to a million of population, as against 5 to the million in 1872. The report of the United States Commissioner of Education for 1898–9 enumerates 447 fellowships in 52 institutions—in each case excluding strictly professional schools. Of this number 293 are reported from universities within this Association. This is exclusive of scholarships, many of which are given to graduate students. In the last academic year sums were expended reaching from $15,000 to $25,000 by different universities for fellowship stipends. In the methods of handling these considerable funds there is quite a number of diversities.

170

The amount of the stipend attached to the fellowship differs within quite wide limits in different institutions. In some the tendency seems to be toward a large number of fellowships with a resulting small stipend, in others toward a smaller number of fellowships yielding each a stipend relatively larger. Again, in some institutions the fellow is expected to render some service in return for his stipend, while in others there is no such requirement. Another difference lies in the exemption of fellows from the payment of tuition, thus in fact to that extent increasing the amount of the stipend—an exemption not granted in all universities. On the whole the preference seems now to be given in most places to students who have already done some graduate work, though there are still some appointments made from those who have just taken the bachelor's degree. The date of making the annual appointment varies. Action seems general in the spring months, but in some institutions comes a month or two later than in others. Finally, some universities require from appointees an agreement to make the doctorate at the institution appointing, this being by no means a general rule.

The mode of making appointments implies uniformly an application filed by candidates, and appointment at the best discretion of the University from the list of applicants. Under the existing customs it seems possible usually for a candidate to file his application in more than one place. He may have several strings to his bow, and failing of success in one institution he may still succeed in another. There is the further possibility that he may receive an appointment from more than one. In this case of multiple appointments the candidate has the privilege of electing the fellowship which seems to him the more eligible. It has more than once happened that, an appointment being made and duly published by one university, a month or two later the same person is tendered elsewhere a fellowship carrying a larger stipend, which naturally he is inclined to accept. Of course the university whose appointment is declined is at some disadvantage subsequently in filling the vacancy. It is not impossible in such cases that the fact of an appointment being made in one place to a certain extent aids the authorities of the other in coming to a conclusion more readily. Perhaps it is deserving of consideration whether it is worth while to encourage this drag net process of applying for fellowships; whether multiple appointments become the dignity of universities; whether, in fact, it is desirable for institutions to enter into competition for the privilege of paying a fellowship stipend to a given candidate.

The primary purpose of giving fellowships at present seems still to be to recruit the ranks of candidates for the degree of doctor of philosophy. In some few cases fellowships are established for the encouragement of research. In these the appointee must usually be already a doctor of philosophy, and in some instances there is no limitation of residence in a specific place.

It may be noted in passing that usually fellowships either are not given in schools strictly professional, like those of law and medicine, or at least that the number of fellowships in such schools is relatively small.

The query naturally rises, is not the graduate school after all really professional, perhaps quite as much so as schools of divinity or law? By far the larger number of graduate students are fitting themselves to teach. They hope for a college place. Many of them have to be content with high school appointments. Moreover, the conditions which once prevailed with reference to teaching places are now radically altered. The colleges expect as a matter of course that young men whom they appoint shall be doctors of philosophy. Secondary schools are more and more making the same requirement. I am convinced, indeed, that the time is in sight when it will be only in exceptional cases that a position can be secured in a secondary school unless by a thoroughly trained specialist.

This being the case, a second query suggests itself. Is there now the need for subsidizing the preparation of specialists for teaching more than the preparation of specialists in law and medicine? Teaching can hardly be said to be a more important or a more humanitarian profession than that of medicine. The demand for experts now exists. It is sure to create a supply, without artificial stimulus. Has not the system of bounties largely served its purpose?

Association of American Universities (Chicago)
27 February 1901

MASON

All these aids are important as additions to the encouragement that the University must offer to superior students at every level.

President's Report 1925–26

HUTCHINS

In this connection I may say that no increase in the tuition charges should be allowed to operate as a selective factor. When, if, and as made such increases should be accompanied by proportional increases in the scholarship funds, so that no man of ability will be kept out of the University of Chicago for financial reasons.

Student Assembly, 20 November 1929

BEADLE

We must give increased attention to our student aid program at both the undergraduate and graduate levels, especially in the divisions of school sciences and humanities. It is important that we find more fellowship support.

State of the University, 6 November 1962

BEADLE

Last week a news story in the New York *Herald Tribune* began somewhat as follows: "Everyone talks about doing something for the Humanities, but the University of Chicago has done it." This referred to the establishment now of fifteen additional graduate fellowships for study in the Humanities, these to be augmented by thirty more within two years, each providing a stipend equal to the most attractive graduate fellowships offered in the sciences. This program, suggested by Provost Levi and supported by special Trustee funds, I predict will initiate a whole series of competitive programs in other top institutions and thus stimulate scholarship in the Humanities way out of proportion to the funds initially invested by this University.

Trustee-Faculty Dinner, 8 January 1964

BEADLE

My guess is that tuition rates are likely to level off and that, aside from additional students, increases from this source will therefore be relatively modest.

State of the University, 10 November 1964

BEADLE

Along with the relatively high faculty salaries, the University, when all sources of student aid through the University are taken into account, has been providing more than eleven per cent of its total budget in various forms of student assistance. So far as I know, this is unequaled in any comparable institution. In dollar amounts, this means that Chicago is putting back in un-endowed scholarship aid about 30 per cent of the tuition it re-ceives, or approximately $4,000,000, and then adding another $8,000,000 for student aid in various forms from restricted sources.

Student Assembly, 18 November 1966

LEVI

I have paid this much attention to the enrollment figures, in part because this is the area where the deviation from the original 10-year projection is the greatest. A part of this deviation, as with the College a few years ago, was intentional, and was based upon the capacity of the student residence halls at that time. A good deal of the variation is a reflection of changing federal pol-icy on student aid. Federal fellowship aid to students at The University of Chicago, for example, has declined on the average of $500,000 a year for the past four years as part of the national policy to substitute federally aided student loans in place of di-rect subventions. The transition has had a substantial conse-quence, and particularly within the private universities. It is doubtful whether the policy under these conditions took account of the need not to damage the places which had achieved some sort of critical mass in terms of intellectual standards and ex-perience.

State of the University, 8 April 1974

HARPER

A very large number of the students support themselves wholly or in part by the aid of the Employment Bureau. Hundreds of students are enabled to secure work of one kind or another which contributes toward their expenses. This work is of various kinds, including: stenography and typewriting, clerical work, manual labor, dining-room service, bill collecting, canvassing, bookkeeping, lighting street lamps, distributing newspapers and circulars, folding Sunday papers in newspaper offices, domestic service, reading to aged people, serving as companions to children and youths, inspecting city gas lamps, acting as ticket clerks at suburban railway stations, or telephone switchboard operators, or stereopticon lantern operators, making lantern slides, reporting for newspapers, and clerking in stores. There have been more demands for young women to do housework than could be supplied. As a rule these places are not desirable. There have been also more openings for students to do canvassing work for book houses, and college novelty houses, than could be filled. The average student does not take kindly to this sort of work, although some men who are naturally adapted to the work secure good returns from it. Perhaps as many as three hundred students each year receive some help from this Bureau.

Decennial Report, 1 July 1902

THERE ARE NEVER ENOUGH GOOD PLACES TO LIVE IN, NEVER, NEVER

HARPER

There was some question in the minds of the Trustees as to the merits of the so-called "Dormitory System" of college life. Effort was made on the part of certain educators at the time of the opening of the University to show that the dormitory life was a survival of the Middle Ages, and that it was something entirely injurious to the development of a proper manhood and womanhood. Our own experience has been exactly the opposite. With each recurring year the demand for residence on the grounds is greater, and the results of such residence are more clearly apparent. This is especially true in the case of women. The accommodations for men, however, have been so meager and unsatisfactory as to give small opportunity for judgment. The avidity with which the rooms in the new Hitchcock Hall have been taken, contrary to the expectations of many, shows conclusively that proper accommodations cannot be secured outside of the halls of the University, and even when it is possible to secure them, there is an attraction about life in a University building which is not found in isolation from the University grounds. The only exception to this is in the case of the Fraternity Houses, which after all can hardly be called an exception, for they represent really only an intensification of the dormitory system. . . .

The distinguishing factor in the social life of the University has been the so-called "House System." This system was established during the first year of the University's history, and its purpose was to provide social units so constituted as to give freedom for individual development. . . . The theory of the system may be summed up in the statement that the University is one family, socially considered, of which the President is the head; that groups of six or more students living together constitute official Houses, for which the President appoints a Head, who is responsible to him. Such groups of students are for the most part self-governing, each group selecting an Executive Committee and some member of the University Faculty as Councilor. The rules of each are thus what the House itself adopts after approval by the University Council. As shown by the report, three classes of Houses have thus far been organized. The first class includes the groups of students occupying University Houses on the Quadrangles. These groups comprise from forty to seventy students each. The second class includes groups occupying Fraternity Houses. The third class includes students having a parlor or sitting-room on the University grounds, made up, however, of students whose homes are in the city. The plan has had a varying success. The life in some Houses has been almost ideal; in others, exceedingly unsatisfactory. On the whole, the scheme has been successful, and the later stages of its development have exhibited many encouraging features. The proposed enlargement of the plan by the unanimous vote of the Junior College Faculty to include all Junior College students is perhaps the strongest evidence of its practical success. Other facts pointing in the same direction are to be found in the recent successful organization of Hitchcock House and the reorganization of Snell House under the auspices of the Young Men's Christian Association. . . .

The history of the Fraternity System in the University is one of more than usual interest. Much anxiety existed in the minds of a majority of the members of the Faculty lest the introduction of Fraternities might bring disturbance of many kinds. The facts show that their presence in the University has been a source of great advantage rather than of disadvantage. In almost every case the Fraternities have contributed each its share, not only to the social life of the institution, but to its general welfare. Some criticism has been presented against the policy of the University in reference to Sororities, the organization of which up to present time has been prohibited by the University. This is not the place in which to present the considerations which explain this attitude on the part of the University. It is, perhaps, sufficient to say that the opinion is still a strong one that the social life of the University has developed more satisfactorily than would have been the case if Sororities had been introduced.

Decennial Report, 1 July 1902

BURTON

The Housing Commission has undertaken an investigation of the Housing conditions of the members of the Faculty and of the student body for the purpose of making recommendations to the Board of Trustees for the improvement of housing conditions. Preliminary to a final report which will make recommendations for a definite policy in regard to the housing of each division of the University over a period of years, the Commission has been occupied during the present year in the attempt to serve the present housing conditions. The first move has been to start co-operative building and co-operative ownership of apartments for members of the Faculty. A group of fifty-five families are now actively interested in the consideration of plans for building or buying apartments for next year. It is hoped that within a year these plans will have been so far carried into effect as greatly to relieve the situation.

Of the student housing problems the most pressing one is that of the married graduate student, who finds the cost of suitable apartments burdensomely high. While an immediate solution of this problem is not in sight, attempt is being made to improve conditions, and to work out a plan whereby this class of students can be provided for.

There is need also of proper provision for the large number of students who now live in outside lodgings. Final solution of this problem must wait, however till the Commission on the

Colleges has made its report embodying an educational policy for the undergraduate Colleges.

The study of these matters has brought the Commission and the University face to face with the question how far the housing of students and faculty is to be considered a part of the educational policy of the University; whether for example we are to pay no attention to the life of the student outside of the class-room, and to allow him to shift for himself, or whether we are to attempt to make his life here a part of his education. What the eventual answer to this question will be there can be no possible doubt.

Convocation, 17 March 1924

BURTON

We need new buildings for the residence of students. Far too many of you live in lodgings round about the University, where you inevitably miss many of the real benefits of University life. We hope before long to begin to meet this real need by buildings across the Midway. I hope we shall not call them dormitories, because we want them to be more than places to sleep. We hope they will be so built and organized and conducted as to be powerful factors in the process of education. Perhaps we shall incorporate into them some of the best features of the college of Oxford and Cambridge. We may even call them colleges, for it is our ambition to develop at the University of Chicago a better type of undergraduate life and education than is now provided here or anywhere in America.

Anniversary Chapel, 1 October 1924

BURTON

Independently of any special theory of the educational development of the colleges it is evident that we urgently need additional buildings for the residence of our students. More than 1600 students who are living in lodgings in the vicinity of the University would be receiving their education under conditions far more conducive to the best results educationally, if they were living in University houses, properly organized and conducted.

The property of the University facing north on the Midway is well adapted to such residence buildings, and is probably the best place for them.

With a view to determining by experimentation what measure of separation of the work of the colleges from that of the graduate schools is educationally most favorable to the work of both the colleges and the graduate schools, and precisely through what period such separation is most conducive to educational efficiency it is desirable to erect on the south side of the Midway a building which can be devoted to undergraduate work and which can serve as the center of undergraduate life in its more academic aspects. This building might well be erected on the block bounded by University and Greenwood Avenues and 60th and 61st Streets, the rest of this block being reserved for further buildings of similar purpose. Residence buildings for women could then be built on the blocks east of University Avenue and for men on those west of Greenwood Avenue.

Since the purpose of these buildings is to conduct under the most favorable conditions an experiment in undergraduate education, they should embody the best ideals that we have yet reached, and the most promising type of experiment, and be so constructed as to be as easily as possible modified if experimentation requires this.

The first educational building should contain rooms for study and reading, class rooms, and other rooms designed and equipped for whatever experiments in undergraduate education it may seem desirable to undertake. In addition there should be the necessary administrative offices and rooms for undergraduate activities of semi-academic character, such as the Undergraduate Council, the Honor Commission, *Cap and Gown, Maroon*, etc. It should be built with a view to future expansion if the experiment should call for it, and to such modification as experience shall show to be necessary.

The residence buildings should not be mere dormitories, but places of humane educational residence. They should provide opportunity on one hand for personal contacts, under the most favorable conditions, with older persons and fellow students, and for the silent influences of good books and art. They should provide for a library, a common room and a dining hall in each unit. They should provide rooms also for resident fellows or tutors and perhaps other members of the faculty, making more intimate personal conversation possible with individuals or small groups than is practicable in more public rooms. The aim should be to preserve the best features of our fraternity houses and women's halls, but with better facilities for the exertion of intellectual influences. All should be planned with a view to uniting as far as possible, the two lines of influence which in our American colleges have been unfortunately separated in large measure as numbers have increased, namely intellectual activity on the one hand and friendly contact with persons on the other.

It is not very important whether these residence halls be called colleges or halls. They will certainly not restrict the residents of a given house to any election of courses offered by any limited number of instructors who are associated with it—this plan has been abandoned at Oxford—but on the other hand each of them will aim to develop a real social and intellectual life of its own, and they will constitute a recognized part of the educational equipment of the University.

"The University of Chicago As It Should Be in 1940:
A Confidential Statement by the President," 1925

BEADLE

We are well aware of the need to add to the number of units available for student housing. Last year we added both George Williams College and the Broadview for single student housing, adding 293 units, and we also acquired and remodeled 53 apartments for married student housing. The renovation of the 78 apartments for married students in the Piccadilly should be completed this year. We are endeavoring to complete plans for a six-story building containing 24 three-bedroom apartments, to be located at 57th and Dorchester Ave. We hope this building will be available for single student housing by next October first. In the meantime, the architects are busy with plans to further implement the report of the Blum committee for the cluster of undergraduate housing—the so-called village plan—on the four-block area west of Greenwood and south of 55th. Present plans call for the construction of units which will house approximately 720 undergraduates, and which will also have twenty townhouses for faculty or graduate students. We are trying to develop this area so that it will include also the much-needed new music and art building, and the theatre. These facilities, a short distance from the Regenstein Library, will give to the University an unparalleled center for the Humanities; at the same time they will relate the new residence halls to the cultural life of the University. We hope a prospective donor or donors will share our enthusiasm for this extraordinary opportunity.

Student Assembly, 18 November 1966

BEADLE

A major disappointment to many of us in our physical planning and building is our failure to make more progress in providing for desirable and adequate student housing. You are well aware of student complaints in this regard. But you may not be aware that the failure is not for lack of trying. The Walter Blum Committee made an exhaustive study of the matter during which the views of faculty members and hundreds of students were sought and carefully considered. Working closely with Edward Larabee Barnes, an imaginative, sensitive, and highly competent New York Architect, their recommendations were translated into a most attractive and practical student village concept to be turned into reality on the two block area west of Greenwood Avenue between 55th and 56th Streets. The village provided for a diversity of housing adjacent to the proposed art-music theatre center and next to the athletic center to the west.

Unfortunately with a changing student population plus confusion, uncertainty, and unrest among the current generation of students as to what is wanted, it has not been possible to raise the funds to build what seemed to so many an ideal provision for comfortable, attractive and even gracious student living on campus. We must continue to try and this is now being done.

Incidentally, I want you to know that despite the large unanticipated increase of some 600 students over estimates for this fall, and contrary to allegations of some protesting students, the University housing offices have never yet failed to provide University housing for all who have requested it. True, much of it is not ideal and must be replaced. While there are still about a dozen students in doubled up dormitory rooms who have said they would like singles, this will soon be corrected. *But,* contrary to highly vocal complaints by students who allege that they want apartment living and can't obtain it, there are now and have been forty-six unoccupied apartments, subsidized and controlled by the University, available to students. They can house almost 100 students, but there are no takers.

State of the University, 5 November 1968

HARPER

One of the most practical, as well as difficult, problems of University life is involved in what may be called the food question, and it is inseparably connected, not only with the intellectual life, but also with the social life of the institution. In the Women's Houses the University has been able to provide a Commons which includes four dining-rooms and makes provision for about two hundred students. During the last year of the first decade a small café for men was established at the corner of Fifty-seventh street and Ellis avenue as an experiment. Only breakfast and luncheon are served. The results have been more than satisfactory. In the new Commons which will be finished within a few months, facilities will be provided for furnishing table board to five hundred men and café accommodations to three hundred in addition. This will probably meet the demand of the immediate future, so far as men are concerned, but it leaves the women who are not in University Houses still unprovided for.

Decennial Report, 1 July 1902

HUTCHINS

Your views on other matters through the years I have fully shared. I wish it were possible to eliminate the mechanics of institutional life. In a large institution, for some reason, the rooms can never be nice enough, the food can never be good enough, the lights can never be bright enough, the buildings are either too hot or too cold, the processes of registration, examination, and graduation are too protracted and too complicated.

I have carefully studied the various expressions of student opinion on these subjects as they have appeared since 1929 and have agreed with them all. There must be something refractory about the material out of which a university is made, or perhaps my efforts have been too modest and too intermittent. At any rate I have concluded that there is something about institutional life, at least on a large scale, that makes it impossible to do anything about it, just as I have concluded that the food in the various faculty clubs is identical, even though the clubs are as far apart as New York and Palo Alto, and that nothing can ever be done about it. One of the reasons why I would favor the development here of the Oxford and Cambridge system of small residential colleges that are federalized into a university is that I believe the smaller the unit the less institutional the institution.

Student Assembly, 2 February 1951

ACADEMIC CHALLENGE: FREEDOM TO LEARN

HUTCHINS

The educational program of Chicago, though not hard—not, in my opinion, hard enough—is more time-consuming than it used to be.

Undergraduate Assembly, 12 January 1940

JUDSON

The University has no desire to have the largest college in the country. It is anxious that its college work should be of a high grade, and that its benefits should be confined to those who are capable of availing themselves of them. It is to this end that the faculty has been so rigorous in eliminating students within the first year who have not come up to the required standards, and it is to the same end that a plan recently adopted will seek to eliminate those who are not likely to reach those standards hereafter before they are admitted at all. In short, we are anxious for students who are serious-minded and capable, and not for great numbers.

Convocation, 11 June 1912

BURTON

The elimination of students not likely to profit from a college course as early in the course as possible: It seems to be the case that about one-half of those who enter as Freshmen fail of grad-

183

uation, and that almost all of those who thus fail drop out within the first two years. Of these, one half again are incompetent students. It is believed that these incompetent ones could be discovered within the first month instead of falling out gradually throughout the first two years. Their prompt elimination would be a great advantage to the college and probably on the whole to those who are eliminated. Of course this process of elimination must not be carried on in a mechanical and heartless way, or on the basis of fractions of a per cent as shown by a marking system. The moral earnestness of a student is of more significance than high marks. Even capacity as shown in extra curriculum activities is not without significance.

"The Future of the University." University of Chicago Senate, 24 February 1923

HUTCHINS

But we are looking for waste. And we see that even at Chicago we have a vacation system that is a symbol of an age that is gone. Our students work harder than the students at some other places, but if they worked forty-four hours a week, they would all get A's, or graduate in half the time, or both. Nor has the weekly schedule of classes made the best use of the student's time or the maximum use of the plant. We should set about reducing vacations. We should consider the example of the College and going on a Monday Wednesday Friday cycle. We should examine the possibilities of late afternoon, evening, and weekend teaching. And we should put on the walls of every lecture hall, dormitory room, and office in the University the words of Dr. Johnson: "I never knew a man who studied hard."

Assembled Faculties, 7 January 1942

HARPER

Upon the whole, the relationship between student and professor has been a close one. It is ordinarily not expected that in an institution with city environment, and in an institution of so large a size, a great degree of intimacy is to be secured. Such intimacy is indeed frowned upon in certain of the larger institutions. It has been different with us. A large majority of the professors have cultivated close personal relationship with the

184

members of their classes. Undoubtedly many an individual has passed out of the institution without entering into such intimacy even with a single officer, but this is not true of a large number, and when true is to be explained in most cases by the peculiar character of the student himself. In some cases officers of the University have held themselves aloof from students, but these cases also have been few, and in general as close a relationship exists in the University between student and officer as might be expected or as is really called for. The student who comes to the University after two years of residence in a college, the faculty of which numbers twelve or fifteen, should not complain if, after his first year in the University, he is not personally acquainted with more than thirty or forty of the three hundred instructors. His acquaintance is three times as extended as it was in the smaller college, although he does not yet know more than 10 per cent of the officers of the University. The fact that he cannot become acquainted with a larger number means nothing, for he already knows a much larger number than he would have met in the smaller institution.

Decennial Report, 1 July 1902

Burton

The University will stand—more I think in the future than in the past—for interest in and concern for the individual. We are determined to escape from the tendency to a mere mass education, which is so strong today and the almost inevitable result of the great demand for education. We do not expect to know you as so many hundred freshmen. We expect that in the case of each of you there will be at least one officer of the University who will know you as an individual and counsel with you as a friend whom he knows and understands.

Anniversary Chapel, 1 October 1923

Burton

I am pretty certain that we are going to lay more stress on personalities and individuals than heretofore, devising some way of forming smaller groups the members of which come into closer contact with one another and with members of the faculty. Education cannot successfully be accomplished by wholesale, or

185

quantity production. It is a personal process and personalities must be recognized. There is a great deal in that old ideal of the college—Mark Hopkins on the end of a log and a student on the other. In my own student days I had many teachers, but only a few who knew how to teach, and among them all one man who really stood out as the preeminent teacher—a man the mention of whose name today though he has been years in his grave—stirs the heart of every man or woman who ever came into his classroom.

I was in a group of three alumni the other day and we were talking about this matter of personal influence—and after I had spoken of my great teacher, one of the three said quietly—"It was Chas. R. Henderson that made me" and another said, "It was W. R. Harper in my case," and the third said, "I had several teachers but the greatest of them was Von Holst."

I shall not be satisfied till we have organized our college education so that every student has a chance to come into close personal touch with at least one great teacher—one great personality with life-giving power in his touch.

And finally I suspect that we have something to learn from Oxford and Cambridge from which we got our first idea of the American College. Perhaps someday we are going to find a way of grouping our thousands of students into smaller groups, that will to a considerable extent share a common life—be something like the old mediaeval guild of scholars, where pupil and teacher mingle together and you do not always know who is teaching and who is being taught.

Alumni Gathering (New York), 1923

MASON

We've been trying to break down the barrier between the undergraduate and the faculty. The student seems to think of the faculty as an opponent, or at least as a referee. I know of students who have been in college two or three years and feel they have no friend on the faculty. My interest is heartfelt in humanizing the whole establishment of education. The University of Chicago has done a great work towards breaking down these barriers—they have no place in a brotherhood of learning.

"Some Statements by President Mason"
University of Chicago Magazine
December 1925

MASON

Students should share with the Faculty our advances of knowledge. I do not mean that a Junior can take a research problem in Celtic or in calculus of variations. I know very well he cannot. But I do know how much it means to the youngster to be around a group doing real things; and if he does nothing more than carry a bucket of water for a man who is performing an experiment in physics, if he does nothing more than help typewrite or arrange sheets or photostats, he gets the spirit of scholarship and can be left to his own devices to satisfy his curiosity. The methods in the colleges, to a very great extent, are those of many decades ago, when it was difficult to obtain the information which constituted a college education. Today you can hardly turn without seeing some very good means by which a man who wishes to educate himself can do so. Libraries are at every turn, self-helps, correspondence schools; there is no need now to furnish merely the helps to education, and there is certainly no reason for the continuance in an undergraduate college of methods which dull the edge of curiosity. I am convinced that students come to the University of Chicago from the high schools with far higher ideals than we give them credit for; that many of them are looking toward the experience as an intellectual adventure. They are easily deflected. They are young. We do not hold as many of them as we might, and I hope that we can hold more. The answer is not in using the college as an instrument to dull curiosity. The answer is in using the college as an instrument to stimulate and feed curiosity and interest; then we can safely leave the rest to the youngsters themselves. If we can work in that direction, we can accomplish an infinite amount of good in American education.

We lack here the economic urge which makes necessary good performance in scholarship in Europe. It is the tradition of America that the able youngster can make good. He does not need his training. Those days may pass soon. We are no longer a pioneer country, and the need for guidance by the men versed in the technique of their subjects is becoming greater and greater; but the economic urge will not be present with us for some time to come, and I believe we must make up for it in some way. America needs more than anything else appreciation for the life of scholarship, and that involves us in quite a turn of events. It means that we shall have to be sympathetic with youngsters who have not had that spark of enthusiasm, that we shall not limit our interest to those who show an early interest in scholarship. I am not sure that the normal boy can be expected under present conditions to plan to be a productive scholar for a profession on entering the University, but we shall get a good many of the best men in the world if we can make our methods more interesting to them. Here are normal, wholesome, sound, American youths with interest in everything from athletics to music. We must make our work more their work, and hold out to them through an honor system such a performance in later years as will throw them certainly and definitely into daily participation with great scholars whose names perhaps they already know and from whom they can obtain that spark of interest that will make it unnecessary for anybody to teach them. They will teach themselves.

Trustee-Faculty Dinner, 12 January 1927

HUTCHINS

But it is said, teachers have great influence on the young. At every age adults have a way of over-estimating the pliability of their juniors. As a result many people seem to have the notion that the student is a sort of plastic mass, to be molded by the teacher in whatever likeness he will. It is for this reason that parents feel they can solve their domestic problems by turning them over to the educator. In secondary school work I have observed this phenomenon time and time again. A lady once presented to my headmaster her son, nineteen years old, saying, "He has been terribly spoiled. He has never done any work. I didn't like to push him. Now you take him, and make a man of him, and interest him in his studies." And my headmaster replied substantially in the words of Tennyson, "Late, late, too late, ye cannot enter now." It is sad but true that at eighteen or nineteen or graduation from high school it is too late to take a boy and make a man of him and interest him in his studies. He has solidified, too often in more ways than one. But even if it were possible physiologically and psychologically, the college should not attempt the job. Because of its size, because its funds were given to it for another purpose, it can only to a limited degree spend its time and money in supervising a student's conduct, in regulating his daily habits, and in forcing him to improve his mind and body against his will. The college is there, with all its opportunities. Broadly speaking he may take it or leave it. And what this comes down to is that if a man hasn't character, if he hasn't the germs of intellectual interest, if he doesn't want to amount to anything, the college can't give him a character, or intellectual interest, or make him amount to anything. It may complete the task, but it is too late to begin it.

Alumni Club of New York, 6 April 1936

HUTCHINS

You remember the ancient oriental proverb: "Why hast thou created me," said the ass, "seeing that thou hast also created the Turk?" "Verily, we have created the Turk so that the excellency of thy understanding and character might be apparent." This, with modifications, almost seemed to me to be the reason the *Maroon* thought the faculty was created. But I was rapidly relieved of this unfortunate impression by an editorial shortly thereafter attacking the students. Apparently both students and faculty left something to be desired. Since that time I have learned that the organization of the course of study and the regulations surrounding it are far from perfect; and the administration even farther because it is doing nothing about these matters.

Upon its stand on these questions the student press deserves the congratulations of the University, for all the suggestions it makes are in the direction of higher standards, more intellectual effort and independence, and better men and women, student and faculty. With the net result it reaches therefore I am in entire accord; for if I were to attempt to state a policy, I should say that I favored the best faculty that could be obtained, teaching the best students that could be found, with a curriculum intelligently adjusted to the needs of the individual. That means that I agree that there are students here as in every university who should not be here. It means I agree that there are teachers, as in every university, who are not the most inspiring in the world. It means that I am heartily opposed to restrictions that fetter the intellectual freedom of the student who has an intellect to free. When I was an undergraduate and a law student I sometimes had a momentary fleeting notion from time to time that perhaps there was something to be got out of these professors and their curriculum if one only knew the way to go about

189

it. Sometimes it even occurred to me that one might perhaps prepare oneself for something, I didn't know just what, if one could only get behind this business of required attendance, regular classes, ten minute papers, weekly tests, and term examinations, and utilize what intelligence God had given one in one's own way to learn something or other. It almost seemed possible that the curriculum might be as interesting as the extra-curriculum if it were as well organized and called for the same effort and intelligence.

Student Assembly, 20 November 1929

HUTCHINS

Since all Chicago professors and students think, the difficulty must come, if at all, at the point of understanding. And this brings us back to the question whether there are any issues in education. If the object of the schools is social adjustment and that of the universities specialized training, the hope that either professors or students will be able to understand one another, or that they will even be interested in doing so, is slim indeed. The College of the University of Chicago, the divisions, the various interdivisional committees, the Federated Theological faculties, and the numerous formal and informal groups of professors and students at Chicago are all attempts to get rid of the barriers to understanding and to lay the basis for communication.

Alumni Assembly (Chicago), 9 June 1951

KIMPTON

How much of a student's time do we give to the required curriculum of broad and shared training? Some say that three-quarters of his time should be allotted to obtaining acquaintance with those fundamental ideas and facts which create the basis of mutual understanding and communication. Others insist that any such allotment is ridiculous and preposterous. If a student has to waste a quarter of his time obtaining a smattering of a lot of things, perhaps this is allowable, but certainly three years should be given over really to learning something about something. The rope on which the pulling and hauling occurs in this tug of war is the poor student, and sometimes, I regret to say, he is stretched all out of shape by the exercise.

Convocation, 13, 14 June 1958

LEVI

The burden which each student carries is personal. The education which he seeks cannot be given to him; he must reach for it with himself. And though he seeks stars to steer by, he cannot escape the self-involvement which is essential if the process of education is to take place. The scholar is not so different. The contribution which he can make to his students and to the world of learning is of himself. It is not external to him. Intellectual powers wither through disuse, and are misguided or ineffective without the agonizing search for perfection which is the mark of the craftsman. The university community finds its fulfillment only through the work of the individual scholar and the individual student; and self-concern, which is not self-indulgence, is an essential ingredient.

University of Tulsa Presidential Inauguration
10 November 1967

EMOTIONAL CHALLENGE: FREEDOM TO MATURE

LEVI

The student is going through a process which is intended to change him and to perfect his intellectual powers. It is a time of testing and emotional growth. The greater the education, the more disruptive the experience may be.

University of Tulsa Presidential Inauguration
10 November 1967

HARPER

The relation between individual members of the Faculty and their respective students has been conspicuously close. In no other institution of this size, I am persuaded, has the intimacy

191

between instructor and student been more zealously cultivated. On the other hand, the interest of the members of the Faculty in amusements and recreations controlled by the students has not been as clearly manifested. There seems to have existed a strong disposition to leave the students to themselves in their various plans for social improvement, the Faculties restricting their energies largely to their own membership. To put the matter in another form, there has been a lack of co-operation between the Faculties as such and the student social interest, while at the same time many individual members of the Faculty have taken large part in connection with these interests. The separation referred to has been due in part to the large numbers which make up the Faculties, it being inevitable that the first movement in a social way shall be within the circles of the Faculties themselves; in part also to the fact that in these first years the members of the Faculties were strangers to each other, and their social interest has been entirely occupied in forming friendships in the new environment. On the other hand, indications of an increasing co-operation between the Faculties and the students have shown themselves, as, for example, in the readiness to unite in the celebration of Washington's birthday.

... The individual spirit has shown itself in so many ways that the history of individual enterprise is perhaps the most pathetic chapter in the history of the University. The strong development of the individual which has been encouraged by the institutions and regulations of the University has been gained at some cost to the spirit of the mass, but this individual spirit, which is characteristically the spirit of the university as distinguished from that of the college, has in proper ways subordinated itself to the more general spirit, and this without detriment to itself. The presence of so large a number of graduate students has influenced to an appreciable extent the general character of the undergraduate student body, and this has not in all cases resulted in disadvantage to the latter. Furthermore, the individual freedom of the graduate student has been shared by every undergraduate student, and while this has to some extent prevented the massing of the students together for certain purposes, it has nevertheless proved to be a distinct source of advantage to the individual student.

... The number of cases requiring discipline has been surprisingly small, and the cases of the most serious character have occurred in the graduate schools rather than in the colleges. There has been the usual number of instances of cheating in theme work and in examinations. No student has been arrested by a police officer during the history of the University, and no student has been dismissed for drunkenness. Cases of immorality which have come to the notice of the authorities have been exceedingly few. In cases of discipline of the most serious character, the President, in consultation with the officers most nearly connected, has acted without bringing the matter to the attention of the Faculties. In ordinary cases the Faculty has taken action. But in nearly every case students have returned after the term of suspension and finished their course of study. Rules of conduct have been few, the general requirements being those ordinarily expected of men and women living in good society.

Decennial Report, 1 July 1902

HUTCHINS

It regards its alumni as adults. It would find it difficult to defend any other attitude; for its students are treated as adults, and it could hardly assume that life and education rendered its graduates less mature than the Freshmen under the New Plan.

Alumni Assembly (Chicago), 24 September 1941

HUTCHINS

But I will tell you in the privacy of this gathering how to make the most apathetic students radical if you really want to do it. The way to do it is to suppress them. This policy has never yet failed to have this effect. The student resents the suggestion that he is not able or cannot be trusted to think about anything but football or fraternities. Most of the student Reds I have heard about have been manufactured by the hysterical regulations of the institutions in which they are enrolled. They are not Reds at all and do not know what it means to be one.

I am far from denying that there are radical students. I suggest that we shall not find the reason for their attitude in the teaching they have received. We shall find the reason for it in the world in which they have had to live. That world is one of chaos.

Alumni Club of New York, 6 April 1936

193

HUTCHINS

For though I do not concede that the students can determine the curriculum, the tuition fees, or the activities in which the University should or should not engage, I do insist that they are entitled to express themselves on these or any other subjects; and I should be the last person in the world to deprive them of the opportunity of doing so in the most pointed and effective manner.

Undergraduate Assembly, 12 January 1940

HUTCHINS

Maroon's problem
a. What to kick about when nothing to kick about
b. Yale *Daily News* wonderful time with required attendance, compulsory chapel, and credit system
c. Climax reached when *Maroon* forced to kick against freedom students elsewhere have been fighting to win, and to complain about being treated like adults when students elsewhere are in rebellion against being treated like infants.
Answer: let's get some better students

Maroon Banquet, 19 May 1937

KIMPTON

The primary business of an educational institution is to educate. I would not deny this for an instant. But it is also the function of an educational institution to provide a full life for a student, outside the classroom and library as well as in. I do not mean that it is the function of the University of Chicago to give a student a manner in any Ivy League sense. I wouldn't mind seeing him have some manners, but I am not sure that is our problem. In suggesting to our students that they conduct themselves in a way consistent with the standards and morals of our society, we are not suggesting any intellectual conformity, but the standards of good taste. It has been the long-standing policy of the University of Chicago to encourage intellectual and social maturity through the greatest possible freedom of expression and behavior on the part of students. If you compare the elaborate

194

dormitory rules of most institutions with our own, you will understand what I mean. If you take a look at our residence hall advisory system, our student health program, and our Counseling Center, you will note that it is our desire to aid you but not to coddle you, to protect you but not to regiment you, and to advise you but not to think for you. This does not mean that you can do anything you want to do at the University of Chicago. You share this situation with the Chancellor of your University and indeed with all the citizens of any civilized community.

Student Assembly, 28 January 1952

HARPER

In accordance with the action of the faculties taken in the Winter Quarter, the students of the Junior and Senior Colleges in their various divisions, have selected representatives who together have constituted the Student Councils. ... These Councils have considered in connection with the student body several important questions. Among these are (1) that of the honor system, the adoption of which would do away with all inspection of examinations on the part of instructors, (2) the relations of The University to other universities in matters of intercollegiate oratorical contests and debates, (3) the question of fuller student representation in the management of the athletics of The University. No definite action has been taken by the student bodies upon these questions, but the discussion which has followed their presentation has already exerted a good influence.

Convocation, 1 July 1896

HARPER

It is generally conceded that the Student Councils have contributed very largely to the *esprit de corps* of the student body. These Councils were intended to serve in each case as an Executive Committee, and thus to represent the students. It has been our custom to present all matters of importance which concern the student body to the Councils for their consideration, and to receive from them recommendations embodying the desires and opinions of the student body. The records show that in nearly every case the recommendations of the Councils have been of such a character as to warrant their acceptance and approval by the University ruling bodies. The growth of these Councils in influence has been steady, and already they have come to occupy a high place in the esteem of the students. Membership is regarded as an honor, and in almost every case those elected to membership have shown faithfulness in the discharge of their duties. The possibilities of the Councils are without limit; each year will add to the dignity and effectiveness of the service.

Decennial Report, 1 July 1902

KIMPTON

Student Government, when an object of real student interest and concern, can be democracy at work. It is sometimes alleged that it has no real power, and is only a puppet with its strings pulled by the administration. I can assure you that a responsible student government on this campus will have all the authority it can use. Perhaps I should mention in passing that it would be very gratifying to hear as much discussion about student responsibilities as I now hear about student rights.

Student Assembly, 28 January 1952

BEADLE

Last spring a special committee, chaired by Professor Harry Kalven of the Law School, examined this general question, and wrote a report which the Academic Council voted unanimously to circulate to faculty members and students. It was published in the *University Record* issued on November 3. I hope you have studied it.

The Committee's report amplifies and clarifies a policy that has been recognized and followed by the University from its earliest years. In 1899 the "Congregation" of the University unanimously resolved:

1. That the principle of complete freedom of speech on all subjects has from the beginning been regarded as fundamental in The University of Chicago, as has been shown both by the attitude of the President and the Board of Trustees and by the actual practice of the President and the professors.

2. That this principle can neither now nor at any future time be called in question.

3. That it is desirable to have it clearly understood that the University, as such, does not appear as a disputant on either side upon any public question; and that the utterances which any professor may make in public are to be regarded as representing his opinions only.

I believe it is fair to say that students in this University have always enjoyed equal rights of nondisruptive dissent and protest. Whether justified or not, student opinion should, I firmly believe, contribute to the educational process, and should be responded to appropriately. Disruptive demonstrations may also contribute something to the educational process, but the lesson they teach is that the emotional climate they create is inimical to constructive educational exchange. This, in addition to other obvious reasons, is why they cannot be defended or tolerated in a university such as this.

State of the University, 7 November 1967

LEVI

All this may well lead to the conclusion that it is good that disruption and unrest have found their way to colleges and universities because, after all, it is a problem for education. And yet for this very reason it is a peculiarly difficult problem for education to deal with. The movements tend to reject reason, which is the way of education. They buttress this rejection by replacing reason with personal qualities thought to be more than adequate substitutes. As always, the corruptions of thought come home to roost. Moreover, coercion and disruption are, in fact, offensive to the very idea of a university. For this reason a university is most vulnerable to them. Over a long period of time it cannot live with them, and to the extent that they are present, they diminish and deteriorate the quality of the institution. And this comes at a time when the quality of intellectual life in our institutions is under attack in any event.

It is not certain there is an answer. But obviously the attempt has to be made. One would hope it can be most appropriately made through a patient reassertion of the universities' own conception of themselves as places for disciplined thought, as academies of the mind, as custodians of our culture, the restorers of eloquence, and the centers of that intellectual concern and unrest which can change the world.

Life Insurance Association of America
(New York), 11 December 1968

LEVI

I have purposely understated the dangers, the harm, the immediate traumatic and the long-term searing effects. There is no single rule for the best handling of these events. But I think this much can be said. Particularly because these festivals are built upon a conception of the world ruled by coercion and corruption, the university's response must exemplify the principles which are important to it. The university must stand for reason and for persuasion by reasoning. Reasoning of this kind requires a most difficult honesty—an intellectual discipline which is self-critical. It is most unfortunate and in the long run disastrous for a university to exemplify expediency which avoids or solves conflicts by the acceptance of ideas imposed by force. So the university must show that it values and respects the individual mind, that discussions can always proceed, but that a threat to the disciplined freedom of the university is a threat to its very existence and purpose. This approach requires candor, consistency, and openness, but also effective discipline. The discipline will be difficult. But the university owes this much to itself, and it also owes this much to the larger society.

American Law Institute (Washington, D.C.)
23 May 1969

IS THERE LIFE AFTER LEARNING?

LEVI

The desire to educate the whole man, meaning by that many of the facets of growing up, was once greeted with great scorn on the Chicago campus in order to give emphasis instead to intellectual skills and the works of the mind.

Association for General and Liberal Education
(Chicago), 25 October 1963

KIMPTON

We have insisted that the purpose of a university is to train the mind, and the inference has been drawn that the rest of the person may go hang so far as we are concerned. We have deplored fun, snorted at anyone who wanted to develop himself physically, and sneered at anyone who conceived of a college education as having any vocational or practical significance.

Trustee-Faculty Dinner, 13 January 1954

HARPER

The full history of the student life during the four years, would be an interesting sociological study. There were, at first, no bonds of association, and only to the slightest extent was there acquaintanceship of any kind. Bold and courageous were those first men and women who began work October 1st, 1892. The recollection of life in the Beatrice, of the removal of the women in the spring to Snell, will never be forgotten by those who took part in these experiences. The divinity men, most of whom had been accustomed to the quiet and seclusion of Morgan Park, were somewhat disconcerted and distracted by the confusion and general looseness which prevailed. The decision of the faculty to discourage the organization of fraternities now seems to have contributed much to the confusion of the earlier years. There was, however, everywhere manifest the presence of an excellent spirit, and the pioneer days performed no slight service in developing character that would not otherwise have been developed. At the beginning of the second year the house system was adopted and immediately social organization began to take form. Meanwhile several efforts were put forth to organize literary societies and these, with the associations formed in connection with the University of Chicago *Weekly*, and other similar efforts, furnished the basis for still further development. The simple division of all undergraduate students into two classes, earlier known as University and Academic Colleges, and more recently as Senior and Junior Colleges, prevented all friction of a traditional character between freshmen and sophomores, and at the same time encouraged a more independent feeling on the part of younger students, as compared with those who had been longer engaged in college work. The large number of graduate students unquestionably exerted restraining influence upon the undergraduates, an influence, however, which was upon the whole good. This same influence was exerted by the life of the houses, especially in the women's houses where graduate and undergraduate women have lived together. The athletic activity was cultivated vigorously from the beginning. Here, more than anywhere else, paternalism may be said to have existed. The University did not wait for the student to organize. The work of the athletic field was placed under the direct supervision of a University officer. The results show that under certain circumstances paternalism is an effective agency. The Monday receptions, instituted soon after the organization of the houses, have contributed perhaps more than any other single agency to the general social life of the students. Mention should also be made of the important contributions from year to year by the Glee and Mandolin Clubs. The annual concert in the city played an important part in the whole history.

Naturally the senior students took in hand the celebration of Washington's birthday, and the custom of Junior College day seems to have become a law. Within two years the exercises connected with graduation have become more and more distinctive, until now certain events of a specific character seem to have become permanent. The more important traditions of student life may be regarded as established.

Quinquennial Statement, 1 July 1896

HARPER

It is commonly understood that in an urban University there exists a great lack of the elements which constitute the basis of social life, and indeed the presence of many elements which are distinctly harmful to such life. Among these latter may be cited, for example, the fact that very many of the students live on the University grounds during only a small period of the day, and also the fact that these same students who live at home are compelled to maintain the social life which is connected with the home. About 40 per cent. of the students have their homes in Chicago; another 40 per cent. live in rooms which are in more or less close proximity to the University grounds; the remaining 20 per cent. reside in the Halls of the University. It is on this ac-

count that the so-called "college spirit" is so slow of develop-
ment in a large community as compared with its growth in a
small community. In the history of our own institution, the de-
velopment of the social life has been somewhat remarkable, in
view of all the circumstances.

In my opinion, the arrangement by which all University exer-
cises are suspended for thirty minutes between 10 and 10:30
A. M. or 10:30 and 11 A. M. has contributed very largely to this
development of social life. This interval has furnished oppor-
tunity for the commingling of students, the holding of meetings
in which a portion or the entire body of students was interested,
and the coming together on stated occasions in Chapel Assem-
bly. I think that no more important institution exists in con-
nection with the University life than this morning interval. If
this respite in the middle of the day were lost by the transfer of
the Chapel Assembly to the first half-hour in the morning, a seri-
ous injury would be inflicted upon the social life of the institu-
tion. . . .

After the first two or three years, suggestions were made for
a Club House for men. This at first seemed something entirely
impracticable, but the force of the suggestion grew in intensity
until it was the unanimous feeling of the Faculties and Trustees
that such a building should be erected. Plans for it were pro-
vided, and upon the recommendation of the Committee having
in charge the designation of the use for which the funds coming
from the Reynolds estate might be employed, Reynolds Hall has
been erected. It is confidently believed that the erection of this
Hall at the end of the first decade will mark a new era in the
social life of the men of the University.

Within the last year, through the efforts of the Dean of Women,
Miss Talbot, and others associated with her, the Women's Union
has been established. This includes from three hundred to four
hundred women, and has already become a center of social life
in the institution. The Women's Union has occupied temporarily
the Disciples' Church on the corner of Fifty-seventh street and
Lexington avenue, and, even with the inadequate facilities thus
presented, the work accomplished has been noteworthy. . . .

There probably has been a less satisfactory development of
the literary spirit among the students than might have been ex-
pected. This has been due in part to the newness of the situa-

tion and to the lack of encouragement and stimulus in certain lines. Great emphasis has been placed on the scientific side of work, and perhaps there has been greater interest developed in the philology than in the literature of a given language. It is also true that in these years the aesthetic side of work has been sadly ignored. A change has already been instituted, and in time the results should show themselves. . . .

The amateur organizations of the University, of Music, Dramatics, etc., have naturally labored under the great disadvantages of being brought into comparison directly and constantly with the professional representatives in these various lines. When members of the University have the privilege of attending the concerts of the Chicago Orchestra at a trifling cost, and when the best plays presented to the American public can be heard almost every night in the year, there is little to encourage the development of the amateur spirit. But in spite of proximity to these exhibitions of the highest art, the local amateur interest has been cultivated with real enthusiasm. The Musical Clubs and the Dramatic Clubs have achieved a large success. . . .

It was very fortunate that in the beginning success attended the effort to organize the religious work of the University upon a broad basis. The Christian Union was so constituted that it should include all religious effort put forth by any particular group of persons. Opportunity was thus afforded, on the one hand, for the work of the Young Men's Christian Association as well as that of the Young Women's Christian Association, and, on the other, for such philanthropic effort as was included in the University Settlement work. There was at first some disappointment that the narrower conception did not prevail in this organization, but today all persons agree that a more satisfactory arrangement perhaps could not have been instituted. The work of the Social Settlement has been genuinely successful. Its success, however, has found its expression not so much in the results accomplished at the Settlement as in the splendid influence which this work has exerted on the membership of the University. The life of the professional student has a tendency to become distinctly selfish. This tendency has been overcome, at least to some extent, through the vigorous effort put forth by the members of the Faculty, including the members of the Women's League, to cultivate in this manner the altruistic spirit.

Decennial Report, 1 July 1902

BURTON

Proper opportunities for extra curriculum activities, social culture and interchange of ideas, and healthful sport: Our purpose should not be to make scholarly digs but broadminded and cultivated scholars and citizens.

University of Chicago Senate, 24 February 1923

BURTON

In a co-operative movement called the "Better Yet" Campaign, twenty-five joint committees, each consisting of two or more faculty members and four or more undergraduates, are studying different suggestions, made in the first instance by members of the Senior Class, as to ways of improving conditions of undergraduate life and work at the University of Chicago.

Perhaps the most important of all these committees is the one which is considering the distribution of students' time. Dante says that nearly all the troubles of the human race come from not knowing how to use time: it is certainly true that nearly all the troubles of the undergraduate body come from this cause. The first task of the committee on the distribution of students' time has been to ascertain the facts as to the ways in which students do actually spend their time. This is being done by use of a very carefully prepared questionnaire which calls for a statement of the time spent by each student in a typical quarter on each of his courses; other studious, literary, or artistic interests; non-athletic activities; athletics; other exercises; class, fraternity, and club interests; religious and social interests; self-support; transportation, etc. Some 2000 of these questionnaires have been returned and the results are being tabulated as a basis for constructive study. . . .

Still other committees which are well advanced in their work are studying the extent of the student desire for instruction in music and the extent to which such instruction is provided elsewhere; the reorganization of the Honor Commission; the distribution of activities among different students in such a way that no student will engage in too many activities and that as many as possible may benefit by the great potential values of such interests; the quality of instruction in large elementary courses; and the question of the adequacy of the women's clubs as now existing to meet the needs of undergraduate women in respect to social organization.

We believe this movement to be notable, not only in its promise of definite and important results in the study of the several problems, but because we believe the informal co-operative association of groups of faculty members and undergraduates in such constructive work to be valuable both for the faculty members and the undergraduates, and to be symbolic of the friendly relations which in general should prevail between the elder and the younger members of the University community.

Convocation, 17 March 1924

BURTON

The University will stand for the ideal of a symmetrical and well balanced life. It is primarily a place for hard work. There is no room for the idler here. Amusement is not our principal business. I once asked a professor in a European University what it was necessary for a student to do in order to get a degree in his University. His answer was, only not to forget what he knew when he came. That is not our spirit.—Unless you have come here expecting to work hard you have come to the wrong place. But we do not expect you to spend all your waking hours in study. There is room here for social contact of student with student, time for you to look after your health, and the cultivation of your manners. We believe in Physical Culture and Athletics, we believe in social intercourse and recreation. But we believe in them all as agencies of education and as concommitants of the principal business of the place.

Anniversary Chapel, 1 October 1923

MASON

We must search for football *function* if we are to validate its monstrous extension. I am as inconsistent in regard to football as every one else. During the season from two to four in the afternoon football is the all absorbing—most important subject of college life. I am out there on the bleachers too. But I must not forget other features possessing unequivocal function. The Dicks' contribution to the control of scarlet fever is more important than all the football games in the world. This rah rah stuff is easily overdone, but as far as it means the happy joyous background of good fellowship and friendship which holds together the real work of the university, I am for it. However, we must recognize the danger of too great enthusiasm for football.

The danger of bookishness is worse. If we could do the impossible and get the bookish student to play football and the football player to study intensively (!)—well perhaps we can.

Alumni of University of Wisconsin and
University of Chicago (Milwaukee), 14 December 1925

HUTCHINS

But you may say, "This is all very fine, but what has it got to do with us? We are undergraduates, not university presidents. What will the abolition of football do to undergraduate life at the University of Chicago?" Think what the University has. In intercollegiate athletics it has had the largest program in the Western Conference. Even without football it has as large a program as any Conference university. It has, moreover, one of the most successful programs in the Conference. In the last six years we have won more championships than anybody except Michigan and have done so in almost every year of the six. The University proposes to continue all the intercollegiate sports it now sponsors and is considering enlarging their number.

In intramural athletics the University maintains a program of eighteen sports. The increase in the participation in them in the last six years has been startling. The number of men in intramurals has gone up 50 per cent. The use of Bartlett Gymnasium has increased by a third. The use of the tennis courts has increased 350 per cent. The University proposes to continue and to expand its intramural program.

Even apart from athletics undergraduate life at the University is so lively that I don't see how you get any studying done. I know from sad experience with some of you that there actually are students here who don't get any done. There are 134 recognized student organizations on the campus. They have 5,600 members. They are putting a serious strain on the facilities of the University. The use of Ida Noyes Hall by these student organizations has increased from 47,000 to 74,000, or more than 50 per cent, in the past ten years.

If you want the answer to the question whether the University is interested in undergraduate life and work, stand on the Midway and look around. In the last ten years we have built the Men's Residence Halls, intended for undergraduates; the Field House, for intercollegiate and intramural sports; and International House, which, I think you will agree, has made an important contribution to the extra-curriculum life of the undergraduates.

I hope that it is not necessary for me or anyone else to tell you that this is an educational institution, that education is primarily concerned with the training of the mind, and that athletics and social life, though they may contribute to it, are not the heart of it and cannot be permitted to interfere with it.

Undergraduate Assembly, 12 January 1940

Hutchins

We insist, indeed, that the most enduring comradeship is that which grows out of participation in the kind of exciting common enterprise which is a Chicago education. We do not admit that the University is deficient in those conventional extra-curriculum activities which go by the name of college life. We assert that Chicago has all these and something more, something which no other university has in equal degree: an atmosphere of intense, strenuous, and constant intellectual activity. Other institutions offer college life; Chicago offers college life, and an education, too.

Alumni Assembly (Chicago), 24 September 1941

Kimpton

The University has been out of football since 1939. We are not in a position to go back into Big Ten football even if we wanted to. Our College, as you know, drops back two years from the traditional four year period, and our young men do not have the maturity to compete in the contact sports with the big leagues.

Let us take stock of our present situation. We have more kids involved in sports than most universities where the whole emphasis is on varsity competition. You'd be amazed to take a good look at Bartlett and the field house on a late afternoon. And we are competing, and doing pretty well, in sports where our

younger men have a chance. We have given the game back to the
kids, and that is something at the moment we can well be proud
of. I think there need to be changes, but I suspect they are more
changes of degree or emphasis than they are changes of kind.
Extra-curricular activities are important in my book. I don't
think they are or ought to be the reason a young man comes to
college, and I am confident that he ought to get a lot more out
of college than is represented by a varsity letter or a fraternity
key. But I don't think we need worry about this at Chicago; the
atmosphere of the place and the quality of the academic work
will take care of that.

Order of the C Dinner, 7 June 1951

KIMPTON

We at Chicago have been so concerned, and properly so, about
the curricular side of our institution that we have paid less at-
tention to the extra-curricular. This has had some obvious ad-
vantages. A student comes here to learn or he doesn't come here.
And he learns something while he is here or he doesn't stay. Our
campus is not a country club, an annex to a stadium, or a drawn-
out poker party, and I can assure you that some campuses are.

. . . But in the process of getting the extra-curricular into
proper perspective, we need to be careful that we do not close
our eyes altogether to things which are of value. We are rather
a violent institution; we have been known to over-correct an
abuse—it's hard on the baby, but we often pour him right out
with the bath water. An extra-curricular program that works
closely with the curricular to round out a student's development
is a very good thing indeed.

Student Assembly, 28 January 1952

KIMPTON

The students need a more active extra-curricular environment in
the college as well as exposure to classroom education. This
means enhanced opportunity for participation in everything
from basketball to Bach, from social dancing to Shakespeare.
We need increased participation in athletics, and fortunately we
are safe from the pitfalls of highly commercialized college
sports. We need broader opportunities for student participation

in the arts, in music, the theater. We need a free and responsible student press. To get the latter, perhaps we ought to return to commercialism at least to the extent of encouraging a press that operates under the hard rules of capitalism and pays its own way, and may even return a profit to its executives. In our extra-curricular doings we have perhaps gone too far in our devotion to pure learning; in avoiding raids on girls dormitories, we may have avoided some of the valuable social climate that is an accepted part of college life.

Alumni Gathering (Chicago), 4 June 1952

KIMPTON

We must stop this schizophrenic nonsense about the extracurricular. At one moment we insist that we have a rich and varied extracurricular program for all our students and then immediately afterward we deplore the very existence of the extracurricular and deny that it is our responsibility. If we are as good as we think we are, why can't we give the life of our students outside the classroom character, depth, and distinction?

Trustee-Faculty Dinner, 13 January 1954

LEVI

I must confess a constant worry as to the necessity for an enrichment of the quality of student life at the University. If one wants to describe student life at the University, I suppose one might begin by pointing out that book circulation per capita by students at The University of Chicago is the highest in the nation among university libraries. Then one can add that the University has what is one of the country's best intramural athletic programs: 4,000 students took part last year in 21 sports on 600 teams, and this from a population of 7,600 students. One difference between the book circulation and the use of the athletic facilities must be mentioned. We have a magnificent library; the best in the country. Nothing like that can be said of our athletic facilities. They are woefully inadequate. The most recent athletic facility is the Field House which was dedicated in 1932. The women's gymnasium—in Ida Noyes—was built in 1916, the men's gymnasium in 1902. We do not have enough handball courts, enough indoor tennis courts, no adequate swimming pool, an insufficient number of basketball courts, and no good court. I should add that the complaints come not only from the students but the faculty as well, and they are continuous. Thus, in the second stage of the drive we propose to add to and upgrade these facilities. I believe it will be difficult to raise these funds. I suppose this is because Chicago, for many years, has been less well known for spectator sports.

About two-thirds of the undergraduates live on campus; over 30 percent of the approximately 5,500 graduate students live in University single or married student housing. I believe that the introduction of senior members of the faculty as Resident Masters, living in the residence halls, the sponsorship by Professor Wirszup, one of the Resident Masters, of a lecture series which has attracted at times hundreds of students to hear Saul Bellow or Richard McKeon or Milton Friedman, the growth of music programs both in the residence halls and elsewhere on the campus, and the revitalization of University theater are all steps in the right direction. We have an enormously talented student body. As one looks at our alumni, one should think of our present students. If 37 Nobel Laureates have been associated with the University, the more important figure is that ten of these were our students. If our faculty has a reasonable ranking, as it does, in the National Academy of Sciences, perhaps it is more important to note that a recent survey of the baccalaureate origins of the membership of the National Academy of Sciences placed Chicago as second, and third in the listing of institutions from which the highest degree was obtained. Twenty-three of the recipients of National Science Foundation Fellowships for 1974–75 have chosen to pursue their work at The University of Chicago. This places us fifth after the Massachusetts Institute of Technology, Stanford, Harvard, and Berkeley. It is perhaps easier to give this kind of accounting in the scientific areas, but if one looks to the arts, the humanities, the social sciences, or the professions, one will see the same results. It is a diverse student body. Over time, 10 percent of the students have come from foreign countries.

I am sure the University has been correct in the priorities which it has given to the academic programs, but I hope the second stage of the drive will bring us a few more of the amenities which in fact, are helpful to the programs.

State of the University, 8 April 1974

THE FUTURE
A GOOD OLD VISION OF A GOOD LIFE

HARPER

I desire to make the following suggestions with reference to the student body now in residence and to those who are to come:

1. In view of the satisfactory work of the Student Councils, and in accordance with their development, larger and larger responsibility should be laid upon them. There seems to be no good reason why a considerable share of the government may not be placed with proper restrictions in their hands. This means a development of the plan of self-government. The more fully this plan can be worked out with common consent and satisfactory guarantees, the better for the life of the University both social and educational.

2. More halls for the residence of students should be built. Experience shows that up to a certain point such halls will be occupied as rapidly as they are provided. Nothing will contribute more largely to the development of the proper spirit and life than the provision of student houses on the quadrangles, or in close proximity.

3. Provision should also be made, in accordance with the recommendation of the Junior College Faculty, concerning those students whose homes are in the city and who do not desire a sleeping place at the University, for the erection of halls in which accommodation for groups of twenty-five or thirty should be arranged. These accommodations should include study-room, toilet-room, and lunch-room, and every undergraduate of the University should have his own place at the University.

4. Larger plans should be worked out for the management of the Employment Bureau. There is practically no limit to the amount of work which such a bureau can secure for those who need assistance. No fee is charged the students. The salaries of that office are a part of the University expense; but a larger corps of strong men should be employed to take charge of the work.

5. Additional scholarships should be established, and the present scholarships of the Junior and Senior Colleges extending for one year should be made two-year scholarships with proper limitations.

210

6. Something should be done to encourage a larger interest in literary work of a creative character. Whether this can best be done by prizes may be a question.

Decennial Report, 1 July 1902

THE PROBLEM OF ATHLETICS
SOMETHING LOST AND SOMETHING GAINED?

BURTON

Of course, all these things may fill too large a place. In a college as elsewhere education is not for amusement but amusement is for education. But sport, manly sport, sheer fun and social life will always have its place in college life.

Alumni Gathering (New York), 1923

KIMPTON

I'd like more athletics on this campus, but in a manner that would meet the approval of the great old man, Alonzo Stagg.

Order of the C Dinner, 7 June 1951

HARPER

The athletic activity was cultivated vigorously from the beginning. Here, more than anywhere else, paternalism may be said to have existed. The University did not wait for the student to organize. The work of the athletic field was placed under the direct supervision of a University officer. The results show that under certain circumstances paternalism is an effective agency.

Quinquennial Statement, 1 July 1896

HARPER

The success of the Athletic work of The University has been more marked than ever before. The eastern trip of the ball team was upon the whole fairly satisfactory. I make no apology for referring to the work of the team in this official statement. The athletic work of the students is a vital part of the student life.

Under the proper restrictions it is a real and essential part of college education. The athletic field, like the gymnasium, is one of the University laboratories and by no means the least important one. The parent whose son has distinguished himself in an athletic team has good reason to be proud of the son's achievement. It may not be denied that evils arise in connection with the work, but this is the fault of the management, not of the work itself. I congratulate the parent whose son is on the baseball team or the football team, as I will congratulate myself if my son should be accorded the honor. But here as elsewhere much depends upon the attendant circumstances. If the work is not amateur work in the strictest sense, nothing that I have said is true. If the life of the men is not of the highest character, all the higher because of peculiar temptations resisted, nothing that I have said is true. If the intellectual work of the men in their various departments is not of high order, nothing that I have said is true. That in The University of Chicago the first of these requirements will be observed, we may well trust the Board of Physical Culture and Athletics, whose business it is to guard with jealous care the purity of college athletics. In the director of the work, Mr. Stagg, we have an example of earnest and conscientious manhood which exerts a powerful influence upon the men themselves toward right conduct and right living. Of the twelve men engaged on the baseball team, including substitutes, one has had the record of A, six the record of B, four the record of C, one the record of D.

To our guests, the members of the Brown University team, we extend our heartiest welcome. Their coming to Chicago marks an important step in the history of college athletics. The good spirit which has prevailed and the character of the work of both teams is something of which the Universities represented may well be proud.

Convocation, 1 July 1896

HARPER

No larger interest in athletic matters has grown up than would naturally have been looked for. The refusal of the University to adopt the policy of other institutions in going out to search for athletes and to persuade them to enter the University by holding out inducements of many kinds is so thoroughly recognized that the athletic management has been severely criticised both by the students and the alumni for its lack of progressive enterprise in this respect; and yet in spite of this so-called failure to do the proper thing, a reasonable number of candidates for athletic honors have presented themselves, and the record of the institution for ten years may be called good. It is at all events singularly above reproach.

. . . Ground should be secured for the intercollegiate athletic games at a point not far distant from the University, but distinctly separated from the University buildings. The possession of such a field would (a) furnish an additional practice field, which is already needed and will be much more needed in future years; (b) relieve the libraries and class-rooms of the noise and distraction of the games, which has come to be something exceedingly serious; (c) secure better arrangement for the transportation of those attending the games. Nothing could be much worse than the present Marshall Field from this latter point of view.

Decennial Report, 1 July 1902

FOR THE LOVE OF IT

JUDSON

In the modern college the subject of athletic exercise and competition affords an interesting and important feature. Such things are not to be regarded as mere recreation. The fact that they are sport and that they are interesting does not militate against the further fact that they are exceedingly helpful in the development of physical health and strength. Gymnastic training and exercise are valuable no doubt. At the same time, the keen interest and zest connected with outdoor sports gives them, when properly conducted and within certain limits, a very much greater value. It is because of this value that it seems desirable as an educational policy that every member of a university, including both faculty and students, should have some form of outdoor sport in which he is particularly interested. Indeed, we do not need to stop with faculty and students. It has been my privilege at times to meet even dignified members of our Board

213

of Trustees on the golf field, and I am quite sure that the sobriety and intelligence with which they perform their important functions as trustees has not been injured by the greater or less degree of skill which they have attained in that manly sport. During the last year considerable progress has been made in the direction of extending and popularizing these outdoor activities among students in the University. The organization of the small colleges in particular has afforded a convenient outlet for such contests, and a greatly increasing number of young men and women have become interested. I am sure that this is a healthful and hopeful tendency and one by all means to be encouraged.

Intercollegiate contests have occupied much attention for some time past among all college authorities. These contests have met with an extraordinary amount of public interest and have excited the keenest activity within the colleges. For a few years past, however, such contests have been surrounded by circumstances and conditions apparently quite beyond the control of the best-intentioned managers, which have tended very greatly to injure their usefulness. The main evil has not been so much the physical dangers to which the players have been somewhat exposed, but rather another class of evils which have in fact an undoubted moral bearing. With these circumstances and conditions the faculties of the nine Middle West universities during the past winter have been grappling, and as a result have agreed unanimously on certain important and far-reaching changes. These are in the direction of eliminating the tendency to professionalism from amateur contests, of doing away with the unseemly dissensions between institutions which have been too frequent in the past, and of substituting genuine amateur sport for the bitter and unfriendly rivalry which from time to time has been obvious. Recently these changes have been supplemented in our case with an arrangement between the Universities of Minnesota and Chicago for athletic contests on an entirely new basis and one exactly in line with the intent of the new regulations. Mr. Stagg, our veteran and valued director of Physical Culture and Athletics, catching the exact thought of the faculty, formulated a plan which was promptly and sympathetically accepted by the authorities of the University of Minnesota and unanimously ratified by the authorities of the University of Chicago. It is sincerely believed that this arrangement with Minnesota is in the direction at least of a new era in ath-

letic sports. The rehabilitation of these contests and their pres-
ervation on a high plane of clean, wholesome, manly, and
honorable conduct is in my opinion far preferable to their abo-
lition. The latter course, which has been favored by some, is
simply a confession of impotency on the part of both faculties
and students. I do not believe in the necessity for such surren-
der. The value in the sports is too great to give up without a
serious and intelligent effort to preserve the value and at the
same time to do away with the attendant evils.

It is perhaps not saying too much to point out that the new
arrangement with Minnesota, and the policy of extending an
interest in athletic sports among the great body of students
within the walls of the college entirely aside from intercollegiate
competition, are the two points which mark the policy of the
University of Chicago in this matter. With this policy as em-
bodied in these two principles our director is in entire accord,
and in carrying out that policy I think I speak for my associates
in saying that he will have the united and hearty support of all
the faculties.

Convocation, 12 June 1906

JUDSON

The athletic policy of the Conference of the Middle West has
again proved its value. The important changes in the whole
attitude of the student body and the public toward athletics
caused by the reforms of the Conference can with difficulty be
appreciated by those not familiar with the old system. The
limitation on number of games, the restrictions on membership
in competing teams, especially in disqualifying graduate and
unclassified students and students in the first year of the col-
leges, and the elimination of the training table have altogether
worked very efficiently in the direction of securing real amateur
sport. Intercollegiate athletic contests are an interesting feature
of student life and an interesting outlet for student enthusiasm.
When not permitted to become the principal thing in college
these contests have an undoubted value. The Conference has se-
cured a large gain in the direction of the right distribution of
values among student activities. It must not be thought, how-
ever, that nothing remains to be done, or that all possible dan-
gers have disappeared. There continue features, especially in

football, which are dangerous to life and health. These must be substantially eliminated if the game is to continue.

The President's Report 1909–10

JUDSON

For the next two years it is the intention of the Board of Trustees to proceed with the construction of four buildings which are imperatively needed at the present time, and on which the Board believes it necessary to proceed without delay. These buildings are: . . . A Gymnasium for Women. The present quarters, provided in 1903 as a temporary matter, with the full expectation that four or five years would see a permanent building ready, have outlived their usefulness. The splendid provision for men in the Bartlett Gymnasium, as well as in the Reynolds Club and the Hutchinson Commons, are in marked contrast with the very inadequate and wholly unaesthetic one-story group known as Lexington Hall. Our women deserve better, and the time has now come when the existing situation must be ended.

Convocation, 11 June 1912

BURTON

In my own undergraduate days I took no part in Athletics, for two reasons, first I was physically incapacitated for active exercise by an injury to my back, and secondly there were no athletics in my day to take part in. Football had not yet come in and my college course fell in a period of the temporary decline of Baseball.

But I have always believed in Athletics, especially since I became acquainted with Mr. Stagg over thirty years ago. I believed in them even in the old days of the massed play, not because of the physical injuries that resulted from it, but in spite of them. I believed, not chiefly because of its physical but chiefly because of its moral value. I believe in that whole-souled devotion of one's self to what one is doing, which I have heard Mr. Stagg express in the phrase, *Put it all out.* I believe in the spirit and practice of team play—that devotion to the institution or the group or the nation to which one is attached, and that forgetfulness of self that Football perhaps above every other sport develops. I am not fond of ladylike men, and I have no use for an individualist.

I know what the C men did for their country in the Great War, and how rapidly they forged to the front, and I have no doubt that the qualities to which they owed their advancement were largely learned under Mr. Stagg's instruction.

Football Dinner, 15 November 1923

PROPORTION IS ALL

BURTON

Physical development is an essential accompaniment of the intellectual life, and sport is a natural companion of study. This is especially true of the life of undergraduates, although the present generation is recognizing as previous generations in America have not that play belongs to all periods of life. College athletics have their difficulties and intercollegiate contests have been by no means an unmixed good. Yet the remedy is not the abolition of either intramural or intercollegiate athletics, but the cultivations of both in due proportion and relationship and under proper regulations and supervision. Many a student of the University of Chicago has looked back on his college days with the feeling that athletics and Mr. Stagg did more for him than any other influence of his whole course.

If then we are determined to bring into the colleges the best possible influence and educational methods, this carries with it the decision to retain athletics as a part of the educational equipment of the University and to administer them from the point of view of their educational value to the student body and the public.

With Bartlett Gymnasium already built on Stagg Field, and with the demand for land in the vicinity for University and other purposes rapidly increasing the University finds it necessary now to decide what its course shall be for some years to come.

With these facts in view and with the hearty concurrence of Mr. Stagg, the following policy has been adopted by the Board of Trustees.

The Field House

Careful study has convinced Director Stagg and others concerned that the first undertaking should be the erection of the field house. This building is an immediate need in order that indoor sports and intramural athletics may continue to develop. The capacity of Bartlett Gymnasium has been repeatedly overtaxed. Interest in intramural athletics is growing at the university, and the encouragement of them is considered essential to the better development of the colleges. Director Stagg has for a long time urged the erection of a field house. The plans for it are founded upon a personal inspection he recently made of the best structures of the kind in the country.

Many details remain to be worked out, but the decision has been reached that the field house shall stand between Bartlett Gymnasium and 56th street, practically filling the space there available. By vote of the trustees, immediate steps are to be taken looking toward the erection of this building. While its use will be primarily for the department of athletics, it will also serve the purpose when needed, of a large assembly hall and as a banquet room for alumni gatherings.

Increase in Seating Capacity of Stagg Field

In dealing with this question, the Committee on Football Seating, Director Stagg and others have examined various proposals with a view to the general educational policy of the university, present and future. Projects involving removal of the field to an entirely new location have been among suggestions offered. The decision reached is that further development of athletics shall be on and about Stagg Field. The reasons for this decision are: the necessity of reserving land already owned by the university for the carrying into effect of its educational policy, and the desirability of having the athletic field in close proximity to the educational and residence buildings.

The definite plan adopted for improvement is that the football field shall be turned about so that the gridiron will be at right angles with its present status. The main axis of the field will then extend from east to west, instead of from north to south. A permanent grand stand will be erected along 56th street. The present temporary stands along the east and south sides of the field may continue in use, but the former will eventually be replaced by permanent stands in front of Bartlett Gym-

218

nasium and the field house. When the present west stand is linked up with those on the north and east sides of the field, there will result a U-shaped stand, which will have a total seating capacity estimated at 51,490 seats, as compared with the present capacity of 31,000.

The temporary stands at the south end of the field, will be increased [to a] total capacity [of] over 60,000. Whatever the form of this construction along 57th street, it is considered that it should be low enough to leave open a view to the south.

The cost, both of the field house and of the improvements on Stagg field can be met from athletic funds. *No appeal is to be made to the alumni or public* for the financing of either project.

"The University of Chicago As It Should Be in 1940:
A Confidential Statement by the President," 1925

MASON

I was a member of the track team, and I have never lost interest in competitive sports. All of us feel the reality and naturalness of that outlet of surplus energy and the physical pleasure in athletic contest. My idea is that intercollegiate athletics should become more thoroughly the climax of a more general participation within the student body. Have more of them engaged. As a character builder men everywhere speak of their appreciation of Director Stagg.

"Some Statements by President Mason"
Magazine, December 1925

MASON

Beauty aside from use and the perception of use can scarcely exist. If fifty years ago we put Bobby Jones on a platform to demonstrate the proper stance in golf the audience would have laughed at the full swing and contortions of hip and arms. Whereas now we say—how beautiful—how graceful—because we recognize that each motion is the correct one for the purpose for which it is employed.

We must search for football *function* if we are to validate its monstrous extension. I am as inconsistent in regard to football as everyone else. During the season from two to four in the afternoon football is the all absorbing—most important subject

219

of college life. I am out there on the bleachers too. But I must not forget other features possessing unequivocal function. The Dicks' contribution to the control of scarlet fever is more important than all the football games in the world. This rah rah stuff is easily overdone, but as far as it means the happy joyous background of good fellowship and friendship which holds together the real work of the university, I am for it. However, we must recognize the danger of too great enthusiasm for football.

The danger of bookishness is worse. If we could do the impossible and get the bookish student to play football and the football player to study intensively (!)—well perhaps we can. If you alumni will permit me I will show you how ridiculous are the demands of the alumnus expecting his college or university to win every game every year. In the Big Ten one school plays six Big Ten games. Its chances to win all six games, considering that the same type of young men go to all schools, is one in sixty-four. You may really expect to see what you every year demand if you will only be brave and patient and wait for sixty-four years. The thing I hope for is that we shall use our common sense in regard to these things and give each phase of university work its rational place.

Alumni of University of Wisconsin and
University of Chicago (Milwaukee)
14 December 1925

NOT A HASTY DECISION

HUTCHINS

Suggested Program for Meeting of Regional Advisors,
Evening of Tuesday, October 16
[Outline]

1. Is the problem of getting students at the University more acute now than it was ten or fifteen years ago, and if so, why?
2. What about scholarships? Should our efforts be directed mainly towards getting students who can pay their own tuition?
3. In what ways are the educational opportunities at Chicago superior to those of most other schools?

4. Is it true or false that the undergraduate school at the University is becoming less important, and should we sell the University mainly on the basis of its graduate schools?
5. What is the attitude of the University towards fraternities and women's clubs?
6. What is the attitude of the University towards competitive athletics?

Alumni Dinner (Chicago), 16 October 1938

MR. HUTCHINS KICKS BACK

HUTCHINS

I am told that there is a good deal of speculation about why I am speaking to you today. Plenty of answers could be given. At the Freshman receptions I have no chance to talk. At Convocations the students want to grab their diplomas and run. As for the annual dinner that the *Maroon* holds every four or five years, one never knows whether the *Maroon* is going to get around to holding it. And, when it is held, I have to spend all the time allotted to me correcting the misinformation the *Maroon* has distributed since the last dinner. My class, in which there are some fifty undergraduates, would be all right except that there the students keep interrupting me all the time. What I have been wanting is a chance to talk to students when they couldn't talk back.

I have lately heard, moreover, that some of you have felt that a recent decision affecting your life here was deliberately if not maliciously announced when you were away for the holidays in order to prevent you from registering an instant and vehement protest against it. If the charge were true, it would give you just cause for complaint. For though I do not concede that the students can determine the curriculum, the tuition fees, or the activities in which the University should or should not engage, I do insist that they are entitled to express themselves on these or any other subjects; and I should be the last person in the world to deprive them of the opportunity of doing so in the most pointed and effective manner. I cannot permit any of you to labor under any misapprehension about the reason why the

Trustees made their announcement when they did. I shall there-
fore state their reason for that. In addition, I shall give the rea-
sons for their decision; and, since I don't know when I shall be
able to get you to listen to me again, I shall give my views of
the present and the future of undergraduate life and work at
the University of Chicago in general.

The reason why the decision of the Trustees was announced
on December 22 was that it was reached on December 21. For
almost three months the Board had been discussing the subject
without coming to any conclusion. On December 21 it did come
to a conclusion. Having concluded, it had to announce its con-
clusion, for in view of the inordinate public interest in the sub-
ject, it could not hope to keep its decision quiet until the opening
of the Winter Quarter. Nobody connected with the administra-
tion is so naïve as to think that you might forget about football
or cool off about football between December 22 and January 2.
We all know that this is the kind of thing men don't forget and
the kind of thing people can and do stay hot about for years.

So much for the date of the announcement. Now for the rea-
sons for it. Football can benefit the participants and the uni-
versity which sponsors it. To the participants it supplies, in
addition to exercise and recreation, training in co-operation,
sportsmanship, and fair play. For the university it may unify the
student body, weld the alumni and the university together, and
interest the public.

These advantages are so clear that most people begin, as I
began the long series of meetings culminating in the decision of
the Board, with a feeling that football, if it can be conducted on
a proper plane, is a good thing for a university.

On further reflection, however, many people have come to be-
lieve, as I have, that these advantages are of two sorts: either
they are not peculiar to football or they accrue only when the
football team wins.

Though football is a wonderful game for the spectator, it is
not as good for the participant as many other sports. It cannot
be played after graduation, except professionally. It is time-con-
suming, and the time is consumed just when the player ought to
be devoting himself to the new courses begun with the opening
of the academic year.

Other sports develop co-operation, team spirit, sportsman-
ship, and fair play just as well as football.

Between thirty and forty men have played intercollegiate football at the University of Chicago. Their activity has attracted attention, inside and outside the University, out of all proportion to their number. It has distracted attention from other games and from our excellent and comprehensive program of intramural sports.

On the effect of football on the University I will take the word of President Wells of Indiana University, who has said, "Football unquestionably has an effect on the spirit of an institution, *provided it is winning football.*" Unless the football team wins a fair proportion of its games, it does not serve as a rallying point for the undergraduates. It irritates many alumni instead of making them enthusiastic. And it is difficult to see how a football team that loses most of its games can attract students. It is true that the University of Chicago had the largest Freshman class in its history last year, but nobody has so far suggested that the record of the football team was responsible.

If the peculiar advantages of football arise only from winning football, the question is: Could Chicago win? We have an undergraduate body of 3,400. The undergraduates outnumber the graduate students. The number of undergraduates is larger than it was in the days of our football glory. If Chicago could win then, why can't it win now? The answer may be simply stated. Many of the universities with which we have competed are much larger now than they were fifteen years ago. The proportion of transfer students here has been steadily increasing. These students are always ineligible for a time and are usually not interested in devoting themselves to football. The proportion of self-supporting students has increased. The educational program of Chicago, though not hard—not, in my opinion, hard enough—is more time-consuming than it used to be. It is estimated that 50 per cent of the football players in the Big Ten are enrolled in schools of physical education. Most of these have grown up since the war. The University of Chicago has none.

There is, of course, one way in which we could win. We could subsidize players or encourage our alumni to do so. Most of you have seemed to feel that the only good football was winning football and that the University should take this path to victory. In your latest poll you voted overwhelmingly for football and overwhelmingly for subsidization. Many of the students and alumni with whom I have talked have urged upon me what they

called "legitimate" subsidization. I am sorry to tell you that
there is no such thing. The Big Ten rules are as follows: "Rule
6, section 4. . . . . No financial aid shall be given to students by
individuals or organizations, alumni or other, with the purpose
of subsidizing them as athletes or of promoting the athletic suc-
cess of a particular University." The test of legality must be
whether the student would be assisted if he were not an athlete.
It is hard to believe that enough competent players could be
legally assisted under this rule to affect materially the record of
our football teams. The University could not break the rule. I
am sure that no self-respecting person connected with it could
seriously want it to.

In short the only kind of football you wanted was a kind in
which the University could not engage. It therefore determined
to give it up. What are the results? In the first place, I think it
is a good thing for the country to have one important university
discontinue football. There is no doubt that on the whole the
game has been a major handicap to education in the United
States. If you win, you must keep on winning. The president of
a state university which had championship teams once told me
that all the people in his state were interested in was the foot-
ball team and that, if it ever lost, his appropriations would be
cut in half. If you lose, you are in the position described by the
following pathetic sentences by President Valentine of Roch-
ester. He said in speaking to his students the other day: "I real-
ize only too well how much of the good work which you or I or
many others slowly and painfully achieve for this university is,
in popular opinion, undone in two months by a disastrous foot-
ball season. It ought not to be that way, but it is that way, and
we might as well be realistic about it."

The greatest obstacle to the development of a university in
this country is the popular misconceptions of what a university
is. The two most popular of these are that it is a kindergarten
and that it is a country club. Football has done as much as any
single thing to originate, disseminate, and confirm these miscon-
ceptions. By getting rid of football, by presenting the spectacle
of a university that can be great without football, the University
of Chicago may perform a signal service to higher education
throughout the land.

Undergraduate Assembly, 12 January 1940

ANSWERING THE ARM-CHAIR QUARTERBACKS

HUTCHINS

"Eighteen Points about the University"
[Outline]

1. University best—not second or third.
2. Chicago Plan—most important contribution to undergraduate education in last fifty years.
3. Every professional school making unique and pioneering effort in its field.
4. Graduate and research work most effective, man for man, of any in U. S.
5. Texas-Chicago agreement most significant step in university organization in last twenty-five years.
6. University has as varied and stimulating undergraduate life as any in country.
7. Discontinuance of football may mark beginning of higher education in U. S.
8. Discontinuance of football most popular step ever taken by University both with public and alumni.
9. Professors and students politically too apathetic and conservative.
10. President in his official acts is merely representative of Trustees and faculty. . . .

Alumni Meetings (Illinois), 25 March 1940
10 April 1940

HUTCHINS

For example, big-time, industrial football, the symbol of the non-educational aspects of educational institutions, confuses the public mind about what education is and contains elements of injustice, hypocrisy, and fraud that run counter to the high ideals that our educational institutions profess. It is perfectly possible to be against football of this type and to be for health and exercise. As for me, I am for exercise, as long as I do not have to take any myself.

Modern Forum Inc. (Los Angeles), 19 April 1950

225

KIMPTON

Our campus is not a country club, an annex to a stadium, or a drawn-out poker party, and I can assure you that some campuses are. We caught the unsavory bouquet of big-time athletics long before our sister institutions did, and I believe I can say without fear of reprimand by even Mr. Sharp that none of our students has accepted a bribe to throw a game. May I pause parenthetically to tell you my attitude upon football, about which there has been so much interesting conjecture of late. I have no objection to football qua football. I played it badly a bit in college, and have been an enthusiastic Sunday morning quarterback in my time. It is a good game as games go, and as games go that get all out of hand, it properly went. I have no intention of trying to reestablish us in big-time football. We couldn't even reenter the big game if we wanted to because of our college arrangement of years, and we don't want to. If at some point there is enthusiasm on the part of some substantial segment of the student body to play intra-mural football or even to engage in extra-mural, non-paying, uncoached games, the possibility will be given appropriate consideration. I know of no such enthusiasm at the moment, and I have no intention of encouraging it. At the same time, I do not feel that it becomes us to throw our weight about and tell our sister institutions how to solve their problem. We have solved ours in our own Chicago way; let them work theirs out in their way. We developed the first chain-reacting pile on a field that might have produced a team for the Rose Bowl; I am perfectly willing to leave it to history to determine which was the more important.

Student Assembly, 28 January 1952

KIMPTON

I feel very much honored to be asked to address the Order of the C. To my mind, you are a particularly important part of our alumni group. You have remained loyal to Chicago through some pretty tough times, and I honor you for it. And through the years, and perhaps through the very process of being kicked around, you have evolved as sane a notion of the meaning and value of college athletics as any alumni group I have ever known, and I honor you for this, too.

It might be of value for me this evening to outline my own conception of the meaning and value of athletics in a college program. I hope you will not think me presumptuous when I say that I am not unacquainted with college athletics. I had the distinction of being the most awkward and inept freshman ever to turn out for football at Stanford, my own alma mater. After watching me for a week, old Pop Warner, who had played professional football with my uncle, urged me to take the academic life seriously. After that, I was limited to impoverishing myself each fall weekend by betting far more than I could afford on a series of teams that never quite came off as a ball club. My first contact with Chicago athletics was indirect. As a Stanford alumnus, I was instrumental in bringing Clark Shaughnessy and Marchie Schwartz to Palo Alto from Chicago. We looked pretty good on that one when Stanford won the Pacific Coast championship and the Rose Bowl game in their first season. I must admit that since then I have not been nimble enough to keep up with Shaugnessy, but I had a long and pleasant association with Marchie. Stanford lost a good man when he quit. Some years later, I served at Chicago as faculty representative on the Western Conference until by mutual agreement we dropped out, and I still regard as some of my best friends Tug Wilson, Pappy Waldorf, and our own great athlete, Fritz Chrisler. I have recently served in a similar capacity, representing Stanford on the Pacific Coast Conference, where, you will be pleased to know, I roundly defeated Pappy Waldorf in a limerick recitation contest for which I won a bottle of scotch and the prolonged applause of the Conference.

I have been associated with college athletics for many years, and because I like athletics, I don't feel very happy over what has been happening. Intercollegiate competition is not the same thing it was when most of you were playing on Chicago teams. It is as far as possible from Alonzo Stagg's dream. We can all be sorry that this is the fact.

The University has been out of football since 1939. We are not in a position to go back into Big Ten football even if we wanted to. Our College, as you know, drops back two years from the traditional four year period, and our young men do not have the maturity to compete in the contact sports with the big leagues.

Let us take stock of our present situation. We have more kids involved in sports than most universities where the whole emphasis is on varsity competition. You'd be amazed to take a good look at Bartlett and the field house on a late afternoon. And we are competing, and doing pretty well, in sports where our younger men have a chance. We have given the game back to the kids, and that is something at the moment we can well be proud of. I think there need to be changes, but I suspect they are more changes of degree or emphasis than they are changes of kind. Extra-curricular activities are important in my book. I don't think they are or ought to be the reason a young man comes to college, and I am confident that he ought to get a lot more out of college than is represented by a varsity letter or a fraternity key. But I don't think we need worry about this at Chicago; the atmosphere of the place and the quality of our academic work will take care of that. I would like to see even greater participation in athletics, and I would not mind seeing more good intercollegiate competition at our own level. We can well pioneer, and I think we are now, in what the proper role of athletics and intercollegiate competition is in a real college education. You may reply that we haven't any athletes. Well, why don't you send us some? I am not worried about any money passing under the table in this case. In fact, it can be passed over the table; why not establish some scholarships for good athletes who are also good students? The Big Ten can't do this because everyone knows it will be abused. We can, and everyone knows it won't be abused.

Order of the C Dinner, 7 June 1951

SPORTS FOR THE STUDENTS, NOT FOR SHOW

KIMPTON

The presence of the "Old Man" on our campus this evening is filled for us with sentiment and meaning. It reminds us of a day when "On Chicago" meant something, and meant something that no sane person can laugh off. But it reminds us also of a time when football was played by students who were amateurs and played for the love of the game. This was what the "Old Man" stood for, and if he were forty-five instead of ninety, football would still mean this for us and for the Middle West.

I have received so much advice, both solicited and unsolicited, on the question of our return to football that I should like to speak to you very frankly on the subject this evening. There are three general questions that must be answered prior to any decision. First, does our Board of Trustees wish to reenter the game? I can only answer that the Board Committee on Student Interests is currently devoting a great deal of attention and thought to the subject. Second, does our faculty wish us to reenter the game? A strong faculty committee has been appointed and is currently considering the matter. Third, does our student body wish to reenter the game, and are they prepared to play it? I have a petition signed by some three hundred students who say they wish to see Chicago reenter football, and we are establishing classes in intra-mural football next year to see if they mean it or not.

I suppose there is a fourth question, which is what the administration of your institution thinks about reentering the game. May I list the arguments for and against that are currently being pondered. On the side of the reasons for our return to football, may I list these: First, it is a great game—to watch and to participate in, and I am aware that you cannot develop a first-rate program of athletics without football. Second, it serves as a rallying point for students, alumni, and citizens which no other activity—intellectual, social, or athletic—can produce, and we need some rallying points. Third, there are many students whom we want at Chicago who do not come, because of, or even who are repelled by, the lack of glamour in our athletic program. We get them as graduate students, but we need them as undergraduates so that we will not need to make so many repairs in their education.

These are strong arguments, but there are some equally strong arguments on the other side. The first is that you want winning teams—and so do I. If you bribe a boy to bring him here and I close one eye or even two to admit him, we cease to be the University of Chicago; and I want no part of it and neither do you. Second, it costs money to reestablish football, and we don't have it. Stagg Field is obsolete and some of it is almost ready to fall down. And uniforms and travel and coaches are more expensive than they were in the "Old Man's" day. Finally, whom are we going to play if we reenter the game? It is fantastic to consider playing institutions of the size of Illinois, Wisconsin or Michigan. At the moment, we have an undergraduate body of 1,500, of whom 200 have not yet graduated from high school and 350 are girls. This places us in competitive quantity with institutions with which we do not compare ourselves in quality. I do not wish to malign either you or our sister institutions in the Mid-West, but I do not confidently expect you to yell yourselves hoarse at a game with Siwash College.

It is in the light of these considerations that a president of a large Mid-Western public university told me the other day that we must be nuts to think of reentering the game. But, nuts or not, we are giving it thoughtful consideration at the present time. I can tell you rather quickly and easily where I stand. It is a good game and I like it. I would like to play comparable institutions, such as Harvard, Yale and Cornell, but I see little or no chance of being included in the Ivy League. I do not want to play in the Big Ten, first, because we cannot compete, and second, because if we tried to we would have to do some things that I don't care to do. Whether this leaves us any reasonable alternative, I do not know. I can only tell you that our decision will be dictated by what we believe to be best for the great university of which we are all a part. I will even add that I hope it will be a decision with which the "Old Man" would agree.

Order of the C Dinner, 2 June 1955

KIMPTON

Your dinner tonight honors the past and the future. Nellie Metcalf entered the picture at just the time athletics was leaving it, and we have given him a very rough time as a result. In this difficult situation he has performed with dignity and with honor. In the face of enormous apathy, if not downright hostility, he has kept going an extremely active program of athletic participation and we owe him a great deal.

Walter, I have welcomed you before, but may I do it officially before the Order of the C, and I hope and believe that we will give you a better time of it than your predecessor had. I never have been able to understand the deemphasis on sports in the context of the University of Chicago. We have professed to admire the Greeks, and they invented the Olympic games well in advance of the first "great book." We have admired the program and the life of the older British universities, and the undergraduate at Oxford and Cambridge is the most avid sports enthusiast, both as observer and participant, that I have ever known. It has even been said that we were soft on communism, and the Soviets do an all-out job on athletics that makes even our Southern football leagues look like a group of rank amateurs. At least we ought to be consistent. I believe, Walter, that during your tenure of office there will be a resurgence of interest on this campus in sports. For the moment, at least, the faculty has said "no" to our reentry upon the football scene, but as I interpret their negative, it is without passion and with no enormous conviction. I believe they are saying that we ought know what we are doing before we do it, and, particularly, that we ought to have some undergraduates around here who are genuinely interested in playing the game. And this is where the Order of the C comes in. Instead of bemoaning the past, I urge you to give thought and take some action for the future. Send some young men—yes, and some young women too—here who have an interest in participating in and witnessing sports. Now don't misunderstand me. I have been wondering for quite a little while when the Pacific Coast Conference was going to explode, and it finally has. We never have purchased athletes and we never will, if for no other reason than that the Old Man would never have tolerated it. But we have a very important educational job to do in the United States at the present time. It is to show that a university—and a great one—can participate in all sports and maintain at the same time its dignity, its integrity and its standards. If we are a pioneering institution, if we really take seriously the idea of setting ourselves up as a model to others, let us pioneer in this direction too and set up a model in an area in which it would really do some good. Intercollegiate athletics, including football, are here to stay in the pattern of American education. Let us show that some sense can be made of it by an institution that prides itself upon making sense. This is your job, Walter. You will receive my support and, I know, the support of these loyal and dedicated men who make up the Order of the C.

Order of the C Dinner, 31 May 1956

KIMPTON

Q. Chancellor, one of the most controversial aspects of your career was your ardent desire to bring back football to the University of Chicago. How do you feel about that now?

A. Where did you get the impression that I had an ardent desire to revive football?

Q. Not desire, an impression—let's put it that way.

A. Well, this was certainly just an impression. I have never been an ardent enthusiast in terms of football. This gets fairly complicated, but I really believe it is a great American college game and I'm not at all clear that the solution to that problem is to leave it. I still believe that a case could be made that we ought to play football and play it decently with other comparable and decent institutions to show that it can be done and done correctly and decently, which would serve then as a model for other institutions. I might go on to say I would not want to re-enter football except under those conditions and I have no interest in the Rose Bowl or beating Minnesota.

Farewell. Press Conference, 29 March 1960

BEADLE

In 1892 William Rainey Harper said, "Sports will be conducted for the students, not for the spectacular entertainment of enormous crowds of people." Ever since, participation sports have been firmly entrenched in the University's program.

Last year 4700 students participated in twenty-one intramural sports on the campus. In addition, close to 200 students competed in eleven intercollegiate sports.

Construction of a new athletic field got underway during the year to replace Stagg Field. The new Stagg Field contains: a 440-yard running track, a combination football-soccer field inside the track, a baseball field, four touch football fields, and ten regulation size tennis courts.

The new field is part of a proposed athletic complex which it is hoped will eventually include a new gymnasium and swimming pool.

State of the University, 5 November 1968

THE HIGH COST OF PRINCIPLE

LEVI

The most recent athletic facility is the Field House which was dedicated in 1932. The women's gymnasium—in Ida Noyes—was built in 1916, the men's gymnasium in 1902. We do not have enough handball courts, enough indoor tennis courts, no adequate swimming pool, an insufficient number of basketball courts, and no good court. I should add that the complaints come not only from the students but the faculty as well, and they are continuous. Thus, in the second stage of the drive we propose to add to and upgrade these facilities. I believe it will be difficult to raise these funds. I suppose this is because Chicago, for many years, has been less well known for spectator sports.

State of the University, 8 April 1974

4

SLAVES OF THE SLAVES OF LEARNING:
Founder, Trustees and Chief Executives

JOHN D. ROCKEFELLER

LEVI

Mr. Rockefeller gave more than money to the University of Chicago. He and President Harper developed the vision of a great university. Mr. Rockefeller's refusal to interfere in the operations of the university gave the university its essential character and freedom, in sharp contrast to many other institutions at that time. The claims of history are such that it is well to recall President Harper's decennial report in 1902, when he said, "I wish to add . . . that whatever may or may not have happened in other universities, in the University of Chicago neither the trustees, nor the president, nor anyone in official position has at any time called an instructor to account for any public utterances which he may have made. Still further, in no single case has a donor to the university called the attention of the trustees to the teaching of any officer of the university as being distasteful or objectionable."

Class of 1971 Assembly, 24 September 1967

HARPER

It is a pleasant task to recall to your remembrance the promise made a few weeks since by our friend and founder, Mr. Rockefeller, of $500,000, payable in four quarterly installments beginning July 1st of the present year, provided the conditions of the

234

gift of Mr. Ryerson were fulfilled. This means a million dollars for the University July 1st if between now and that time $225,000 new money can be secured. It is not safe under all the circumstances to be very confident as to the success of the effort. Any one who is to-day familiar with the condition of the financial world knows that this amount of money can be obtained only with the greatest difficulty. At an early date the canvass will be begun. The assistance of every friend of the University will be required. If successful, the University will have a million dollars for general equipment, and thus the third step in its establishment will have been taken. The first was the endowment of instruction, the second, the provision for buildings, the third, the equipment necessary to make this instruction and these buildings available. The gift of so large a sum as half a million, to be used outright for the purchase of equipment, was a gift under all the circumstances not to have been expected from Mr. Rockefeller. He had plainly indicated that he would care for instruction, and he had also expressed the hope that Chicago would care for buildings and equipment. He realized, however, the peculiar situation in which we found ourselves—the financial stringency which defied every effort to secure money. Seeing our necessities and appreciating all that we had tried to do, he has come forward in a new and unexpected way, and the University has stronger evidence than ever before of his deep interest in its work. I said a moment since that to-day our greatest need is a heating and electrical plant. A week ago our greatest need was books. It seemed hardly possible to continue work without large additions to the various departmental libraries. But how could these additions be secured until the success or failure of the effort to raise the million dollars, and on the other hand how wait until July 1st? The problem was a serious one. It was presented to our friend in New York City. He recognized its serious character and believing that the million dollars would be raised, knowing that in any case the books were needed and must be purchased, he has arranged for $50,000 to be spent at once for books and equipment. The distribution has already been made, and the several departments are now at liberty to make their orders in accordance with the appropriations designated. Did ever institution have a better friend?

Convocation, 2 January 1894

HARPER

It is a delicate and somewhat difficult task to undertake to make a statement on the relations of the founder of the University to the institution, for much that I should like to say must of necessity be omitted. The story of the beginning of Mr. Rockefeller's interest in a college or university in Chicago is a long and intensely interesting one. The main features of it will probably not be made public until after the death of those who were the principal actors in it. His association with the Theological Seminary at Morgan Park was the occasion of his later interest in the larger work. His keen insight into the future led him to select Chicago as the center of the educational work which it was in his mind to foster. His study of the situation was one extending over several years, and only after he had given the subject a prolonged consideration was a decision finally reached. The fundamental principle in his policy from the beginning to the present has been to render assistance in such a way as that the responsibility for giving may not be taken from others. The wisdom of this policy has fully demonstrated itself. The fact that the list of donors contains so large a number of names is in large measure due to the working out of this important policy. The method was one which has at times seemed severe, for Mr. Rockefeller has been very conscientious in carrying out his contracts, doing only what he has agreed to do, and compelling the other party to do his share according to the agreement. But the good results of the method are fully apparent, and the fact that the University has received in gifts $17,000,000, and that this sum has come from over three thousand donors, is in itself sufficient evidence of Mr. Rockefeller's wisdom in this whole matter.

If any feature of his relationship has been more marked than another, it has been the steady perseverance with which he has pursued the purpose originally outlined. So far as I understand the case, he has not wavered. His attitude has always been that of intelligent interest. But this has never led him to interfere in any way with the educational details of the work. Much ado was made on a certain occasion with reference to the resignation of a professor, it being asserted that this resignation had come about through the influence of the University's patron. It was said at that time, and it may be repeated again, that the representations to that effect were absolutely false. Mr. Rockefeller was not even aware that such a professor was in the University until he saw in the newspapers an account of his resignation. . . .

On two occasions only has Mr. Rockefeller found it possible and convenient to visit us. The first was the celebration of the Quinquennial, and the second that of the Decennial. On both of these occasions his public addresses were so well conceived and so admirably expressed, and their adaptation to the situation so evident, that with one accord all who heard or read them were delighted. During both of these visits he has shown a keen appreciation of the kind and courteous expressions made to him by the friends and Trustees of the University. In no year of the University's history has he given more substantial evidence of his abiding love for the University and of his deep interest for its future than during the year closing June 30, 1902.

This statement would be incomplete without a full recognition of the part which has been played by the wife of the founder. From the first hour to the present her heart has been full of sympathy for the work, and on many occasions her words of encouragement have been a source of great service. It would indeed be difficult to determine whether the husband or the wife is the more strongly interested of the two.

It is an occasion for regret that arrangements for celebrating Founder's Day have never been satisfactorily completed. The Trustees at first designated Mr. Rockefeller's birthday, July 16. Afterward it was thought best to designate the day on which he first visited the University, July 1, 1896. Neither of these days seems to come at the right season of the year, and up to the present time a combination of Convocation Day and Founder's Day has been made. The relationship between the founder of the University and the Trustees has been at all times a most cordial one, and every step in the progress of the University has been one of common agreement.

I desire to present the following suggestions:

1. The Trustees should take steps in the immediate future to secure a bronze or marble bust of the founder of the University. The painting by Eastman Johnson is of course a most important treasure, but this is not sufficient, and we cannot be satisfied

237

until there is placed in its proper position a more lasting representation of the founder.

2. The question of a permanent day to be set apart as Founder's Day, and to be celebrated as such every year, is one which should now receive careful consideration. In the earlier years it was thought best not to press this question for decision until a larger experience might be secured. The question of holidays and celebrations is one of great importance in the calendar of the University, and no permanent holidays in addition to those already established by law should be granted until this question has been settled.

3. It would seem to be proper and altogether appropriate that the University, whenever assembled in Convocation, should send a communication to the founder. These meetings of the entire University are not complete without some recognition each time of the great and splendid service which has been done the cause of education in the Mississippi Valley by the foresight, courage, and magnanimity of this one man. A proper acknowledgment of this fact in such form as may be adopted from time to time is a tribute to which he is entitled.

4. An effort should be made by the Trustees to secure a visit from the founder each year of the remaining years of his life. Such a visit would always bring with it inspiration and increased zeal in the furtherance of the work, and such a visit, I am persuaded, would likewise prove to be a source of real satisfaction to the founder. An urgent appeal to him would perhaps secure his favorable consideration of this suggestion.

5. Provision should be made for acquainting the students of the University, not only with the relationship of Mr. Rockefeller to the University as founder, but also with the elements in his character which make him prominent among the men of modern times. Respect for his modest reserve would perhaps lead to the postponement of any direct action along the line of this suggestion for the present, but the matter is certainly deserving of consideration in the near future.

Decennial Report, 1 July 1902

JUDSON

May I quote from the letter of the Founder of December 13, 1910?

"In making an end to my gifts to the University, as I now do, and in withdrawing from the Board of Trustees my personal representatives, whose resignations I enclose, I am acting on an early and permanent conviction that this great institution, being the property of the people, should be controlled, conducted, and supported by the people, in whose generous efforts for its up-building I have been permitted simply to cooperate; and I could wish to consecrate anew to the great cause of education the funds which I have given, if that were possible; to present the institution a second time, in so far as I have aided in founding it, to the people of Chicago and the West; and to express my hope that under their management and with their generous support the University may be an increasing blessing to them, to their children, and to future generations."

Convocation, 11 June 1912

Burton

I was told today a very extraordinary story by one of your members that I want to repeat here for the sake of banishing forever the thought connected with it. He told me that he recently met a gentleman in Chicago who had lived here for fifteen years and who was under the impression that John D. Rockefeller maintained the University of Chicago as a private enterprise for the profit he could derive from it. (Laughter.) I should like to mention the fact that Mr. Rockefeller has given to the University of Chicago, and, in so doing, given to this western country, thirty-five million dollars, and that he does not derive one quarter of one penny's dividend from that. If he has any dividend, it is the satisfaction of having made a contribution to the higher life of the world. When he made his last promise of contribution, which was thirteen years ago, and which promise was completed three years ago, he said: "I have done for the University all I have contemplated doing." He will never give us another dollar, for the reason, as he said, that the University is located in Chicago, it belongs to the citizens of Chicago and he must commit it to their care. It is committed to the care of Chicago and this western country. It is our earnest desire so to conduct it upon the policy originally laid down, a policy which I have endeavored to state to you today, a policy of education in every aspect of life.

The Executives' Club of Chicago, 27 February 1925

HUTCHINS

We were founded as a university and had few of the labor pains that have afflicted institutions in New England. Mr. Rockefeller, in less than twenty years, gave us $35,000,000 of free money, and $35,000,000 of free money is worth more than $70,000,000 tied to specific objects. Mr. Rockefeller's gifts could be used to advance the total effectiveness of the University in any way the trustees saw fit.

Chicago Association of Commerce, 29 January 1941

HUTCHINS

The Baptists were right. They wanted a college in Chicago because they knew the city was the capital of the Middle West, and that the forces which would mould the life of that vast area would emanate from Chicago. Mr. Rockefeller was right. He decided in favor of Chicago, though he had never lived here and had no sentimental connections with the place. He decided in favor of Chicago because he knew that the University would gain strength, power, and influence from it.

And so it has. The chief characteristics of the University are independence and courage. These qualities, as much as the vast sums it has received and as much as the educational and scientific excellence of the staff, have made the University great. If we ask ourselves why the University has shown the independence and courage which have distinguished it, we must ascribe it to two things, the attitude of the Founder and the spirit of the City.

There is no precedent, as far as I know, for the attitude of Mr. Rockefeller. He must have invented the doctrine that a donor who wishes to advance education and scholarship should leave them to educators and scholars. Other universities founded at about the same time have scarcely equaled the eminence of the University of Chicago. One reason is that each of them had to contend with the educational convictions or eccentricities of its founder or his representatives. Mr. Rockefeller must have had some educational convictions; he may have had some educational eccentricities. He never revealed them. There is no record that he ever made any suggestions about or criticisms of the program of the University. Opponents of certain professors appealed to him in vain to suppress teaching which they regarded

240

as heretical. He gave no sign that he had heard. Mr. Rockefeller's restraint is surely unique in history and surely accounts in large measure for the rapid rise of the University. It could have had as much money—and even more—and done a mediocre job. The reason it did a good one was that it was free to do it. It was free to use all the independence and all the courage that it had.

> University of Chicago Citizens Dinner, 26 September 1941

Kimpton

Rockefeller Memorial Chapel. This Chapel was built by the University's great benefactor as an expression of the centrality of religion in the life of the University. The University of Chicago was founded on principles of religious belief and in its rise through sixty years to a position of world prominence, the religious basis on which it stands has ever been maintained.

> Hillel Foundation (Rockefeller Chapel)
> 13 January 1952

Kimpton

Perhaps I can tell you a story in that regard which has always amused me. After Rockefeller had underwritten these deficits for some years he finally called a halt and said that he would make a final gift to the university and that from here on out the university was on its own. Of course, while he was willing to talk to Mr. Harper in the future, he would not talk to him about deficits . . . Harper, of course, agreed.

At the end of the fiscal year Harper went to New York to see Mr. Rockefeller. He called him up and Rockefeller said that he was glad to see him but that he would not talk about deficits. Harper agreed and when he walked into Rockefeller's office he said, "Let us pray." That, of course, was the custom of the day. So, they knelt down and prayed, and Mr. Harper told God all about the deficits. [Laughter] However, as you can well imagine, Mr. Rockefeller patiently underwrote Mr. Harper again.

> University of Chicago Citizens Board, 25 June 1953

Levi

Whether true or not, there is a lot of history in that story.

> Class of 1971 Assembly, 24 September 1967

LEVI

The emphasis on research was a declaration of faith in the power of the individual mind. It carried with it a profound conviction of the importance of freedom for the mind to inquire, to know, to speak. John D. Rockefeller set the tone through a policy of noninterference. As one commentator has recently written, "No contrast could be greater than that between the early years at Stanford and the beginnings of the University of Chicago." The results in the early days showed the difference. The sharing of the new learning gave Chicago its interdisciplinary stamp and its sense of unity. It was one university.

University of Chicago Citizens Board
16 November 1967

KEEPERS OF THE TRUST

HARPER

The history of these years shows conclusively that the attitude of the Trustees toward the Faculties of the University has been broad and liberal. It is understood that all questions involving financial expenditure fall within the province of the Trustees and are to be considered by them; that all appointments to office in the University are made directly by the Trustees upon recommendation of the President; and that on questions of fundamental policy, involving the establishing of new Faculties and the change of statutes as established by the Trustees, final action is reserved for the Trustees themselves. But it is a firmly established policy of the Trustees that the responsibility for the settlement of educational questions rests with the Faculties, and although in some instances the request of a Faculty has not been granted for lack of the funds required, in no instance has the action of a Faculty on educational questions been disapproved. It is clearly recognized that the Trustees are responsible for the financial administration of the University, but that to the Faculties belongs in the fullest extent the care of educational administration. During the years covered by this Report there has been no case of an appeal to the Trustees by a minority in any Faculty or governing Board against the action of a majority or against the action of the President.

The history of the growth of the University is in itself the best testimony of the largeness of view taken by the Board of Trustees. With a body of Trustees less intelligent or less able, such progress would have been impossible. It is fair to say that in the breadth of view which has characterized the work of the Trustees there is to be seen an expression of the spirit of the city of Chicago—a spirit to which the University is indebted for many of the important elements that have entered into its constitution. Justice compels me to refer particularly to the work of certain of the Trustees. To Mr. Martin A. Ryerson, the President of the Board during ten years of its history; to Mr. Andrew McLeish, the Vice-President, who has on several occasions in the absence of the President assumed his duties; to Mr. Charles L. Hutchinson, the Treasurer of the Board during the entire period; to Mr. Frederick A. Smith, the Chairman of the Committee on Instruction and Equipment; to Mr. George C. Walker, who has served on various regular and special committees; to Mr. Thomas W. Goodspeed, the Secretary of the Board of Trustees; and to Mr. Edward Goodman, the Treasurer of the Baptist Theological Union, the friends of education in Chicago and the Northwest are indebted for a service in each case without which the University could not have accomplished its work, and for a devotion which, I make bold to say, has not been surpassed in connection with any educational movement in American history.

Not least among the virtues of the Trustees has been the measure of sympathy and support which has uniformly been accorded by them to the President of the University. It may be said that such official support is to be expected on the part of Trustees, and that without it nothing can be effected. This is, of course, true; but I have in mind, in addition to this, the personal help which as individuals the Trustees have accorded me, and without which I could not possibly have endured the strain involved in the work of organization, or maintained the courage needed in the face of so many difficulties. There has been no moment in the ten years when I have not felt that each Trustee was a warm personal friend to whom I might go for that intangible help which a cold officialism does not furnish, but which exists only in connection with personal friendship.

I desire to present the following suggestions:

243

1. The University should procure the portraits of those who have served as Trustees during these first ten years. Whatever may hold true of future decades, it will always be recognized that special responsibilities rested upon the Trustees of the first decade. The name of each Trustee is so closely associated with the work in all its parts and as a whole as to justify the demand that his portrait should be one of the possessions of the University to be transmitted to later years.

2. Since the period of first organization has now passed, and the work of the University is better comprehended; and since also the details of the work are growing with great rapidity and will continue so to grow, it should be considered whether the present plan of organization in committees will prove in the future to be the most effective. This plan undoubtedly possesses many advantages, chief of which is the fact that the work and responsibility are thus divided, and the various members of the Board are enabled to become more thoroughly acquainted with certain divisions of the University than they could possibly become with all its divisions. But it is a question whether by this organization sufficient unity is secured; whether, as in the case of the ruling bodies of large cities, it would not be better to throw the responsibility of all the details upon a smaller number of men who might be able or willing to give a larger share of their time to the work; and whether, as in the case of business concerns, larger responsibility may not be placed upon the administrative officers. Such a smaller body would constitute an Executive Committee, to which might be given large powers in the intervals between Board meetings. It is perhaps true that in the case of no institution in the country are details presented to the Board of Trustees to such an extent as in the case of the University of Chicago. This policy has surely justified itself in the past, but with the growth of the University it may be doubted whether such men as are desired to serve as Trustees will have the time, aside from their other duties, to consider the work of the University in so great detail.

Decennial Report, 1 July 1902

BURTON

And a third great asset is our new President of the Board of Trustees. I have spoken of the two great Presidents of the University. We are not less fortunate in our two Presidents of the Board of Trustees. It was a noble service that Mr. Ryerson rendered for thirty years as President of the Board of Trustees. And we who know Mr. Swift, and have seen the keen intelligence which he brings to the great problems of the University, and the generosity with which he spends his time and his money, and the sympathy with which he enters into every situation are sure that the reign of Harold the Swift will be in no respect inferior to that of Martin the Silent.

Alumni Gathering (New York), 1923

MASON

I would like to make an entire speech, long and singular, to show my appreciation of the wonderful body of men who compose the board of trustees of Chicago. Mr. Harold Swift, Mr. Martin A. Ryerson, Mr. Donnelly and all the other trustees, it seems to me, give more than half of their time, their best thought and their fortunes to serve the University and through it humanity. Chicago is a free school. There were no restrictions attached by its founder to his generous gifts, the only thought being how he could best serve. So with all the men who have so wonderfully given of themselves to further the university.

Alumni of University of Wisconsin and
University of Chicago (Milwaukee), 14 December 1925

MASON

The University of Chicago is most fortunate in its body of Trustees, as well as its faculty. These groups are remarkable in their spirit of frank, sincere, and friendly co-operation. The Trustees are a devoted body of eminent citizens who at great personal sacrifice in time and energy insure the success and stability of the institution.

Convocation, 12 June 1928

HUTCHINS

Legally the University is the Board of Trustees; they are responsible for the selection of the staff; they determine their salaries and tenure, and control the institution in such detail as they wish. They have greater powers than the directors of an ordinary corporation; they are self-perpetuating, and there are no stockholders.

The public concern with the University is shown by its incorporation under the laws of Illinois and the tax-exemption conferred upon it by the Legislature. It may be suggested that the public regards the Board as its representative, with the duty of seeing to it that the University is conducted in the public interest. This may be urged particularly in regard to the teaching of very young people; it may be said that the Board has a special responsibility to guarantee that the instruction at these levels is the kind the community would like to have, or at least that it is not the kind that the community would not like to have. In this view the Board has an obligation to keep the University in tune with the life of the community, with its aspirations and ideals, and must exercise such supervision over education and research as to insure this result.

Since the University is a corporation, and one spending millions of dollars a year, it is easy to think of it as a business. If it is a business, there must be employers and employees, with the usual incidents of that relationship. In business an employer ordinarily would not tolerate an employee with whom he seriously disagreed, or whom he disliked, or who, he thought, was bringing the organization into disrepute. In this view the Trustees are the employers of the faculty and have the right, if not the duty, to discharge those who in their judgment discredit or embarrass the University.

In attempting to analyze functions in a university it should be noted that a board of trustees is a unique American organization. Since the Middle Ages the European Universities have been controlled directly by the state, without the intervention of a board of any kind, and the British universities have been controlled by the faculties. The universities of colonial America were not universities at all; they were professional schools, designed to train ministers for the churches which founded them. Some of the trustees of these institutions were teachers in them; but they were all clergymen, who were doubtless charged with the duty of making the education given by the college conform to the wishes and needs of the denomination. Since the colonial period the major universities have outgrown their original purpose and have become institutions concerned with research, general education, and all varieties of professional training. The sole object of the Harvard of 1636 has become a minute fraction of its activities today. . . .

I should argue that society has thought it worthwhile to set apart men who are to search for knowledge impartially and to communicate it in the same spirit. It has thought it worthwhile to provide a haven for the individual specially qualified to pursue the truth and to protect him from the community, from influential citizens, and even from his colleagues. In this view a university is first of all a group of professors.

If ideally a university is a group of professors, what is a board of trustees? A board of trustees is a body of public spirited citizens who believe in the aims of the professors, namely, the development of education and the advancement of knowledge. They have undertaken to relieve them of two responsibilities they cannot carry: the responsibility of managing their property and the responsibility of interpreting them to and defending them from the public. They fix the salary scale in order to make sure that the university's money is not squandered. They find out all about the faculty in order to interpret them to the public. But they have renounced for all practical purposes any right to pass on their qualifications to be professors. The faculty is not working for the trustees; the trustees are working for the faculty. The analogy of business or what an employer may do in business is therefore inapplicable.

"Report of the President 1934–35" (Unpublished)

KIMPTON

Its Board has always included the ablest and most public-spirited men of Chicago, and, as Harold Swift has said many times, it is undoubtedly the hardest working board in the country. They are devoted trustees, who take the time to know the University in detail and to give their energy, intelligence, and influence to its welfare. The chairmen of the board through the years testify to its distinction and devotion: Martin A. Ryerson, Harold H. Swift, and Laird Bell have all made the welfare of the University their primary concern.

Women's Club (Chicago), February 1952

KIMPTON

A friend of mine in the same line of work once said that the head of a university must pose before his Board as a scholar and before his Faculty as a businessman—and then pray that never the twain shall meet. Once a year, within the honored tradition of this University, the twain do meet and, as a result, I do not enjoy this occasion as much as most of you. One always wonders what secrets are being exchanged at these happy tables. With the assistance of alcohol, the wall built by the Chancellor between the Board and the Faculty may be successfully breached. Using the strategy that the best defense is an offense, I have decided upon this occasion to reveal some secrets too, and tell the Board something about the Faculty and the Faculty something about the Board.

Some day, when you have nothing better to do, I urge you to engage in the interesting academic exercise of reading the *Articles of Incorporation*, the *By-Laws*, and the *Statutes* under which this University is presumably run. After a quaint preamble in the *Articles* about how the Board should operate academies, preparatory and manual training schools, there is a specific charge to the Board, and I quote: ". . . to establish and maintain a university, in which may be taught all branches of higher learning, and which may comprise and embrace separate departments for literature, law, medicine, music, technology, the various branches of science, both abstract and applied, the cultivation of the fine arts, and all other branches of professional or technical education which may properly be included within the purposes and objects of a university, and to provide and maintain courses of instruction in each and all of said departments; to prescribe the courses of study, employ professors, instructors, and teachers, and to maintain and control the government and the discipline in said University, and in each of the several departments thereof . . ." End of quote. And just to be sure that there is no monkey business about all this, these articles are signed by John D. Rockefeller and Marshall Field, among others.

I hope all of you get the full meaning of this statement. It is the Board's problem to provide instruction, to prescribe courses, to employ professors, and to control the government and discipline of the University. I dare the Board, individually or collectively to do any of these things, although there certainly is no question it has the power. Can't you see the report of the AAUP if the Board of Trustees decided to *exercise* some of its authority?

Under the *Statutes* of the University, arrangements are made by which the Board shakily delegates some of this power, and the Chancellor is portrayed as quite a fellow. He is the executive head of the University in all its departments; he is the presiding officer of all ruling bodies; he makes appointments to the academic staff of the University. Oddly enough, the *Statutes* make no reference to the only real power the Chancellor possesses, namely, the resignation he carries in his pocket to all Board and Faculty meetings. At this point instead the *Statutes* change the subject. It is said that the Chancellor is responsible for carrying out all measures officially agreed upon by the Faculty in regard to matters committed to them by the Board, but it doesn't say, of course, that anything *is* committed to them. And where did the Faculty get into this picture in any case? Up to now, one could have assumed that the Board owned the University and the Chancellor operated it. This would be the time, I suspect, for the magnificent chorus in *Porgy and Bess* to sing: "It Ain't Necessarily So." It is a strange situation when the legal power structure of the University is exactly the reverse of the one which actually holds, but such indeed is the case.

Let me describe for the benefit of the Faculty what our Board really is and what it does. It is a group of business and professional men who have a great respect for the academic world in general and for this institution in particular. They understandably feel at home in dealing with the fiscal, physical, legal and real estate problems of the University. There is no one of them who does not put in many hours each month on these important aspects of our affairs, and the sole payment to them for these services is the privilege of buying our dinner this evening. There is no faculty member present who is not richer through the studied financial unorthodoxy of the late Edward Eagle Brown, who served for years on our Investment Committee. Our Treasurer tells me that, if each member of this Investment Committee were paid on the same basis as a director of a mutual investment trust, he would receive $20,000 each meeting. And you would be amazed to know how much legal advice we need, and how much free legal service we get. The hours of free real estate expertise that go into the purchase of a single building on Hyde Park Boulevard would locate and plan a new suburban shopping center for Marshall Field & Company. There is no brochure we issue that does not have sufficient talented time devoted to it to launch a new product for General Motors. And the poor Chairman of the Board—he should really, like Harold Swift, be a wealthy bachelor, for he renounces for the duration all family ties as well as all visible means of support.

But—and this may surprise you—the real interest of the members of the Board lies in the academic. It is strange and wonderful, at affairs such as these, to hear the faculty member talking about his E & E budget, trying to remember the last quotation on Bell & Howell stock, and fumbling to conjure up something bright to say on the subject of high interest rates, while the trustee wants to talk about anti-matter and the progress of the Epigraphic Survey. . . .

. . . They love this University, intensely admire this Faculty, and are dedicated to their welfare. And the Faculty, though the Board is shadowy and remote, return this admiration and this trust. They know the power of the Board and they respect how gently the reins are drawn. It is a world they never made, but the Faculty understands and appreciates the stature of each Board member and the measure of his devotion. Harld Swift, Laird Bell, Edward Ryerson, and Glen Lloyd are known with respect and affection by all scholars who know this University.

It is one of the elementary laws of administration that when something is going along well, you leave it alone. And I recall from earlier and happier days in the study of philosophy that one never probes any genuine mystery too deeply; faith is a precious though a fragile thing, and too rigorous an analysis may make it altogether disappear. It was Tertullian, in the early confused days of the Third Century, who said stoutly, "I believe because it is absurd." Something like this blind commitment seems to motivate our Board and our Faculty in their respect for each other and in their common dedication to research and education. And the reward, like that of Tertullian, must lie in heaven for those who devote their lives, their money, and their energies to a cause which none of us fully understands but in which we all deeply believe. May we on both sides of the great divide continue to enjoy and to deserve the limitless confidence and esteem that each has always felt for the other.

Trustee-Faculty Dinner, 14 January 1960

BEADLE

Finally, I should like to say a word about our Board of Trustees. I have seen several Boards, some at close range, and I can say that I have never seen a more effective one. Its members have supported the University magnificently in many ways, many of which you are as familiar with as I am—and many of which, I dare say, you are not. Perhaps one way you are not familiar with is the recent establishment of a special fund for strengthening the University. This has been done quietly, anonymously, without public announcement, and through wide participation on the part of Board members. It is officially called the President's Suspense Fund. It might better be designated the Selective Eminence Fund, for it is to be used to bring additional outstanding scholars to the University—and for keeping those we have. It is "high potential" money and we must not reduce it to low potential by using it for increases in budgets across the board.

This fund puts us in a position financially to bring to the University now those ten to twenty selectively distinguished scholars who would raise to eminence eight or so additional departments, increasing the total to twenty, or five more than Stigler's goal. At the same time, we could double or even treble the number of departments at the top in national competition.

Trustee-Faculty Dinner, 10 January 1962

BEADLE

One important part of a university that outsiders do not often rate—at least I do not know of any serious attempt to do so—is the Board of Trustees, or its equivalent. I do know from personal observation something about such bodies in six major universities or colleges, so I'll try. I put our Board first by a wide margin among those I know, and if I were a betting man, I would stack high odds on ours against all others—in competence, in understanding of what an institution of higher learn-

251

ing should be, in genuine interest, and in performance. And I don't say that on this occasion just because the Trustees have personally for forty-five years carried on the special, and I believe unique, tradition—wonderful, delightful and generous as it is—of hosting magnificent dinners such as this. . . .

I have done some checking on the history of these dinners. They go back forty-five years to the time of Judson as President and Martin Ryerson as Chairman of the Board. At first they were held at Hutchinson Commons (there was no present Quadrangle Club in 1920). When that proved too small, Ida Noyes became the site, then, in succession, the Women's Gymnasium, the South Shore Country Club, the Stevens Hotel (as the Conrad Hilton was then called), and now here.

I estimate that 40,000 meals were enjoyed—like the one we have had tonight. I can't say how many cocktails were drunk, for in the early days that practice was frowned on. Besides, no one counts the drinks. They began at the South Shore Country Club, where you bought your own in the cocktail lounge.

Speaking of cocktails at the University, Emery T. (Tom) Filbey tells me that their precursor was beer, served in 1942 to a group of military officers in training at the University for service in captured territories. Tom arranged a dinner for them at which he wished to serve beer. He tried the Quadrangle Club, International House and Ida Noyes. All said, "So sorry, no beer, even to Army officers as a special exception." So he asked Ernest Colwell, then Dean of the Divinity School, if he could give the dinner—with beer—in Swift Hall Commons. "Sure," said the Dean. Takes a divine to rise above petty principle and, if necessary, invoke Biblical precedent.

Trustee-Faculty Dinner, 14 January 1965

NOW, A WORD ABOUT OURSELVES
AND ONE ANOTHER

HARPER

This is also true of the words of the President of the University, which should never be taken as an official statement of the University itself, unless he distinctly utters it as such and indicates that particular body, Trustees or Faculty, for which he speaks. All other utterances are of an individual and personal character, and he should be given permission, as is every other professor, to make utterances for himself.

Decennial Report, 1 July 1902

KIMPTON

It is peculiarly my job to explain the University, to make clear our nature and our role.

Order of the C Dinner, 7 June 1951

HARPER, WITH TONGUE IN CHEEK . . .

HARPER

About three thousand years ago there came into existence a new profession—that of the prophet. The early history of this profession had much in common with the rise of a profession coming to be recognized as such for the first time in the present generation—that of the college president. In the earliest days of prophetism the incumbent of that office was not infrequently termed "mad." The presence in its ranks of certain men occasioned great surprise for it became a proverb, "Is Saul also among the prophets?" Not infrequently these prophets in their enthusiasm stripped themselves of their clothing and fell down in a trance. At one time in this early period, we are told, there were about four hundred of them.

It is somewhat the same in these early days of the college president. He is not infrequently treated as "mad." Very common is the phrase, "Has Jones also become a college president?" Instead, however, of stripping himself, he labors without ceasing to strip others. The number is the same, about four hundred. The analogy between the ancient dervish and the modern college president might be pressed even more closely; but it is unnecessary.

A superficial observer will find much to substantiate the very common accusation that the college president is professionally a prevaricator. Do not members of a college faculty distinctly recall many occasions when the president has promised promotion, or increase of salary, or a special appropriation for books and equipment; promises that he has forgotten as soon as the door was closed upon the interview? Is it not true that on many occasions, students, summoned to the president's office to meet charges made against them, have left the office wholly satisfied that these charges had been shown false and firmly convinced that the president was on their side, only to find the next day that the verdict declared them guilty rather than innocent?

How often, too, it has happened that the president in talking with one person, or group of persons, has seemed to entertain a given opinion, whereas, in conversation with another person, or group, strangely enough a different opinion on the same subject was expressed. It is reported that the president of a New England college not long since gave up his position because his statements on the same subject to different people varied so radically; in other words, because the truth as he represented it was so multiform. To be entirely just to New England, it must be added, reports of this tenor are not restricted to that section of the country.

The president of a college or university who succeeds at times in concealing his real thought concerning this man or that subject is politely called a diplomat. Is it diplomacy, or is it lying? Or may a more euphemistic phrase be found to describe the policy which must characterize his dealing with all classes of men if he is to remain a college president?

A closer study of the case and the examination of specific instances will furnish evidence that the professor who thought he had been promised promotion or an increase of salary made petition to this effect, was received courteously, and mistook courteous treatment for a business pledge. The student, it will be found, forgot that the president was his judge. A judge is silent until sentence is to be pronounced. The student mistook that silence for acquiescence in his own statement. It is easy enough to imagine that the person to whom one talks has in his mind the thought of the speaker. The next step is easier still, actually to believe that the listener has approved the words of the speaker, or perhaps that he has spoken them.

Possible it is, to be sure, that the president in expressing his desire that such and such a thing should be, sometimes makes a statement that is open to stronger interpretation than he intended. It would be strange if he did not occasionally consent to a proposition which, upon later consideration, might appear to be impracticable; or which, however urgently he might present it to the powers that be, would fail to secure their approval. Does he likewise sometimes forget? Unquestionably, for he is human. Does he sometimes really undertake to do the impossible? Surely, and he discovers this fact to his cost. In all these cases, from the point of view of the other man, he is, in the language of the street, a liar. And yet, I dare say, he still supposes himself worthy of the confidence of his fellow-creatures.

The college presidency is a profession in which a large percentage of one's time and energy is occupied in saying "no." Real risk is taken when, for the sake of variation, even in a small proportion of these cases a kindly interest is shown. To be brutal may not be so good a policy at the time, but in the long run it probably pays. One of the most distinguished university presidents now living was noted during a large portion of his career for his extreme brutality. It is altogether probable that the high success which he has achieved is due in no small measure to this fact. He is said to have become greatly softened in his later years. One can afford to practice policy in later years which would spell ruin in the early career.

It is contended, with some show of plausibility, that the modern college president is, first and last, a "boss." Does he not have almost unlimited power? May he not exercise this power at his own pleasure? Does he not set up and pull down? Can he not brow-beat and threaten? Is not the life of every professor in his hands? Does he not make and break careers? Is not the administration of a college or university in these times an example of one-man power? It is so maintained, and we must confess there are some facts which seem to favor this contention.

If the existence of one case of this kind, or even of several, would warrant us in supposing that it was generally true, the question would be settled. Perhaps there has not been known in recent years, a more typical instance of despotism than that which is said to have existed in a certain State University. The writer is fully aware of the fact that this same word "despot" has been applied both good-naturedly and ill-naturedly to his own administrative policy. But it is interesting to observe that within a few months there has been appointed the *first* president of the University of Virginia—a significant fact in the history of education, showing that the extreme democratic policy initiated by Thomas Jefferson is regarded as a failure. It is probable that Mr. Jefferson, if living, would himself recognize the failure of his cherished idea. In these last years has Harvard outstripped Yale? If so, is it not partly because at Harvard the president is given larger power?

To what extent is the college or university of modern times a business enterprise, requiring the adoption of business methods in the transaction of its affairs? If this point of view is provisionally assumed, light may be shed upon the question from the study of the tendency in modern business concerns. As institutions grow larger and more complex, is there not inevitably a tendency towards specialism in administration, and a necessity for organization which will definitely locate responsibility? The departmental professor in a college or university is ordinarily wholly occupied with the affairs of his own subject. The responsibility rests upon him to develop that subject as best he can. He is, to be sure, an agent responsible for the institution as a whole, and any policy that would injure the institution would be felt by his department. At the same time, the departmental interest is uppermost in his mind, and his judgment in decisions of questions of general policy is necessarily biased. Decisions made even by many persons of judgment more or less biased and without a personal knowledge of the questions at issue, are not likely to be wise decisions.

Should not the president of an institution of learning be restricted in his power? Shall the highest educational interests of a great republic be placed in the hands of men who may be called czars? A close study of the situation will show that, when all has been said, the limitations of the college president, even when he has the greatest freedom of action, are very great. In all business matters he is the servant of the trustees or corporation; and his views will prevail in that body only in so far as they approve themselves to their good judgment. In educational policy he must be in accord with his colleagues. If he cannot persuade them to adopt his views, he must go with them. It is absurd to suppose that any president, however strong or willful he may be, can force a faculty made up of great leaders of thought to do his will. The president, if he has the power of veto, may stand in the way of progress, but he cannot secure forward movement except with the co-operation of those with whom he is associated. If there is one institution in which the president has too much power, there are ten in which he has too little.

The office of the college president is an office of service. Everything good or bad which connects itself with service is associated with this office. True service everywhere involves suffering for others. In no other profession, not even in that of the minister of the Gospel, is vicarious suffering more common. But one cannot be suffering for another unless one suffer also with that other. A fundamental characteristic of the president must be a sympathetic nature. He is doomed to failure unless he is able to place himself in the position of others with whom and for whom he has been called to work. In the truest sense the position is a representative one. He does many things, not of his own choice, but because he represents his colleagues. He may not do this or that thing according to his own pleasure or his own sense of what is proper. The decision to do or not to do must rest largely upon the possible effect, helpful or harmful, to the institution of which he is head. In short, he is the slave of his environment and must submit to the drudgery as well as the misery of that slavery.

And, besides, another feeling which gradually grows upon the occupant of the presidential chair is that of great loneliness—the feeling of separation from all his fellows. At certain times he realizes that in all truth he *is* alone; for those who are ordinarily close to him seem to be, and in fact are, far away. On occasions of this kind courage is needed; strength, of a peculiar character. An ordinary man, and after all the college president is an ordinary man, cannot thus be cut off from his associates and fail to experience the sorrow of such separation. The college presidency means the giving up of many things, and, not least among them one's most intimate friendships. Moreover, this feeling of separation, of isolation, increases with each recurring year and, in spite of the most vigorous effort, it comes to be a thing of permanence. This is inevitable, and it is as sad as it is inevitable.

While it happens that the words as well as the actions of the president are misunderstood by those about him; even by those of his colleagues who stand nearest to him, he is indeed fortunate if a worse thing does not come—the wilful effort to misrepresent him. He cannot exercise the functions of his office honestly without disturbing at times some even of these whom he believes to be his friends. And when this happens, these friends, perhaps unconsciously, will cease to find back of his actions the motives which he himself entertains. It is sometimes pitiful to see how easily men will misunderstand each other and how complacently the misrepresentations of another's thought are spread from mouth to mouth. The reader will say that such things do not happen. Let me assure him that experience demonstrates not only the possibility but the frequency of their occurrence. Three cases of persecution through misrepresentation, which was actually malicious, have occurred within a year. The names of these institutions are well known.

There come likewise times of great depression when one contemplates in all its details the bigness of the task which lies before him. In many instances this bigness becomes overwhelming, because of the exacting nature of the demands made, together with the number and magnitude of the difficulties involved. So numerous are the affairs of a great university; so heavy are they, in the responsibility which they impose; so delicate and difficult, in the diplomacy which their conduct requires; so arduous, in the actual time required for their management; so heart-engrossing and mind-disturbing, that there is demanded for their adequate supervision a man possessing the strength of a giant and an intellectual capacity and a moral courage of the most determined character. One, indeed, possessed of strength, feels himself weak when he is brought face to face with all that is demanded; and one becomes sick at heart when he contemplates how much additional strength is needed to enable him to fulfill his duties as his conscience tells him they should be fulfilled.

Besides all this, there is found in moments of greatest encouragement a feeling of utter dissatisfaction with one's own work. To what definite thing can the president point and say—this is my work? Does he not find his highest function in helping others to do the things which he himself would like to do? Yet he must stand aside and see others take up this very work which in his heart he would desire to handle. The head of an institution is not himself permitted to finish a piece of work. It is his business to find ways and means by which others may be helped to do their work. Some presidents never learn this difficult art—the art of letting others do things which one wishes himself to do. And for this reason not a few men fail to fill satisfactorily the office of president. There are two common maxims which, if quoted in a form exactly the opposite of that in which they are in vogue, must regulate the work of the chief officer of a university if that work is to be successful. The first of these is this: *One should never himself do what he can in any way find someone else to do.* It is fair to presume that, with a single exception, there is no function of the presidential office that cannot better be performed by one or another member of the staff than by the president himself. I mean by this that for each particular function there can be found a man who has the peculiar ability to do that service better than the president can do it. The one function which may not be included in this statement is the selection and nomination of new members of the staff. Further, *the president should never do today what by any possible means he can postpone until tomorrow.* Premature action is the source of many more mistakes than procrastination. No decision should ever be reached, or at all events announced, until the latest possible moment has arrived, for how many are the instances in which new evidence has been introduced when, alas, it has been found too late to make use of it.

But there is also a bright side to this picture. How can one fail to find great satisfaction in a work which brings him into close association with life confessedly higher and more ideal than ordinary life? If in any environment idealism reigns supreme, it is in that of the university. There one works for and with young manhood and womanhood; and nothing in all the world is more inspiring than work in such association. It is the period in human life of greatest inspiration, of most intense enjoyment, and of loftiest aspiration. The sadness of life is for the most part a thing of the future. Ambition is the keynote; and affection is in its best and purest mood. The life of a university officer is in many respects the most ideal that exists. The minister meets everywhere sorrow and sickness and death. The lawyer struggles against dishonesty, dissipation, and fraud. The physician is almost wholly occupied with want and pain and suffering. With the college professor and the college president it is essentially different. They have to deal with all that is uplifting in life, with the constructive and not the destructive forces of life. The satisfaction which this brings no one can describe.

How does the president of a university spend his time? Largely in seeking ways and means to enable this or that professor to carry out some plan which he has deeply at heart—a plan, it may be, for research and investigation, or for improving the work of instruction. If it is not service for an officer of instruction, it is service for this or that student whose needs, to him at all events, seem very great. If one is selfish, he grows weary of it all; but, if in his heart there is an earnest desire to do for humanity the several services which in his position it is possible for him to render, he learns sooner or later that to no man in any position is there given greater opportunity for service. In a few cases those with whom one comes into contact appreciate keenly and cordially the unselfish service which has been rendered.

A few, I say; I did not say only a few, because if even a few feel such appreciation, and in proper form express it, the gratitude of these few will be good return for the loneliness and misrepresentation and despondency which have been his lot. The words spoken from the heart, of even a small number, will prove to be good compensation for one's devotion to the interests of an institution. A single utterance of sincere gratitude uttered by one who has been helped will continue through many days and weeks, and even months, to counteract the depressing influence of words of criticism, reproach, and ridicule. In no realm of life does a man feel more quickly the response to effort which he may have made than in the realm of student life. Nowhere else, it is true, is criticism more sharp; nowhere else is real conflict more easy. At the same time, nowhere else is friendship closer, or words of appreciation more sincere.

The college president deserves the support of the intelligent man of modern times. His position is a trying one; his burden is heavy, and the reward is, at the best, meager. His effort is always intended to serve the interests that make for truth and the higher life. He is not usually a "liar" or a "boss." He may sometimes seem to be too self-satisfied; one could name a few such. But for the most part he does his work, conscious that he has the short-comings which mark his kind, realizing keenly that his tenure of office, unlike that of his colleagues, is quite uncertain, yet fully resolved to perform his duty without fear or favor and to allow time to determine the question of his success or failure.

"The College President." *Magazine*
November 1938

Reprinted from The *William Rainey Harper Memorial Conference Held in Connection with the Centennial of Muskingum College*, October 21–22, 1937, by permission of Muskingum College and The University of Chicago

Hutchins

I will tell you a professional secret, which I would not venture to reveal if I were not leaving the profession, and that is that he can do as little as he pleases or as much as he can.

A university president may take the estimated income of the university, and after due allowances for reserves for every conceivable contingency, divide it among the academic applicants for it on a per capita basis. To those who complain that they got too little he can explain that he has exercised no discrimination: each has got his share of what there was. He can automatically approve the recommendations for appointments and promotions that come to him from the departments, pausing only to make sure that they are within the budget. He can abstain from the consideration and discussion of educational issues and content himself with explaining, if he can, the educational programs of the various departments and schools. If he does these things, and if he raises money, he will be a great success.

He cannot seek to distinguish among individuals, projects, and ideas without alienating successive blocs of his constituency. Whatever the disagreements among these groups on other matters they will unite in holding that he has very bad judgment.

The financial requirements of universities have steadily risen; and money raising has become the preoccupation of presidents. In some quarters it is thought that the only qualification of a university president is his ability to raise money. Since raising money is by no means an academic specialty, university presidencies have gone more and more to men without academic standing and even without academic interests. Why should academic qualifications be insisted on when the man has nothing to do with academic matters? The question is: has he the reputation and temperament that will gain him access to sources of funds?

I must confess that all this is a mystery to me. I do not see

---

Press. Samuel N. Harper, son of the first president, makes this comment: "In the examination of the family files for material which might appropriately be placed in the log cabin where Dr. Harper was born, this unpublished manuscript was found. It seemed proper that this article, prepared in 1904, be read at the centennial dinner, when former presidents of Muskingum College and Muskingum alumni who had headed educational institutions were being memorialized." (Original note.—Ed.)

what raising money has to do with managing a university. A university president is remotely analogous to the conductor of a symphony orchestra. The analogy is not close, because in a university every man is a soloist, and the conductor cannot tell him what to play. But the analogy is close enough to suggest the absurdity of saying that the capacity to raise money has any bearing on a man's qualifications for a university presidency. Would you think that a man should be selected to conduct a symphony orchestra merely because he could get the money to finance it? Yet somebody raises the money for the orchestras of the country.

I could understand the notion that university presidents should be judged by the money they raised on one of two hypotheses. If the finest educational and scholarly program could be expected to result from adding up the offerings of the departments, then nobody needs to worry about the score the university is playing. Or, if there are no educational issues, then nobody needs to concern himself with the resolution of such issues.

The first hypothesis amounts to saying that a university is a collection of professors, located more or less in one place, using certain common facilities, like libraries and heating plants, that would be too expensive for them to pay for individually. The university provides these conveniences, but beyond that it has no purpose. It has no purpose of its own. Many notable examples can be given of this type of institution, and it may be that the hypothesis on which they are founded is correct. It is perhaps sheer vanity that has led me, as a university officer, to hope that there was a purpose for my institution, and incidentally for myself, beyond that of academic housekeeping. Academic housekeeping has ever failed to hold my attention.

Alumni Assembly (Chicago), 9 June 1951

OUR CONSCRIPT FATHERS

KIMPTON

It is the role of your new chancellor to protect and nourish the great tradition of the University of Chicago and to attempt to solve the problems of our day within that tradition.

State of the University, 14 October 1952

HUTCHINS

The president of a university represents both the trustees and the faculty. At Chicago this is made explicit by the practice of having the President nominated by a joint committee. One of the president's duties to both the faculty and the board is to act as chief interpreter of the University. One of his duties to the trustees is to see to it that they have all the information about the University they will consume. Another is to prevent the faculty from wasting the university's funds. One of the president's duties to the faculty is to help the trustees so to understand the university that they will not be tempted to use their financial control to control the educational and scientific work of the university.

"Report of the President 1934–35" (Unpublished)

KIMPTON

The University was an exciting project, because of Mr. Rockefeller, and even more because of the man who accepted the task of organizing it and leading it. William Rainey Harper had big and original ideas, and because of notions that seemed fantastic to some, he provoked considerable ridicule and attack as well as enthusiasm. The University was described as "a foreign intrusion in the life of the city," and as "Harper's folly." But there was no folly about it, as the succession of new buildings and the acquisition of distinguished members to its faculty rather quickly demonstrated. . . .

The University has always enjoyed great leadership. Dr. Harper was a genius in education. He had a fresh and original approach, and did more to establish the university idea as we know it than any other man. To his remarkable ability he added energy, enthusiasm, and the talents of a promoter, essential to a new enterprise of the scope he envisaged. He ran the University with thumping deficits each year which were patiently underwritten by Mr. Rockefeller. . . .

His successor, Harry Pratt Judson, performed a particularly important service for the period in which the University found itself after the death of Harper. He was able to meet the demand of Mr. Rockefeller that the University consolidate its gains and establish an educational and financial equilibrium. There are still many people at the University who recall with admiration and affection the third president, Ernest DeWitt Burton, a saintly scholar suddenly lifted from a peaceful life to take on the strange work of an administrator. This Dr. Burton did with a vigor and skill that astonished even his friends. It was under him that the University became aware of the fact that it had tended to become isolated from the community and that the changing world made the endowment of the University inadequate for the times and its needs. In the few brief years in which he served as president, Dr. Burton engendered a renascence of spirit and effort that still prevails.

Max Mason, his successor, stayed here only a couple of years before he became president of the Rockefeller Foundation, but in that short time he displayed a real talent for charming wealthy citizens into giving money for the expansion of the University. Some of them, fascinated almost to the point of hypnotism, collapsed in relief when he went away, recognizing they now would be able to keep the remnants of the money that otherwise he would have taken from them.

I scarcely need do more than remind you of my immediate predecessor, Robert M. Hutchins. He did for education in his time at the University—and it was the longest administration the University has known—what Dr. Harper had done in his day. He took a hard, fresh look at the way education had crystallized in the last half century, and with that clarity which marked all his efforts, arrived at some very sound conclusions. His was a great era, in which the University reasserted its pioneering tradition and renewed its excitement over intellectual problems.

Women's Club (Chicago), February 1952

WILLIAM RAINEY HARPER: PRIMUS INTER PARES

JUDSON

The past year, rounding out the fifteen years since the initiation of the University, has been signalized by a great loss. The President whose large ideas gave shape to the institution, whose energy, buoyant hopefulness, and ready grasp of business made it possible to strike out on new lines and to create that which did not exist, has gone from us. He remains with all a precious memory. He lives and will live throughout the history of the University in the great work which he accomplished and in the virile ideas which he embodied in the University and which will live through the ages. His loss is to us beyond measure. We can only, all of us, take up the work which he initiated and carry it on in the same spirit of fidelity to duty and of hope for what is to come. In that spirit and with that spirit the University will continue to grow in usefulness and in magnitude of resources.

Convocation, 12 June 1906

BURTON

President Harper was by nature and training a leader. Few men of his generation have possessed in larger measure than he those qualities which mark one as made for captaincy, and which make other men willing and glad to enlist under his leadership. But his leadership was always genial, never magisterial. Men followed him instinctively and from preference, not under compulsion. He understood men, he appreciated what was best in them, he loved companionship; his horizon was broad, and his insight keen; he was hopeful, courageous to the point of daring, persistent and self-sacrificing. Withal he was intensely human. His best friends and warmest admirers recognized his faults. But they were the faults of a strong man, fighting a strenuous battle in an imperfect world. None of them was the fault of a weakling, and none of them sprang from self-seeking. In all his ambitions he never intentionally injured another, sought always those things that were helpful to others.

Dr. Harper was eminently a companionable man. He loved his fellows, and he loved to associate them with himself in work and in play, in planning and in executing. In the multitude of those enterprises in which he engaged as President of the University of Chicago, and of its Divinity School, as head of the department of Semitic languages, as editor of the journals with which he was connected, in the conduct of the American Institute of Sacred Literature, he delighted to work in association with others. Even in his study he enjoyed the fellowship of another mind, and in authorship associated himself with others, dividing work and responsibility with them. With a keen discernment of the ability and character of other men, which en-

265

abled him to recognize the particular work which each was adapted to accomplish, his judgments were characteristically those of appreciation, not of depreciation. He usually rated a man higher than the man himself did, and believed him capable of larger things than he would himself have undertaken. As a rule, the outcome justified his faith. And if sometimes the future belied his judgment, if sometimes a man proved unworthy of the confidence reposed in him, this testified rather to President Harper's healthy faith in humanity than to a judgment habitually faulty.

It was in no small measure this appreciative discernment of the peculiar strength of individual men that enabled him to associate with himself in the various departments of the University, and the varied forms of his activity, men of widely diverse temperament, tastes, and even convictions. With each of them he had his point of contact and sympathy. And men who would never have been drawn into co-operation by any attraction for one another found themselves able, through their common relations to Dr. Harper, harmoniously to co-operate for a common end.

He was particularly successful in developing the abilities and ambitions of younger men. He would talk with them at length concerning the possibilities of their own particular line of work and career, often outlining plans that would require years to accomplish. Sometimes the young man himself failed to perceive the necessity of the time element, and grew impatient at the President's apparent failure to bring about the fulfilment of his own prophecies. With the man of real ability and promise he had all the patience and faithfulness of a father in correcting mistakes and imparting ideals and inspiration.

No one who has had the experience of being a member of one of those groups of men, sometimes large, often small, that gathered in the President's office or study, to confer and plan together with the least possible formality, will ever forget how under his leadership horizons were broadened, impossible tasks became wholly practicable, and hard work a pleasure.

Most fertile in suggestion of new plans himself, most original in devising new methods of work, he was at the same time most hospitable toward every suggestion put forth by his associates, and quick to express appreciation of it. Most ready to discard an old and favorite method of accomplishing a result, when that method had outlived its usefulness or could be displaced by a better one; most keen to perceive any change in conditions, demanding a corresponding change in means or methods, he yet welcomed the sharpest criticism of new plans, and carefully weighed every objection. Invincibly persistent when he was sure that he was right, willing to wait weeks, months, years, if need be, for the fulfilment of his plans and his dreams, but never willing to admit that what ought to be could not be, there was yet nothing of obstinacy in him. The mere fact that another disagreed with him, though that other was his warmest friend, or one for whose opinions he had most respect, could not change his own opinion, had little effect indeed upon that opinion. But he could be dissuaded from immediate action by the dissenting judgment of others, and argument or reconsideration sometimes led to a real change of mind.

Nothing was more characteristic of Dr. Harper, nothing more clearly marked him for leadership, than the largeness and boldness of the plans that shaped themselves in his mind and often came to expression in informal conferences with his colleagues. The demand thus made upon those who were associated with him was large, but it was never a mere imposition of burdens upon others. He always insisted upon taking a full share of the load himself, and showed a real appreciation of what he was asking of others. If the great burdens that he bore sometimes made it impossible for him to perform all that he undertook, or if plans in which others took a share with him sometimes had to be postponed again and again from sheer lack of time or of opportunity to carry them out, he never despaired, but cheerfully set forward the date for the achievement of the effort, and pressed resolutely and hopefully forward.

A man of large ambitions, he was singularly free from self-seeking. For the University, for the Institute of Sacred Literature, for the Religious Education Association, for the journals which he edited, for all these he had great hopes and great ambitions. To these, and the other agencies through which he could serve his fellow-men, he gave himself in reckless self-forgetfulness and generous self-sacrifice.

To work with such a leader was an education in all that makes for noble leadership. To have worked with him is a precious memory, and an inspiration to live earnestly and generously while life lasts.

"In Association with His Colleagues."
Biblical World, March 1906

KIMPTON

Unlike most of our sister institutions of learning in this country, which began as simple colleges for the training of a learned ministry, Chicago began as a great University. It drained the resources of even a Rockefeller, and decimated the ranks of teaching and research talent in several American universities to do it, but William Rainey Harper would not settle for less. He may have been an ordained Baptist minister, but he wanted no part of a small Baptist college to which Rockefeller thought he was committing himself.

Convocation, 16 December 1966

KIMPTON

Harper was a dynamo who spilled forth educational ideas at the same rate that the new industries of Chicago were spilling forth products. He was one of the first to see that Gilman was transforming Johns Hopkins into the first modern University, and this concept of a modern university he brought to the Middle West while Yale and Harvard slumbered in sleepy little New England towns. Chicago never became a University; under Harper's direction it began as a University. He developed a great research center and drew up a blueprint of what later became the College of the University of Chicago. He invented the correspondence system of adult education and the quarter system. He established the first university press in the Middle West. He converted his educational dreams into expensive realities so rapidly that not even the Rockefeller fortune could keep up with him.

Convocation, 12 June 1953

BURTON

President Harper was a man of great originality. Not all of his ideas have proved practicable. Not all of his schemes succeeded.

But he was so fertile in producing them that he could fail in enough things to have ruined another man, and yet succeed in enough to make him eminently successful. Not all of his ideas were new, but an astonishing number of them were, and those that were not new were so reborn in his mind, and were set forth with such new clearness and force that they had all the inspiring quality of absolute novelty.

For the benefit of some of you who perhaps never knew him and do not appreciate how much of what you found at the University and what you perhaps took for granted, was really due to him and was new, I should like to mention certain elements of the University's life which were born in his brain.

1. The three major system. I mean the plan according to which each student in general pursued only three subjects at a time. This policy of concentration was produced at a time when under the influence of the comparatively recent introduction of electives, students were accustomed to carry on any where from five to ten subjects at once.

2. The four quarter system, the elimination of the long summer vacation, which all colleges had inherited from the days when the boys had to go back to the farms to reap the harvest in summer time. This gave a chance to the student who wanted and was able to do so to carry on his work through the year with only four vacations of a week each, afterward changed to two short vacations and the month's vacation in September. But much more important was the fact that it opened up to thousands of teachers in all the colleges and universities and high schools of the west the opportunity for advanced study. . . .

3. The emphasis on the Graduate School and research. This was not wholly new—Johns Hopkins and Clark had blazed their path in the East. But it was quite new in the West, and coupled with the continuance of work in the Summer Quarter constituted a tremendous contribution to the development of higher education not only in the West but throughout the country.

4. But while President Harper exalted the graduate work and research, he was not less earnest in his insistence on the duty of the University to the community at large. With an emphasis and clearness that I am sure had not up to that time been equalled he insisted that the duty of the University was not simply to its students and through them to the country, but directly also to those that could not come inside its walls.

This thought of the duty of the University to the outside public took form in two features of the life of the University, both of which were almost wholly new then—University Extension—instruction by public lecture and by correspondence—and the University Press—by which the results of the research were made accessible to readers throughout the world.

President Harper died without reaching his fiftieth birthday. But he left behind him a marvellous record of achievement in several fields. But his greatest achievement—his largest contribution to the welfare of the country was the ideas which he wrought into reality in the University of Chicago and the permanent impress he had made on American education.

Alumni Gathering (New York), 1923

BURTON

One other element of the present policy of the University was a result of these ideals which Dr. Harper embodied in the original constitution of the University. I refer to the removal of the restriction which was put upon the presidency. Eventually it came to be seen that the University must be able to look anywhere, not only for its instructors but also for its president. This actually came about only in 1923, but it was in reality a product of Dr. Harper's ideals.

Alumni Gathering (Los Angeles), 1925

HARRY PRATT JUDSON

BURTON

President Judson was of a different temper and temperament, but he met the needs of the University as Dr. Harper had met those of an earlier day. In the seventeen years of his administration he gave to it stability and confidence in its future, and he left it not only larger and richer than he found it, but especially established on more solid foundations, its future secure against any storm that is at all likely to arise.

Anniversary Chapel, 1 October 1924

BURTON

I do not know how many of you have come to know President Judson personally. I hope that many of you have done so. But probably none of you can have known him as well as I, who have been his colleague for over thirty years and have served under him as President for seventeen years. Perhaps, therefore, I may venture to say to you some things about him on the basis of my more intimate acquaintance with him.

The world knows him as an author, and as an educational administrator of unusual ability, as a member of important Boards and Foundations, and as representative of these Boards and of the national government on important Commissions to foreign lands. But I, who may claim to have known him as friend, should like to speak to you of two or three of his more personal qualities.

President Judson is eminently a just man, one who in all the complex questions that come before the executive officer of a great university could always be relied upon to see all sides of a question, to weigh all considerations judicially, and to be pre-eminently just in his decisions.

In the second place he is an absolutely unselfish man. I remember his saying to me once in the confidence that he might show toward a colleague of many years, "No one has any right to take this office in any other than a spirit of absolute self-sacrifice." In that spirit he administered his office. No tinge of self aggrandisement ever marred his administration.

In the third place, Mr. Judson is a very kindly man. To be just is not always to be kind. There is a justice that is cold and severe. To be unselfish is not necessarily to be kindly. The martyr, who is ready to lay down his life for a cause, may be harsh and hard to live with. Mr. Judson is not only just and unselfish, but kindly. Not that he carries his heart on his sleeve, not that he is emotional or gushing. He is neither. But all those who have really come close to him have found him to be a most genuinely kindly and sympathetic man.

A president has to do many things that are not pleasant for him to do, and that are not welcome to those who are affected by them. It is a great thing to have in the presidential chair a man whom people trust because they know that he is just, unselfish, kindly. I congratulate you that you in your gift today are honoring a man who not only has been a scholar and administrator, but a man whom his friends admire and love because of his high personal qualities.

Convocation, 12 June 1923

KIMPTON

President Judson was twenty years stabilizing the institution financially and shaking it down academically.

Convocation, 12 June 1953

BURTON

President Judson was as great as a conservator and as a builder as President Harper was as an originator. For cut off in early middle life President Harper left many things incomplete—their future unassured. He had extended his lines, he had not in all cases consolidated his gains. President Judson took his office in an hour of grave difficulty, not to say peril. The situation that confronted him was wholly different from that which Dr. Harper had faced. Seeing this with clearness he addressed to it with a clear perception of its nature and has wrought nobly and well. He took an institution which was like a building well begun but with many parts still incomplete, open to the weather, exposed to peril. He left it rounded out, solid, substantial, far beyond the reach of danger.

Alumni Gathering (New York), 1923

BURTON

The main purposes of President Judson's administration were conservation and stability—the consolidation of the gains achieved and the establishment of the University on a firm foundation. For his work in this direction the University will always be deeply indebted to him. And it should be remembered that in his administration there was also a large increase of resources, and a notable growth in the number of students.

"The University of Chicago As It Should Be in 1940:
A Confidential Statement by the President," 1925

BURTON

The magnitude of the service which President Judson rendered to the University is indicated by the following figures within his presidency:—the endowment of the University increased from $8,639,000 to $30,268,000; its total property from $17,892,000 to $53,342,000; its annual budget from $1,214,000 to $3,315,000 and its annual enrollment of students from 5,079 to 12,748.

Alumni Gathering (Los Angeles), 1925

ERNEST DE WITT BURTON

BURTON

These two notable [Harper and Judson] administrations have themselves prepared the way and created a demand for a period of which the key words shall be discovery and betterment—discovery of truth in every field, betterment of every phase of our work.

"The University of Chicago As It Should Be in 1940: A Confidential Statement by the President," 1925

BURTON

On these foundations it is the manifest duty of the University to build. We should not honor but dishonor our predecessors if we should content ourselves simply with holding what they handed down. Our faces, as theirs were, must be to the future.

Anniversary Chapel, 1 October 1924

BURTON

The presidency of the University of Chicago is a great honor and a great responsibility, and neither of these was ever among my ambitions, still less among my expectations. Mindful of the statutes of the University respecting retirement, and of the dangers of overstaying one's welcome, I had had it distinctly in mind that I would, at about this time, retire both from teaching and administration and devote those years which a long-lived ancestry encouraged me to hope for to certain tasks in scholarship and book-making which I had long ago begun or planned. About a year ago I notified the Dean of the School in which I have done most of my work that my notification of retirement was at his disposal at any time when he preferred to fill my place with a younger man. Yet when last January the Board of Trustees requested me to take the position of Acting President, I found myself irresistibly drawn to accept it, in large part for the same reason that influenced me some years ago to accept the office of Director of Libraries, because it promised an opportunity to fulfil a long cherished ambition, to be of service to the whole University and not simply to one division of it. And I freely confess that the interesting character of the work, and the cordial cooperation of Trustees, Faculty, Alumni and friends which I have enjoyed since February, have more than offset the arduousness of my duties. It is therefore, on the one hand, with a deep sense of responsibility, and on the other, with a not less keen appreciation of opportunity, that I now publicly, as I have already privately, accept the office to which I was elected by the action of the Board, taken July 12.

Acceptance of the Office of President, 31 August 1923

BEADLE

The history of that time suggests that, had not Ernest DeWitt Burton succeeded Harry Pratt Judson as President, undergraduate work might indeed have been abolished.

Immediately on succeeding Judson in 1923, Burton set out to revive interest in the College.

Trustee-Faculty Dinner, 11 January 1967

KIMPTON

Unfortunately, he lived only a year and eight months after his selection as President and during that time he laid the foundation and began the great medical organization that now occupies a group of buildings on the campus of the University of Chicago.

University of Chicago Citizens Board, 25 June 1953

CHARLES MAX MASON

KIMPTON

In the very brief tenures of Burton and Mason the University moved forward once again, building from the blueprints which Harper had left behind him as unrealized possibilities.

Convocation, 12 June 1953

KIMPTON

Max Mason, [Burton's] successor, stayed here only a couple of years before he became president of the Rockefeller Foundation, but in that short time he displayed a real talent for charming wealthy citizens into giving money for the expansion of the University. Some of them, fascinated almost to the point of hypnotism, collapsed in relief when he went away, recognizing they now would be able to keep the remnants of the money that otherwise he would have taken from them.

Women's Club (Chicago), February 1952

MASON

Support for the work of the University is being granted in increasing measure, and I feel that there is no limit to the support if this Faculty maintains the performance of which it is capable. I believe that there lies within this Faculty the power to promote education and research even to a higher degree than in the past. There is the power to create a university of a new kind in America, of a grade vastly different from that of today. The opportunity is before us to bring back the Harper days of pioneering and to give a second impetus to the life of scholarship in the whole country.

Trustee-Faculty Dinner, 12 January 1927

HUTCHINS

These matters have received earnest attention at the University of Chicago and elsewhere for many years. In 1927–28 great

275

progress was made here in the development of a collegiate curriculum and of rules for its regulation. It is impossible to refer to the educational aspects of the present reorganization without referring to the background which these studies provided. Without the work that went into the investigation then conducted the plan now in effect would have encountered difficulties that were resolved three years ago. The University's program is simply a development of that worked out at that time.

Convocation, 23 December 1930

ROBERT MAYNARD HUTCHINS

KIMPTON

Then, as you all know, Robert Hutchins came on the scene—a young man, barely thirty years old. In fact, I think that he was not quite thirty when he assumed the Presidency of the university and his tenure lasted for some twenty-two years.

University of Chicago Citizens Board, 25 June 1953

HUTCHINS

I have been asked by the indomitable chairman of the Committee in charge of this affair to state—not to exceed ten minutes—my impressions of the University of Chicago. My first impression is that an awful lot of public speaking is going on here, particularly this week, and that something ought to be done about it. From Evanston to Flossmoor, from the Planetarium to Oak Park the cry goes up that Hutchins has talked enough. I'll say he has. Since you have all listened to me, or at least been in a position where you could listen to me on many previous occasions, I shall assume that you are gathered here to listen to the other speakers and shall startle the chairman by being the first speaker anywhere who ever stayed within a time limit.

As you know, I came to Chicago from the country. I had heard of the eminence of the University, but I did not understand what it meant. I knew that a university could not be really successful unless it had winning athletic teams, large quantities of magnificent fraternity and sorority houses, and a student body that looked as though it had been elected solely from photographs. Indeed when I was, through an inexplicable concatenation of accidents, elected to my present post the reforms that at once occurred to me as the major planks in my educational platform were these—winning football teams, bigger and better fraternity and club houses, and the selection of students solely on the basis of their photographs. Imagine my embarrassment when I found on my arrival here, that these reforms had already been instituted. The present freshman class had been filled with carefully selected athletic material. My own fraternity had built a house almost as luxurious as our theological seminaries. And Mr. Woodward had inaugurated a system whereby the ladies were admitted to the University only after he had made a personal examination of their portraits.

Alumni Meeting, 7 June 1930

HUTCHINS

Some weeks ago I agreed to appear today to destroy the hallucination that I do not exist. I was much flattered by your interest in my existence. During my four years in college I did not see the President and did not want to. My policy with the President was live and let live. As long as he didn't bother me I was content not to bother him.

Undergraduate Assembly, 12 December 1933

KIMPTON

It is to Mr. Hutchins' credit that, recognizing the greatness of the University of Chicago in terms of its great research workers and scholars, he should decide to take undergraduate education seriously and this is precisely what he did.

He decided that a great university must be rated in terms of its great scholars but also it must do a significant, a real and a valuable job at the undergraduate level of education leading up to the Bachelor of Arts degree.

This, I would say, is his great contribution to the University of Chicago, though there were many others, and it was this interest which led to the formation of the College of the University of Chicago, which I propose to describe today.

University of Chicago Citizens Board, 25 June 1953

KIMPTON

It took twenty-two years of the reign of Robert M. Hutchins, however, really to bring into existence what Harper had planned, although Hutchins naturally modified Harper's ideas in the light of his own times, and added to them his own original insights. The accomplishments of Hutchins during the last quarter century are so many that I cannot pause to catalog them. I want to talk today only about the system of undergraduate education that was the dream of Harper and the realization of Hutchins. It is one of the most remarkable experiments in the history of American education.

Convocation, 12 June 1953

HUTCHINS

On January 1 the horrid thought came to me that I had been in university administration for ten years. It occurred to me also that on any statistical analysis I could hold out much longer, and that it might be wise for me to deliver my valedictory remarks on this occasion in order to make sure that they were delivered. I might then be perfectly content to die by assassination or otherwise, serene in the consciousness that I had not been deprived of the last word; I should have spoken it in advance. And so I determined tonight to give my conclusions as to professors and Trustees on the basis of my extended and varied connection with them. But do not be alarmed. I have changed my mind. Since a cause of action in libel or slander does not survive the one who utters it, I shall postpone my most important and interesting suggestions to the posthumous publication of my diaries.

But still I am ready to share with you certain fruits of my vast experience and certain conclusions at which I have arrived as a result of my sojourn here and elsewhere in the higher learning. That sojourn convinces me that the opportunity and the responsibility of the University of Chicago are greater than ever before. . . . If this is so—and you may take it from one who has been a university president longer than you have that it is so—the question is how can the University of Chicago carry its responsibility and rise to its opportunity? And the first answer is that for light and leading we must rely upon ourselves. We cannot look to England or the Continent. We cannot look to New England or New York. We must rely upon ourselves. This is nothing new: with a few minor aberrations we always have. The ideas on which the University was founded were not imitative. The University made its reputation because it did things that had never been done. A reputation for leadership can be acquired only this way. Doing things that have never been done of course involves some risks. It is safer to wait until somebody else has taken those risks and pointed the path to safety. But if this University is not prepared to take some risks we may give up hope for the higher learning in America.

Trustee-Faculty Dinner, 12 January 1933

HUTCHINS

You will say that I am living in a world of dreams, that everybody knows that the primary responsibility of the head of a university is to raise money and promote public relations. I say that this is what is wrong with the higher learning in America and that it is time somebody did something about it. I say that the primary responsibility of the head of a university is to lead the attack on its intellectual problems. If he does not do this, it will not be done. And if it is not done, the University may get money, but it will be none the better for it. It may have resplendent public relations, but they will be little but fakery. The only problems that money can solve are financial problems, and these are not the crucial problems of higher education. Money is no substitute for ideas. We see on every hand institutions that demonstrate the fallacy of economic determinism in education. They are very large, very prosperous—and completely meaningless.

The University of Chicago can use, and it ought to have, much more money than it has today. But it must have that money for its program, and its program is more important than the money; for if the money is to do any good, it must be attracted by the program. The development of the program is the responsibility of the Chancellor; the trustees, together with officers appointed for the purpose, must assume the responsibility for raising the money. If they say that because the Chancellor wants it he must raise it, the result will be some very rich endowments and a very poor university.

Trustee-Faculty Dinner, 10 January 1951

LAWRENCE ALPHEUS KIMPTON

HUTCHINS

One of my more spectacular successes is the new Chancellor of the University.

He has held three or four of the most important posts in the University, and several elsewhere. He has ideas and character, and a combination of tact and firmness that is as rare as it is necessary. His popularity with the faculty and the trustees is great and with those who are seriously interested in honest administration and in the improvement of higher education it will always remain so.

Alumni Assembly (Chicago), 9 June 1951

KIMPTON

I first saw these gray towers a quarter of a century ago during the frenetic days of the War, and I knew at that moment that this was the only real university I would ever know and love.

When the war was over, Bob Hutchins asked me if I thought the Great Books were great, and when I forthrightly answered "yes," he made me a dean. I deserted for a time to bask in Stanford's sunshine, but after three years I begged to come back. I was crowned sixth head of this University in this awesome chapel, and it was the highest honor that ever will or could come to me. The activities of my administration were marked by exigency; there were some dirty jobs to do involving money, neighborhoods and the College, and I did them, and somehow held the place together in the process.

Convocation, 16 December 1966

BEADLE

If a great university will not stay and use its knowledge, wisdom, and power to help solve a critical problem, who will do it? There is talk of a Peace Corps and of other grand schemes to help underdeveloped nations in far parts of the world. We should, of course, do everything possible in that direction—but

280

in doing so we should not forget that we must somehow learn to cure the sickness of poverty, unemployment, and racial discrimination that blights the hearts of our great cities.

In our own surroundings, a magnificent start has been made through the combined efforts of the University, the local community, the city, the state, and the federal government. We owe a deep debt of gratitude to Lawrence A. Kimpton for taking the lead in this enormously difficult and often discouraging undertaking. We must keep up the effort, for if we succeed, we will have established a pattern for the rest of the nation to follow. This is a noble goal for a noble university.

Inaugural Address, 5 May 1961

KIMPTON

Some time I hope to have the pleasure of being with you throughout the evening. The faculty takes such an enormous pleasure in casting me each year in the Revels as a janitor, a mail carrier, or a tractor driver, that I shall probably never be able to make it. Some day the faculty may become genuinely convinced that the Chancellor really does occupy a menial position about this university, and they won't feel so obligated to caricature it.

Order of the C Dinner, 31 May 1956

KIMPTON

Things are better, there is no denying it. Our undergraduate program is reorganized, our economy is stabilized, and our neighborhood is in the process of improvement. In all these things we take satisfaction, and for all these things we give thanks. But the time has come to remind ourselves that great universities are not built merely by balancing budgets, reorganizing curricula, and improving neighborhoods. This is only to remove the underbrush which has been stifling our growth and development, and at last we begin to see the sun. But our really important problems lie before us. We have suffered during this period of readjustment, and we all know it. We have lost some good men; we have been unable to appoint young people who will build the university of the future. We have not been able to expand our laboratories and our classrooms to meet the coming need. Our Library has suffered in its acquisitions and its services to our faculty and students. We have not been able to keep salaries in pace with our inflationary times. We have repaired our house, but our real task is to build a city. It is my hope that we have not become so conditioned to meeting the problems of the moment that we have lost the ability to plan our future. The experiences of the past have thinned and tightened our ranks. Our problem now is to march forward. Our objective is a fairer city—a new and greater University of Chicago.

State of the University, 23 November 1954

KIMPTON

I suppose I have been generally educated too around the University of Chicago. I have certainly been exposed to a wide variety of experience in somewhat the same way as yourselves. The problems of a university of this kind—and in a sense I have been involved in them all—range from the impact on archaeology of the rising waters of the Nile caused by the Aswan Dam to the value, cost and operation of a 12½- billion-volt accelerator. I doubt that I now understand all these things as thoroughly as you have come to understand the materials in the general courses; a chancellor, by the very nature of his job, must pose as an authority on all sorts of matters that, when you come right down to it, he doesn't know much about. A general is a generalist by definition, but what I have lost in depth I have perhaps compensated for in this matter of methodology. I am proud of what I have learned at the University of Chicago about methodology in recognizing problems and finding solutions to them. Over the last nine years we have actually repaired neighborhoods, regained financial solvency, changed the College around, and rebuilt the professional schools. The big accelerator is in good hands, fairly well financed and on schedule, and we are even pondering a crash archaeological program in the disappearing valley of the Nile.

I am not sure that I have changed as much in matters of taste as I hope you have. Perhaps these things are for the young, and one becomes increasingly inflexible as his arteries harden. I have tried to like beatnik poetry and prose and have even worked at understanding this strange cacophony of sounds called modern jazz, but without success. As for folk songs, I sadly agree with the man who remarked that the only trouble with them is that they are written by the people. I still like Shakespeare and Dickens and Beethoven and Brahms, so I'll have to write this part of my general education off, but let's wait a hundred years before making a final aesthetic judgment on who is right.

I do believe, however, that in having to do some things one doesn't want to do, I am way ahead of you. You may have had to learn some mathematics even though you deplored the stuff or had to analyze a modern poem which you found incomprehensible; but I have had to repair neighborhoods, say pleasant things to unpleasant people, and enter into all manner of activities for which I had no talent or initial concern. I am sure the discipline was good for us both and constitutes an essential part of our general education.

Convocation, 10, 11 June 1960

KIMPTON

I have submitted my resignation as Chancellor of the University of Chicago to the Board of Trustees, through their chairman, Mr. Glen A. Lloyd. I had two reasons for resigning.

When I was elected Chancellor in April, 1951, I set myself certain goals. Some were directly concerned with education; some concerned the general welfare and strength of the University. Among the educational goals were the reorganization of the College and the improvement of several of the professional schools. Both have been achieved.

Externally, the existence of the University was threatened by encroaching slums. That had to be stopped—and it has been stopped. The University needed more money, for endowment, for new buildings, for faculty salaries. The University has found a great deal of money since 1951—$100 million of it.

My second reason was that I believe the head of this University can make his greatest contributions to it in a relatively short time. Its history shows that each of my predecessors brought an era of new vigor and intensity. I think the time has come for a new man. The University means more to me that I can say, and despite my conviction, I have found it hard to come to my decision.

Press Conference (Retirement), 29 March 1960

KIMPTON

My most brilliant decision came through the realization that I had been cast in a certain role, and that when the role was played, I should make way for a new group that could do a new job.

Convocation, 16 December 1966

GEORGE WELLS BEADLE

BEADLE

One afternoon last November I sat in my office at Caltech when my secretary buzzed and said, "President DuBridge on line 1."

"Hello."

"Say, there's a Mr. Lloyd here from the University of Chicago. Could you see him?"

"Gee, I'm sorry," I said, "there's a seminar coming up in a few minutes and the speaker is a personal guest. I am to introduce him and it would be quite awkward if I were not there. I'll be out by 5:30. Could I see him then?"

"No, I'm afraid that is too late."

"If it's very important, I might be able to get out of going to the seminar."

"No, don't bother, maybe he can see you another time."

So, thinking Mr. Lloyd might be a salesman for the *Encyclopaedia Britannica* or the Great Books, I went on to the seminar.

On returning after the seminar, I found a well-dressed and very distinguished-looking gentleman waiting at my office door.

As I thought, "My, they do select fine people to sell these books," I said, "Oh, hello, are you Mr. Lloyd?"

"Yes," he said, "I just thought I'd try and catch you for a minute."

"Sure. I'm sorry I was tied up."

And then I added, "Say, why don't we walk over to the house. It's just across the street and we can have a quiet talk there. I think my wife will let us in."

So we walked over. I asked my visitor if he'd mind sitting down in the patio for a minute, I'd check and see if Mrs. Beadle was prepared to receive a visitor.

"Sure," he said.

I went in and said, "Say, Honey, there's a man here from the University of Chicago. I don't know if he's a salesman or a professor. Can we come in for a drink? Maybe we should ask him to have dinner."

"Sure," Muriel said, "I have chicken and we can spare a wing for him."

So there we were.

I asked Mr. Lloyd what he did at the University of Chicago.

"Oh," he said, "I'm the Chairman of the Board. We're looking for a Chancellor to replace Larry Kimpton and I just wanted to know if you had any suggestions."

"Sure," I said, "Why don't you get McGeorge Bundy?"

"Goodness," Mr. Lloyd replied, "that's the 789th time Bundy has been suggested. I'm afraid he's out. We hear Mr. Kennedy has him all signed up for Washington."

I tried again. "How about Dick Nixon?"

"We have him on the list."

"Good man." I said, "Maybe he belongs to the wrong political party for the University of Chicago?"

"We are broadminded at Chicago."

Well, we spent a very delightful evening.

Mr. Lloyd is a broadminded man. Despite the chicken wing, he called me six weeks later and said, "Would you come back to Chicago for a visit?"

"Sure."

Finally, Mrs. Beadle and I came for a second visit. That settled it. The Board and the Faculty Committee agreed that with her beauty and charm and brains, the Chancellor wouldn't matter much so why not sign us up.

But, first we had to see the Chancellor's house. We did.

Muriel got me in a corner and said, "Let's go back to California, Honey."

But, as I said, Mr. Lloyd is a good *salesman*.

So here we are.

And the Chancellor's house is all redecorated, repainted, and we love it.

We came for a quick reception in January. Then I came permanently in February and settled down in the Quadrangle Club until the house was fixed up.

One evening I went in to eat at the round table. There was one very distinguished gentleman setting there—a top professor, no doubt. I sat down and he said, "I'm Mr. X, who are you?"

"I'm George Beadle."

"How do you spell it?"

"B-E-A-D-L-E."

"What are you doing here?"

"Oh, I'm trying to be the new Chancellor."

"That's wonderful, have a drink on me."

We've had a wonderful welcome here. Chicago *is* a friendly place.

The first day I was here, I met Abe, the paper man, Izzy the laundryman, and Mitzie, the flower girl—and was immediately accepted as a fitting and proper member of the community.

One morning, I got to the office early—insomnia you know!

On the steps I met a young man carrying a suitcase.

I asked if I could help.

He said he was here for an interview—he'd taken the train in from Iowa and he was coming to see the Admissions Office. I took him up, he waited, and when the office opened he had his interview.

"How'd you find the Admissions Office?" the young lady in charge said.

"Oh, I met a nice man in shirt sleeves on the first floor. I guess he was the custodian. He brought me up."

The other evening, about 10:30, after we'd moved into the Chancellor's house, the doorbell rang. We'd retired early—the day had been rough.

Muriel put on a dressing gown and went down, after being warned that she should put the night chain on—those Chicago burglars you know. I came part way down in protection, a flower pot in hand as a weapon.

It was a policeman.

"Are you the housekeeper here?" he said.

"Yes," Muriel replied.

"Why aren't your lights on?"

"Why because we've all retired."

"You must leave the outside lights on—don't you know that?"

"No. No one told me!"

"Well, you must do better hereafter—young lady."

That's what we like about Chicago. Everyone accepts us for what we are—PEOPLE.

This morning, Miss Olson, my able secretary inherited from Larry Kimpton, said, "Now if you'll just stay home and tend to the routine matters and let your wife make all the speeches, you can't miss!"

Inauguration Luncheon, 4 May 1961

BEADLE

Some weeks ago, the keen-eared Doris Olson heard, through the slightly opened door of my office, grumblings that went something like this: "Why the so-and-so must the President of this University give so many speeches, year after year after year—on the state of the University in November; at Convocation in June—always in duplicate; on a dozen other occasions each year; and on top of all those, at the annual Trustee-Faculty dinner in January, where tradition says he does it each year—while trustees (with the exception of our speaker tonight) and faculty members do it once in a lifetime. Why can't we be like other universities?"

Came the muffled but clearly audible comment back through the partly open door: "Why do you think Hutchins and Kimpton resigned?"

Trustee-Faculty Dinner, 11 January 1967

BEADLE

I leave the President's Office with the knowledge that the unsolved problems will be approached with the perception, sensitivity, and understanding that Edward Levi brings to the Presidency. As a continuing Courtesy Professor of Biology and a resident of Hyde Park I shall observe future progress at close range and with very keen interest.

State of the University, 5 November 1968

EDWARD HIRSCH LEVI

BEADLE

More than any other single person, Provost Edward H. Levi is responsible for our continued progress in academic strength.

287

He knows what academic excellence is and is tough, uncompromising, persuasive and effective in getting it. And I want to emphasize that this is not easy.

Trustee-Faculty Dinner, 14 January 1965

BEADLE

We all know that no university can be stronger than its faculty. William Rainey Harper not only recognized this more clearly than most university heads, but he did something about it—dramatically and successfully. Provost Edward H. Levi understands this equally well and, both as Dean of the Law School and as Provost for the past twenty-eight months, has emulated Harper in persuading top scholars to join our faculties. It has been an inspiration to me to observe how his rare combination of talents enables him to accomplish this. First of all, he has an amazing and uncompromising sense of what constitutes academic excellence. His persuasive talents are strengthened by his honesty in describing both the strengths and the weaknesses of the University. I have personally experienced the skill with which he presents the latter as challenges and opportunities. He combines tough-mindedness in judging academic quality with a sense of human understanding that far transcends shallow sentimentality. He is realistic about the importance of academic facilities and material needs of faculty members. Although we much prefer to emphasize academic excellence, I do point out that a recent report, based on AAUP records, puts the average academic salary at the University of Chicago among the top four academic institutions in the nation—along with those of Harvard, Stanford, and California Institute of Technology. . . .

Provost Edward H. Levi, in his capacity as Acting Dean, has prepared for consideration a plan for modifying the organization of the College. His proposal, made after a series of conferences with College faculty members, students, and others interested in the College, suggests that there be created five Collegiate Divisions, four paralleling the four graduate divisions—Biological Sciences, Humanities, Physical Sciences and Social Sciences—and a fifth called the Division of General Studies.

State of the University, 10 November 1964

288

BEADLE

Since the mid-fifties, when the University of Chicago was in deep trouble in neighborhood, in faculty, in students, and in finances—all of these, of course, interrelated—the faculty has increased markedly in both numbers and stature. This has been so, especially in the four and a half years that Provost Levi has been on the job.

His dedication to the welfare of this University, his good judgment, his persuasiveness, and his willingness to push financial resources to the limit for top academic quality, have been in large part responsible for an increase in faculty of forty to fifty each year, with many outstanding scholars among those added.

State of the University, 1 November 1966

BEADLE

We are confident that, under Edward Levi's leadership as President, the University of Chicago will further strengthen and consolidate its position of leadership in higher education. While the success of the three-year financial Campaign for Chicago will assure a minimal financial base for that leadership in the immediate future, long-term success will require even greater efforts.

Convocation, 7, 8 June 1968

LEVI

I trust I will be forgiven a personal word. I approach this unlikely moment with many memories. I come to it also with understandable concern. I do not misconceive the importance of this office which has changed through the years. Rather, the goals, achievement, and tradition of this university are disturbingly impressive. Our university has had a standard of extraordinary leadership, difficult to maintain. I am grateful to Chancellor Hutchins, Chancellor Kimpton, and President Beadle for their presence today. They will understand my anxiety. It is not that we fear mistakes. Perhaps we should fear not to make them. President Hutchins in his address—given forty years ago

—spoke of the university's experimental attitude, its willingness to try out ideas, to undertake new ventures, to pioneer. In some cases, he said, the contribution was to show other universities what not to do. Let me say, with rueful pride, since that time we have made many similar contributions. I hope we always will.

It is natural for this university to believe it believes in pioneering. After all, this university came into being as a pioneering first modern university, borrowing ideas from Germany and England, building upon the New England college, joining undergraduate instruction and a panoply of graduate research in what, some said, surely would be a monstrosity—all this done with middle-western enthusiasm and a confidence the best could be obtained here if only it could be paid for. Much has been written of the financial arrangements of those days, the creative use of material resources generously given. But the basic faith was not in material resources. The faith was in the intellectual powers of the mind. It was considered important, more important than anything else in the world, to uncover and understand the cultures of the past, to appreciate the works of the mind, to penetrate the mysteries of the universe, to know more about the environment, the societies, and the nature of man. The university's seriousness of purpose was proven from the first by its insistence upon freedom of inquiry and discussion. Intellectual tests for truth made other standards irrelevant. Schools for the propagation of special points of view might exist, Harper wrote, but they could not be called universities. The emphasis on the need to question and reexamine, both as part of the inquiry of research and the inquiry of teaching, established a basic unity for all of the university. The basis of that unity underscored the relationship between teaching and research. That unity encouraged discussion among disciplines. It supported the individual scholar as he crossed accepted boundaries of knowledge. It made possible—even compelled—continuing debate concerning the place of professional, specialized, general, and liberal education within the university. It made the university self-critical.

"On an occasion such as this," as Mr. Kimpton stated on a similar occasion, "the important roles are not played by those who are present. . . . Our efforts are given importance by the opportunities and responsibilities . . . we inherit." So I have stressed those virtues which from the beginning and until now have characterized our institution: a willingness to experiment, a commitment to the intellectual search for truth, freedom of inquiry, and a concern for the educational process as though the freedom of man depended upon it. This is our inheritance. It is an inheritance preserved and strengthened, indeed made possible, by the action and faith of many who are present today.

Inaugural Address, 14 November 1968

LEVI

Q: Are you aware there are stories that you may not even exist—that people never see you?

A. I have wondered about that and I have asked myself a couple of questions about that, but the answer always seems to come back that if I am not for myself, who is, you know. And I—I exist.

Interview in *Maroon*, 26 April 1974

5

PARTS OF THE WHOLE

No academic structures will ever be built which will long satisfy the dreams and aspirations of our University.

KIMPTON

THE COLLEGE

HARPER

Large emphasis has from the beginning been laid upon the graduate work, and this not without good reason; but it has been also intended that the work of the colleges should receive its proper share of attention. The time has not come in America to separate the college from the university; the line between the two has not been clearly drawn. The Colleges of the University of Chicago are and will be as strong as the best instructors and the best equipment can make them.

(First) Convocation, 1 January 1893

HARPER

The origin of the present Board of the Senior College of Arts, Literature, and Science is described in the statement on "Administrative History," p. xliii. The work under the charge of this Board was originally a part of the work of the General Faculty, later the work of a special Board of that Faculty, still later the work of a special Faculty, and at present the work of a Board which serves as a standing committee, on the one hand, of the Faculty of Arts, Literature, and Science, and, on the other, of all of the Faculties including in their enrolment students of the rank of Senior College students. The terms "Upper" and "Lower" were at first used, but after two years these were changed to Senior and Junior College. The Senior College work at present includes eight possible groups, viz.: Arts, Literature, Science, Law, Medicine, Commerce and Administration, Divinity, and Technology. All but the last of these have been organized. The membership of the Board is constituted as follows:

1. The President and the Recorder.
2. The Deans concerned with Senior College students.
3. Two representatives each of the following groups of departments: (a) Ancient Languages and Literatures; (b) Modern Languages and Literatures; (c) Philosophy and the Social Sciences; (d) Mathematics and Inorganic Sciences; (e) The Organic Sciences; (f) Each professional or technical Faculty having students who are candidates for the Bachelor's degree; namely, the Divinity, the Medical, the Faculty of Commerce and Administration, the Faculty of the Law School.

The reports show that the number of students classified as members of the Senior Colleges actually in attendance at any one time has varied from 31 in the Spring Quarter, 1893, to 326 in the Spring Quarter, 1902; and that the various Bachelor's degrees have been conferred in any given year on from 15 to 286 candidates, the latter number being reached in the year closing June 30, 1902.

A large minority of the Faculties of Arts, Literature, and Science would probably favor the policy of granting one Bachelor's degree rather than, as at present, three, but a majority has always been in favor of the policy outlined at the beginning; and if the suggestions made elsewhere in this Report should be adopted, the degree of B.D. as well as that of LL.B., and perhaps others, will be given to represent in general the same time-requirement as is now represented by the other Bachelor degrees.

Much difference of opinion has existed as to the advisability of conferring the Bachelor's degree on graduates of affiliated colleges after three months' residence. It is evident that this practice seems at first sight to discriminate in favor of those who do not come to our own institution, but considerations may be presented which largely relieve the difficulties in the case.

A remarkable fact is shown by the Dean's Report in reference to the number of students entering the University of Chicago from other colleges. Probably in no other university does the principle of migration in undergraduate work play so prominent a part.

More or less doubt has existed as to the advisability of continuing the plan of Division Lectures. Upon the whole, it is probable that the plan, or some improvement of it, will remain a permanent institution of the undergraduate work. The same statement may be made concerning the weekly Chapel Assembly.

The requirement that students who have not taken courses in Psychology and Ethics shall be expected to take one Major each in the Senior College work is one which has approved itself by experience. These courses really are Junior College courses, and the student who enters the Senior College without having taken them is treated as conditioned in them.

The flexibility of our system is seen in the fact that a student may reduce the time of his work, if he so desires, in either one of three ways:

1. By selecting, as his Senior College subjects, courses in the Professional School—a step which shortens by so much the time required in the Professional School.

2. By continuing in residence during the whole or part of the Summer Quarter.

3. By securing permission to take a fourth subject in addition to the regular three.

In this way the University regulations adjust themselves to the needs and to the desires of different individuals, but in no case is there a lowering of the standard.

I desire to make the following suggestions:

1. A larger number of scholarships should be established, and incentive should be given students in the smaller colleges to finish their work in the University by the provision of such scholarships.

2. Scholarships awarded to students who have done their work in the Junior Colleges should cover the entire period of the Senior College, namely, two years, instead of one.

3. Effort should be made to classify in the undergraduate colleges a larger number of those who come to us as Graduate students, because, (a) as a matter of fact, the work of many of these students is such as in the University of Chicago is regarded as undergraduate work, and (b) the student thus secures the Bachelor's degree of an institution which will be everywhere recognized as valuable.

4. Every effort should be put forth to treat alike students of the Senior College rank, in whatever group or college they may be registered. In other words, the same requirements should be made of Medical students, Law students, and Divinity students who have the rank of Senior College students as are made of Arts, Literature, and Science students.

5. Provision should be made by which a student doing work of high character might be excused from a certain number of

Majors, the number of Majors being apportioned to the degree of ability shown in the work already done.

6. The plan already adopted in the Junior Colleges of naming members of the Faculty who will consent to serve as advisors of students should be adopted in the Senior Colleges, and should be urgently recommended from time to time to the student body.

7. There should always be kept in mind the desirability of preserving a unity of feeling among the Senior College students, and every opportunity should be taken to emphasize this unity as over against the great diversity of Departments and groups represented.

8. The present policy of granting the Bachelor's degree to the graduates of affiliated colleges after three months' residence in the University should be modified to include a provision that the students intending to take such a degree shall (*a*) matriculate at the University at least six months before they enter the University for the residence of three months, and at the time of matriculation present a full description of all college work which they have done up to this time; (*b*) register at the University simultaneously with the registration at the college for the courses of instruction offered during these two Quarters; and (*c*) present through the proper executive officer of their college all examination papers which they have prepared and all special papers which they have written during these Quarters, for the inspection of the Departments concerned. . . .

The Junior Colleges

The following statement made in the President's Annual Report for 1898–99 will perhaps best present the thought underlying this distinct division between the Junior and Senior Colleges. This statement also furnishes the considerations offered for the establishment of the so-called title or degree termed, for lack of a better word, "University Associate":

Upon the recommendation of the Faculty of the Junior Colleges and of the Senate, and upon the approval of the University Congregation, the Trustees have voted to confer the title or degree of Associate upon those students who finish the work of the Junior Colleges. The action in the Faculty of the Junior Colleges and in the Senate was practically unanimous—the action in the Board of Trustees was entirely unanimous.

From the point of view of the student, the following considerations have had influence in determining this action: (1) The fact, very generally recognized, that no important step is taken at the end of the preparatory course. The work of the Freshman and Sophomore years in most colleges differs little in content and in method from that of the last year of the academy or high school—except that it is somewhat more advanced; but, on the other hand, (2) at the end of the Sophomore year a most important change occurs according to the organization of the larger number of institutions—for it is at this point that the student is given larger liberty of choice, and at the same time higher methods of instruction are employed. For the last two years of college work the university spirit and the university method prevail. A new era in the work of the student has begun. (3) It is evident that many students continue work in the Junior and Senior years of college life whose best interests would be served by withdrawal from college. Many continue to the end, not from choice, but rather from compulsion, because of the disgrace which may attend an unfinished course. If it were regarded as respectable to stop at the close of the Sophomore year, many would avail themselves of the opportunity. (4) Many students who might be courageous enough to undertake a two-years' college course are not able, for the lack of funds or for other reasons, to see their way clear to enter upon a four years' course. Many, still further, feel that if a professional course is to be taken, there is not time for a four years' college course. It is for this reason that, in part, our professional schools are made up so largely of non-college students. If a student who had in view ultimately the medical, or legal, or pedagogical profession could make provision to finish a course of study at the end of two years, he would be much more likely to undertake such a course than the longer four years' course. (5) On the other hand, many students who are thus led to take the two-years' course would be induced at the end of that time to continue to the end of the fourth year, and in this way many students of the very highest character, at all events, would be enabled to take the entire college course by whom, under the present arrangements, such a course would be regarded as impracticable.

From the point of view of the University, the following points have been considered: (1) Many academies are able to do, at least in part, the work of the Freshman and Sophomore years. The high schools in some states are ready to do such work, and in at least one state the university of the state recognizes the work of the Freshman year when performed in approved high schools. (2) It cannot be denied that, until young men or young women have shown some maturity of character, it is wise that they should not be sent very far away from home. If, now, the academies and high schools could so perfect their work that Freshman and Sophomore courses might be offered, many young people would be enabled to pursue their education to at least this higher point. (3) A large number of so-called colleges, which have not sufficient endowment to enable them properly to do the work of the Junior and Senior years, should limit their work to that of the Freshman and Sophomore years. In many cases the officers of these colleges recognize most keenly that they are not doing justice to the students in the higher classes. In reality they are defrauding the students who pay their fees in lower classes in order to obtain a meager sum of money with which to provide an entirely inadequate course of instruction for the higher class of men. These institutions in many cases would be disposed to limit their work to the lower field, if it were made possible for them to do so. They find it necessary, however, to give a degree. If they could follow the example of a large institution and give an appropriate recognition of the work of the lower years, they would be ready to adopt such an arrangement. (4) It is a general law of educational work that in seeking a college, students rarely go farther away from home than a hundred miles. Ninety per cent. of all the students in American colleges will be found in colleges which are within a hundred miles of home. If a fair proportion of these institutions were to limit themselves to the work of the Freshman and Sophomore years, at the end of this time the students who had finished this work and desired to continue would be compelled to go away from home to some distant institution, perhaps a large university, where library and laboratory facilities might be found which would make possible the doing of good work. If, on the one hand, the academies and high schools were elevated, and if, on the other hand, the scope of work done by many colleges were limited, and as a result institutions developed which would do that work thoroughly, there would come to be a recognized distinction between college and university which does not now exist.

In order, therefore, to encourage a movement in the direction thus mentioned, the proposed degree has been established. It is believed that the results will be fivefold: (1) Many students will find it convenient to give up college work at the end of the Sophomore year; (2) many students who would not otherwise do so, will undertake at least two years of college work; (3) the professional schools will be able to raise their standards for admission, and in any case many who desire a professional education will take the first two years of college work; (4) many academies and high schools will be encouraged to develop higher work; (5) many colleges which have not the means to do the work of the Junior and Senior years will be satisfied under this arrangement to do the lower work.

The work of the College has passed through three stages in its method of administration. During the first year the work was conducted by a Board under the General Faculty, and while this Board was really a committee, it had very largely the power of a Faculty. Upon the division of the General Faculty, a special Faculty was established for the management of this College, which was made up of all instructors offering courses intended primarily for Junior College students. In the spring of 1902 a definite effort was made to bring the Junior College work under the immediate supervision of the General Faculty, and thus to take away its independence. The arguments for this position, although strongly presented, did not prevail, and the policy already in vogue was strengthened. After nearly ten years of trial the plan of a separate and distinct Faculty, with independent powers, received the approval of the majority of the Congregation. Certain changes were suggested in the constitution of the Committees whereby the various groups of Departments should have proper representation. On the basis of an action of the Congregation taken January 31, 1902, additional steps were taken in April for the better distribution of the work of the Faculty and for the assignment of larger responsibility.

In November, 1901, the Advisor System was adopted, with the understanding, however, that it should be entirely voluntary on the part of the students. The members of the Faculty came forward quite unanimously and heartily to offer their services to the students who might desire the same. Up to the present time, however, the results of the plan have not been encouraging.

A serious question has confronted the University, and especially the Faculty of the Junior Colleges, in connection with the growing scarcity of lecture-room and laboratory space in the buildings thus far erected. It has come to be quite clear that it will require the entire space of the central quadrangles to make provision for the Senior College and Graduate work of the various Departments. The Science laboratories, although very large, are already practically full. Two or three possibilities seem to present themselves: (1) either that of enlarging the present buildings, without reference to the architectural effect; or (2) that of removing certain Departments to adjoining quadrangles; or (3) that of separating a certain portion of the work of all Departments furnishing elementary courses and assigning this work a place on the outside quadrangles. The third plan commended itself to the largest number. It was, indeed, unanimously adopted as the opinion of the Junior College Faculty. It was, therefore, decided by the Trustees, upon the recommendation of a special Commission to arrange for Junior College work outside of the central quadrangles. . . .

It seems to be the unanimous desire of the Junior College Faculty to lay an emphasis upon the House system even greater than that which it has thus far been given. It is proposed, moreover, to require every member of the Junior Colleges to be a member of some House. Provision will be made for all the Houses that may be required. These Houses will fall into two classes, those intended for residence, and those planned only for the use of students whose homes are in the neighborhood. Provision will be made in the latter case for clubs of thirty or forty students, which will include a study-room, a parlor, and a dining-room, together with a toilet-room and a cloak-room. It has been calculated that such provision can be made for two or three dollars a Quarter. In this way every student will have a home on the University grounds. The suggestion has also been made, and considered with some degree of favor, that in the non-resident Houses luncheon shall be served in the University every day and the expense made a regular part of the Quarter's bills. . . .

I desire to make the following suggestions:

1. The Adviser System has not yet been given a satisfactory trial. Too great emphasis has been laid upon the voluntary side of the matter. The Faculty has been somewhat slow to force the service of its individual members upon the students. If necessary, the Trustees should take action upon this matter, and thus make it certain that those who are to be students in the first year of college work shall have a more careful supervision than is now received. It is almost pitiable to note the indifference and ignorance of many students in reference to all questions relat-

ing to the essential factors in a college life. It is not supposed
that a fuller introduction of the Adviser System will remove all
this indifference and ignorance, but the more rigorous intro-
duction of the system would contribute much in this direction.

2. While good results have been secured through the Division
Lecture plan, these results have not been so marked as could
have been desired. An important advantage was secured when
arrangements were made by which men accustomed to do pub-
lic lecturing, for example in connection with Extension Lecture
Work, were assigned to this task. As experience has shown, many
good instructors fail entirely in an effort to profit or interest
students in a subject for which credit is not given or an exam-
ination demanded. The original thought of securing a substan-
tial correlation of subjects in the mind of the student has been
largely lost sight of in the actual execution of the plan. There is
opportunity in this matter for an important contribution to the
subject of college training. Something outside of the regular
class-room work and the religious gathering is needed to secure
a unity of spirit and a unity of thought in the student body, to
furnish a common element which shall be of service to all.

3. The number of Chapel Assemblies in the Junior College
should be increased. At least two meetings should be held each
week. Without question, better results are gained by holding
separate sessions for men and women. Here again experience
shows that the voluntary element is not a very important con-
sideration. Not only in this respect, but in others, it may be
questioned whether a larger compulsory element should not be
introduced into the work of the early college years.

4. Within two or three years a growth of interest has been
noticed in the graduating exercises of the Junior College. This
should be encouraged. Every effort of the student body to make
public expression of its corporate existence should be strongly
cultivated. There is little danger that there will be found too
great an exhibition of true sentiment.

5. The number of scholarships open to Junior College stu-
dents should be increased, but a matter of still greater impor-
tance is the extension of the time during which scholarships
assigned may be enjoyed. At present no scholarship continues
longer than one year. Every Junior scholarship should be as-
signed for two years, with, of course, provision for a modifica-
tion in case the work of the student does not seem satisfactory.

6. It will soon be necessary for the Dean of the Junior Colleges to devote his attention exclusively to questions which arise in connection with instruction and the staff of officers, together with those questions of a general character which relate to the student body as a whole. The Deans in the College, who are essentially Assistant Deans, should be sufficient in number to take the supervision of the work of individual students. In general, there should be a Dean for every one hundred students, and perhaps, by the plan just suggested, as many as one hundred and fifty students could be profitably handled by a single Dean. This would certainly be true if the Adviser System were properly introduced.

7. Since the scope of the work of the Junior College will continue to broaden, and since technological students and others are soon to be admitted, care should be taken to hold in one great body all the students of the Junior College grade. A single set of traditions should prevail. No line should be drawn between the classical students, on the one hand, and the scientific or technological students on the other. All should work under the same general regulations, and effort should be made to draw together these various groups and to hold them in close connection. The work of the Junior Colleges will be successful in proportion as it is a work characterized by unity of purpose and unity of spirit both on the part of instructors and students.

Decennial Report, 1 July 1902

THE BEGINNINGS OF SECOND THOUGHTS

JUDSON

The Colleges have become firmly established as an essential part of the University, and while of course they may at any time be, and ought to be, compelled to adapt themselves to changed conditions of social and educational life in the country at large, at the same time the apprehensions which have been expressed annually in the last twenty years that the University may do away with the Colleges altogether have no more likelihood of being realized at the present time than they had at the outset. The University has no desire to have the largest college in the country. It is anxious that its college work should be of a high grade, and that its benefits should be confined to those who are capable of availing themselves of them. It is to this end that the faculty has been so rigorous in eliminating students within the first year who have not come up to the required standards.

Convocation, 11 June 1912

JUDSON

The history of the American college has shown a very interesting and peculiar development, resulting from social conditions in our own country. While originally planned on the model of the English college, the evolution has taken a different line, and the institution now is in its essentials unlike that of any other country. The great development of the physical sciences and of the social sciences, the introduction of the elective system, the growth of large colleges, and the organization of technical work, have all tended to create totally different conditions from those in the early years of the college. Meanwhile the development of the high school, tending to take over the earlier years of college work, and the development of the university, whereby the later years of college work tend to become specialized and professional in character, are presenting entirely new possibilities of college organization. In the meantime the form of the old organizations is continued, without being well adapted to new requirements. The American college problem as it exists in these opening decades of the twentieth century has not yet been solved, and needs a very careful and intelligent study. It would not be surprising if the result of that study should be some quite startling changes in the existing organization.

Report of the President 1909–10

JUDSON

There is possibly another way in which this matter may be regarded. I suppose if the student in our American college, not intending necessarily to become a lawyer or a physician, should elect certain studies of legal character, or studies in science or in medicine, that these elections might be regarded as useful toward his general education. Surely, as a part of liberal training, certain legal studies would be quite applicable. Many students

302

in college elect to take science courses quite largely—their tastes lie that way—and they take chemistry, zoölogy, and bacteriology to a very considerable extent. If a student in the choice of his electives selects them in these ways, can it be fairly said that his course will be injured under the elective system? Then the student taking his college degree—his first degree—under those conditions comes up to his professional work, and the professional school finds that the college has already fitted him largely for this work. He has done in college perhaps a third, or a quarter, or a half of the entire work of the professional school. That being the case, is it not a fact that the professional school may justly require less of him? It may easily be said that if the student would choose something else, he would have another year, and he would be older, and would know more. He might, so far as that goes, take still another year, and be still more valuable. But after all is it worthwhile to protract preparation for a profession to that extent? Many think not, and I must admit that we in our part of the country are inclined to look at it in that way. Of course, students enter our law school after they have taken their Bachelor's degree—quite a number of them. At the same time, students may choose their electives in such a way that they eliminate the first year in the professional school. It is because that has been done throughout the Central West, that these colleges of which President Eliot spoke have made to many of us the propositions in question. But in substance this is our way of looking at it, that a student in college may elect in such a way as not to injure his course, and yet, on the other hand, to fit himself for professional work. He does just as much in the way of general training in four years. He does just as much in the way of special training. And he wastes no time.

"Discussion of Mr. Wilcox's Paper." Tenth Annual Conference of the Association of American Universities (Ithaca), 7 January 1909

AN HISTORICAL REVIEW

BEADLE

Chauncey Boucher, who was Dean of the College [from 1926 to 1935], says, in his book, *The Chicago Plan*, that after the first

World War, undergraduate work at the University ". . . was grossly neglected; even worse, the College came to be regarded by some members as an ill-begotten brat that should be disinherited."

There was then apparently general agreement that the entire undergraduate program—that is, the College—should either be strengthened or abandoned. The considered opinion of the University Senate in 1922 seemed to favor the latter, for it officially advocated continued and increased emphasis on the graduate programs, with further limitations on those at the undergraduate levels.

At about that time, instruction in the Junior College—the first two years, in which general education was given most of the limited emphasis it had—was delegated in large part to graduate teaching assistants—100 of them each year, with an annual turnover of forty per cent.

The history of that time suggests that, had not Ernest DeWitt Burton succeeded Harry Pratt Judson as President, undergraduate work might indeed have been abolished.

Immediately on succeeding Judson in 1923, Burton set out to revive interest in the College. He appointed Ernest Hatch Wilkins as Dean of that unit. Together they introduced a series of proposals and changes that were the beginning of a period described by Daniel Bell in his 1966 Book *The Reforming of General Education* as " . . . the most thoroughgoing experiment in general education of any college in the United States."

Incidentally, in case you have not already done so, I strongly recommend you read Mr. Bell's book. It summarizes general education at Columbia, Harvard and Chicago, which, as the author says, have provided the three basic models of general education that hundreds of other colleges have adopted, with or without modifications.

Mr. Bell knows the Chicago situation from first-hand experience, for he was an instructor in our College from 1946 to '49—the period of the fully developed Hutchins plan—and he is this year a Visiting Professor from Columbia University in the current Levi-Booth College, and in the Department of Sociology.

But to return to the Burton era: He and Wilkins revived a proposal of Harper's that envisaged a junior college combining the last two years of high school and the first two years of college. Plans were drawn up to build this physically across the

Midway on what is now known as South Campus, with an instructional quadrangle and sixteen residential units which would house 1200 of the 1500 expected students.

Dean Wilkins proposed the survey course plan that reached a high peak of distinction in the Hutchins College of the thirties.

Burton initiated a fund-raising campaign for carrying out his plans, which succeeded in adding $10,000,000 to the assets of the University—a tremendous sum for that period.

No one can know what would have happened had Burton not died after two years in office.

As it was, his South Campus College never materialized, though the idea persisted for some years, and the present Burton-Judson dormitory units, housing about 350, were built with the possibility still open that it might come to be. Under Burton's successor, Max Mason, College planning went forward to the extent that, when Hutchins succeeded Mason in 1929, some of the ground had been prepared for the developments of the next twenty-one years, which, as you all know, were at once among the most exciting and controversial in the University's history.

Professor Bell recognizes five essential characteristics of the Hutchins College as it was fully developed by 1942:

First, a clear break in the traditional 8-4-4 sequence of elementary, secondary, and college programs, substituting the 8-2-4-3 sequence of elementary, secondary, college, and master's degree programs. The fourth component, the three-year master's program, was never fully accepted in all disciplines. This plan regarded general education as an end in itself, for at that time only some twenty per cent of the Chicago students went on to postbachelor degree work.

Second, a completely prescribed curriculum of general education.

Third, all knowledge organized into a comprehensive number of fields designed to give the student basic organizing principles, rather than mostly factual knowledge.

Fourth, a completely autonomous college, with a separate faculty not holding appointments in graduate areas, and a system of staff-taught courses in general education, with no use of graduate student assistants.

Fifth, a system of placement and comprehensive examinations administered by a special staff under the direction of a University Examiner, the comprehensive examinations to be taken whenever the individual student felt qualified, without reference to formal course work or class attendance.

A short time ago, I tried taking a set of these. I almost passed, that is, in Biology.

Although the Hutchins College was not universally cheered within the University, I know from personal friends who attended it, that it was praised to the skies by many. Theodore Puck, now a well-known biophysicist at the University of Colorado Medical School, had told me that the early Hutchins College at the peak of survey course success was the most exciting and rewarding educational experience of his life. James D. Watson, of DNA fame, can speak with equal eloquence about the later version of the same College—the era of staff-taught general education courses.

During the Kimpton regime, the Hutchins College began to undergo modification. First, the four-year general education sequence was shifted in time. The assumption of regular entrance after two years of high school was abandoned, but provision was retained for early entrance of some especially qualified students. This change was necessitated because the idea of entrance after two years of high school never won wide acceptance. Even in the Hutchins College the proportion of such early entrants was never higher than one-fifth of the class.

But the shift to the conventional timing of entrance while retaining the four-year general education concept ran into difficulty too—because it did not provide for the specialization demanded by eighty per cent of its students who went on to graduate work, this in contrast to some twenty per cent two decades earlier.

As a result, provision for specialization was provided by reducing general education requirements and by the College faculty collaborating with the graduate divisions in providing for subject majors.

In more recent years, the trend has been to strengthen that collaboration by encouraging joint College-Graduate Department appointments, and even fusion of College and Graduate Department faculties. This has the great advantage of bringing into the College many highly competent graduate department faculty members who otherwise would not teach at the general education level in the College.

The question of why the Hutchins College was not continued in its final form will, I am convinced, never be answered to the satisfaction of all its proponents.

One of the important reasons given for its demise is: That it was not accepted by other universities and, hence, that its early-awarded B.A. degree did not serve as a qualification for graduate work. Even at Chicago, three-year M.A. programs designed to complement the early B.A. degree were never fully developed in all graduate areas.

I was on a general educational policy committee at Stanford in the late thirties or early forties. Ray Lyman Wilbur, then President, argued for adopting the Hutchins plan there. But his proposal never got to the point of serious debate. I have often wondered what would have happened had it been implemented at Stanford. I think the plan might then have spread and become national. It is also possible that, if the plan had matured a half century earlier, in Harper's time, when it was first thought of and before the present junior college movement had gained momentum, it might then have spread rapidly and widely.

That is all fascinating speculation, but since it is past history, we shall never know the answer.

Trustee-Faculty Dinner, 11 January 1967

REAFFIRMATION OF THE COLLEGE

BURTON

None of us would, I presume, think of anything except going forward and doing our best to produce the best kind of a college for our part of the world that it is possible to produce. Yet because it has been suggested in some quarters that we should abandon college work and restrict ourselves to Research and professional work I should like to mention three reasons which seem to me to be decisive in favoring the policy of retention and improvement rather than abandonment.

1. My first reason I have already touched upon. We need the colleges to complete our educational laboratory. "We do not yet know how to educate." Alongside our research work in the physical and biological sciences, in the social and philological sciences we must also continue the investigation of education itself.

The experiments and studies that are now in progress in the University may eventually result in the reduction of the college course, for most students, to three years instead of four as at present. If so this will of course not be done by lowering the standard for graduation, but by squeezing the water out of the pre-college curriculum in such a way as to make room in the high school for at least one year of the work which is now done in college and which is not really of college quality. But the point I am now making is that [in] our function as a School of Educational Research which aims to make genuine contribution to educational theory and practice which will be of benefit to all the schools of the country we must include not only the practice school of Elementary and Secondary grade and the Graduate School of Education, but the connecting unit furnished by the colleges.

2. A second reason for retaining the Colleges is that they are needed to prepare students for the graduate schools. If the latter are to be of the quality which they ought to attain, the university cannot depend wholly upon other universities to furnish it students for graduate work, but must maintain college work of a kind which will insure a good body of thoroughly trained students for the graduate schools.

3. We must maintain our friendly relations to our environment. We must cultivate Chicago not by following a wrong educational policy, but by doing thoroughly well that part of educational work which most strongly appeals to a community like that of Chicago. From this point of view the discontinuance of college work would be a fatal mistake.

But if we are to retain our colleges, as we undoubtedly must, the very reasons which I have named for retaining are also reasons for improving our colleges to the highest possible point of educational efficiency.

To this end it is incumbent upon us to make a thorough study of all phases of college work. What the outcome of such a study would be I do not at all profess to foresee. I venture however in a purely tentative way to suggest some results that might follow.

(a) The elimination of students not likely to profit from a college course as early in the course as possible. It seems to be the case that about one-half of those who enter as Freshmen fail of graduation, and that almost all of those who thus fail drop out within the first two years. Of these, one half again are incompetent students. It is believed that these incompetent ones could be discovered within the first month instead of falling out gradually throughout the first two years. Their prompt elimination would be a great advantage to the college and probably on the whole to those who are eliminated. Of course this process of elimination must not be carried on in a mechanical and heartless way, or on the basis of fractions of a per cent as shown by a marking system. The moral earnestness of a student is of more significance than high marks. Even capacity as shown in extra curriculum activities is not without significance.

(b) A second effect that must follow from our studies is one already touched upon viz. the remanding of work which is really of secondary school character to the secondary school where it belongs, and the eventual shortening of the college course by one year or even two. But whatever may be the result in this respect I feel strongly inclined to believe that we shall come in time to

(c) the devising of quality tests and methods of enabling men of different ability to pursue their course at the rates adapted to their ability. Each man should be constrained to do his work as rapidly as is consistent with good quality and should be graduated not solely on the strength of a certain number of courses taken with a passing grade, but on the basis of some final test of the kind of scholarship he has achieved. To this I am confident that we shall also add

(d) Much more careful attention to the individual student than any American college is now giving.

(e) Some method of grouping men according to the type of graduate or professional work to which they are looking forward in such way as to exclude random election and so give the advantages of reinforcement of zeal by the interest that comes with pursuit of a definite goal.

(f) A due consideration of men who will not go further in school than the A.B. Degree. We must not repeat the mistake our American schools generally have made of shaping the curriculum wholly for those who will go on to the next stage in the educational process.

(g) Proper opportunities for extra curriculum activities, social culture and interchange of ideas, and healthful sport. Our purpose should not be to make scholarly digs but broadminded and cultivated scholars and citizens.

309

If I state these points tentatively, well aware that they must run the gauntlet of criticism and experimentation, I make my next and last suggestion with still greater modesty. Yet I cannot abstain from raising the question whether the best type of college work does not require a measure of segregation alike from the High School on the one side and from the Graduate School on the other. In the typical American college, such as Harvard and Yale were and as Williams and Amherst are, the college is not only the centre but the whole circle. And even to-day in most of our Universities the college fills the centre of the stage. With us it has been and is quite otherwise. Undoubtedly we have gained by this fact. We have escaped some of the traditional defects or vices of the American College by the emphasis that from the beginning was laid by us on Graduate work. Yet I think it must also be conceded that our gain at this point has been offset by a measure of loss. The undergraduate at Williams or Princeton, at Beloit or Carleton, gains something that the University of Chicago student does not usually get. The advantage is not wholly on our side. Undoubtedly our conditions in a large city are so different from those of a small city or village that we could not reproduce the small college of the small town if we wanted to do so. Be that as it may, I raise the question whether a larger measure of differentiation between the life of the undergraduates from that of the graduates than we have hitherto brought about might not be achieved without sacrificing the advantages which we now possess. What I have in mind might be in a measure accomplished by erecting on the main quadrangle (or immediately adjoining it) if space can be found, a college building or a group of buildings which should be devoted wholly to undergraduates and should constitute the center of their life at the University. But quite possibly there is a better plan. What I suggest is an ideal rather than the method of achieving it.

In this autobiography to which I referred above Professor Michael Pupin speaks of the esprit de corps of our American colleges as being one of their best features. The University from which he gained this impression was, when he was a student in it, essentially an undergraduate college. Has the college in a university lost something of this spirit, of which many of us had an experience in our own college days similar to that of Professor Pupin. Is it possible to restore it?

310

I remember President Harper telling me that he had great difficulty in inducing the Board of Trustees in 1891 to enlarge the campus from the three blocks of which it was originally intended that it should consist, to the four blocks of our present main quadrangle. He won and then supposed that he had secured all the land the University would ever need. In that belief the original plans provided for Chapel, Library, laboratories, lecture halls, and residence buildings, for graduates and undergraduates, for men and women—all on the one four-block tract. The record of that point of view appears in the residence buildings at three of the four corners of the quadrangle. Fortunately, but not soon enough, President Harper foresaw how much larger an enterprise he had undertaken than he at first supposed and the outlying blocks were provided. Some things done at the very beginning we probably cannot change. But I venture now to raise the question whether before any more buildings are built we should not take another look into the future, and reassuring ourselves as to the permanence of the colleges as a part of our University plans, consider under what physical conditions the life of the colleges can be most effectively developed. For, I repeat, the very reasons that require us to retain the colleges require us also to make them the best possible. Can we not produce here in Chicago colleges that will have the advantages of a Balliol or a Williams, yet also the great advantages of close contact with the graduate and Research work to which out main quadrangles will be especially consecrated?

"The Future of the University." University of Chicago Senate, 24 February 1923

WHAT SHOULD COLLEGES DO?

BURTON

That the Colleges of the United States have rendered an invaluable service in the past, no one who knows their history will deny. That they are capable of great improvement and ought to be improved is equally beyond doubt. The University of Chicago recognizes in these facts a challenge, which it earnestly desires to meet by developing a type of college better than any that is now provided in the United States and adapted to meet present day needs and to give to college students the best possible kind of education for the period of advancement which they have reached.

The University cannot afford to leave this work entirely to others to do. While prosecuting with all vigor the work of its graduate and professional schools there are decisive reasons why it should side by side with them maintain its colleges, as an integral part of the University. The two levels of education are best prosecuted, not indeed intermingled, but under the same administration, and not too remotely separated. The colleges profit from knowing something of what is going on in the graduate schools, having a pride in their achievements, and stimulated to higher type of college life than is likely to prevail when no such influence affects their ideals and aims. On the other hand the maintenance of the colleges by the University is distinctly in the interest of the graduate and professional work.

Historically the Colleges of Arts, Literature and Science are the foundation and center of all our American University education. Johns Hopkins University indeed undertook to dispense with them and to build up a Graduate School without a college, but presently supplied the foundation with which it had first thought to dispense. The University of Chicago was built on the lines of the common American tradition. It was originally expected to be a college only. And though before it opened its doors in 1892, in accordance with the plan evolved by President Harper it had been determined that graduate work should fill a large place in the plans and work of the new institution, its colleges have always been an integral and vital part of the University.

Not only because this is our tradition, but more especially because after mature deliberation it has been decided that the policy is a wise one, it may now be considered settled that the University will continue to maintain its college work. Whatever changes are requisite to make the work of the colleges more effective it will stand ready to make, but it does not contemplate abandoning them. The work which they do in preparing men and women to be useful and effective members of society, broadening their horizon and sympathies, quickening their power of thought and maturing their judgment is itself ample warrant for their continuance. Situated in a city of three million people and having within a radius of 500 miles half the population of the United States which normally sends to college each year thousands of young men and women, the University cannot be indifferent to the needs of these youths and to the opportunities of its environment.

It is from the colleges, its own or those of other institutions—that the University must derive its supply of students for all the graduate and professional schools. Without them these more advanced schools would speedily close their doors. It is in the Colleges as a rule that the ambition for scholarship or professional achievement becomes a real force in a young man's life. From the colleges furthermore come the great body of educated men and women who create and support the sentiment in favor of education. Nor can the University safely depend entirely upon other institutions to render this service. It must itself take part in this work and conduct colleges of its own. They are needed to supply to its graduate and professional schools men and women, who, trained under its influence, will give character to these schools; to facilitate research, and make reasonably complete its research, in the field of education; and to supply a real need of its immediate environment and constituency.

But it being settled that the University is to continue to maintain its colleges it is self-evident that it must make them the best possible. Much serious thought has been given to the question how this can be done, and while many aspects of the matter remain to be further investigated and made the subject of experimentation some things have emerged with unmistakable clearness.

First, the aim of the college must be nothing less or narrower than the development of personalities, the providing of a kind of life in college which will fit the student for a rich and useful life in after-college days. It must take account of the fact that some of its students will go on to further study in graduate or professional school, and that for others college days will end, not education, but education in school. It must, therefore, concern itself with the needs of both classes.

Second, it must set and maintain high standards of scholarship and steadfastly discourage the notion that college is a pleasant interlude between school days and the serious business of life.

Third, it must recognize the possibilities and conserve the values of the out-of-class hours and activities of the student. It must take account of the educative influence of companionships, recreation, and athletics.

Fourth, it must deal with its students as individuals. Mass education is not adapted to produce the highest type of personality. It is better than none; it is far from being good enough. The University must, therefore, provide opportunities for easy and intimate contact not only of the students with one another but with more mature men and women of high character and scholarly interests, yet interested also in people and sympathetic with youth and patient with its impatience.

Even this brief statement of the matter is sufficient to make it clear that the colleges of a University which is made up in no small part of graduate and professional schools call for intent attention and constant study, lest their requirements and possibilities be overlooked, and for treatment in important respects different from that which is given to the other divisions of the University. Some men can do good work both for college students and for graduates. But the practical exigencies of the situation will usually require most members of the faculty to devote themselves to one class and largely to give up work in the other field. Good college work is the essential basis of good graduate work. Neither must cut the nerve of the other. Research must not be sacrificed to large college classes, but neither must college teaching be entrusted to men whose only interest is in scientific problems and to whom undergraduate teaching is a perpetual bore. College teaching is a highly dignified and important service worthy to stand on its own merits, and to be conducted in the best possible way, not as an incident of work supposedly or really more important.

On the other hand there are undoubted advantages in conducting college work in close relationship with graduate work. It broadens the horizon and vision of the student. It keeps him from thinking that four years will give him a complete education. It injects into the college the spirit of research, which, though it cannot be cultivated in college for its additions to human knowledge, is essential to the best atmosphere of the college.

These considerations suggest, what we have come to believe, that we have at the University of Chicago a rare opportunity to develop a kind of college life and education, which for our situation will surpass any that has yet been evolved, and will be a real contribution to American education. They carry also the suggestion that while the unity and continuity of all the work of the University should be conserved, before and in and after undergraduate days, yet some measure of separation and some diversity of method should differentiate the several stages of the educational process.

To these educational considerations local conditions of the University of Chicago add important elements.

(a) The University is fortunate in possessing on the south side of the Midway facing the Medical School, the Library, the Chapel, Ida Noyes and the School of Education, land which is still unoccupied by permanent buildings. On this land buildings for the colleges can be erected in which they can develop their own life according to the best plan which our students of education can suggest. Fortunately, also, the development of the colleges on this tract is in the interests of the rest of the University. The development of graduate and professional work which may reasonably be expected in the not distant future will call for all the space in the main quadrangle and on the blocks east and west of it, not occupied by such general buildings as the Chapel, Library, and Administration Building, and by the Athletic Field and buildings. There will of course be a considerable period before this result will be fully achieved and some kinds of work for undergraduates, such as Chemistry and Physics, may perhaps remain permanently in the same buildings in which the graduate work is done. But broadly speaking the interests alike of the Colleges and of the Graduate and Professional Schools suggest that the University north of the Midway should be a graduate institution, and the Colleges should have a free field for their best development south of the Midway. Perhaps nowhere in America is a physical situation so favorable to the best possible development of a University containing both Colleges and Graduate Schools and so adapted to allow each to develop according to its own genius yet in mutually helpful relationship.

"The University of Chicago As It Should Be in 1940:
A Confidential Statement by the President," 1925

A COLLEGE EQUAL TO THE CHALLENGE

MASON

One of the greatest duties that we have to perform is to create in the University of Chicago a university in which scholarship is sought and appreciated by the undergraduate body. Because of the research activity of this institution there seems to be clearly indicated a type of performance in education which it is our duty to try: education by participation in research. We cannot drive that to the limit. Students must obtain the technique for that participation, and there must be means for obtaining general information. Provided that the goal of participation in some really vital research problem appears as a reward to undergraduate students for successful performance in their work, they will become a part of our general program in a wholly new spirit. I am reminded of a true tale that was told me a short time ago about a little boy who, a great many years ago, when bread was five cents a loaf, was given five cents with which to buy anything that he wanted. He went downtown with his mother, and he looked over everything. It took him a long time, and after all of his shopping, after he had studied everything in the stores for an hour, he ended up by buying a loaf of exactly the same bread that they served every day on the table and which he had up to that time been very unwilling to eat. A rather surprising thing for a youngster to do. He bought it, put it under his arm, and took it home. He sat down for supper, and he said, "No, I don't want any of the other supper. I want my bread"; and he ate his bread and nothing else. "My," he said, "isn't that good bread?" I think there is a good moral in that story. That spark of interest will lead our undergraduate students further ahead than any other method which we can devise, and it is in keeping with our program.

Now how shall we work it out? Mr. Swift said I had plans for this University. I have lots of problems in connection with this University, but we must all work out the plans together. I believe there is more than a mere visionary desire in the statement that we can make this to a greater degree than heretofore a university in which training and education occur by participation in the performance to which the Faculty is devoting its life. Students should share with the Faculty our advances of knowledge. I do not mean that a Junior can take a research problem in Celtic or in calculus of variations. I know very well he cannot. But I do know how much it means to the youngster to be around a group doing real things; and if he does nothing more than carry a bucket of water for a man who is performing an experiment in physics, if he does nothing more than help typewrite or arrange sheets or photostats, he gets the spirit of scholarship and can be left to his own devices to satisfy his curiosity. The methods in the colleges, to a very great extent, are those of many decades ago, when it was difficult to obtain the information which constituted a college education. Today you can hardly turn without seeing some very good means by which a man who wishes to educate himself can do so. Libraries are at every turn, self-helps, correspondence schools; there is no need now to furnish merely the helps to education, and there is certainly no reason for the continuance in an undergraduate college of methods which dull the edge of curiosity. I am convinced that students come to the University of Chicago from the high schools with far higher ideals than we give them credit for; that many of them are looking toward the experience as an intellectual adventure. They are easily deflected. They are young. We do not hold as many of them as we might, and I hope that we can hold more. The answer is not in using the college as an instrument to dull curiosity. The answer is in using the college as an instrument to stimulate and feed curiosity and interest; then we can safely leave the rest to the youngsters themselves. If we can work in that direction, we can accomplish an infinite amount of good in American education.

We lack here the economic urge which makes necessary good performance in scholarship in Europe. It is the tradition of America that the able youngster can make good. He does not need his training. Those days may pass soon. We are no longer a pioneer country, and the need for guidance by the men versed in the technique of their subjects is becoming greater and greater; but the economic urge will not be present with us for some time to come, and I believe we must make up for it in some way. America needs more than anything else appreciation for the life of scholarship, and that involves us in quite a turn of events. It means that we shall have to be sympathetic with youngsters who have not had that spark of enthusiasm, that we shall not limit our interest to those who show an early interest in scholarship. I am not sure that the normal boy can be expected under present conditions to plan to be a productive scholar for a profession on entering the University, but we shall get a good many of the best men in the world if we can make our methods more interesting to them. Here are normal, wholesome, sound, American youths with interest in everything from athletics to music.

We must make our work more their work, and hold out to them through an honor system such a performance in later years as will throw them certainly and definitely into daily participation with great scholars whose names perhaps they already know and from whom they can obtain that spark of interest that will make it unnecessary for anybody to teach them. They will teach themselves.

Education by participation in research. It is not too much to hope for. It is not too much to study to see how far we can go, and as I have talked with some members of the Faculty I have been startled to find to what an extent that is already in existence in various departments of the University. Our true program, it seems to me, is an intensification of the program we have always had: the research work of the Faculty centered in the most vital problems which they can find. We must cut the lines of departments when necessary, in centering groups of men in common effort on a problem—for the problem is the real thing, the department the artificial thing. We need a set of problems of vital importance under solution co-operatively by this great group of men, with graduate students as many in number as can well, enthusiastically, and ably co-operate in that problem of research performance, far less course-giving and course-taking than is at present the habit. The curse of the American student is taking courses, and the difficulty for the Faculty is giving courses. I speak, naturally, in exaggeration and very extremely when I say that I believe half of the energy of the Faculty can be saved from course-giving if we allow participation, but I believe that that is not very wild as a guess—not for tomorrow, but when we learn this game a little better—and I believe that the students will profit from it.

I have talked at length about the undergraduate training to-night because it is the worst thing we do. We do not wish to do graduate work, research, and undergraduate work as a whole and do any of it poorly. I think we all agree that the undergraduate work has been done more poorly than anything else here at the University. Now that is not because it is done poorly by comparison with work in other institutions, but because the graduate work has been done in such a wonderfully outstanding way. I am appealing to you, then, frankly for an interest in our whole problem in the spirit in which Mr. Arnett spoke: That all of the work of the University is important; that we can bring to this institution well-qualified, responsible youngsters of good personality; that we can make scholarship attractive to them by giving them posts for responsible work as rapidly as we can; that we can merge into a program of productive scholarship a program of graduate and senior college instruction and create here in Chicago an instrument which will show the way out of this muddle of mediocrity that at present exists over the land in our ordinary undergraduate college.

In every undergraduate body you have a substantial group of able and enthusiastic young men and women who will go out into the work of the world as able citizens really influenced by their college experience. But with that group is a large body of indifferent young men and women. My thesis is that it is not necessary that these individuals be indifferent, and I hope that by study and by thought we can make our research here, our spirit of productive scholarship, the leading light for our educational method. I do not want to infer that I am more interested in undergraduate education than in any other kind; but we have that as part of our program, and do not do it as well as the rest. Our main effort will always be for creative scholarship.

Trustee-Faculty Dinner, 12 January 1927

THE HUTCHINS IDEA OF THE COLLEGE

HUTCHINS

Since the object of the University is to advance knowledge, it is clear that the College can only be justified if it contributes to this end. The College will contribute to this end, I believe, and in three ways.

First, it should give a good general education. We know that general education has hitherto been spread all through the four years of junior and senior college and has even spilled over into the graduate schools. At the end of the College period hereafter the student should have a solid foundation upon which he may base his specialization. In the second place, the College will contribute to the advancement of knowledge by removing those barriers which have in the past discouraged less determined people than you from becoming scholars. How courageous you were, when you come to think of it, to be willing to spend seven years fulfilling to the letter requirements of course after course, semester after semester, year after year. In spite of your natural brilliance you could not go much faster. You could not go much slower. Even before the end of sophomore year you may have wondered if this ambition of yours to be a scholar was worth the price you paid in monotony and scattered effort. We cannot tell whether the absence of a scholarly atmosphere in American colleges is the result of the kind of students we get or the kind of colleges we run. Doubtless the responsibility is divided. The kind of college we hope to run is one in which every incentive and opportunity are offered even to the freshman who cherishes scholarly ambitions.

The College faculty has abolished time requirements, credit requirements, and course examinations. It has agreed that the sole criterion for exit from the College shall be the general examinations, which will not be given by the College faculty but by an independent board. These examinations may be taken by the student at the end of any quarter in which in his opinion he is ready to take them. The brilliant student may, therefore, if he is brilliant enough, present himself for the College examinations at the end of one quarter in residence, and begin his specialization in one of the upper divisions. He is not retarded by the ignorance or indifference of his associates. His progress depends on his own attainments.

In the third place, the College of the University of Chicago will contribute to the advancement of knowledge because it will be an experimental college. If this were not so I should recommend its abolition. We cannot maintain a college at Chicago on the ground that we should produce jolly good fellows or even good citizens. There are enough institutions already engaged in these activities. Few institutions in our area can do what we can do in collegiate education, and that is to experiment with it with the same intentness, the same kind of staff, and the same effectiveness with which we carry on the rest of our scientific work. Education is a branch of knowledge. Our College must contribute to it.

At the same time we shall agree, I suppose, that those who are going into college teaching may well be familiar with the latest developments in that field. Some such familiarity our own College should supply, and in supplying it may help us to meet whatever criticism may be directed against our method of educating college teachers.

"The Chicago Plan and Graduate Study." Association of American Universities (Chapel Hill, North Carolina) 13 November 1931

HUTCHINS

Although the reorganization of the University of Chicago affects administration and research as well as education, I shall confine my remarks to the educational aspects of the plan. Few of you, I imagine, are university administrators and still fewer research workers. Most of you, however, have either been graduated or expelled from college, or if you have not had either of these delightful experiences, you have children for whom they are in store. Perhaps some of you are high school students, and consequently cherish a natural desire to know whether under the present organization of the University of Chicago you would be more likely to be graduated or to be expelled.

In order to shed light on this and other important questions it is perhaps best for me to begin by stating exactly what the reorganization is and how far it has gone. But even before doing that I should like to point out that though the plan now in effect is experimental in the sense that it is new in conception and application, it is not experimental in the sense that it is reckless or ill-considered. Many parts of the program have been under consideration at the University of Chicago and elsewhere for several years. Still other parts of the program have actually been tried, and successfully tried, here and at other universities. We have attempted to combine in one large-scale venture the best thinking that has been done in other institutions and within our own quadrangles in regard to educational problems. Enough trial and error has gone on at Chicago and elsewhere for us to be reasonably confident that our present plan will produce better educational results than any we have been capable of in the past. We shall modify the plan from time to time in the light of experience, but we do not expect to be compelled to depart from any essential principle involved in it; for we think those principles have been shown to be entirely sound.

The reorganization of the University abolishes the Graduate Schools, the Senior College and the Junior College. The institution now consists of the professional schools and of five divisions in Arts: the Humanities, the Social Sciences, the Physical Sciences, the Biological Sciences, and the College. The College is an entirely new kind of educational unit. It is constructed to attempt to discover what a general education ought to be and to administer it thereafter. No degrees are to be awarded in the College. The student who wishes only a general education may leave the University with a certificate showing that he has one, after he has passed the general examinations testing general education. If in addition he can show that he is qualified for advanced study he will be admitted to one of the four upper divisions, or eventually, perhaps, to one of the professional schools. All degrees will be awarded by these divisions and schools. In order to secure breadth of training, students will be recommended for degrees by an entire division and not by one department.

The educational object of the reorganization therefore, was to provide in the College, first, a sound general education; second, preparation for advanced study in one of the divisions or in a professional school; to provide in the divisions opportunities to the students to specialize in one of the major fields of knowledge and at the same time to secure breadth of training. The faculties of all the divisions are now re-canvassing their course of study and the regulations governing it. Since the staff had three years ago given much attention to these matters in the College and since the College is basic to the whole enterprise, it is not remarkable that the first definite action was taken by that division. It has voted that effective with the entering class next fall, credits and time requirements are abolished as the criterion of intellectual maturity, and that comprehensive examinations shall be developed to reflect the completion of general education and qualification for advanced study. The other divisions, which are now reconsidering their course of study, are free to experiment with it, and that freedom implies that if they so decide they may leave things as they are.

One important step, however, has just been taken which may have great effect on the course of study in the upper divisions. The Faculty has decided that plans should be made for the award of degrees in fields cutting across not only departmental lines, but also divisional lines. This involves specific approval of a plan presented by the Division of the Social Sciences for conferring the degrees of Master of Arts and Doctor of Philosophy in International Relations. Under this scheme students desiring advanced work in this field as preparation for research, teaching, diplomacy, or foreign trade will be able for the first time to avail themselves of all the opportunities offered at the University for the study of international affairs.

When the College Faculty had determined to abolish class attendance, course examinations, and course credits, and to develop comprehensive examinations to be taken by the student when in his opinion he was ready for them, it at once became clear that the problem of student advice and the problem of establishing, administering, and testing comprehensive examinations were very serious and very important. On December 17, therefore, it was decided to appoint a new officer to be known as Dean of Students and University Examiner, who should be responsible for the organization of the best possible advisory service for students, and responsible as well for the installation of the best possible system of general examination. This officer will see to it that every student has all the advice that he can stand, that he is thoroughly familiar with what the University expects of him, and with the courses offered in the University as a means of achieving it.

This, then, is the reorganization of the University of Chicago to date. Whereas the institution was formerly composed of the professional schools and forty departments, we now have the professional schools and five Divisions: the Humanities, the Social Sciences, the Physical Sciences, the Biological Sciences, and the College. In the College the traditional methods of measurement, which have always been stated in terms of courses taken and years spent, have been abandoned. Beginning with the entering class next fall the student will be expected to prepare himself in the College for a general examination which he will normally take at the end of two years, and which will test both his general education and his ability to do advanced work. Passing such an examination will not entitle the student to any degree, for all degrees will be awarded in the upper divisions, and only on the basis of a general education plus advanced study. Passing the examination testing the completion of general education will secure for the student a certificate indicating that he has honorably finished the work of the College. If he passes in addition the examination qualifying him for work in one of the four upper Divisions, or perhaps in one of the professional schools, he may go on with advanced professional or non-professional study. In the upper divisions he must show qualifications to be determined upon by the Division as a whole and not by one department. Throughout his course he will have an adviser whose business it will be to understand his problems and to indicate to him how he may best prepare for the examinations. The construction of these examinations is such a serious matter that a new officer has been appointed at the head of the examining system.

But you may ask why it was that the University of Chicago felt compelled to make such sweeping changes in its educational methods. The answer is that when we looked at the education that the University was administering we saw that the system we had gradually developed was not quite accomplishing our educational objectives. Doubtless because of the large number of students with whom they have had to deal American universities have hit upon the scheme of dealing with them as though they were identical. A university that had enough bookkeepers found it fairly simple to determine the intellectual stage which any given student had reached. It depended entirely on the number, not the quality, of the courses he had attended, the years he had been in residence, and the grades he had secured. Since the student got these grades from the instructor who had taught the course, they were more likely to reflect careful study of the professor than of the subject. Since the examinations were course examinations, the student tended to memorize isolated fragments of information that would be useful on examination; he was not compelled to co-ordinate his information or his thinking about it. Most universities have taught most courses from the Freshman year on as though every student in the course were preparing to devote his life to a study of that particular field, even though ninety per cent of them were clearly taking the course to fill out requirements for graduation, or because they wished to know a little something about the subject.

Universities have been insisting on small-group instruction at great expense for all students in all fields when instruction through lectures would have been better for those who did not intend to specialize. They have insisted on assuming that all tools would be equally useful to all students. They have, for instance, put those in the sciences, including the vast hordes that never expect to do anything in science but who wish to learn something about it, through laboratory routines that were admirably calculated to train the future scientist and to deaden the interest of everybody else. That this system was not without unfortunate effects on American scholarship cannot be doubted. The student entering the Freshman class with a vague notion that perhaps he might like to be a scholar could look forward to seven years to be spent in the painful accumulation of sixty-three courses, perhaps under sixty-three different instructors, involving the acquisition of skills and techniques he would never use, and intensive application to subjects in which he had only a general interest. Since this system was of necessity provided for the pace of the average man, the student of solid worth who was slow to adjust himself to new surroundings might find himself counted a failure. The student prepared for a faster pace must linger with the majority of his classmates; and those who wished to become scholars might well conclude long before receiving a degree that if this was scholarship and education they had had enough of it.

We could see that these things were true with students at all educational levels. In addition, students at each level had certain difficulties of their own. Men and women who have spent three years or more in taking courses and carrying on research in the Graduate School as preparation for college teaching have heretofore been recommended for the degree of Doctor of Philosophy by one department, in which they have done almost all their work. There has been a good deal of complaint from the colleges that these Doctors of Philosophy have not had the general education needed for college teaching. Without debating the truth or falsity of this allegation, we can at least concede that a system of independent departments lends itself to narrow specialization, and some device that will produce breadth without superficiality is called for. Furthermore, these students in graduate schools have supposedly been investigating important problems. It is hard to think of any important problem that can be studied in one department alone. As these problems cross departmental lines, it is certainly desirable that students follow them in their passage without being detained at the departmental boundary. For a student who wishes to devote himself to International Relations, for example, to be compelled to enlist under the banner of one department and fulfill to the letter its requirements for a degree, is to deprive him in a modern university of many of his finest opportunities to understand his problem.

The professional student, too, has had difficulties of his own, resulting chiefly from the constantly increasing length of his education. Professional study may well be started, presumably, at the end of a good general education. But we have assumed first that all of college work was general education, and second, that the longer a man stayed in college the better his education was. Consequently in the effort to get better students in schools of law or medicine we have constantly raised the number of years in college required for entrance to them. This process has in many professions extended the period of training to quite disproportionate lengths. The graduates of some of the so-called best law schools cannot start practice before they are twenty-five, and the graduates of some medical schools of the same grade cannot begin to earn a living until they are past twenty-seven. It has never been established that there was anything mystical about these particular ages or this particular background. Whether four years of strenuous attention to football and fraternities is the best preparation for the study of law, for instance, has never been seriously investigated. When it is investigated, I predict the most startling results.

In the colleges we have been doing two things under one roof: general education and advanced study. These are distinct functions, but have been somewhat confused in most American colleges. Although in many of them there has been a theoretical shift in interest from general education to advanced study at the end of the student's first two years, the collegiate atmosphere, which might well have been confined to the period of general education, has carried over into the period of advanced study; and the junior or senior has felt slight change in his environment, or in his curriculum, or in the attitude of his instructors toward him. There has been almost no provision for the student who wished or perhaps deserved only a general education. He has received instruction based on the idea that he wished or ought to wish something more. The universities have in general treated every incoming freshman as an aspirant for the bachelor's degree. Many Freshmen, perhaps, would not have desired it except that there was no curriculum leading to a dignified terminus at an earlier period. The reorganization of the educational work of the University of Chicago, therefore, was based on the desire to adjust the University to the individual, to individual needs, and to individual merits at each educational level.

Now that we have seen what the reorganization is and what the reasons for it were, we are in a position to determine how it will affect the individual freshman entering the University of Chicago in the fall of 1931. Our entrance requirements have been simplified, so that a student who graduates from high school in the upper half of his class and receives the recommendation of his principal may gain admission to the University. Students recommended by their principals who are not in the upper half of their graduating class may gain admission through passing supplementary tests administered by the University. The entering freshman will appear next fall a week before the University opens for what is known as Freshman Week. In this period he will be assigned to an adviser who will follow him and his work throughout his entire College career. If he wishes only a general education he will be advised to attend lecture courses designed to give him one. If he has the idea that he would like to go on to the bachelor's degree, but does not know in which field he wishes to do advanced work, he will be advised to attend general lectures until he makes up his mind. If the Freshman thinks at entrance that he wishes to go on to the bachelor's degree or even beyond it, and knows the field in which he wishes to specialize, he will be advised that he may qualify for work in small groups designed to prepare him for advanced study. He will be told about lecture courses that in addition should give him a general education. He will be told about laboratory courses and language courses that he should attend if he plans to qualify for one of the upper divisions in which language or laboratory work is desirable. Printed outlines of all courses offered in the College will be shown him. Sample examinations showing the kind of thing that will be expected of him on completing his college work will be given him to study. In the light of his own particular background and his own particular interests he and his adviser will determine the best way for him to prepare himself for the examination that marks the end of general education and qualification for advanced work. Since attendance at classes will not be required, he will be able to prepare himself in the way that is best for him, in and out of the classroom, on and off the campus.

The student may present himself for the college general examinations at the end of any quarter when in his opinion he is ready to pass them. The student's adviser will give him the benefit of his opinion as to whether he should attempt the examinations or not. Since the examinations are of a new sort, every possible device will be resorted to that might assist the student in knowing how to face them. In all his work he will be given papers and quizzes at least once a quarter which will indicate to him what progress he is making, although they will not affect his chances of graduation. They will be purely for his information and for that of his adviser and instructor. If the student fails in the comprehensive examinations at the end of the College, he may take them again, and may repeat this experience as many times as he cares to, unless and until he becomes a public nuisance. It is therefore clear that the new system adopted in the College is a complete adjustment of the institution to the individual. If the student wishes a general education only, he may secure it. If he wishes to prepare himself for work in the upper divisions, he may do so. If he is slow, he may take as long as he likes to prepare himself for the College examinations. If he is brilliant, he may present himself for these examinations at the end of one quarter in residence.

We expect the average student to spend two years preparing himself for the College examinations. In other words, we do not expect the College course of study to take a much longer or shorter period for the average man than the Junior College course of study has required of everybody in the past. All students will be carefully advised as to the courses they should take. Students preparing themselves for work in the upper divisions will be in small classes in which they will receive a great deal of personal attention. The University is now erecting on the south side of the Midway two dormitories for eight hundred students. The first of these, to accommodate four hundred men, will be ready for occupancy next fall. Faculty members resident in those dormitories will be equipped and expected to give educational guidance to students under their charge. The theory that under the scheme now to be introduced students will wander homeless and alone, trying to figure out what is expected of them, is therefore quite unfounded. Students will receive even more personal attention than they have in the past and will have every assistance in determining the best way to prepare themselves for the examinations.

The student who has passed the College examinations may leave the University with a certificate indicating that he has, insofar as the University is able to determine, a general education. If he has shown himself qualified for work of an advanced character, he may go on into one of the divisions, either into the Humanities, or the Social, Physical or Biological Sciences. Although the professional schools have not yet modified their entrance requirements, it is expected that sooner or later a student who has passed the College examinations, and shown himself qualified for advanced study may enter one of the professional schools on the same basis as he is now permitted to enter one of the upper divisions.

The student on entering one of the upper divisions is prepared to specialize. He has a general education and a good grasp of the main ideas in the field of learning to which he wishes to devote more time and attention. Here again with his adviser he will study printed outlines of courses through which he may prepare himself for the general examinations offered in the division for the Bachelor's, Master's and Doctor's degrees. It is expected that the average student who wishes to secure all these degrees will spend as much additional time in the University as he does at present, namely, five years. The slower student may take a longer time; the brilliant student may present himself after he has been in residence a year for the comprehensive examinations qualifying him for the degree he wishes to obtain. Until June, 1932, students may enter the Junior year of the University of Chicago by transfer from other colleges on exactly the same basis as in the past. After June, 1932, no student will be admitted to one of the upper divisions unless he has either a degree from an accredited college or has passed the examinations for entrance to the division administered by the University of Chicago.

We have now seen what the reorganization of the University of Chicago is and have learned what the reason for it was. We have observed how it will affect the educational process as it is experienced by any given student. It remains for me only to state what I believe will be the principal educational results of the new system. They are four; and the first of them is that students will be educated in independence. This system is one of opportunity, not compulsion. The student will have all the advice he needs and all the personal attention he can bear. He will not be compelled to develop his character or his intellect. He will be advised as to the best method of doing both.

The second educational result that we expect to achieve we hope to accomplish through general examinations. Instead of passing course after course, forgetting the one he has passed as he passes on to the next, the student will be required to coordinate his information and his thinking about it through general examinations at the end of his course. These examinations will not be mere tests of his memory for facts. They will test rather his ability to organize, to create, and to think.

The third educational result of the reorganization affects the Faculty. We shall now be compelled to think ourselves. We shall have to know what we want a student to know and what we want him to be able to do, instead of contenting ourselves as in the past with discovering what he has been through. We shall have to devise, in other words, an entirely new course of study designed to accomplish our objectives. We can no longer say that a student is educated when he has passed thirty-six courses with a minimum average of sixty-five.

The fourth and final result of the reorganization is that the University is adjusted to the individual. Because it is the most spectacular feature of the plan, the newspapers have quite naturally directed the attention of the public to the fact that under the reorganization of the University of Chicago a student may obtain the Bachelor's degree in less than four years. People all over the country, therefore, have had a picture of the student spending a casual week-end on the Midway and returning to his home in South Dakota with all the degrees that the University of Chicago can award. I beg to call attention to the fact that under the new scheme no student may present himself for any comprehensive examination until he has been in residence a quarter, and no student may present himself for any examination leading to a degree until he has been in residence a year. It is true, however, that since the student under the old scheme, no matter how brilliant he might be, could not leave the Junior College until he had been in residence two years and could not secure the Bachelor's degree until he had been in residence four, the time required for these operations may be materially short-ened for some students. The reverse, however, is equally true and equally important. Whereas in the past a student who for any reason was not prepared to go along at the average gait would find himself on probation or perhaps expelled, under the new plan he will be able to take a longer time to complete the work of the College or the work for any degree.

The object of the reorganization was not to speed up the edu-cational process for all students. It was to adjust the educa-tional process and the speed thereof to the needs and equipment of each individual. The results of such a plan are that in the case of some students more time will be required. In the case of others a shorter time may be needed. In the case of the aver-age man we expect the reorganization to have no affect what-ever on the time devoted to education. Education for many peo-ple, perhaps for most people, is a slow process. We must not be deluded, however, into thinking that it is equally slow or equally fast for all people. Differences in preparation and ability are enormous. By recognizing them and providing for them we hope to give a better education to everyone.

"Education and the University of Chicago"
Radio Address (WGN/Chicago) 2 January 1931

HUTCHINS

Events have won some battles for us. One is the battle of liberal versus vocational education. It is clear that training people for jobs will not help them to avert the next war. It is equally clear that if we do avert the next war the activities of the bulk of the population will be so highly mechanized that a few days' train-ing on the job will be more effective than anything the educa-tional system can accomplish. Everywhere, even at Harvard, it is now admitted that liberal education is the most pressing need of our time. Here at Chicago we think we have a pretty good idea what it is. We know what to teach. We have some notions about how to teach. What we do not know is whom to teach. And yet the answer is clear. The answer is everybody. If every man is to be free, then every man must be educated for freedom.

In these circumstances it can give us only partial satisfaction to think that we are having fair success with high school valedic-torians. Who is going to show how the other 99 and 44/100 per cent of the population is to be educated? Perhaps we shall find that we cannot do it at Chicago, that the education of students of one level cannot be combined in one institution with the education of students of another without damaging the education of both. I would not sacrifice the education of the valedictorians in order to achieve a mediocre result with the rest. We appear to have within the scheme of the College sufficient flexibility to protect students with high I. Q.'s from students with low ones. The special interest sections, remedial sections, and the privilege of taking examinations when in the student's opinion he is ready to take them would seem to be enough to guarantee that the education of one student need not interfere with the education of another. Perhaps these devices are not adequate. But I am sure that we have not yet exhausted our ingenuity in working out other devices to the same end. We are committed to democracy, by which every man rules and is ruled in turn for the good life of the whole community. This conception is a tragic illusion unless through education every man acquires the moral and intellectual training which democratic participation assumes.

Trustee-Faculty Dinner, 9 January 1946

BACK TO BEGINNINGS AND NEW BEGINNINGS

KIMPTON

The College of the University of Chicago is another example of the pioneering experimental quality of the University, and there is nothing wrong with it that several thousand students would not cure. The Board of Examinations has recently completed a study of our College graduates, comparing them with graduates of traditional four-year institutions on an examination for which there are national norms. On four of the tests of general education, 98 per cent of our College students exceeded the median for seniors elsewhere, while in the remaining four tests, 86 per cent or more exceeded the median. On the General Education Index, which is an average of the performance on the eight tests of general education, 99 per cent of our College graduates exceeded the 70th percentile on the national norms. Even on the tests for specialized knowledge, our College graduates, whose training has been only in general education, did remarkably well. Those who took the advanced test in biology, for example, exceeded the median for senior students who have majored in biology. On the sociology advanced test, 95 per cent of the College graduates taking it exceeded the median of college majors in sociology. In history and literature four-fifths of our students who took the test exceeded college seniors who majored in these fields. This is a remarkable record of performance and bears witness to the success of the College in creating a program which is both broad and thorough. The College continues to develop and refine its academic program but is turning increasingly to the problem of the total life of its students within the Quadrangles. One of the important aspects of this new emphasis is to attract more students to the College. It is distressing to note that, if we disregard the G.I. enrollment, the numbers in the College have fallen off by some four hundred students since 1948.

State of the University, 14 October 1952

KIMPTON

What, then, are the educational values which the College sought to realize over the past twenty years? It began upon the simple premise that there is an education that should be common to all intelligent people. If men are to communicate, they can only understand and appreciate one another's ideas against a background of common knowledge. It is this education which we call general education as opposed to that specialized training through which men develop expertness within a special field of knowledge. How can such a program of general education best be devised and taught? This was so large and important a question that a separate faculty was established which would have as its exclusive concern the creation and teaching of a curriculum in general studies. It was to be a basic education providing a background for communication, a basis for the enrichment of personal experiences, and a foundation for good citizenship. In order to create this separate faculty and clothe it with the stature and dignity necessary for its important job, it was granted the privilege of awarding the most valued of undergraduate degrees, the Bachelor of Arts. Along with this interest in devising a program of general education went a strong interest

333

in the problem of high school education and its relationship to the process of higher education. Time is wasted in the junior and senior years of high school and its program is unrelated to the system of higher studies beginning at the college level. These are the fundamental considerations which brought about the program which we have come to call the College of the University of Chicago.

Other innovations were introduced which educators had long talked about but had never really done anything about. Placement examinations were used to evaluate the student rather than the chicken tracks of the registrar's transcript. Comprehensive examinations were devised by a separate Board of Examinations to measure the student's mastery of the skills and content of the courses in general education, and these were given often enough so that the student could take them when he felt himself prepared. Students were admitted to the program any time after they had completed the sophomore year of high school and were granted the degree of Bachelor of Arts for the completion of the program of general studies.

But certain problems, both practical and theoretical, developed in the actual operation of this program, and the changes that have just been made are designed to solve these problems. Let's start with the practical problems. The College began at the eleventh grade to point up dramatically the weakness of the high school program. This move, understandably, did not generate any lively enthusiasm, to say the least, among the people in the field of secondary education. The program cut their activities in two and drained off their students at the junior and senior levels. They did not counsel their students to enter the program at the first year level of the College, nor did they send their teachers to the University to learn the content and techniques of general education so that the high school programs could be upgraded in quality and material.

The second problem that developed concerned our relationships with our sister institutions of higher education. It was the original expectation that many institutions of higher education would shortly follow us in awarding the Bachelor of Arts degree for general education at the end of the fourteenth grade or traditional sophomore year in college. But none of them did. The result was embarrassing. A graduate of the most distinguished program of general studies in the country was often admitted to another institution as a junior. When we protested such treatment, and proved by the Graduate Record Examination that our students were equal in training and competence to any in the country, it was pointed out that our own Divisions required three years beyond our Bachelor's degree for the Master's degree, so that we were treating our College graduates as juniors too. A variation of this annoying problem was that students who entered the College program after graduation from high school—and most of them did enter at this level—were generally set back a year by the placement examinations. Consequently there were six years between high school graduation and the Master's degree. And thus a system that had acceleration as one of its original virtues began to operate in reverse.

This unfortunate relationship with secondary schools and with institutions of higher education, including our own, pointed up a problem that starts as a practical problem but shortly becomes one of genuine educational importance. The University of Chicago has always prided itself upon its ability to communicate. It has organized itself through divisions and institutes and committees so that the traditional departmental barriers of knowledge have been broken down, and ideas and techniques and people move easily over the great range of knowledge which is the University of Chicago. It has been our pride also that our communication with the world beyond our walls has been as good as that within them. Perhaps no institution in the United States has more profoundly influenced the educational scene in sixty years. In our early days tents were set up on the Midway and special trains were run from Texas so that teachers in other institutions could come and learn, and, having learned, return to their communities and incorporate the new materials and techniques into their local educational systems. But our traditional pride began to fall. We were not communicating what we had learned to the high schools, to our sister institutions of higher education, and, indeed, to our own institution. This, then, was our next great problem. How do we better relate ourselves to the total educational process—to the secondary system of education in this country, so that we improve and upgrade it by the things that we have learned; to our sister institutions of higher education so that they may profit by the program of general studies that we have devised; and, finally, to our own divisions of specialization.

335

The final problem I wish to discuss with you is the most fundamental of all, since it is essentially one of educational philosophy. The problem arises from the fact that the phrase "general education" has become a national slogan, and once a phrase becomes a slogan it takes on so many meanings that it runs the danger of losing any clear meaning, even to those who shout it. In fact, it is fairly safe to say: the louder the shouting, the fainter the meaning.

But we at the University of Chicago must know what we mean. We are in the profession of general education, and, indeed, we think we did more than anyone else to establish it as a profession. We have two questions that we must always ask ourselves. What is the meaning of what we are doing? Are we doing what will bring out the best in us—and in you?

What is the meaning of what we are doing?

Of the many meanings attached to the term general education, let us concentrate on the two that seem most fundamental to us. An education that gives its students a *general* view of the important intellectual achievements of man is indeed general education. It is concerned in imparting an understanding of both the interrelations among these achievements and their differences in materials and methods. Its aim is to produce men and women who know that nothing is alien to them which is of fundamental importance to humanity. The men and women whom I know and respect have this first general education—a wide view of human achievements, but also something in addition—a special grasp of some field of human endeavor in which they move with confidence and purpose, adding to it contributions of their own. The second concept of general education, therefore, is the combination of an understanding of the achievements of others and at least a start toward self-achievement. It is a general education because it is the kind of education generally needed by those persons like yourselves who come to our University. This I take to be a truth that will be even clearer when we examine the second question we ask ourselves.

Are we doing what will bring out the best in us—and in you?

Our College is not a municipal junior college. It is not a privately endowed liberal arts college in a small town. It is an organic part of one of the great universities in the world, and an organism takes on part of its definition from its environment. Students pass by many municipal junior colleges and country liberal arts clubs to come here to do their undergraduate work, and many who don't should. What is the best we have to offer students for travelling farther and, unfortunately, paying higher tuition? Two things—two things, however, that should meet in one. First, a college that, we think, gives better than any institution in the country a large view of the history of humanity's efforts to humanize itself; and, second, investigative minds now engaged in making part of the history that will be studied by the next generation. And some of those making this history on certain hours of the immediate present would gladly stop to teach undergraduates.

I turn to the question of what is best in you. The best in our graduates has made us one of the best universities in the world, and it was your quality that brought you here in the first place. For objective evidence accumulated through the years makes clear that students come to the University of Chicago because someone recognizes that they have unusual gifts, because someone senses early that the mark of leadership is upon them. We should not let such students go without first acquainting them with what humanity has done for them and then giving them at least some preparation to do something themselves.

I come now to the decisions arrived at recently by the Council of the University Senate, "the supreme academic body of the University," decisions arrived at after more than a year of study of the problems, both practical and theoretical, that I have just outlined. In restating the Council's decisions, I shall try to emphasize their structure and rationale, on the assumption that what circulates most freely and widely are small, scattered pieces of decisions and not their large intentions and connections.

Point Number One. Hereafter, all programs leading to Bachelor's degrees will provide a general education in the two basic senses I have previously defined. They will give the student a broad understanding of man's most important scientific and humanistic achievements; in addition, the student will be given at least a start toward the mastery of a field in which he shows special interest and promise. Since the student will be given both, he will have the kind of education, *generally* speaking, that should bring out the best in him and in us.

Point Number Two. Several different Bachelor's degrees will be given hereafter, but basically they are of two sorts. The College will award a B.A., the program for which will consist of the present College program plus approximately a year of intensive study in a general field. The second Bachelor's degree will be jointly administered and awarded by the College and the various Divisions. The proportion of general and specialized work will vary with departments, since some, such as the foreign language departments, must begin with students who commonly have little command over any language other than their own, whereas a department such as philosophy recognizes that our College gives its students unusual preparation in its field. But in no case will students be awarded a Bachelor's degree without demonstrating a thorough grasp of the main fields of knowledge and the main forms of communication.

With these degrees, the University will draw a wide diversity of students. Those who wish to take the full College program may still do so, and we hope that many can and will. But there are able students who are short of money or short of time, especially as the result of military service. There are also able students who, although wishing a wide background, have early been especially curious about one part of the intellectual scene and are impatient to start exploring it. Most of these will probably find the second of the degrees more suitable.

With only one fixed undergraduate program we were becoming unwittingly more exclusive in certain senses than many eastern schools. But it was the intention of this mid-western university from the beginning to ask only that its students be able and willing, and to think that it was more a part of the land on which it stood if its students were poor and rich, young and mature, left and right, and odd and even.

Point Number Three. All the new Bachelor's degrees are four-year degrees in that they begin at the traditional freshman level rather than at the eleventh grade. Our program, therefore, will be related to the total American educational process, and we can begin to train teachers in secondary schools in our materials and techniques. But in two important senses they are not four-year degrees. We shall continue to test performance by placement and comprehensive examinations, and therefore not the calendar of Julius Caesar but ability and preparation determine the time needed to complete the program. Moreover, we have no four-year degrees in the sense that students must complete four years of high school before being admitted to the College.

338

Students are admitted into the College on the same basis as they complete it—on the basis of ability and preparation as demonstrated by examination. The University is forever concerned about the able youngster who is wilting on some high school vine. He should come here immediately and bear fruit.

These, then, are the main changes that have been made this year in our undergraduate education in order to relate it more closely to the University and to the American educational process as a whole. This move is worthy of our great pioneering and innovating tradition that began in 1892 and will continue so long as this University remains great. To change if it is done wisely is to progress. To resist change is to bear witness to the quality and distinction of what we already possess. So long as we do both these things with vigor and with vehemence you need have no worries about the future of your alma mater.

Convocation, 12 June 1953

BEADLE

The important question now is: how is the present College doing?

Wayne Booth says its prospects have never been brighter, in quality of students or in morale of the faculty. He ought to know, for he was an Instructor in the full-fledged Hutchins College in 1949–50, and is now the Dean of its 1967 successor.

I assume you all know the present organization, first proposed by Provost Edward Levi, which subdivided the College into five Collegiate Divisions, four of which correspond in name to the graduate divisions, Humanities, Physical Sciences, Social Sciences and Biological Sciences. The fifth, especially designed to permit flexibility and experimentation, is called the New Collegiate Division. Each Collegiate Division is headed by a Master.

Unlike Cambridge and Oxford Colleges, our Collegiate Divisions are not residential but are intellectual units which eventually are expected to have separate academic home bases.

Students of the four subject Divisions will share a core of four courses in general education, these the equivalent of one academic year's work.

Each of the four Divisions includes provision for course sequences that will constitute a more-or-less conventional subject major.

339

With the permission of James Redfield, Master of the New Collegiate Division, and on the basis of his personal and unofficial report, I shall now attempt to describe how several College faculty members are going about devising and teaching an experimental course, called *Liberal Arts One,* for a group of sixty-one first-year students who volunteered to take this course instead of the two regular general education courses in humanities and social sciences. Thus, it is the theoretical equivalent of half the total first-year course load.

Six regular faculty members teach the course—Booth, Redfield, Levine, Sinaiko, Schwab and Playe. Each except Playe works with a graduate assistant of his own choice. There are six sections, five of eleven students each, and one of six taught by Playe.

The topics to be covered, the calendar, and the format of the course were worked out by the staff last summer. As an example, the assigned readings this term include selections from Plato, Aristotle, Freud, Kierkegaard and Nietzsche.

The course, as developed in Redfield's section, in which "Mike" Denneny is the Assistant, works like this:

Monday mornings:

A two-hour meeting of the eleven-student section. The Professor and Assistant alternate in leading the discussion.

Monday afternoons:

One-and-one-half-hour meeting of the total staff of the entire course—six faculty members and five Assistants—in which the significance of the readings is discussed.

Tuesdays and Wednesdays:

Two-hour meetings of half sections, five or six students with each instructor, for discussion of papers students have written—usually two per week. Professor and Assistant play equal roles.

Thursdays:

All staff and students—some seventy-five—meet for two hours, one for a lecture, and one for a discussion in which staff members do most of the talking.

Grading for the record is on a pass-or-fail basis, but advisory grades on an A, B, C, etc., basis are given on all written papers, these for student and faculty use only.

One sees immediately many advantages:

The Professor and his Assistant participate as equals. I cannot imagine a more effective training experience for the Assistants.

Staff members know their eleven students well, and none is ignored.

Students work hard on papers—twelve to fourteen hours per week. All papers are read carefully and critically, and individually commented on.

Student morale is high.

Staff members find the course extraordinarily challenging and stimulating.

We can be sure Liberal Arts One will be seen through many interested and critical eyes. I hope it will at least destroy the widespread myth that graduate teaching assistants should not be used in beginning general education courses. I like to believe the experiment already supports the view I have long held, that the effectiveness of such assistants is largely a matter of how they are selected and how they are used. Many of them will become the inspired and effective teachers of the future, and we certainly need more of that kind.

Liberal Arts One is not the only new development in general education at the University. Recently Roger Hildebrand told me about the highly satisfying experience he and Mark Inghram had last quarter in one of the three sections of the first-year general education course in the Physical Sciences. Roger gave the lectures and Mark had charge of the laboratory. Five graduate teaching assistants collaborated in the course. Students were so enthused that many of them attended extra evening sessions, some designed to teach them rudiments of the calculus that would aid in understanding physical principles.

Ray Koppelman tells me similar enthusiasm is being generated in the first-year general course in Biological Sciences, with a thorough curriculum revision nearing completion.

All of this seems to me to add up to two conclusions; first, that the present College is generating a level of enthusiasm equal to or surpassing that of any of its predecessors; and, second, that if intelligent, informed and competent teachers are enthusiastic about what they are teaching and how they are doing it, the enthusiasm is pretty likely to be transmitted to students.

We have an abundance of superb teachers, and the 1967–style College of the University will give them ample opportunity and encouragement to make full use of their talents.

If next year I really do resign to get out of speaking, I think I'll sign up for the new College—if they'll take me—and see if I

can do better on those examinations, at least the one in biology.
Trustee-Faculty Dinner, 11 January 1967

A WORD FROM A CREATOR

LEVI

Because I may sound critical of certain tenets of liberal or general education, I should say at once that I admire the College of the University of Chicago. I believe that the College has made the intellectual tradition the challenging and question-inducing focus of campus life. It is not unique in that, of course, but it has been persistent and pioneering. It collected its thoughts on what education was about when it was popular to leave that to the students. It developed one of the first general-education courses, "The Nature of World and of Man," and when that caught on, changed its direction to cultivate the required broadly gauged, group-taught courses in the basic disciplines and skills of the liberal arts. I would not say that all of this was done with the greatest modesty in the world, nor was the Message to the Gentiles always as pleasing or as persuasive as it might have been. But a certain amount of tension is good in education as elsewhere. The excitement among the faculty and, therefore, the students has been real. If at times the College has loved excitement more than winning ways, this reminds us that not even at Chicago can one have everything. And the influence has been widespread and good for American education. Surely, not many schools can point to such a record of contribution to collegiate life.

But I have some questions about general and liberal education which, even though they are not directed specifically at the College, are intended to apply there as well as elsewhere. In any event, perhaps it may be useful to express doubts concerning some widely and deeply held views.

Since I am an ex-law school dean, it is not surprising that I should have some doubts concerning the legitimacy of the fears of professionalism and specialization which seem endemic to liberal arts and general studies programs. Some of the fear is

342

justified, of course, but I think this depends on the way professionalism and specialization are approached. In any event, it is a fact that law schools, perhaps erroneously, often think of themselves as giving a kind of liberal education at the graduate level. It is a program of great intensity, made more intense because there is a seriousness of purpose in part derived from an awareness that a craft is being learned and that craftsmanship makes a difference and must work. We did not believe that the fact that there was seriousness of purpose, and involvement in doing, rather than solely an appraisal of what was being done, detracted from the liberal arts training, nor did it occur to us that there was any particular handicap that the education was at the graduate level. All that I am saying, if I am correct, is that professionalism and specialization by themselves may not be incompatible with liberal arts education. The arts and techniques for law school work are reading, reasoning, and speaking, an ability to relate values and concepts in operational structures and to make judgments which involve justice in action as the result of the application of the general to the specific. These seem to be of the liberal arts, and while it is not strictly germane to my theme I think some recognition should be given to the part which professional schools play within universities, because they now represent a merger of the teaching and research traditions when this merger is so important and so much needed. Possibly I may be forgiven with this misshapen background if I wonder at the assumption sometimes made that the liberal arts and general studies are solely undergraduate matters, and that freedom from specialization in depth is perhaps not a desired but an inevitable element in a successful liberal arts and general studies program.

By now it is, of course, clear that I do not know what the liberal arts are, and I am not sure what is intended by general studies. Somehow there seems to be something unsatisfying about the roster of liberal arts if by that is meant grammar, logic, rhetoric, geometry, arithmetic, astronomy, music, and perhaps medicine and architecture. It is difficult to be against these items, but they do not seem to be the precise categories for identifying the skills and techniques necessary for intellectual and cultural life. The categories seem to be a matter of history and therefore of treasured learning, and they suggest, but I wonder if they identify, the ways of thought and the technical skills necessary for modern knowledge and intellectual creativity. In any event, I doubt if many would think these categories spell out a curriculum. I am not sure the matter is helped much by adding the concept of general studies, if by that is intended (and I realize there are other meanings) the exposure of the student, usually through the required grouping of courses, to the major ingredients in the major fields of knowledge characterized as humanities, social sciences, and the natural sciences, with some additional work perhaps in mathematics, history, and language. And all this to be accomplished primarily in the first two years of a college program. One can say of the liberal arts approach that it is of the essence of any intellectual education, for its concern is the working out of the theoretical framework which gives meaning to an unruly subject matter, the ability to work this framework, and to understand through the competition of other disciplines the relationships of compatibility or incompatibility arising out of the purposes for which these structures are used. But I am not sure that these lessons can be learned in what are essentially survey courses, even though the name is now anathema, and survey courses in subject matters which are not themselves organized—in some instances at least—with any unity of theory. The conflict between disciplines within the unorganized subject matters would be highly educational if there were time and opportunity to explore in depth. But a social science course which touches upon some economics, some psychology, some sociology, and some supreme court cases may turn out to be education in the liberal arts when it becomes an exercise in reading and rhetoric. But it does not have time to explore the structures in depth, and it can never know what the competition among the disciplines really is.

In short, I doubt whether the guided trip through the various subject matters can be accomplished in the spirit of the liberal arts. It is necessarily superficial, even though it may give training in reading, speaking, and writing of a limited kind. There is, therefore, perhaps a lack of seriousness, or a failure of craftsmanship, not in terms of the instructor but in effect, which should be devastating to any liberal arts conception. Moreover, I fail to see why the complete guided tour is necessary either from the standpoint of a roster of skills or techniques or in order to make of the student a decently balanced individual.

344

The desire to educate the whole man, meaning by that many of the facets of growing up, was once greeted with great scorn on the Chicago campus in order to give emphasis instead to intellectual skills and the works of the mind. One may wonder at the necessity for the exclusion of the creative arts and other omissions which placed history and language in limbo. But it surely was not desired to replace the whole man with the evenly educated man—with the smattering well balanced, although of course worse things than that could happen to a student. All of us naturally, I think, tend to overemphasize formal instruction and the place of examinations in the educational process. A proper university or college would have many lectures, concerts, plays, and discussion groups. And interactions within the university community, if matters are properly attended to by the faculty, can fill many of the gaps which will save a student from the dreadful consequences of not having had a formal course covering the more superficial aspects of art, poetry, or the Supreme Court's view of segregation, to take some examples where I clearly mean no offense. What I am arguing for is exploration in depth and an appreciation of craftsmanship and of technical skills of all kinds, including the grubbiest, where mechanical contrivances are seen as extensions of works of the mind, with the responsibility of the professional felt deeply because the structure is not merely observed but is made to work. Of course, I am not saying that all survey or superficial approaches should be ruled out. But I doubt if they do much for the liberal arts, and I am pleading for some room for intensive study, which, if sufficiently pursued, will bring many subject matters together. I am aware that possibly I am urging a form of education which the red brick universities of England are deserting, but while these universities are no doubt very good and should be encouraged, I am not certain we must follow them.

I do not believe the specialization of craftsmanship is provided by the system of majors in the last two years of college work. Specialization requires its own unity and determined purpose. The bazaar of the first two years of college life, during which the departments in effect flash their wares at the students, is replaced by a cafeteria in which the student is allowed to pick and choose from a bewildering array of courses and programs, and where, although I am sure it frequently occurs, one cannot be sure that any community of scholars exists with which the student can identify and which identifies with him. I am not so much concerned about the freedom of the student to pick and choose, but his lack of opportunity to find the coherent and intensive programs which I suggest should be at the center of his education.

Just as I think it is impossible to organize all knowledge for the student in his first two years, unless the thrust is a philosophical program in depth, which has its own form of specialization, I also think it is important that the separate subject matter courses of the last two years form part of a coherent whole, which results from organizing a discipline in its main dimensions. There ought to be a faculty which feels a commitment to this organization and is concerned about the progress of the student in the field as a whole. And because there is a relevance in other disciplines, and because education is not merely specialization, such a faculty should feel a concern, too, to see to it that the exposure of the student to subjects and arts outside his main field continues at this higher level.

One theme which runs through what I have said is the relevance of research to teaching and learning. The structures of the intellectual world can be admired, but they are never truly known until they have been worked with, used to comprehend new knowledge, and refashioned to repair the damage done to them by new facts or theories not previously accounted for. There is a unity to knowledge to be sought after, and the community of scholars adds to the successful pursuit of research when it tries to explain the framework contemporaneously arrived at by the separate disciplines. This generalizing and explanatory function can be one of the great contributions of the liberal arts college to the research drive of a university. There should be a natural affinity, therefore, between the liberal arts and the research functions of the university. Possibly a better organization of undergraduate study would break down the barriers between undergraduate and graduate work not because the college is regarded as preparatory but because participation in research illuminates the field of study. And because the competition of many disciplines is wholesome and revealing in increasing measure as greater competence is achieved, it should be possible and important to do much more with the liberal arts at the graduate level.

In these remarks I have, no doubt, overstated my case such as it is. I am not suggesting that a student's college education should be kept within the narrow bounds of one discipline; indeed, I would urge intensive exposure to more than one discipline. Nor am I suggesting that all work within all areas must be undertaken with intensity. I am urging that some greater emphasis be given to the possibility of earlier specialization, and that specialization itself be more broadly conceived and given greater unity within a larger discipline. I agree, of course, there are definite values to an education in common. My question is whether this idea of a community of learning cannot be further developed in the last two years of college life and also, if necessary, be somewhat modified in the earlier years to permit new unifying programs to develop. I mean to raise questions whether all the work of the first two years must be of a nonspecialized type and whether there is any necessary order from the general to the more limited as the college curriculum progresses, whether in some cases an inversion of this order might not be more profitable, and whether there is not an exciting opportunity for the development of four-year liberal arts programs developed vertically throughout the period, illuminating and including specialized studies.

I am under no illusion as to the limited importance of curricula and the greater importance of faculty and students capable of creating an intellectual community among themselves. But if any particular curriculum is not so important, the existence or the lack of existence of a viable and responsible community in which membership signifies pressure, duties, responsibilities, and the excitement obtained from a certain coherence seems to me to be of major significance. One of the real glories of what is now called the Hutchins College is that it achieved this sense of community and identification. It was inevitable, I think, given the complexities of the modern university or college, that this essential unity should have been changed into something more diverse. And yet that diversity can be reflected in a new coherence of intellectual communities with interaction and common purpose. The university as a whole can hardly discharge its very real leadership responsibilities in the modern world if it is not, in fact, a community of such communities. At the very least we must make certain that our internal structures and the organizational beliefs of the past, which have achieved their purpose, are not hampering us from fulfilling our responsibilities.

Association for General and Liberal Education
(Chicago), 25 October 1963

LEVI

Harper-Wieboldt was rededicated last autumn with ceremonies in which the College eloquently and fittingly explained its past glories, expressed its satisfaction that at last it was getting something of the physical setting it deserved, and looked forward with hope, judging itself to be, in reality, the best undergraduate college in the United States. This is a ceremony which recurringly takes place, as in the past, when the College acquired Gates-Blake and then, later, Cobb Hall. I agree with the College in these sentiments. The rededicated Harper Library adds a magnificence which probably can be appreciated best by those who knew Harper before transient modern improvements removed its elegance. The elegance has now been restored, and is made more noticeable by a kind of medieval informality. Furthermore, both towers of Harper Library seem to be safe—an accomplishment which was denied to our predecessors.

State of the University, 8 April 1974

LATER, AND (SOMETIMES) ADVANCED LEARNING
FOR GRADUATE DEGREES
THE DIVISIONS AND SCHOOLS

HARPER

. . . graduate work, the idea which has more completely controlled the policy of The University than any other . . .

Quinquennial Statement, 1 July 1896

HARPER

On the basis of the ten years of history one may reasonably make certain predictions without incurring the charge of boldness. The most difficult part of the work of organization has been finished. Some traditions have actually been established, and upon these as a foundation others will soon grow up. The essential characteristics of the institution have been determined. The institution promises to become a university, and not simply a large college. Its professional work will be on a level with the so-called graduate work, and will indeed itself be graduate work of the highest order. The Senior Colleges will serve as a clearing-house for the Graduate and Professional Schools; that is, as a period during which the student will work according to his own choice and with his best spirit.

With the Divinity School thoroughly established, the Law School in substantial shape, and the Medical School practically arranged for, there remain only (1) the School of Technology and (2) the Schools of Music and Art. It is hoped that the second ten years will bring these remaining schools, and with them the great Library, with its surrounding buildings for the Departments of the Humanities, a great University Chapel, and the remaining Laboratories of which the institution today stands in such need.

Decennial Report, 1 July 1902

JUDSON

Within the last generation, however, another step has been taken in the development of universities, and two new ideas have appeared. The first is that of the so-called "graduate school," which essentially is simply an organization for training those who have taken their baccalaureate degree in some specialty—geology, chemistry, political economy, law, or what-not. Accompanying this is the idea of research. This implies that one essential function of the university is the pursuit of new truth. Of course the graduate school idea and the research idea are to a very considerable extent conjoined, as the specialist must himself be an investigator. Therefore the university professor is engaged primarily in investigation, and at the same time he is training the graduate students in investigative method.

The definition adopted by the Association of American Universities may perhaps be considered as indicative of the present trend of thought in that direction. In accordance with this definition the American university should have a strong graduate school, and if it has professional schools these must be essentially graduate in character. Now I put the statement in this form understanding distinctly the present limitations in the regulations of the Association whereby "at least one of the professional schools must have a combined course, graduate and collegiate, of not less than five years." Of course the expectation is that ultimately all professional schools will be of such character that the professional degree will be given only after a baccalaureate degree has been obtained, thus making the school essentially graduate. But the graduate idea implies both specialization and research, so that research may be regarded as the heart of the university idea at its present stage of development.

> "The Idea of Research." University of Minnesota
> Presidential Inauguration, 18 October 1911

JUDSON

I am extremely skeptical of the practicability of trying to systematize those courses we call graduate courses. The status of graduate work seems to me to depend on several postulates. Perhaps one of these postulates is a number of students who have had an adequate college course indicated by the bachelor's degree. Perhaps a second postulate would be that these students have about three years of time which they are willing to give in working toward the degree of Doctor of Philosophy. A third postulate would be a faculty composed of men who have had such training that they are masters of their subjects. Admitting these postulates, I am inclined to say that a graduate course is a course of instruction or of study of such kind as a faculty of that character thinks it advisable for such students to follow. That seems to be about as near a definition as can be attained. However, the weight of a doctor's degree depends in the long run on the character of the faculty and the reputation of the institution granting the degree. Doubtless there will be great variety in the way in which subjects are handled in different institutions. That does not seem to me, however, a matter of great importance. Standardizing courses of instruction may be fairly easy in a secondary school, and perhaps in the earlier years of a college. The difficulty, however, increases rather rapidly as we go up in the scale, until in the later years the practicability of thus standardizing fades out. It does not seem

350

to me, therefore, practicable to standardize graduate subjects, nor does it seem to me very desirable.

"Discussion of Mr. Kinley's Paper." Tenth Annual Conference of the Association of American Universities (Ithaca), 8 January 1909

BURTON

The Graduate Schools of Arts, Literature and Science. The University of Chicago was founded as a college, with little or no thought of its being anything else. The first million dollars was raised on that basis. But when Dr. Harper accepted the Presidency he did so on condition that the scope of the work should be broadened far beyond the original thought, and when it actually opened its doors in October 1892, it was already understood that the emphasis of its work would be on the Graduate Schools. It had at that time but one professional school, the Divinity School. By this fact of primary emphasis from the beginning on Graduate work, the University of Chicago is differentiated from almost all other American Universities. Harvard, Yale, Columbia, Princeton, Cornell, California were all founded as colleges, and, while adding professional schools to the college, only comparatively late in their development undertook graduate work with emphasis on research. Johns Hopkins and Clark are the only two schools other than Chicago of which it can be said that from the first their chief interest was in graduate work. It is, I judge, only just to say that financial limitations have seriously hindered the development of these two Universities. What shall we say of ourselves? Has the incoming of professional schools with large numbers of students preparing to become practitioners rather than investigators, and the great increase in the size of the colleges, in any measure thrown Research work into the shade? Certainly we have to our credit a long list of notable achievements. Certainly we have still maintained our ideals, and in no small measure achieved them. The recent action of the Senate in expressing a desire for a fund of one million dollars the income of which may be used for research in the fundamental sciences, and the recent successful efforts to obtain special funds for research in the social sciences shows that some of us at least are awake to the opportunity for a new advance in this field. But if we should without egotism or

351

boasting but with a serious sense of responsibility, at least in respect to the great Mississippi valley, confront ourselves, should we feel that we had attained and needed only not to backslide? Have we been sufficiently on our guard against carrying the methods of the college up into the graduate school? What is our definition of a Seminar? Have we given undue time and attention to that appendix to the college, work for the Master's degree? Have we been sufficiently careful to eliminate the men who are in reality incapable of research work and only waste their own time and that of the professor? Have we with sufficient diligence sought out and encouraged the man who is exceptionally capable of research? Have our fellowships been sufficiently large and numerous to enable us to draw and hold men of this type? Are our library facilities such as they ought to be if research is the thing that we are most interested in? Have we provided adequate opportunity for informal exchange of ideas among research students in the same department and between those of different departments? Have we been sufficiently concerned in making specialists to give them also breadth of outlook and make them cultivated gentlemen as well as technical scholars?

I ask all these as real questions not as indirect affirmations. What I wish to suggest is that if we take seriously our responsibility as possibly, of all the universities of the country, the one that by tradition, by achievements, by possibilities for the future, has the best chance of leading in research, then it is fitting that we should reconsider all our plans, methods and equipment. To this I need only add that I am confident that there are others beside ourselves who look to us to take the place of leadership, and that if we courageously aspire to it we shall find help in achieving our ambitions.

I wish to speak next of the Medical School. We are all familiar with the arrangement with Rush Medical College that was entered into in the latter years of President Harper's administration, according to which the premedical work and the first two years of the Medical course itself are given at the University and the clinical work covering the last two years at Rush Medical College. In 1917 under President Judson's administration the sum of $5,300,000 was raised to make possible the carrying out of a plan believed to have great advantages over the plan previously followed. The new plan included an arrangement

with Otho S. A. Sprague Memorial Institute and the John Mc-
Cormick Memorial Institute and the Children's Memorial Insti-
tute, and made available for the Medical work of the University,
including research and teaching, equipment and endowment, a
sum exceeding ten million dollars. New buildings were to be
built on the south side of the Midway and the full four year
medical course was to be given at the University. At the same
time medical instruction was to be continued at Rush Medical
College but only for graduates in medicine, who having been
engaged in practice desired to return for further study which
should equip them for greater efficiency.

The putting of these plans into execution has been delayed by
the world war and the consequent increase in the cost of build-
ing. It is the judgment of the Trustees that the time has now
come to begin the execution of them. It is expected that con-
struction of the Rawson building at Rush Medical College
which will provide needed laboratory facilities for the school
for postgraduate work that is to be maintained on the west side
will be begun within ninety days. The plans for the school at the
University will be re-studied from every point of view in the
hope and expectation of discovering a way out that will lead to
real if not also rapid progress.

It is understood that the number of students will be limited
and the effort will be made to conduct not a large school, but
one of the highest possible scientific character and professional
efficiency.

We are assured by competent judges that we have the best
opportunity to create a first-class medical school that exists in
the country if not even in the world. This statement sounds a bit
like Chicago boastfulness. But it is not Chicago men that have
made it to me. The peculiar excellence of our opportunity con-
sists not in the possession of enormous sums of money—there
are others that have more—but in the opportunity to construct
a medical school with a full time staff in close connection with
the departments of the University doing advanced research
work of the highest quality—the departments of Physics, Chem-
istry, and the various fields of Biology. Some of you are aware
perhaps that the greatest advances in medicine in the next few
years are likely to come from the department of Physics, and it
is an inestimable advantage to our Medical School that it is to
be in close relationship with Ryerson and Kent and the depart-

353

ments around Hull Court. Harvard's Medical School is in Boston, Cornell's is in New York, Columbia's miles away from the research departments on Columbia Heights. If we do not here in the next few years build up—not the biggest, but the best Medical School in the world, we shall have missed our opportunity and shirked our responsibility.

"The Future of the University." University of
Chicago Senate, 24 February 1923

WHERE DO WE GO FROM HERE?

BURTON

The interest of the University in all its departments is so great that one hesitates to assign preeminence to any one of them. Yet, if one inquires for that which has been the distinguish[ing] mark of the University of Chicago the answer must be found in the emphasis which it has always laid upon graduate work as carried on in its Graduate Schools of Arts, Literature, and Science.

The aim of these schools is twofold—first, research for the sake of the scientific discoveries which will thus be made, and secondly, the education of students in methods of research, with a view to their becoming discoverers themselves and teachers who will train others to follow in their foot steps.

It is the spirit of research, the eager and organized effort to enlarge the area of human knowledge, to replace guesses by certainties, to open new areas of knowledge, to organize data and extract from them new knowledge, that is the most characteristic work of the modern university. We shall still try to know what men of the past thought, because we appreciate that all increase of knowledge comes by an evolutionary process advancing stage by stage, but our emphasis will always be on the facts accurately observed, and our ultimate appeal will always be to them.

The various departments of the Ogden Graduate School of Science have from the first been conducted in this spirit. The names of our faculty have stood high in the list of discoverers in their various fields, and the list of the discoveries made in our laboratories is a long one. Albert A. Michelson, Robert A.

354

Millikan, Thomas C. Chamberlin, Julius Stieglitz, George E. Hale, John M. Coulter, E. Hastings Moore, Leonard E. Dickson, Howard Taylor Ricketts, to name only a few and to pass over many not less honorable, have given the University of Chicago an enviable standing in the scientific world.

But what we have achieved is but a stimulus and a challenge to still greater achievements in these two related fields, discovery and the education of men to be discoverers. Many interesting and promising investigations are now in progress, and there is literally no limit to the service that can be rendered to humanity by such a school as with men and means can be developed at Chicago. To render this service is the aim and purpose of this school.

Three things must be done to enable the University to meet its opportunities in this field. The first and second have to do with men. We must pay larger salaries to men of first-rate ability. We must add men here and there to departments at present inadequately staffed. The increased cost of living, the increasing sense of the value of scientific investigation to the world, and the consequent sharp competition among universities, and between the universities and the departments of research of industrial corporations, all combine to make it impossible to develop and maintain strong departments of science without large increase of resources. The maintenance of an important department of a university, such as Physics or Chemistry calls for an annual expenditure larger in amount than would have been yielded by the sum which in 1890 was thought to be adequate to provide the whole institution as then planned with land, buildings and endowment. . . .

It is the definitely formed ambition of the University, as it believes it also to be its duty, to develop its medical work in such a way as materially to lift the level of medical education and medical practice in the United States. It has great reason to congratulate itself on the progress that has been made in that direction by reason of the fact that within the last year the plans which have been under consideration for a quarter of a century, looking to the development of a high-grade University School of Medicine, have been perfected, and are now definitely on the way toward realization in fact. . . .

The University Medical School is organized within the Ogden Graduate School of Science. This unusual arrangement—a school within a school; a faculty within a faculty—is adopted for the purpose of emphasizing and insuring the thoroughly scientific character of the School. It will indeed be a professional school in the sense that it will offer to college graduates courses of instruction by which they can be prepared to obtain the M.D. degree, and be able to pass the State examinations, admitting them to practice in the several States of the Union. But it will do far more than simply prepare the student for this examination—it will aim to cultivate in him the spirit of research, with the expectation that he will carry this spirit into his practice and deal with every patient as a problem to be solved by the best means at his command. It will offer a much larger number of courses than any single student will be expected to take, in order that each student, following the line of his major interest, may advance far enough in some line of study really to acquire scientific methods and not simply a body of facts to be remembered. It will encourage its professors to carry on research not simply for disciplinary purposes but with a view to making real contributions to knowledge, and will look for veritable and valuable results from their work.

The clinical work for the M.D. degree will continue for a time to be done at Rush Medical College, but when the buildings soon to be begun on the South Side are completed, this work will be largely transferred to those new buildings. Meantime, the Rush Postgraduate School of Medicine will have been developed in the Rawson Building on the West Side. This also will be a School of Medical Science and Research, but will be limited to students who have already obtained an M.D. degree. Probably its student body will consist mainly of physicians who, having spent some years in practice, desire, by further study, laboratory and clinical work, to perfect themselves for general practice or in the treatment of some disease or to fit themselves to become specialists.

It is believed that these two Medical Schools, one on the University Quadrangles and one on the West Side, the former having the great advantage of close contact with the sciences fundamental to medicine, and the other profiting by its nearness to the great West Side hospitals, will admirably supplement one another. Both will aim to make solid contributions to medical knowledge and to the development of a thoroughly competent medical profession, and together they will constitute a centre of medical study with facilities scarcely to be surpassed, if indeed equalled in the world.

But not even these two together will realize the full ambition of the University. Not only does it desire to add to Surgery and Medicine, hospitals for and instruction in Pediatrics, Obstetrics, and Psychiatry, but it looks forward to an early development of a School of Public Health in which men shall be trained for important positions as Public Health Officers, and of a School of Mental Hygiene. Both these schools will probably be organized as the University Medical School will be, within the Ogden Graduate School of Science, and will aim not only to train practitioners in their respective fields, but by research to make steady contributions to the science that underlies the practice and ensures its efficiency.

In the development of the Department of Psychiatry, the University is assured of the cooperation of the Otho S. A. Sprague Memorial Institute, of which Professor H. Gideon Wells of the University faculty is the Director. The University has contracted with the Institute to furnish the land for a building for the Institute, to be located near the Billings Hospital, the Institute to provide the funds for the building, and the University and the Institute to cooperate in raising a considerable sum for endowment additional to that which it now possesses. . . .

On the broad basis of the researches in the fundamental sciences which are conducted in the Ogden Graduate School of Science, the University desires to follow the precedent already set in the matter of Medical Science and to develop advanced work in other departments of Science which are intimately related to professional work. The University will not undertake to maintain trade schools; i.e., schools which aim to prepare men for the practice of a trade or of a profession on the basis of mere training in technique. It will, as far as possible, offer to the ablest men opportunity for that work in the fundamental sciences which will help them to become independent thinkers and creative leaders in their respective fields.

Among the fields in which the University, situated as it is in a great industrial centre, ought to offer special opportunities is Engineering in its various branches, especially electrical and chemical engineering. Until the University receives funds for a completely organized Graduate School of Engineering, a relatively moderate addition to the facilities which it ought in any case to provide in Mathematics, Physics, and Chemistry, would enable the University to make a real contribution at a point where it is very much needed and would be of great value to the

357

community. The purpose of the University would not be to train technicians, but to prepare men for the places of largest responsibility, initiative and leadership. When such a school is organized it should be within the Ogden Graduate School of Science, as the Medical School already is.

The Graduate School of Arts and Literature

The University desires greatly to increase the effectiveness and the scope of its graduate work in the field comprehensively included under the term "humanities." The Graduate School of Arts and Literature in which these studies are pursued, like the Ogden Graduate School of Science, has had an honorable history and made an admirable record of achievement. From it a constant stream of men and women have gone out to fill important positions in the world of education and literature. The names of Harper, Breasted, Angell, Shorey, Tufts, Manly, Laughlin, Small, Dodd, and Goodspeed are well know for the work which they have done as members of our Faculty.

The departments that compose this school are at an interesting stage of their development. Their roots are much further back in the past than those of the physical and biological sciences. They furnished practically the whole not only of the mediaeval curriculum, but even of that of early modern times. Their business was mainly with the facts of history, with appreciations of literature, with the abstractions of philosophy. Science came in as an intruder and a rival, and the term was applied only to the study of the physical and the biological. A laboratory was at first ipso facto a place for research or illustrative experiment in physics, chemistry, or biology. Even to this day the use of the term science in reference to studies in language, literature, or society is sometimes resented by those who wish to keep it to its earlier usage and application to the laboratory subjects.

But it is becoming increasingly evident that the facts of human life in all its aspects are capable of a study substantially of the same character as that by which the earth and the heavens and the sea and their elements and inhabitants can be studied. The conviction, moreover, is growing that such study is an absolute necessity to human progress and welfare; that we cannot afford to know all about the stars and the fishes, the molecule and the atom, and only guess how men react to their environment and what types of human action make for betterment and

358

which for disintegration of society; that it is fatal to go on improving explosives and machine guns and war-planes, and not to look acutely and thoroughly into the operation of the social institutions and agencies that men have devised to accomplish their ends.

The social studies of every type are therefore in the process of becoming sciences, not by slavishly imitating physics and chemistry, but by adapting their methods to the different kind of facts with which the social studies have to deal. The University of Chicago recently received a gift to pay the expense of testing the question whether Chicago could be used as a laboratory of Social Science, with the result that there remained no doubt that it is admirably adapted to this purpose and that very valuable results would be sure to follow the used scientific method in the study of the problems of human society.

This tendency, to deal with social phenomena scientifically, which has already greatly affected our work in these fields, is sure to continue and to work still further changes. There is indeed a serious danger that, carried too far, it will exclude entirely the element of appreciation and destroy the broader cultural values of the old Literae Humaniores. Such a result would be disastrous. Its possibility must be recognized and the result itself avoided. But no such precaution can stop, or ought to stop, the development and application of the scientific spirit in the realm of human life, individual and social. It is thoroughly accepted, in theory at least, in Education, Theology, Sociology, Economics, Commerce and Home Economics. It will not stop until it has dominated them and all the related subjects in fact as well as theory.

But this process is calling and is destined still further to call for enlargement of the faculty to provide specialists and investigators in the diverse lines of work which are opening up as the result of the fact that new discoveries constantly uncover new areas of the unknown which it is desirable to add to the known.

In one field in particular the demand for further organization of research and instruction seems especially pressing. This is the field of politics, statecraft, or statesmanship. We have long had professional schools of Theology, Medicine, Law, and more recently of Education and Commerce. These Schools are becoming increasingly schools of research as well as instruction and professional training. But we have never had in our own University a school of Politics, and it is doubtful whether any other American University has such a school thoroughly organized and equipped. Here in the centre of the Continent, the educational centre of a large part of the United States, there ought to be a thoroughly organized, manned and equipped School or Institute of Politics. Its relation to the Graduate School of Arts and Literature should doubtless be analogous to that of the School of Medical Science to the Ogden Graduate School of Science—a school within a school.

It should make researches into every phase of political life, municipal, state, national, international. It should add to our existing courses in Psychology, Sociology, Economics, History, and Political Science, adequate courses dealing with the many aspects of the political relations of men, and prepare students for practical service in city, state, and national government at home and for consular and diplomatic service abroad.

It will not, of course, profess to be able to make an accomplished statesman any more than the Divinity School can make a great preacher or theologian, or the Law School a great lawyer or judge. But it should and could offer him the opportunity to gain a preparation to serve the state, comparable to that which the Medical School and the Law School offer to those who seek to practice medicine or law. It should include clinical work in its requirements, and aim to make not a mere scholar but a practical and patriotic public servant.

In addition to its work in preparing men for public service, the School of Politics should offer to students who are not expecting to enter politics as a profession opportunities to gain such a knowledge of the political situation and of the political principles as would dispose [them] to accept the responsibilities of citizenship and a sufficient training in practical politics to enable them to meet these responsibilities effectively. . . .

That business administration is susceptible of scientific study, and that by such study it may become more effective and more contributory to the general welfare of the community, may now be regarded as established by the facts of experience. In this field of legitimate University activity, The University of Chicago has taken an honorable part, and desires still further to increase its usefulness.

No one can predict the remote future or formulate a policy for it, but in the endeavor to render the best service in the immediate future, the School of Commerce and Administration will not undertake to be a trade school, fitting men for business by teaching them a standardized technique. It will continue to emphasize broad *education* for business administration rather than narrow *training*, and to build its instruction in the various aspects of business on a broad understanding of the relations of men in society.

In the immediate future, both the undergraduate and the graduate divisions of the work should be strengthened. The undergraduate division will endeavor to give to each of its students the best possible education with reference both to his broad interests as a man and a citizen and to his special career in life. But it will also participate in one of the great educational experiments of the day by helping to work out a better coordination with our secondary education, by aiding in the enriching of the curriculum of the secondary schools, and in rounding out the curriculum which it has organized in terms of the great functions performed in business rather than in terms of technical operations. In this, as in other fields, the service of the University lies in blazing new trails, in scientific experimentation, in broad education for positions of responsible leadership in society.

The opportunity for service on the part of the graduate division of the school is equally clear. Business research, development of research workers, development of instructors in the field of business education, and development of materials of instruction are all pressingly needed. As is true of other divisions of the University, this graduate work is conducted under the control of the Graduate Faculties of Arts, Literature and Science. . . .

The Graduate School of Social Service Administration

The Graduate School of Social Service Administration is one of the more recent additions to the Schools of the University, and has not received that endowment which its value to the University and the Community merits. It is the result of a fusion of the Chicago School of Civics and Philanthropy (founded in 1901 as a part of the Extension Division of the University but operating on an independent basis 1906–1920) with the former philanthropic service division of the School of Commerce and Administration. The original arrangement was for a five year term, but some months ago the Board of Trustees of the University voted to make the work a permanent part of our educational enterprise.

The very name of the school, containing the word "graduate", shows that this branch of our work is being conducted in accordance with the long accepted policy of the University. It is a graduate professional school and not a technical training school. It gives a broad professional education to those who wish to qualify for positions of leadership in our great public and private philanthropic agencies. Such a school can do its work effectively only in a University setting where the cooperation of the basic social sciences may be secured. In our own organization, this cooperation is assured by having the Degree of Doctor of Philosophy in this field granted by the Faculties of the Graduate School of Arts, Literature and Science.

There can be no question of the need of such work in the educational program of our day. Arnold Toynbee has well said, "to make benevolence scientific is the problem of the present day." The promotion of the humanitarian interests of society in an efficient and scientific way is greatly to be desired both on grounds of broad social policy and on those of public economy.

The fields of service immediately before the school are the following: (1) Rounding out the organization of the curriculum and preparation of materials of instruction for use in this and in other schools of Social Service Administration; (2) Research and the training of research workers for positions in educational institutions, and in public and private philanthropic agencies; (3) Preparation of instructors for service in this and other schools; (4) Preparation of a broadly educated personnel that can develop ever better methods in our philanthropic agencies. . . .

In connection with added facilities and better support for the Libraries, mention may also be made of the need of a Library School, chiefly of Graduate rank, for the education of librarians of the highest class. Library service is now properly recognized as a profession, calling for an education quite comparable to that which is necessary for entrance in the teaching profession. For its higher grades, the candidate needs a large knowledge of languages and of literatures, a wide understanding of the constantly widening range of human knowledge, and no small measure of technical skill.

The librarians of this vicinity, and indeed of a larger area, have long recognized the need of a school of somewhat higher

362

grade than any that now exists in America, and there has been a growing feeling that Chicago, with its extraordinary group of libraries of various types, is the best location for such a school. It is also clearly recognized that it should be in connection with a large university, since only thus could its students have access to the necessary courses in language, literature, history, etc., to the bibliographical collections with which they need to be familiar, or the great collections of books which they need for practice. The University of Chicago fulfills these conditions as few other institutions could. Its library is rich in books of almost all classes, its bibliographical equipment is quite exceptionally complete, and its catalogue, though not yet quite complete, is unsurpassed, perhaps unequalled, in America for its scholarly accuracy.

Though the establishment of such a School would involve an element of expansion, it seems the obvious duty of the University of Chicago to meet this need of the vicinity and of the country. . . .

In all the Divisions of the University enumerated above, and in the professional schools named below it must be remembered that the emphasis will always be on the quality of the work, on its thoroughness and acuteness. What the world needs is by no means more products of study which are fairly good, or more men fairly well educated but work which is of the highest quality for accuracy of observation, keenness of interpretation, perfection of expression. . . .

The School of Education

The School of Education became a part of the University in 1901. It has rendered a great service in the education of teachers and the betterment of education in the West. It is in urgent need of more space in which to do its work and of additional endowment to enable it to do that more effectively.

Education as a university department of instruction and research is a recent addition to the group of the Humanities. It developed in response to a demand from the schools of the country for trained teachers and administrative officers.

It is often believed and often said that all that is necessary for the teacher is to know the subject which he is to teach. The teacher of Mathematics or Latin should study these subjects and be satisfied that he will in this way be prepared for his work.

A different view is that which led some three quarters of a century ago in this country to the establishment of normal schools. This second view is that teachers can be prepared to carry on their work by efficient methods if someone tells them the rules of procedure and gives them an opportunity to practice teaching for a time under the direction of a supervisor.

The third view is that there is no such fixed formula of school organization or teaching that any generation can adopt without careful study and reformulation of the practices of an earlier day. Education moves forward; the curriculum broadens in scope, the various units of the educational system receive ever increasing numbers of pupils, methods must change to suit the new and expanding conditions. Each period of civilization faces a new problem if it would realize the purpose which was described at the opening of this paper where it was stated that the aim of Education is to make individuals "capable of the largest participation in the good of life and the largest contributions to society."

Our School of Education is an embodiment of this third view. While teaching the various subjects of the school curriculum with the cooperation of the other departments of the University and training its students in the Laboratory Schools, it devotes its chief energies to constructive studies looking toward the improvement of methods and the enlargement of the content of teaching and at the same time looking toward more efficient organization of the school systems of the country.

As examples of the type of service which is rendered by such a School of Education it may be pointed out that states and municipalities call on members of our staff for help in surveys. Members of our Department of Education have participated in surveys in Cleveland, Denver, San Antonio, St. Louis, Grand Rapids, New York State, Texas and in a number of other centers.

The scientific work of our Department in the fields of Elementary Education is conspicuous. The work of Professors Judd, Gray and Buswell in reading; of Professor Freeman in writing; of Professors Judd and Buswell in arithmetic and the publications of scientific monographs by these men and their students have contributed to the improvement of teaching so greatly that the advice of these men is sought in many quarters in the reconstruction of the course of study. Similarly Professor Bobbitt is one of the leaders in the study of the curriculum. He was called for periods of six months and three months to assist the school systems of Los Angeles and Toledo in reorganizing their High Schools. Professor Morrison and his students made extensive surveys of the financial organization of Illinois schools and Professor Morrison was a member of a national commission on school finance.

Many of the members of the faculties of the Laboratory Schools have contributed to the instruction of the schools of the country by the preparation of text books. Notable among these are the series of books in Mathematics introducing the combination of algebra and geometry and texts on the direct method of teaching foreign languages and latterly text[s] on the sciences.

The opportunity for the University to exercise through the School of Education a wholesome influence on the schools of the country is boundless. What is needed to make this possible is equipment for research. The School of Education has demonstrated its ability to carry on a high grade of scientific work. It does not aim to expand numerically beyond a modest limit. It aims rather to put out a stream of high grade researches and to train a selected group of graduates who will then extend the same type of work to the normal schools, and colleges and university departments of education, especially throughout the Mississippi Valley.

But this calls for enlargement of staff. At present it is strong in curriculum construction, methods and educational psychology. It needs enlargement in school administration, educational sociology and such special lines as secondary education and junior high school education. . . .

The Divinity School

The Divinity School has made a notable record of achievement in the nearly sixty years of its existence, and needs only additional resources with which to increase the scope and effectiveness of its work. In this instance the part is not greater but older than the whole. The school which is now known as the Divinity School of the University was founded in Chicago twenty-five years before the University opened its doors. It was, however, incorporated in the University before the University began its work by a contract which provided that it "shall be taken to be and shall be the Divinity School of the University of Chicago." From the beginning it has been the desire and ambition of the faculty to be in fact, and not in name only, an integral part of the University, sharing in all aspects of its life. The fact that

President Harper did full work as a professor and that his students were largely from the Divinity School, that Dean Hulbert was for a long time Chairman of the Committee on Athletics and took an active interest in the games, and the widely catholic interests of Dean Mathews and many of his colleagues have all contributed to make possible the realization of this ideal.

By the gift of generous donors who have preferred to remain anonymous a building for the Divinity School is now in process of erection. It is hoped that the erection of the Bond Chapel for which Mrs. Joseph Bond provided a generous gift some years ago may not be much longer delayed.

These buildings supplemented by those of the Chicago Theological Seminary, which is affiliated with the University and happily supplements the work of the Divinity School, and those of the Ryder Divinity School, and of the Disciples House, which it is hoped may be built soon, will, it is believed, provide adequate housing for the work of the University in the field of theology for years to come.

But the school is not so fortunate in respect to its annual maintenance. From the opening of the University the Divinity School has aimed to be not only a professional school for the training of men for the ministry but a school of research in all the fields that contribute directly to knowledge and clear thinking in matters that pertain to religion. It has aimed moreover not only to cultivate the investigative attitude on the part of the students within its walls but to promote open-mindedness and sound thinking on the part of the religious public and the youth of the country generally. The list of books which have been written or edited by the members of the faculty is a very long one, possibly surpassing that of any other group of men of equal number in the University, or any other theological faculty in the country. To carry on this double task of instruction and productive scholarship requires a relatively large faculty in order that all the various phases of theological scholarship may be dealt with by men who are able to concentrate attention each on his own field, while also keeping himself reasonably abreast of the progress of scholarship in related fields. . . .

The Law School

We count ourselves fortunate that we have one professional school, which has so far rounded its programme of development,

366

and so far meets the requirements of its situation that its demands for increased expenditure are very moderate.

But it is altogether probable that within the period of sixteen years which this statement undertakes to cover the development of the Libraries and of the departments of History and the Social Sciences, which must always be grouped around the Harper Court will make it highly desirable to devote the Law Building to these subjects and to provide another building for the Law School. Two considerations recommend this course of action. First the building in which the Law School is now held is a free building, in the sense that it was not dedicated by the donor to any special subject. In the second place Law is, more than almost any other subject in which the University conducts education, detachable from other subjects. Its books are law books, which other departments use to a very limited extent, and its students make little professional use of any other books. The change is not a pressing necessity. It probably ought to come about within ten years.

> "The University of Chicago As It Should Be in 1940:
> A Confidential Statement by the President," 1925

THE DIVISIONS BEING BORN

MASON

While accurate subdivision of the field of knowledge is impossible, it is useful to think of a rough division into four major groups: the physical sciences, biological sciences, social sciences, and humanities. I shall briefly review the recent progress in these at the University.

The departments in the physical sciences have always been very strong. Their success imposed a great handicap upon them, particularly in mathematics, physics, and chemistry. Their staff has been inadequate to care for the large number of graduate students, and their physical facilities meager out of all proportion to the importance of the research work which was being done. New buildings, new equipment, and strengthening of staff have been made possible by a grant from the General Education Board, and by the generous donations of George Herbert Jones,

Julius Rosenwald, and Bernard A. Eckhart. Although addition to the endowment and to the buildings has been very great, it is still insufficient, and the necessity for further effort should be clearly felt, for not only does all science rest upon the foundations established in these departments, but knowledge of the nature of the universe from which a broad philosophy of life can be gained, must come from them.

The biological sciences, engaged in the study of living processes, form the foundation for the clinical work in medicine, and both for themselves and for their applications in this field, must receive further support and encouragement. Considerable additions to endowment funds and physical facilities have been made in the new Clinics Building, and additional space has been provided for the Departments of Physiology, Physiological Chemistry, Pathology, Zoölogy. New buildings have in turn liberated space for the Department of Anatomy, in which such excellent work has been done for more than a generation. The Department of Bacteriology and Hygiene is in great need of additional support both for adequate housing and increased income. Some stimulation has been secured in botany but additional space is greatly needed. Work in the biological science departments has been one of the chief sources of strength and distinction of the University and they should be vigorously supported and encouraged. The idea of unity of location must be kept in mind in order that these departments, in fact if not in name, should be a closely related group forming a biological institute.

An important new effort has been made possible in the social sciences at the University. The social sciences are undertaking a new type of attack on the problems of human relations. These groups are pioneering in the study of man and are approaching their problems in the scientific, fact-gathering manner. The urgency of scientific approach is great since we are facing problems of direction of a society which has but recently acquired new control over its physical environment. These new natural forces have made the world an increasingly complex and dangerous place in which to live. The need for understanding of human relations is great since on this understanding only can be built self-mastery and proper direction of social effort. Such understanding, difficult as the problems now seem, does not seem impossible if we look back upon the past difficulties through which natural science has come to its present orderly concepts of the universe. What we need now, and this is the actual effort in the social sciences, is a determined, modest, and continuous program of fact-finding, and later we may expect the large simplicities to emerge. On the basis of presentation of this program great endowment support has already been secured and a laboratory building assured. But much is to be done in increase of endowment for support of effective work.

The addition of Wieboldt Hall furnishes a workshop for the students of modern language. In addition to this stimulation in the field of the humanities, a grant from the General Education Board to be expended over a five-year period has proved to be a valuable aid in accelerating the work. New materials have been collected, research assistants appointed, and members of the faculty relieved from some of their other duties in order that they may rapidly complete studies on which they have been engaged. The Oriental Institute is an outstanding example of productive scholarship in the field of the humanities. Departments which might concern themselves with merely passing on the knowledge of various languages have combined to utilize their techniques in a broad research program which is adding greatly to the knowledge of the derivation of our civilization and culture. The individual projects in this field may be looked upon as units in a co-operative program tracing the genesis of our cultural values. It is a matter of congratulation to the University that the spirit of workers in this field is so thoroughly scientific.

In keeping with the University tradition of training for deeper insight instead of preparing for professional activity by training in techniques only, the professional schools of the University are looked upon as intimately connected with and growing from the group of fundamental sciences. For example, the new departments of clinical medicine at the University and the whole medical effort have been initiated in order that there may be intimate connection between teaching and research in clinical medicine and the fundamental sciences which underlie medicine. The same policy is maintained toward the professional schools growing out of the social sciences.

One of the greatest duties we have to perform is to create in the University of Chicago a college in which scholarship itself is appreciated by the undergraduate body. Dominance of the University by the spirit of performance gives promise for the future as the emphasis is placed still more on opportunity and less on compulsion. Interest thrives on responsibility and opportunities for initiative, and in our undergraduate college, with the background of creative scholarship given by the graduate schools, we may well go farther in abandoning any methods which seem to be based on the assumption that the undergraduate goes to college to resist education. The American undergraduate shows great interest and energy in his self-managed extracurricular affairs—the so-called "student activities." Our goal will be reached, when, in this sense of the word, the intellectual work of the college becomes a "student activity." Under such conditions the undergraduate college will stimulate and be stimulated by the work in graduate teaching and research. In graduate work, and in Senior College as well, students must study subjects rather than take courses. I believe that the University of Chicago has the opportunity of abandoning the childish game of marks and grades, and emphasizing the fact that education is fundamentally self-education, and that the University may well be defined as a set of personalities, capable of inspiring curiosity in students, together with physical facilities which enable students to satisfy their own curiosity by their own effort. While appreciable improvement has been produced in the institution of honor courses, we have still far to go in the direction of stimulating students to independent interest. The more able students in the Senior College may well be allowed participation in minor capacities in research work of the faculty. The ideal toward which it is desirable to work is that of a group of problem-solvers, united in a real fellowship of learning—a group comprised of both faculty and students participating in the solution of problems as their abilities allow, the students inspired to obtain knowledge because of their interest in the application of knowledge and technique which they see around them.

Convocation, 12 June 1928

HUTCHINS

We have therefore many advantages, not the least of which is the temper of the Faculty as revealed in the admirable cooperative work now under way. We should make the most of them by careful and continued attention to the possibilities of extending this type of effort into other fields.

In such developments the place of the professional schools is important. They have a dual obligation, the obligation to experiment with methods of educating first-rate professional men and the obligation to participate with the rest of the University in research. At the present moment there is nothing educational upon which there is less unanimity than the methods of professional training. The divinity schools are so disturbed that they are having a survey of themselves conducted. The medical schools have been in ferment for almost twenty years. The law schools for half a century have been subjected to the bitter criticism of the bar and one another. The schools of education are only now succeeding in making their own universities accept them as educational experts. The schools of business are in grave doubt as to the effectiveness of their educational scheme. In such a situation it is obvious that one function of the professional schools at the University of Chicago is to experiment with methods of instruction which shall in all these fields contribute to the establishment of standards of professional training.

The graduate schools of arts, literature, and science, are, of course, in large part professional schools. They are producing teachers. A minority of their students become research workers. Yet the training for the doctorate in this country is almost uniformly training in the acquisition of a research technique, terminating in the preparation of a so-called original contribution to knowledge. Whether the rigors of this process exhaust the student's creative powers, or whether the teaching schedules in most colleges give those powers no scope, or whether most teachers are without them is uncertain. What is certain is that most Ph.D.'s become teachers and not productive scholars as well. Their productivity ends with the dissertation. Under these circumstances the University of Chicago again has a dual obligation: to devise the best methods of preparing men for research and creative scholarship and to devise the best methods of preparing men for teaching. Since the present work of graduate students is arranged in the hope that they will become investigators, little modification in it is necessary to train those who plan to become investigators. In the course of time it will doubtless become less rigid and more comprehensive, involving more independence and fewer courses. But the main problem is a curriculum for the future teacher. No lowering of requirements should be permitted. No one should be allowed to be a candidate for the Ph.D. who would not now be enrolled. In fact the selection of students in the graduate schools on some better basis

371

than graduation from college seems to me one of the next matters the University must discuss. But assuming that this is settled, and assuming that a student who plans to be a teacher has been given a sufficient chance at research to determine his interest in it, his training should fit him as well as may be for his profession. This means, of course, that he must know his field and its relation to the whole body of knowledge. It means, too, that he must be in touch with the most recent and most successful movements in undergraduate education, of which he now learns officially little or nothing. How should he learn about them? Not in my opinion by doing practice teaching upon the helpless undergraduate. Rather he should learn about them through seeing experiments carried on in undergraduate work by the members of the department in which he is studying for his degree, with the advice of the Department of Education, which will shortly secure funds to study college education. Upon the problems of undergraduate teaching his creative work should be done. Such a system places a new responsibility upon the departments, that of developing ideas in college education. But it is a responsibility which I am sure they will accept in view of the history and position of the University of Chicago. Such a system means, too, that different degrees will doubtless have to be given to research people, the Ph.D. remaining what it chiefly is today, a degree for college teachers. But however opinions may differ on details, I am convinced, as are the Deans of the Graduate Schools, the Dean of the Colleges, and the Chairman of the Department of Education, that some program recognizing the dual objectives of graduate study, the education of teachers and the education of research men, must be tried at the University of Chicago.

Inaugural Address, 19 November 1929

THE GREAT REORGANIZATION AT ITS BEGINNING

HUTCHINS

Although the attitude of the College student may be collegiate, the attitude of students in the divisions should be scholarly and professional. Eventually only those interested in and qualified for advanced study should be admitted to the divisions. As I have often said, the advantage of graduate schools is not in the maturity of students, or in the background of students, but in the segregation of students. If we can confine college life to the College and develop a graduate attitude and graduate habits of work in the first years of the divisions, we shall have students entering a scholarly atmosphere two years earlier than they have hitherto. Here our architectural program, if, when, and as realized, will assist us. We hope to develop the College plant on the south side of the Midway, where the new Men's Dormitories now stand. The passage from the south to the north side of that avenue will perhaps dramatize for the student his departure from college and his entrance into the University.

The first effect of the divisional plan on graduate study is therefore that it brings the graduate school down to the beginning of junior year. The second is that it assists in helping the student to breadth of view and the study of problems rather than fractions of problems. Since departmental categories are historical, the student who is interested in a problem rather than in getting a degree from a department may be somewhat at a loss to know in what department he should pursue it. Such a field is international relations. Another is child development. Another is mediaeval studies. In the first of these the Social Science Division has made arrangements so that a student may take his degree in international relations even though we have no department of international relations. In the others similar plans are developing. Such plans are facilitated, though not made compulsory, by the divisional scheme.

Cooperative research, too, is facilitated though not made compulsory by the divisional scheme. Any program that attempts to coerce investigators into such research will fail. Any program that does not provide the fullest opportunity for such research is reactionary. The divisional organization at Chicago originated in the research committees that were directing investigations of a more or less cooperative type in the Social Sciences, the Humanities, and the Biological Sciences. Since faculty members with common interests from the different departments are now brought together in the divisions as parts of working and planning units, we expect the divisions to give impetus to cooperation in investigation. We do not expect any division to insist upon it as the criterion of professional excellence.

The reorganization of the University, then, should contribute to the advancement of knowledge through attracting, training,

373

and stimulating people who can advance it or train others to do it. The whole plan should re-vitalize the research activities of the University. What else is necessary? A committee of the University Senate studied this matter for a year, and came to the conclusion that, "In the future, as in the successful past, the quality of the staff will largely determine the quality of graduate instruction." We do not suppose that any changes in our machinery will turn stupid students into brilliant ones, poor teachers into great ones, or indifferent investigators into Nobel Prize winners. We do feel, however, that the changes in our organization will make teaching and research more attractive and more effective, and will at the same time adjust the University to the needs of the individual student.

The matter of educating college teachers does not bother me very much. It seems to me a little absurd to produce Ph.D.s, 75% of whom will go into college teaching, without giving them some idea, except through osmosis, of what college teaching is like. But with the new College, with the feeling that all our divisions have on this subject, and with the recommendations of the Senate Committee to whom I have referred, I believe that we shall gradually bring this problem to its solution. That Committee recommended the appointment if and when funds are available in each department which wishes it to be made, of a person thoroughly trained in the subject involved and also skilled in educational experimentation and educational research to guide activities and investigations designed to improve the general training provided by the departments for prospective teachers, and to conduct a seminar on the distinctive problems of teaching the subjects with which the department is concerned. The Committee also recommended that the Department of Education institute for the benefit of all graduate students a course surveying the entire educational system, not with the idea of dealing with distinctive problems of any departments but rather with the notion of orienting the student in the general field of his future work. The University Senate has adopted all the recommendations of the Committee.

I am unalterably opposed to diminishing the amount or quality of the research required for the Ph.D. But I do not believe it necessary to reduce the time devoted to it in order to give the prospective teacher some conception of the developments and difficulties in college teaching. By eliminating all formal course and time requirements we free the good student at least so that he can devote himself to that work which appears to him desirable as preparation for his career.

But if the education of teachers seems to me a question that we shall answer in the natural sourse of events, the question of providing incentives to research presents itself in no such rosy light. The teaching demands of colleges and universities are such that research after graduation is difficult and not always valued. The research requirements for the degree are frequently knocked off in a routine manner. Since the same curriculum, the same examinations, and the same recognition come to the student who is doing graduate work to get a better job and to the student who is doing it because he wants to be an investigator, no real incentives and no real rewards are offered in graduate schools for outstanding excellence in research. The potential investigator may be overloaded with routine work, and doing that in classes largely composed of people who have no interest in investigation. Because of the time he must give to this majority the instructor cannot give the potential investigator the guidance and attention he deserves. Admitting that much can be done to improve the education of teachers, we should concern ourselves primarily with the discovery of some method whereby we may give a new impetus to creative scholarship in this country.

I have thought for some years and still think that one way to do this and one worth trying would be to differentiate the curriculum, the examinations, and the recognition of the prospective research worker and the prospective college teacher. I think this would be simple and effective. But I am the only person in the University of Chicago who thinks so. And although my prejudice in favor of my own ideas is extreme, I must confess that such overwhelming testimony against this one gives me pause. At any rate the question is with us academic in every sense; for the Senate Committee I have mentioned definitely rejected the proposal, and its action was confirmed by the Senate. The problem, however, as a solution of which the proposal was advanced, remains.

We are, we think, working toward its solution through the reorganization of our administration and our curriculum that I have described. We do not believe that we have reached ultimate truth in any of these matters. I hope that the reorganization of the University of Chicago may never cease. I shall continue to think that we are making progress as long as we are dissatisfied. I trust that my grandiloquence today will not mislead you into thinking that we believe that we have accomplished anything significant. We are simply beginning a long process in which we need nothing so much as your candid criticism and advice.

> "The Chicago Plan and Graduate Study." Association of American Universities (Chapel Hill, North Carolina) 13 November 1931

A GENERATION LATER: A CAUTIONARY NOTE

KIMPTON

It has been a source of pride to us at Chicago that we have recognized once again that knowledge is one, and have tried to organize the University accordingly. The divisions are large, and within the divisions little is made of departmental boundaries, at least as barriers in the pursuit of knowledge. And between the divisions there are committees and institutes that bring together the biologist and the physicist, the sociologist and the classical scholar. This is one of our greatest achievements. It has produced some of our best research, it has made us a community of scholars, and has made of our community one of the most intellectually exciting places in the world. Even the food at the Quadrangle Club is made tolerable by the atmosphere. I do not wish for an instant to diminish this achievement or depreciate the value of this atmosphere; I wish only to raise a slight warning signal. How far can this spread go without becoming thin? How general can we get without losing touch altogether with reality? Plato sent his Philosopher King back into the cave at a certain point to grub about on specifics, and thus avoided the mistake that Hegel later made when he shoveled all knowledge into the architectonic of the dialectic and made a fool of himself thereby. It has been my observation, for whatever it is worth, that some remarkable strides forward have been made, from time to time, by knowing an awful lot about an awful little. A second problem at the divisional level is the institutes. It has been our pleasant and productive custom to single out some area of new knowledge that needed the special attention of a cooperative team of investigators from

376

related disciplines and call the resulting assemblages of men, machines, and museums institutes. The results have been good; new knowledge has been produced in fields ranging from ancient man to the atom. But problems can result. We must constantly be alert to the danger that by such a heavy concentration of men and resources, we run a serious risk of unbalancing our broad line of attack. The department must not be starved to feed the institute, and it must not be so loaded with the routines of teaching and administration that it cannot make its own proper contribution to the conquest of knowledge.

The Professional Schools, with one rather conspicuous exception, have customarily received a good deal of criticism at the University of Chicago. It has been suspected that they lacked any subject matter content of their own, and such content as they have pilfered from departments of the University has been debased by giving it low vocational applications. Some have sought a balmier climate of opinion by retiring into the purer air of the divisions, and others have braved it out by wrapping about them some joint appointments. In spite of all this, or perhaps partly because of it, the Professional Schools have done a remarkably good job. But hasn't the time come to change this attitude? Content is none the less good if it is freely borrowed from other disciplines and reorganized to bear upon a profession. And what is wrong with making a living out of the mastery of a field of knowledge? If the school teaches only the tricks of the trade rather than the broad principles of the profession, of course it is bad, but none of our schools does this. I feel no sense of shame in saying right out loud that our Medical School trains doctors, our Law School lawyers, our Business School business men, our Library School librarians, and that this is a good thing. When this training is conducted in conjunction with a lively program of research designed to enlighten and elevate a profession, a real contribution is made to the world, thoroughly worthy of the best efforts and the deep respect of a great university.

Trustee-Faculty Dinner, 9 January 1952

KIMPTON

The Humanities share with the Physical Sciences the institute-division relationship problem, though for historical and occasionally hysterical reasons it takes a somewhat different form.

377

The Oriental Institute is not a part of the Division, but most of its members are through appointment in the Department of Oriental Languages and Literatures, and an interesting kind of shell game is occasionally played in which a responsibility to both is used to avoid an obligation to either. Lest this be interpreted as reflecting upon the quality of the Oriental Institute or the Department of Oriental Languages and Literatures, may I pay tribute to the sound scholarship of both?

But I can assure you that we do not intend to join the conspirators in complaining about the position of humanities in the world today and then leave them to their fate in our University. It is true that we count on many of the Division's young men to fulfil their promise in the next few years; but the Division and Dean Wilt in turn may count on the full support of the University in their aim to attain, in the not-too-distant future, a position worthy of the humanistic origins of this and all great universities.

It is not easy to say what a good professional school should be, or what its relations should be internally to the parent university or externally to the profession it presumably serves. We seem at the University of Chicago to be evolving our own definition of the professional school, and, though it violates many of the rules of success elsewhere, we like it, and it uniquely fits the local scene. Our professional schools must be very much a part of the University, drawing their substantive content from the basic areas that surround them; the relationship to the profession, on the other hand, must be equally close. The teaching of the School, drawing for its material upon the basic disciplines, still must have a relationship to the actual practice of the profession; and the research of the School, relying upon the knowledge and techniques of pure research, must still be relevant to the immediate and long-range needs of the profession. It is a fine line these professional schools must walk, clinging fast to the ivy as they extend the other hand in friendship and cooperation to the busy practitioner who often accepts it none too cordially.

Our School of Medicine is the archetype for the Chicago definition of the professional school. I have already discussed it, since it is inseparable from the Division of the Biological Sciences, and, if the basic departments of that Division may seem to have lost some of their past luster, one of the reasons, at least, is that some of the fundamental work in biology is being done by the medical men. This emphasis on fundamental investigation, one of the distinguishing characteristics of the School, has been valuable to medical education and significant to the medical profession, with which there is an increasingly closer relationship. Perhaps the best symbolic summary of all this is the widespread professional acceptance and use of certain surgical knowledge and techniques invented by a physiologist who in our unique environment slid easily into surgery and, incidentally, en route became one of the most polished speakers in the country.

Law, under the remarkable leadership of Dean Levi, who, parenthetically, had no qualifications for the post, except being bright and difficult, has followed in this same Chicago tradition. It has drawn deeply upon history and the behavioral sciences to enlighten its research and teaching, and it commands the respect and esteem of the national and local bar who ten years ago erroneously had written it off as lost. That this plan of a professional school finds favor in the eyes of the best legal scholars has been proved by a series of brilliant appointments in recent years and last year by the appointments of Professors Francis A. Allen of Harvard and Nicholas Katzenbach of Yale. But the Law School has its fair share of problems. It shares the precarious instability of all truly good things, and, like Cinderella, it broods about some possible stroke of midnight. But most of its problems are of a physical nature. With its new staff, activities, and students, it has outgrown the building that Theodore Roosevelt delicated in 1903, and it still lacks the final million dollars to undertake the new building across the Midway.

Our center for theological training and research, called the Federated Theological Faculty, has flowered under Dean Jerald Brauer into a professional school in the best Chicago tradition. For reasons that are unclear, it lost for a time its relationship with the University and its connection with the Protestant pulpit and lived an obscure and esoteric life of its own. But in more recent years, as the University and the church have come to know it better, it turns out to have a group of young men who have been welcomed by other parts of the institution and by the councils of American Protestantism. These young men have created one of the biggest problems for the school, as first Union and more recently Harvard have coveted their neighbor's possessions. Another problem that will yield perhaps to time and retirements is the organizational one. Four schools are tied together by a loose bond of federation that is no stronger than

379

the sentiment of good will that each may choose upon occasion to feel for the other, and this bond, like that of the atom, is periodically strained by internal collisions. But with all its difficulties this important school gains in stature daily as it strengthens its ties with the University and with its constituencies.

Our School of Social Service Administration had the distinction of making a profession of social work, and it has remained the outstanding center for such training in the country. Its fault, if any, has been too close a connection with the profession it created and too exclusive a dedication to filling and guiding its needs. With the encouragement of the University and, more important, the Field Foundation, it has embarked upon an ambitious program of research drawing upon fundamental knowledge from sociology and psychology and so satisfies the criteria for a strong professional school. It has been weakened and saddened, however, by the loss through retirement of Helen Wright and the tragic death of Frank Flynn, and it has found difficulty in replacing such distinguished colleagues.

The School of Business is one of the oldest of our professional schools and in its time has walked on both sides of this fine line drawn above. It was conceived by Leon Marshall, as good a theoretical economist as we have ever had, and it produced such distinguished industrial leaders as J. O. McKinsey, who taught his classes in the early morning hours to avoid conflict with his extensive consulting practice. Under the new leadership of Allen Wallis and James Lorie, the School has made a most promising fresh start. We are a great University in a great business community, and the School proposes to be the bridge between the two. It is a sad fact that even the best of our nation's business schools have limited themselves to selecting youngsters bound to succeed in any case and to training them in business practices outmoded by progressive corporations ten years ago. The enlightened intention of our newly reorganized Business School is to provide real leadership for American business by remaining closely related to basic research, on the one hand, and to the needs and interests of our great Chicago business enterprises, on the other. It remains to be seen whether the School can successfully walk the fine line and not become another department of economics or, alternatively, a management consulting firm with low fees. It needs more money for even more new appointments than it has made, and it badly needs a new building to house its enlarged staff and its substantially increased student body. The Ford Foundation has been approached on these matters and on a scale that startled even these dealers in substantial philanthropy. We feel about our Business School and indeed all business schools as the New Englander did about his ailing wife when he remarked, "I sure hope Nellie gets well soon or something."

State of the University, 5 November 1957

AFTER ALL, DOING MAY ALSO BE LEARNED . . .

Kimpton

What is the place of the professional school in a university of the kind I have described? A professional school is usually thought of as that part of a university which receives its knowledge ready-made from basic areas and translates it into new configurations necessary for the practice of a profession and the training of students in it. Our answer is our School of Medicine, which, strictly speaking, is not a school at all but a part of the Division of the Biological Sciences, its faculty, like any other faculty in the University, avidly in search of new and fundamental knowledge. Our other schools, with variations appropriate to their history and subject matter, have followed this same guiding principle, and they are as oriented to basic research as are our Divisions. But, nonetheless, we should always worry about them. Air-conditioned palaces across the Midway could—though they need not—separate the schools from the *Geist* of the University, and their success might—though it has not—separate them from the scholarship of the University in general. At the risk of being misunderstood, I should remind you that we air-condition only the dogs at Billings Hospital, and perhaps this has some value as a symbol of our dedication.

State of the University, 3 November 1959

Levi

In the popular lexicon of higher education it is commonplace to denigrate professional schools as merely vocational. This indicates a misconception of the proper role of the professional school. It probably also indicates a misconception of the place for the purely vocational school. The downgrading of vocational schools is again a mistaken response to democratic values which, in fact, would be supported through the growth of some vocational schools. We ought not pretend they are something else. But the character of a professional school must be quite different. The professional school which sets its course by the current practice of the profession is, in an important sense, a failure. It cannot be this narrow and pedestrian and at the same time be effective. The professional school must be concerned in a basic way with the world of learning and the interaction between this world and the world of problems to be solved. This is true in medicine, in law, in engineering, and even in training for the ministry. It is true in other professions, including the profession of business, when it is viewed in this way. And because a profession is involved, a culture—a responsibility and an artistry—must be inculcated. It is not easy to create a new profession. This is indeed one of the problems of the social sciences. Viewed in terms of its larger responsibilities, the professional school inherits and exemplifies much of the disappearing tradition of the liberal arts college. As such it represents some of the highest values in a university. When a professional school does not exemplify these values, it suggests there is not only something basically wrong with it, but with the university of which it is a part, for the loss to both is great.

"The Choices for a University." University of Tulsa Presidential Inauguration, 10 November 1967

LEVI

Yet all would agree that somehow ideas must be made more relevant to present problems.

This is the function of the professional school and of the professions. It is through the professions that ideas developed and discussed within universities find their way to treatment and application. It is through the professions that a better conception of problems to be met is brought to the universities for analysis. The relationship is intricate and continuing. The profession itself is involved in the creative process. It develops institutions of its own to facilitate the bringing together of ideas and problems. It has its own customs, its own sense of group responsibility and purpose. It develops the craftsmanship necessary for understanding and application—a craftsmanship which itself reflects a group judgment as to what the main problems are. It is concerned with the continuing education of its members and the training of successors. The professional schools within universities reflect this concern; at the same time they represent the profession in the examination of basic problems and relevant ideas. The prototype of the overall relationship can be seen in the field of medicine, where the physician, the institutes, the hospitals, the medical schools, and the universities form an interrelated complex. When the system operates properly—and this is a problem for any profession—the exchange of ideas as to problems and theories is continuous. The physician, whether or not he is on a medical school faculty, or in a university hospital, or in a group clinic, or in practice by himself, has a relationship to the continuing research of the universities and institutes. And the profession provides group action for the solution of problems—that, after all, is what a hospital is.

> "The University, the Professions, and the Law"
> University of California Legal Center Dedication
> (Berkeley), 2 January 1968

GOING BEYOND OURSELVES:
THE OLDEST, BIGGEST, BEST PRESS

BURTON

In our emphasis on research, and on the physical contiguity and intellectual unity of the University we ought never to become academic or monastic. After all science is for men not men for science. Human beings may be the subjects of research, but the ultimate purpose is not research but human betterment. To *crescat scientia* we add at once *vita excolatur*.

Nor can the University be content to make its contribution to human betterment solely through the students whom it brings to these quadrangles and on whom it confers degrees. Knowledge demands publication as truly as discovery. Hence we must maintain an agency of publication, our journals and our press.

> "The Future of the University." University of
> Chicago Senate, 24 February 1923

HARPER

The work of the University Press, the third division of the University, has been organized in three departments: The department for the purchase and sale of books, the printing department, and the publishing department. Already the type has been purchased for work of a high order and merit, and journals have been issued in the name of the University. THE JOURNAL OF POLITICAL ECONOMY, THE UNIVERSITY EXTENSION WORLD, and THE BIBLICAL WORLD have appeared, and arrangements are being made for the publication of others. The obligations of the University extend beyond its campus; and through the Press, in close alliance with all departments of the University, it is hoped that important results may be accomplished.

Convocation, 1 January 1893

HARPER

The work of the University Press is classified roughly into four departments as follows: for Publication, for Printing, for Books and Apparatus, and the bookstore.

In no part of The University's work has there been greater progress than in the publication of journals.

It seems hardly necessary to call attention to the fact that the work of the three great divisions of affiliation and cooperation, the extension and the press are virtually three phases of a single work. It is through these three channels that The University comes in contact with the outside world. This outside world of The University includes the institutions working in affiliation or cooperation, the individuals attending lectures or classes, or preparing recitations by correspondence, and, last of all, the more general and more distant public which can be reached only through a printed page. It is true that all of these channels have their source in the work and life of The University at its center. Through these channels, the heart-blood of The University finds its way to the men and places more remote. Without these agencies The University of Chicago would repeat the history of many another institution, the history of many another individual, characterized by utter selfishness. Nor is it true that The University exhausts itself by thus giving its heart-blood to those who are far distant. By giving, it receives back again much more than it has given.

Quinquennial Statement, 1 July 1896

HARPER

The *University Record* has been published weekly during the quarter. It has included important articles which were thought to be of interest to those directly or indirectly connected with educational work. It has aimed to give officially the life of The University in its various departments. The *Record* is intended to supply the trustees, the members of the faculties, the students, and particularly the friends of The University at a distance, with a correct statement concerning everything of importance which transpires at The University. The expense of publication has been greater than was anticipated. It will be necessary that the subscription list be largely increased if the publication is continued. It is expected that every alumnus will become a subscriber to the RECORD in order that he may thus keep himself in touch with the work of The University. Is it too much to hope that the friends of The University who are interested in its progress, and who desire to become acquainted with its work, shall also become subscribers for the periodical?

Particular attention is invited to the special numbers of *The Biblical World* and *The School Review*, published in June. The subscription list of every journal of The University is growing steadily. The work of the Department of Publication has become so large that the facilities at our command have proved to be utterly inadequate. One of our greatest needs is a building or portion of a building for the presses, composition room, bindery, and proper provision for the editorial work of The University publications.

Convocation, 1 July 1896

HARPER

The first organization of the University Press was in the form of a stock company independent of the University, with which the University entered into a contract. The head of this company was Mr. D. C. Heath, of D. C. Heath & Co., Boston. It soon became apparent that the relationship was not sufficiently close, and although the management of the company was entirely satisfactory, and there had arisen no friction of any kind, all parties concerned were agreed that it would be best to transfer the rights of the company directly to the University. The interest and enthusiasm in those early days of Mr. Heath and Mr. R. R. Donnelley cannot be forgotten. After two years, the contract was mutually changed in July, 1894, and the property of the company was purchased by the University. The Press has been under the successive management of Mr. Charles Wells Chase, Mr. Hazlitt Alva Cuppy, Mr. Ned Arden Flood, and Mr. Newman Miller. . . .

The Press is conducted on the basis of a Constitution adopted by the Trustees, which classifies the work under the following departments: the Manufacturing Department, the Publication Department, and the Purchase and Retail Department.

The following departmental journals are published by the Press:

Journal	Departments Connected	Issues per Year	Average Pages per Year
The Biblical World	Biblical Faculties	12	985
The American Journal of Theology	Divinity School	4	900
The American Journal of Semitic Languages and Literatures	Semitic Languages	4	265
The School Review	School of Education	10	710
The Elementary School Teacher	School of Education	10	860
The American Journal of Sociology	Sociology and Anthropology	6	870
The Journal of Geology	Geology	8	820
The Botanical Gazette	Botany	12	930
The Journal of Political Economy	Political Economy	4	605
The Astrophysical Journal	Astronomy and Astrophysics	10	710
The Manual Training Magazine	Private owner	4	256

The following series of studies are published, numbers being issued from time to time:

1. "Studies in Classical Philology." Three complete volumes and one number of the fourth volume.
2. "Germanic Studies." Three numbers.
3. "English Studies." Five numbers.
4. "Economic Studies." Five numbers.
5. "Political Science Studies." Seven numbers.
6. "Bulletins of Anthropology." Four numbers.
7. "Divinity Studies." Two numbers.
8. "Historical and Linguistic Studies in Literature Related to the New Testament." Two numbers.
9. "Publications of the Yerkes Observatory." One volume.
10. "Contributions from Walker Museum." Three numbers.
11. "Contributions from the Hull Botanical Laboratory." Forty numbers.

The following statement shows the output of books and pamphlets by fiscal years:

1892–93	2
1893–94	3
1894–95	11
1895–96	8
1896–97	31
1897–98	27
1898–99	22
1899–00	28
1900–01	28
1901–02	40
Total	200

The following statement shows the output of books and pamphlets by Departments:

Department of Philosophy and [Psychology]	10
Department of Education	41
Departments of Theology and Religion	7
Department of Political Economy (complete)	31
Department of History	7
Department of Semitic Languages and Literatures	44
Departments of Science	58
Miscellaneous	2
Total	200

The most ambitious undertaking of the Press outside of the publication of the journals is the manufacture and publication of the two series of volumes celebrating the Decennial of the University.

The growing appreciation of the work of the Press on the part of the Trustees is shown in the fact that a new building for the use of the various departments of the Press has just been completed at a cost of $110,000. This building is constructed on modern principles and furnishes a very satisfactory headquarters for the work of this very important division. While at present occupied in part by the Library and the Law School, in the very near future the entire building will be devoted to the work of the Press.

The mechanical equipment of the University Press at the close of the fiscal year ending June 30, 1902, was valued at $10,521.77. This amount is represented by the equipment of the composing-room, with the exception of a job outfit including two small presses, paper cutter, type, etc. For the work which has been attempted the plant is thoroughly equipped.

In addition to this the plant includes a smaller press of modern body type amounting in the aggregate of the various sizes to about eight thousand pounds. In the job department are about two hundred fonts of sufficient size and variety to handle a large volume of work. There are also large fonts of Greek in five sizes, Hebrew in two, Nestorian Syriac, Arabic, and Ethiopic. With the addition to these special fonts of a most thorough equipment of mathematical, astronomical, and other signs and accents, the University Press has been able to produce work possible in very few printing houses.

The question has been raised whether the cost to the University of the printing of its journals and books was not greater by the present policy than if the work were done by contract. This question is a difficult one to answer conclusively without going into a very elaborate explanation, because it is a matter which is affected very largely by conditions. The question must be considered from a theoretical standpoint, practical comparison being impossible because prior to the present time the work has been divided, a part having been done on contract and a part at first hand. However, experience has demonstrated that, so far as concerns the work done by the Press, it has been put out at a less price than the same work would have cost on contract with an outside firm.

The question resolves itself into an inquiry, as to whether it is possible for the University to operate the various departments of the University Press as economically as the same work could be administered by another party. Granting that it is possible to secure competent administrative ability, there is no reason why the conditions should be different in connection with the work done by the University Press from what they would be if it were executed by a private corporation. The item of labor is the same in all parts of the city. Printing stock has a marketable value which is easily ascertained, and with the volume of its business the University is able to secure as low prices as those granted to any publishing house. These and many other items of expense which might be mentioned are practically the same for all printers and publishers, and if the administrative ability of the affairs of the Press is competent, the business will show a profit. The principal saving, therefore, to the University lies in the amount of profit which would accrue to any commercial corporation engaging in the same class of work.

Aside from the saving of the regular commercial profit, there are many incidental advantages which result in an actual saving of money to the University in the operation of its own printing and publishing plant. It would be impossible without a great loss of time and money to carry on the volume of printing and publishing now conducted through the University Press if the manufacturing and publication activities were not closely associated with the local interests of the University itself. Under the present conditions, while a great saving of time is effected in the doing of all of the composition at first hand, an expense of about $1,200 per year is incurred in the item of cartage, which would be saved if all of the work could be done at first hand. It is doubtful if such work as characterizes most of our journals and books could be secured on contract with any such degree of accuracy or speed as that with which it is now accomplished. These results can be reached only by the employment of workmen trained to our particular class of work, in order that they may know in an emergency just what to do and when and how to do it. Only the editors of the journals and those in direct charge of the publication of the official documents of the University can appreciate the great convenience of having the work done on the ground at first hand.

It goes without saying that the money spent on much of the printing done by the University Press means a direct benefit to the University; and it would seem that the results of the expenditures must be measured very largely by the promptness and accuracy which accompany the issue of all printed matter. To those acquainted with the printing business the result of continuous requests for accommodations by a customer of a printing house is well known. An average printing firm cannot be induced to favor one customer as against others without using the situation as a basis for increased charges. The University has many times felt the result of situations of this kind without being in a position to remedy the difficulty. The possibility of doing all the work in its own plant would eliminate embarrassment of this sort.

The affairs of the Press have been conducted by a Board appointed by the Trustees from the different Faculties, nominated by the President, and in addition the Director of the Press and the editors of the journals. This Board conducts the work through four principal committees, namely: (1) Manufacturing Committee, (2) Publication Committee, (3) Purchase and Retail Committee, (4) Official Publications Committee. The Trustees in the regular Budget of the University make a special appropriation for each journal; also appropriations for particular books or studies.

I desire to make the following suggestions:

1. A better organization is needed for that portion of the work which includes the purchase of apparatus and equipment for the University. The connection between this work and that of the Press has not been as close as it should be. Of necessity each Laboratory must exert a large influence, not only on the character of material purchased, but also on the selection of the particular place of purchase. All of this work, however, should be conducted through a central agency, and this agency may more satisfactorily be connected with the University Press than operated as a separate division of the institution. This work requires a larger force of assistants, and deserves more careful and detailed consideration in the future than it has thus far received.

2. Provision should be made for keeping in New York city at least a small stock of the publications of the Press. Our publication list is from every point of view a most respectable one, and includes not a few books which have created for themselves quite a large demand. An arrangement can easily be made for the care of such a stock in connection with the University's of-

fice already established in New York city to handle the advertising of the Press.

3. One advertising representative cannot do the work both in the East and the West. It would be profitable to establish in Chicago, as well as in New York, an office for securing advertising for the journals. To this office also might be committed the care of such announcements in the magazines and papers as the University desires to have made from time to time of its various Departments, as well as the advertising business of the Press itself.

4. It is important for the sake of the University as well as for the success of its publications that proper representation of the Press be secured in England and on the continent. Nothing that has been done thus far seems altogether satisfactory. One of two policies must be decided upon: either to concentrate the representation of the Press and select one representative for the work of all the Departments in London and another on the continent; or to place different books and journals with different dealers in England and on the continent. On the whole, the former policy seems preferable. An effort should be made to secure a proper arrangement within the near future.

5. It will be necessary within a year to give to the Press a larger proportion of the Press Building than it now occupies. If the Law School can be transferred to its new building October 1, 1903, the space now occupied by it can be satisfactorily used by the Press and a small portion of it perhaps given to the Library; but it is necessary, from the point of view of the Press, that the erection of the new Library Building be finished as early as possible. At the present rate of progress the Press will require within three years every foot of space afforded by the present building.

6. The members of the University at large should cultivate a closer sympathy with the work of the Press. As individuals and as a University they are to derive from it great benefit. The measure of this sympathy, however, may be determined by the degree of knowledge which is possessed by members of the University. It seems important, therefore, that regular reports should be made by the Director of the Press to the Congregation of the University, such reports to cover in general the work of the Quarter closing at the time of the meeting of the Congregation.

Decennial Report, 1 July 1902

A GENEROSITY OF MIND

BURTON

Let me just say, in a few words, respecting dissemination, that the university recognizes that its duty is not only to find out truth, but to give to whatever it discovers the widest possible publicity. No university professor patents his discovery. From the foundation of the University, there was incorporated, as an essential part of it, the University Press, and from the beginning honor has been given to the man who publishes the results of his work, in other words, to the man who having discovered something which can be of use to the scholars of the world, puts it on the printed page and sends it out to the world.

"The Business of a University." The Chicago Association of Commerce and The University Club of Chicago, 1923

BURTON

In the founding of the University, President Harper emphasized as complementary functions of a university, discovery, education, and dissemination. It is the business of a university not only to instruct its students, but on the one hand to discover new truth by research and, on the other, to give it to the world by publication.

This conception demanded the creation of a University Press; for publishing houses conducted for pecuniary profit cannot be relied upon or even expected to publish the results of research, many of the most valuable of which will never pay the cost of publication, still less yield a profit.

The University Press had a long period of struggle and difficulty, but it is now firmly established, the largest and most successful University Press in America, not yet equal to those of Oxford and Cambridge, but on the way to rival them. Its contribution to the effectiveness of the University by furnishing an outlet for publication of the scholarly studies of the faculty, and by its maintenance of the University's twelve scientific periodicals, has been almost incalculable. It is happily no longer necessary to ask for money to support it or to draw upon general funds to meet deficits. But it still offers an admirable oppor-

392

tunity for those who would promote the publication of financially unprofitable but scientifically valuable books to contribute to the University subsidy fund to make such publications possible. Such funds will always be needed and will always be useful.

"The University of Chicago As It Should Be in 1940:
A Confidential Statement by the President," 1925

KIMPTON

The University of Chicago Press, the oldest university press in continuous existence in the United States, has successfully weathered a personnel storm and moves forward in a most promising way under the new leadership of Mr. Morton Grodzins. Fifty-five new books were published during 1951–52, ranging from scholarly monographs of the most esoteric nature to a national best seller. The Press continues to dispense knowledge at a proper rate and at an alarming deficit through publishing a large proportion of the nation's scholarly journals. I am pleased to return to our older tradition of having a faculty member as Editor of the Press, and I sense already a closer relationship between the Press and the research and educational activities of the University and of the scholarly world in general.

State of the University, 14 October 1952

THE EXTENSION DIVISION

BURTON

The principle of dissemination led also to the establishment of the University Extension Division, whose work is still going on prosperously.

Alumni Gathering (Chicago), 24 March 1925

HARPER

In many respects the results accomplished in the University Extension Division have exceeded all expectations. The number of centres organized, the number of those who attended the lec-

ture-studies, and the general interest manifested have been al-
most phenomenal. Every effort has been made to restrict the
number of organized centres in the city of Chicago in order that
the reaction in the coming year might not be too great. Up to
this time 122 courses have been given, and these courses have
been attended by nearly 20,000 people. It is gratifying to say
that the work of the class department is steadily increasing. It
is manifest to all that in this class-work, as organized inde-
pendently or in connection with the lecture study work, the real
results of University Extension are to be looked for. The work
is still in its infancy, and no man today can tell us the shape or
form which it will assume in later years. It is enough, however,
to know that by means of it the University is enabled to give
intellectual stimulus to many thousands, and, in turn, to receive
the sympathy of those thousands in its educational work. The
gulf between the University and the masses has grown wider
and wider in the years that have passed. There will always be
such a gulf, but the future will see it greatly narrowed. We all
see dangers in this work of University Extension. It will be a
serious matter indeed if our friends make the mistake of sup-
posing that the work thus done is really university work. Would
that it were such, but, in the nature of things, this is impossible.
Unless in the future a larger proportion of those who attend the
lectures do the actual work prescribed, and take the examina-
tions, there is danger that these lecture studies will partake
more of the character of entertainment than of instruction. Until
the University Extension audience will consent cheerfully to at-
tend courses of twelve lectures, it being understood that in
these twelve no more ground is to be covered than some of our
lecturers now pass over in a single lecture, it must be confessed
that a high standard has not been reached. But these things will
come. The age in which we live is an age in which every intelli-
gent man demands instruction. Who are so able to give it as
those selected for that purpose by the University? What agency
so well adapted to guide this work as the University? The men
who do it must be strong men and cautious; strong in their
ability to grasp the subject of which they treat, cautious, lest in
the presentation of it wrong impressions be conveyed. I deny
that a popular presentation of a subject is necessarily unscien-
tific; some may preach truth in many departments without be-
ing technical.

The work of University extension is a great work, and although we may not be able to foretell in detail the form which it will take in the future, it is, I make bold to say, a permanent work; one which will grow in dignity and which will assume an importance larger than many of the educators to-day conceive possible.

Convocation, 1 April 1893

HARPER

It was expected that this year the University Extension lecture work would show a marked decrease. So great was the interest manifested throughout the first year of the work, that a reaction seemed to be inevitable. The continuance of the World's Fair until late in the Autumn, postponed, of course, the establishment of work in the old centres and the organization of work in new centres. But contrary to expectation and in spite of hindrances, the lecture study work is greater than during the corresponding season of last year. The number of centres supplied from the University during the Quarter has been thirty-three and the number of courses given thirty-five. The number of different individuals attending these lectures has been six thousand. A most gratifying feature of the work is the fact that there has been great increase in the amount of reading in connection with the lectures and in the number of the papers prepared. The work takes on more and more the character of a permanent institution in the towns which have adopted it. The purpose of the Extension lecture work is becoming better understood. It is now seen that the aim is not primarily the assistance of non-residence students towards the completion of a college course and the conferring of diplomas and degrees, but rather the directing and stimulating of the reading and study of those who wish to read and study under direction. In every community there are many who desire to maintain systematic intellectual activity along various lines of literature, history and science. No one supposes for a moment that the University Extension lecture takes the place of the more systematic, laborious and continuous work of the college or the university. But it is clearly becoming evident that the work has an intrinsic value of its own which will insure its permanency as a part of the educational activity of the community. The problem before the University is wisely to meet this demand and to direct the interest already excited in such a way as to lead to permanent results. A steady increase has shown itself in the work of the Corresponding Teaching department, and arrangements have been made for the immediate organization of twenty-two classes in various subjects to meet in different parts of the city in order that thus the advantages of the University may be extended to those who cannot come to it.

Convocation, 2 January 1894

HARPER

When it is recalled that in the ten years the amount of $400,000 has been contributed in small sums of one, two, three, and five dollar fees for the support of a great intellectual movement, and that all of this money, with an additional $100,000 furnished by the University, has been employed in placing before the various Centers men of international reputation in the various departments of study, the significance of the movement will come to be appreciated. The University Extension work has not been conducted as an advertising scheme, and yet it has without question brought many people, old and young, into contact with University thought and life who otherwise would not have known such contact. It is probably true that the work has been appreciated by college graduates more than by any other single class of people. They have found that in the midst of the activities of life something is needed as an incentive and help in stimulating their intellectual development. . . .

The steady advance of the Correspondence-Study work is noteworthy. Very frequently propositions have been made to popularize this work and greatly increase the number of students who have availed themselves of its service, but these propositions have been uniformly rejected. The work done by correspondence in connection with the University is as serious and as strong as any work attempted in the classroom. It is in large measure conducted by those who are at the same time doing the classroom work of the University. It is asserted by the instructors that in most cases twice as much actual work on the part of the student is called for. There is no other correspondence work being done which does not have for its primary object the making of money. Academic traditions have been respected, and the work may justly be said to have been conducted exclusively on an academic basis. In view of the great amount of correspondence work offered in every section of the country, there has been some question in the minds of the University authorities as to whether reproach might not come on our own institution because so large an amount of the instruction elsewhere offered is valueless. On the other hand, we have to recall the fact that hundreds of institutions called universities are offering degrees for work of a decidedly inferior character, but this does not take away the responsibility of institutions attempting to give instruction of the highest order. The friends of the University may rest assured that the Correspondence work done under its auspices is at all times exactly on a par, so far as its character is concerned, with the work done in the lecture-rooms of the institution. It has been a source of satisfaction to note the change of attitude on the part of a large proportion of the Faculty during these last few years. At first the Faculty was rightly suspicious of the whole matter, but as the character of the work became better understood, and as one after another was persuaded to undertake courses for himself, acquaintance with the methods and results led to a change of opinion, and today it may be said that a thorough respect for it and an appreciation of its usefulness in connection with the residence instruction of the University are felt throughout the institution.

I desire to make the following suggestions:

1. If the Lecture-Study work is to hold its place in the future, a larger staff of lecturers must be employed. The present staff is not able under the highest pressure to meet the demands made in the various communities.

2. In order to maintain a staff of Extension men, a premium must be placed upon Extension work. This premium may take one of two forms: either (a) that of a larger salary than is paid the professor who does his work within the walls of the University, or (b) that of a shorter service for the same salary. Ordinarily the Extension professor should be allowed to finish his work in six months and be given a full six months' vacation for study and recuperation. In any case the hardship of traveling over long distances in the western territory must be compensated in some way.

3. It is extremely desirable that the officers of the regular staff of the University should be detached from class-room work and

placed in the Lecture-Study field now and then for a period of three months. The result of this will be twofold. Not only will there accrue a great advantage to the Extension work itself, but the University will be profited in having its lecturers come in contact with life and work outside the University walls.

4. The work of the Correspondence-Study Department will never be thoroughly established until a separate staff of officers shall have been created. It is too much to ask the regular officers of the University to increase their duties, even with extra pay, by conducting individual Correspondence work. Besides, this movement has now reached a point where it deserves the full and continuous consideration of men whose whole time shall be devoted to it. It is important that the Correspondence staff be organized at an early date. . . .

In addition to these regularly matriculated students, during the last two years, after the dropping of the Class-Study Division, a certain number of students has been cared for by the University College in classes away from the College rooms. Very many of these are matriculated students of the University, but many are not. They should, however, be taken into consideration, in the figures of the University College, because many of them are doing the same kind of work as is done at the University College, and they are constantly being drawn into the University College classes proper. . . .

An attempt was made to adjust the courses to the demands being made from time to time, and the result was, taking the fourth year as a typical year, that courses were organized in the various Departments as follows: Philosophy, 5; Education, 3; Political Economy, 2; History, 5; Greek, 2; Latin, 5; Romance, 4; German, 4; English, 7; Mathematics, 2; Physics, 1; Chemistry, 1; Geology, 1; Zoölogy, 3; Botany, 2; Public Speaking, 3; Library Science, 1. At the end of the fourth year it was apparent that a splendid body of students was being helped in this way who could receive help in no other form. Many of these students had classified themselves according to the regulations of the University and were studying for a degree. Already many by means of the opportunity thus afforded have been enabled to receive the Bachelor's degree. At least four hundred students are actively engaged in the prosecution of the full college course with a view to the degree. Only a small percentage of the colleges of the United States have an enrollment of as many students.

The fact confronts the Trustees that at the end of the fifth year, 1903, the term will expire for which the gift was made. There seems to be no question that in no part of the University has a gift of money been used to accomplish so much as in this particular case.

I desire to make the following suggestions:

1. The work of the University College should be continued. It would be wholly inconsistent to give up this work and at the same time continue other work which the University is doing in which the returns are not so great. If, by the expenditure of six or seven thousand dollars, four or five hundred students can be assisted in carrying on their studies for a college degree, the work done as indicated is the most economical of any higher educational work in the country.

2. It is important that more suitable quarters be obtained than those the College has occupied during the five years of its history. These rooms are not as accessible to students from the West and North Sides as is desired. The fact that so large a part of the Studebaker building is occupied by teachers of music occasions constant noise, which proves to be a source of annoyance to those engaged in the usual recitation-room work of the College.

3. There is room for a much larger development than has yet been secured. The provision which has recently been made by the Board of Education for promotion and increased salaries on the basis of examinations passed will prove a great incentive, and whatever other sources of help may be offered to teachers of Chicago by the Board of Education or by other institutions independent of the Board of Education, it is apparent that there is no agency to which the teachers may come with so much profit as to the University College, partly because the work done in the University College will count for a University degree as well as for the examination looking toward promotion and increased salary. The small fee charged will not deter many from entering the classes.

Decennial Report, 1 July 1902

BURTON

Among the plans outlined in the early bulletins of the University is one for the association of colleges in the western cities with the University in a way which should enlarge the usefulness of the University and render a helpful service to the colleges themselves. It was with the same breadth of vision and purpose of making the University helpful to the largest possible number of people that from the outset he [President Harper] also included in his plans a University Extension Division. This phase of the University work, through which it was to send out lecturers and teachers into the cities and towns of the west, and to conduct instruction by correspondence with pupils throughout the world, was looked upon with grave suspicion by some of those who were associated with him in the early history of the University. Men accustomed to feel that university work could be done only in university walls and under the immediate oversight of the resident university professors, could but fear that the attempt to carry the thought or spirit of the university to the people by way of lectures and classes and correspondence lessons would result in a lowering of educational standards and a conceit of knowledge without its reality. But the President never for an instant wavered in his judgment or in the steadfast maintenance of his policy. His previous experience in correspondence work, begun while he was still professor at Morgan Park, and in lectures and class room work conducted by himself in Philadelphia, New York, New Haven, and Boston, had given him unshaken confidence in the possibility of conducting work of this kind effectively and helpfully.

"President Harper—The Educator." *The Monthly Maroon*, January 1906

BURTON

It has always been a part of the policy of the University of Chicago to extend its opportunities of education as widely as possible. At its founding this spirit found expression in what was then known as the University Extension Division, in the Lecture Study Division in which the lamented Richard Green Moulton took a leading and effective part. Later it found a new outlet in the establishment of University College, which since has offered courses of instruction by members of the University faculty in the down-town district in the late afternoon and evening when persons obliged to spend most of their day in earning a living can have opportunity for regular university work. The Dean of the School is instructed to conduct all its work with the same quality of instruction and the same requirements for credit which are maintained in the other colleges and schools of the University. In the year 1923–4, 108 instructors were employed in this college, 197½ major courses were offered, and elected, and 2887 different students were registered.

The opportunity for service of the city through University College is much greater than the University is now meeting. Subject to the provisions that instructors shall not be encouraged or permitted to take on an amount of work which will prevent their doing their work at the University or down-town thoroughly, there should be a great increase in the number of courses offered and of students taking them. It is to be desired that work of University College now conducted in rented rooms at 116 S. Michigan Avenue, should be carried on in a building to be owned by the University, bearing its name and housing all its down-town activities of all kinds, including its business offices. To the work of the University College might well be added popular lectures on science, literature, history and art. Such a building would undoubtedly materially increase the influence of the University upon the City. How much the Art Institute and the Field Museum gain in this respect by being at the front door, so to speak, of the City, is well known.

Of purpose similar to that of University College, but appealing to a still wider public is the Home Study Division of the University Extension. It dates from the founding of the University and for thirty-two years has been giv[ing] to people in all parts of the world who could not come to the University, opportunity for University instruction by correspondence. Its students last year numbered 6912. It is self-supporting except for the space it occupies and heat, light, and janitor service. It is at present housed in Ellis Hall. Before that building is torn down, as it must be soon, the Home Study Division should have permanent quarters in a permanent building.

Of like purpose with the Home Study Division, but working wholly in the sphere of Religion, and employing somewhat more popular methods, is the Institute of Sacred Literature, founded by President Harper in 1889, incorporated in the University in 1905, and conducted with an increasing number of students and a growing body of instructional literature since that time.

"The University of Chicago As It Should Be in 1940:
A Confidential Statement By the President," 1925

WE WILL BE HEARD

HUTCHINS

Northwestern, Loyola, and Chicago have joined with the local broadcasting stations and the national chains to supply a comprehensive program of education by radio in the Chicago area. The Rockefeller Boards and the Carnegie Corporation have indicated a willingness to co-operate in financing the organization. It will provide a clearinghouse for programs and a unified direction of them. The moving spirit in this enterprise has been Mr. Allen Miller, director of our radio work, who will be the executive of the Council when it gets into operation in the fall.

The Superintendent of Schools has been interested in having teachers continue their education. Northwestern and Loyola have developed work which will be very popular; for it leads to the M.A. degree, which is conferred without a thesis on the basis of credits obtained in vocational courses. Our Department of Education rejected similar suggestions; but with the enthusiastic support of the Superintendent it has organized seven seminars in special topics for the leading members of the system in School Principalship in Chicago, Curriculum and Instruction in the Junior Colleges, Curriculum and Supervision, The School and the Social Order, Statistics and Measurement, Educational Administration, and Educational Psychology.

"Report of the President 1934–35" (Unpublished)

THE DOWNTOWN CENTER MATURED

KIMPTON

University College, which offers a unique opportunity to reach our community at the adult level, must employ its teachers from outside our ranks. We do not gladly teach, and certainly not in the evening.

Trustee-Faculty Dinner, 13 January 1954

402

KIMPTON

University College, our center for adult education in the Loop which also operates a lively center for Home-Study, has much in common with the Laboratory School. It has an old and valued tradition going back to Harper; adult education, even if no one understands what it is, is admitted by all to be important; it plays a significant role in our relations with our community; and, finally, it is underpaid, badly housed, and underprivileged. Most of our schools and departments have ignored the opportunity afforded by University College. Some have developed joint programs, but, too often when these programs achieved distinction and success, they have been withdrawn from the College and have gone their separate ways. Dean Maurice F. X. Donohue, who seems to take delight in discouragement, has proceeded to launch new programs and hire new people and has produced in his four years of office a 50 per cent increase in enrolment in University College and a 100 per cent increase in Home-Study. It is said by certain campus purists that some of the courses should belong in no curriculum that bears the name of Chicago and that a good part of the teaching is done by blind who lead the blind. If there is any truth in these harsh words, the answer is an easy one: Dean Donohue would be pleased to have the guidance and services of the Quadrangles to elevate the quality of his program. In the meantime the show, full of zeal and enterprise, goes on, commanding almost as large an audience as our combined graduate and undergraduate campus enrollment. At the present rate of increase, the time will come when it will need to rent and heat Soldier Field to seat its students; and we on the Quadrangles need to give some careful thought to the standards, program, and teaching in adult education.

State of the University, 5 November 1957

KIMPTON

It may or may not be true that every great university has a kind of *Geist*, or character, or unity; I only know that this one has. As I read our history, we had it the day our doors opened, and there has been no significant change since then. All sorts of people, including me, have tried to monkey with it, but nobody can win.

One may like or dislike it, but there it is. It is not too easy to put into words, but its essence is a passionate dedication to pure research and scholarship. Everything else is secondary and derivative. This is the *Geist*, the character, the unifying principle of the institution. Most of our mistakes—if one chooses to call them that—have been the result of trying to make some other objective, however worthy, superior or even equal to this. The old college is an example. It was a superbly conceived and executed enterprise. One can only say in sorrow that it did not suit the nature of the beast. To teach as a part of the quest for new knowledge has its dignity; only to teach has none at this University. And our current difficulties at Downtown College are again related to this problem. Since the turn of the century, we have instructed adults in a Loop location, and most would agree that this activity is important, both in itself and as a part of our service to the community. But, here again, this teaching has not in recent years reflected the *Geist* of the institution; it is not the University of Chicago.

If this is our genius, so be it. It is a mark of maturity to accept one's fundamental character for what it is and proceed to solve life's problems within its context.

State of the University, 3 November 1959

KIMPTON

Another very interesting case that has claimed the Board's attention this year is University College, our downtown adult education center. Without knowing much about University College, the Board has been inclined to think rather well of it upon the grounds that they have been told that adult education is important, they know some people who have profited from work there, and their general impression is that the activity seems to have some public relations value for the University. They were therefore surprised to learn that a faculty committee had unanimously recommended its abolition. I explained that the fundamental criticisms were that the enterprise was costing us money, the work was being done chiefly by non-faculty people, and that most of the courses, though offered in the name of the University of Chicago, did not meet the standards of our faculty.

Trustee-Faculty Dinner, 14 January 1960

BEADLE

As you all know, the University of Chicago pioneered in this area, beginning way back with William Harper and has continued a program of extension ever since. Over the years, participation in the interest of the regular faculty has gradually decreased. Recently, under the leadership of John T. Wilson and Arthur Heiserman this trend has been reversed. A number of activities have been dropped in the program. For example, career development, law for non-lawyers, graphic arts, conversation as an art, parent-teacher programs and reading comprehension and speed.

Most of the credit courses have been moved to the quadrangles beginning this term. These are now the responsibility of the appropriate academic units in the college, in the divisions and in the schools.

The results have been successful beyond the expectation of many. Enrollments have dropped moderately. . . .

The plan now is somewhat different. It used to be three hours once a week, all in one step. It is now two one and a half hour [classes] on two separate nights, which may have some influence.

Also, sections both at the quadrangles and at the downtown center had to be closed because of no more room. Therefore, the registration was artificially held down for lack of facilities and space.

The desire of regular college students to elect late afternoon and evening classes in preference to those given at regular hours has turned out to be far greater than anticipated. Some two hundred students are involved and the number would have been greater had it been permitted.

This year, and the 1963–64 academic year, will be important in determining the demand for extension work as well as the level of interest and involvement of the faculty.

I know that the faculty, administration and Board of Trustees are deeply grateful to Mr. Wilson and Mr. Heiserman and others of the extension department for their very effective efforts in the difficult task of reorganization of a program to which faculty, administration and board have reaffirmed a commitment.

In a world of rapid change, continuing education for adults assumes a greater and greater importance. I hope we can continue to play an effective role.

State of the University, 6 November 1962

405

REACHING OUT INTO THE SUBURBS

LEVI

As one result of these studies, we came to the reluctant conclusion late last autumn that it would be necessary to close the present Downtown Center of the Extension Division. The loss to the University of the operations of this Center has been running at the level of about $300,000 a year.

The University has been a pioneer in the development of extension work. The original plan and first announcement of the University included evening courses in college and university subjects for men and women in and about Chicago whose occupations would not allow them to take the regular work on the campus. They also indicated that correspondence courses would be given in college and university subjects for students in all parts of the world. The correspondence school program continued until 1963 when it was terminated. The copyrights for 55 syllabi were then sold to the University of Wisconsin to supplement the extensive program run by that institution. The lecture-study program developed from 1892 until 1911, when financial losses caused its termination. It had operated through various centers around the city. Extension work, through University College, during that period, was able to sustain a Downtown Center, largely through the subsidy of a private donor. When that subvention was removed, financial losses compelled an attempt in 1906 to transfer the work to Blaine Hall on the campus. In that location the enrollment all but disappeared, and University College in 1908 again returned to a Downtown building. By 1937 as many as 4,000 individuals were taking courses in a degree-granting curriculum or in one of the cooperative programs with other institutions or businesses. The growth of competing extension programs, as was the case also with home study, cut into enrollment; increasingly questions were raised about the quality of the programs. In 1960 the faculty of the University placed the Downtown Center under the University's Board of Adult Education; in 1962 that Board recommended that all programs for credit be moved to the Quadrangles. Non-credit courses continued, however, at the Downtown location, although with declining enrollment. Among the most important offerings which have continued, and for which there is great loyalty, are those of the Basic Program and the Fine Arts Program. I have no doubt that these are excellent programs, not easily duplicated, and worthy of this University's efforts. Plans are being made to make possible their continuance in outlying areas of the city, and also in a different Downtown location which is being donated for this purpose. There will have to be some changes in tuition charges, however, and in methods of operation so that the total saving, if not $300,000, will come close to that level. . . .

In the late sixties, with the help of The Ford Foundation, and under the direction of Professor James L. Cate (and very much in the spirit of the kind of arrangements which President Harper fostered), the University developed a cooperative program with 34 private Midwestern liberal arts colleges. Under this program, 144 students eventually received Master's degrees in the Humanities from The University of Chicago. More recently the University has endeavored to provide special seminars and conferences for members of the faculties of Midwestern colleges and junior colleges. The program has been small, but perhaps it points a direction. More than 100 institutions have been represented over the last three years in brief Humanities Institutes which have been sponsored by the University. These Institutes typically run for four or five days, and may have as many as 75 participants. Last December, under the auspices of the Extension Division, some 65 faculty members from 40 private and public colleges in six Midwestern states came to the campus for three days of seminars and meetings on "The Humanist and the Artist." The major paper was delivered by Professor Leonard Meyer. Professor Easley Blackwood—noted composer and pianist as he is—gave a demonstration session of an artist at work, rehearsing a piece and speaking about it. Professors Sinaiko, Redfield, Ted Cohen, Maddi, and Neil Harris conducted seminars; artists from the Midway Studios, Department of Art, took part. Another example: the School of Social Service Administration last summer, as it had the summer before, conducted a special institute for the training of teachers in undergraduate programs in social work. Teachers from 17 colleges attended.

At the present time, the University has been discussing with the Associated Colleges for the Midwest a Summer Institute in

Far Eastern Studies for the benefit of their students and faculty. Alas, I suppose financing has been the problem, since I remember this being discussed years ago.

In cooperation with the Center for Middle Eastern Studies, the Center for Policy Study sponsored during the present year the Conference on Turkey, 1922–72, which brought together more than 100 scholars from all over the world including our neighboring institutions. Next year in collaboration with the Divinity School, the Center will be sponsoring the three-week celebration of the septicentenaries of both St. Thomas Aquinas and St. Bonaventure, with a series of lectures and discussions by ten leading theologians and scholars.

To these examples of what are, in some cases but not all, extension-type activities, reflecting so many different aspects of the University, let me add that the University, under the faculty Board of Radio and Television, is one of the largest, if not the largest, producers of broadcast time in the nation among institutional broadcasters. Programs we produce and distribute nationally total about 300 hours of broadcast time each week. The Nora and Edward Ryerson Lecture series, which will be inaugurated by Professor John Hope Franklin on April 23rd, is an attempt by our faculty to produce over the years a series of most memorable lectures, worthy of the best we have, worthy of being recorded and played many times.

I have taken this occasion to stress this history, and this kind of ongoing reaching out of educational activities, which the University has so frequently sponsored, because these activities may have a special role today. The opportunity for a continuing or renewed or first-time relationship with a university may be particularly important for many college teachers, for members of a college-trained population whose education ought to be continued, and for scholars who may find the diversity and unity of our University has much to offer as, indeed, these scholars have much to offer us.

State of the University, 8 April 1974

6

THE INFLATIONARY KINGDOM OF MIDAS

MEN MEAN MONEY

BURTON

The last thing I have to mention as a consequence of this emphasis upon quality is the necessity of a strong faculty, the maintenance of the highest possible standards in respect to the men who constitute the faculty of the University. As I mentioned at the outset, President Harper recognized in the beginning that his fundamental policy carried with it the necessity of men of extraordinary ability.

You know, of course, thirty-three years having passed away and the men of extraordinary ability who were selected necessarily being men near middle life, because they could not have proved themselves before that, now having reached the end of their academic careers, these men must now be replaced by men of equal eminence and standing. Of course, we have produced men of that sort within the period, but in no university can you simply breed from within. In addition to the men of ability you may create within the institution itself, you must be bringing in fresh blood and the best possible blood continually to maintain the highest standards, and, inasmuch as it has been our ambition not simply to make a good university but to make the best possible university we must seek also the best possible type of men, and that is a matter that involves an extra addition to our income for, though men of our profession are not particularly avaracious, they do have to buy books occasionally, at least, they do have to travel now and then, at least, to come in contact with their fellows elsewhere and maintain their intellectual standards and enlarge their horizon. While, thirty-three years ago the University paid the highest salaries that were paid in the country, that is no longer true, and other universities are paying far more to maintain these standards, and, in that regard, we must increase our resources.

Fund-Raising Campaign (Chicago), 18 March 1925

DO NOT MUZZLE THE OX

JUDSON

It is true there are still some scholars who, like Agassiz, have not time to make money. And let us thank God for them. But there are very few who do not have to take time to make a living. And so far as I have been able to observe even scholars who are most ardent in devotion to their profession find their ardor glow more brightly under the breezes of favorable material conditions. It is on the whole, I believe, said and thought to be a distinct gain for education that the head of a department in the University of Chicago is now able to earn almost as much as the head cook in a leading hotel.

"University Ideals." Date and Occasion Unrecorded
From the H. P. Judson Papers in
the Joseph Regenstein Library

BURTON

This effort at betterment we shall extend to every part of our educational work and to our research. We shall be continually trying to do all our work better for graduates and undergraduates, in the Colleges and the Graduate School and in the Professional Schools.

If this sounds a little vague, let me point out a few rather concrete things that this will involve.

It will involve considerable increased expense for salaries of professors. Do you have to bribe a man, then, to do better work?

Does it take a larger salary, then, to induce a professor to do his best? No, but it does take money to raise the level of instruction and research in an institution. Men cannot do their best work when they are worried over how to meet the legitimate expenses of their families, and cannot buy books and have to take on outside work and write potboilers. It takes a reasonable salary to enable a man to give his best to the University and to his students.

Moreover, there are only a few really first-class men in each department of knowledge—not enough to fill all the chairs in all our American universities—and when so many of the things that a man needs to enable him to do his best work take money, we cannot complain if the size of the salary has something to do with deciding which call he will accept. It takes money, and more money, to build up a strong faculty, and with our ambition for betterment we cannot be contented with anything else than the best.

Anniversary Chapel, 1 October 1924

BURTON

In all the Divisions of the University enumerated above, and in the professional schools named below it must be remembered that the emphasis will always be on the quality of the work, on its thoroughness and acuteness. What the world needs is by no means more products of study which are fairly good, or more men fairly well educated but work which is of the highest quality for accuracy of observation, keeness of interpretation, perfection of expression.

With this in mind and recognizing that what more than anything else makes a university great is great men, it is proposed to establish ten professorships, carrying a salary of $10,000 each, not to be assigned to any single department, but to be filled by men of exceptional eminence in their respective fields, whatever they may be. To hold one of the "Distinguished Service" professorships would be the highest honor the university could bestow, and to found one of them would be one of the most useful possible ways of employing $200,000.

"The University of Chicago As It Should Be in 1940: A Confidential Statement by the President," 1925

411

MONEY FOR BRAINS

MASON

During the quarter Mr. Frank P. Hixon, desiring to promote a group of Distinguished Service Professorships, offered to endow one if a group of five could be formed. Mr. C. H. Swift has allocated his gift of $200,000, previously reported, for the endowment of one. The previous gift of Mr. Andrew MacLeish, who for many years rendered high service to the University as Trustee and Vice-Chairman of the Board, has been supplemented by gifts from members of his family to a total of $250,000, and allocated to the support of a Distinguished Service Professorship and a Visiting Professorship. Mr. Sewell L. Avery allocates $200,-000 of a gift of $250,000, not previously reported, for a Distinguished Service Professorship, and the group of five has been completed by Robert Law, Jr., who agrees to augment his previous pledge of $80,000 for this purpose.

Convocation, 15 June 1926

HUTCHINS

But experiments in education presuppose men to carry them out. It cannot too often be repeated that it is men and nothing but men that make education. If the first Faculty of the University of Chicago had met in a tent, this would still have been a great University. Since the time when that Faculty gathered student numbers have swollen to an unprecedented extent; tremendous gifts have been made for special projects; and the rewards in business and the professions have mounted to heights never before dreamed of. The increase in student numbers, coupled with the desire to deal with them in small classes, has inevitably led to the expansion of the Faculty. Gifts representing the special interests of the donors have required additional appointments. The University has received $53,000,000 in cash or pledges since 1919. But only $7,000,000 of this sum was free to be used for general salary purposes, in spite of the noble efforts of my predecessors to carry on the University's traditional preference for giving first-rate rewards to first-rate men. As a result the professorial maximum, which is more important than the professorial average, has increased $3,000 in thirty-seven years. Meanwhile more and more of our best college graduates have been dissuaded from a scholarly career by the characteristic American feeling that there must be some connection between compensation and ability. It is hopeless to try to combat that feeling. What we must do is to meet it by paying salaries in education that will attract the best men in competition with business and the professions. Comparisons of salaries among universities are irrelevant and harmful. For the question is: Can we now get the kind of men we want to go into education? Since no university can answer this question in the affirmative, it can derive little satisfaction from the thought that its salaries are as low as those of neighboring institutions. And the expression of satisfaction does positive damage in leading the public to think that this matter has been settled. It will never be settled until America is willing to pay enough to induce its best brains to go into the education of its offspring and stay there. It will never be settled until professorial salaries are such as to make scholarship respected in the United States. This object will not be attained as long as professors must carry on outside work or teach every summer to keep alive. Nor will it be attained if they must live in conditions that scarcely provide them with the decencies of life. Nor shall we come much closer to it as long as our people feel that the scholar receives a substantial share of his compensation in the permanence of his tenure. I do not mean that salaries in education must be identical with those in business. Nor do I want men to go into education to make money. But on the other hand no man should be kept out of education by the certainty that he will have to live in fear of his creditors all his days, or by the feeling that the profession is a refuge for mediocrity. The only method by which we shall approach our goal is by paying salaries that will enable the universities to compete with the business world for the best men. And this policy I believe the Board of Trustees of the University of Chicago will put into effect as rapidly as its funds permit.

It is a policy about which there is nothing revolutionary. It is simply what was done here in 1891. To carry it out we must husband our existing resources, making sure that we are spending them on first-rate men for first-rate work; we must perhaps ask the student in some schools to make a larger contribution toward the cost of his education; and we must focus the attention of the public upon the fact that only through general funds for salaries can a university hope to retain its outstanding men and bring in others to join them. In this way we may carry on the greatest tradition of the University of Chicago. In this way, too, perhaps, we may give strength to its other traditions of experiment and productive scholarship centered upon the problems of our city. So may we make the future worthy of the past. So may we continue to pioneer and set new standards for the West. So may we justify the faith of the Founder, the confidence of the community, and the aspirations of the men and women who have labored here to build the greatness of this University.

Inaugural Address, 19 November 1929

HUTCHINS

At any time under any conditions there is only one way to get a distinguished university. That is to get a distinguished faculty. Whatever we may say about our deplorably small scholarship and fellowship funds, for example, we must grant that the chief attraction to good students is good professors and that if the professors are good enough the students will come to study under them even if they have to spend their own money to do it. If the distinction of this university is to endure it must continue to have a distinguished faculty.

This is, of course, partly a matter of money. Unless we can preserve a competitive level of salaries, we cannot hope to keep or secure a faculty worthy of the University. So we decided that if we could not raise our salaries, which were low in comparison with Harvard, we would at least maintain them. Although I still believe we were right, I must admit that the continuance of this policy depends on almost immediate financial recovery. On the one hand we are losing some of our best people through retirement. On the other we are dissipating our reserves. For the support of the general budget alone we have spent over half a million of those funds and are committed to the expenditure of over $300,000 more in the current year. These two processes cannot go on indefinitely. If the depression lasts much longer we shall lose our gamble on faculty salaries.

Fortunately the outlook is somewhat better than it was when the budget was adopted. Income from all sources has gained appreciably. It must gain more to erase the present deficit, and still more to allow us to enter on any plan of building up the staff. I must therefore beg the faculty to be patient a little longer and beg the trustees to continue their herculean efforts to increase the income of the University.

Important as income is to the development of a university, the example of Johns Hopkins as it used to be shows that money is not nearly so important as something else, and that is the selection of the faculty. It is possible to be very rich and very undistinguished. Perhaps I am hysterical on this subject, but it sometimes seems to me that the whole question of the excellence of a university turns on the nature of its appointments and promotions.

Trustee-Faculty Dinner, 10 January 1935

HUTCHINS

Most of the discussion of higher education in the United States is about money. Money is very important; but we ought to think once in a while about the things that money cannot do. The only problems that money can solve are financial problems. Money cannot make a great university; it can only supply the means to one. We know that millions are spent annually on enterprises called educational that have no educational value. Money cannot even buy men, because the best men will not stay long in an institution that has nothing but money. If an institution has an idea, it can use money to realize it. If it has no ideas, all the money in the world will not help it. The important problems of American education are intellectual, not financial. In this situation there is grave danger in money, for there are numerous instances in which money has been spent for purposes that could not be achieved or that should not be achieved, with the result that the institution where it was spent and the educational system as a whole have been deformed.

We all know that beautiful buildings and expensive equipment do not make a great university. Some of the best work at the University of Chicago has come out of the poorest quarters.

Which would be better, a faculty of a thousand, average fair; or a faculty of five hundred, average excellent? A large and mediocre faculty will cost more than a small but superior one. Its effect is diffuse; its example is uninspiring; and consequently it is difficult to rally the public to its support or its defense.

> "The Freedom of the University." Parents' Association of the Lab School, 1 November 1950
> Hillman Lecture. Columbia University
> 21 November 1950

BEFORE THE GOLDEN 60s, THE WORRISOME 50s

KIMPTON

There is another aspect of the inflationary spiral that I feel obligated to mention. Professorial salaries have never been high, but they have usually been adequate, and a man felt compensated in entering the academic world in large part by the fact that he was doing the work that he loved. Now the universities have not been able to increase salaries to keep up with the increased cost of living, and the problem is becoming acute. It is not unusual for a young surgeon who has chosen a career of teaching and research to be making $4,500 a year. He will be 35 years old, and, in addition to his 4 years of undergraduate work, will have had 3 years of medical school, a year of internship, and 3 to 5 years of residency where his salary has been $90 a month. The average salary at our university for a teacher in the field of the humanities is less than that earned by the average hourly paid worker at General Motors. If this work is worth doing, it is worth a living salary to those who do it.

> "Financing Private Education." Mid-Continent Trust Conference, 9 November 1951

KIMPTON

Faculty salaries are more important than new buildings at this period in our affairs. In this connection, during the four-year period 1949–53 our physical plant operation has had to absorb increased costs of roughly $540,000 because of rising costs of materials, labor, and supplies. During this same period, costs have been absorbed and expenses reduced by a total of $1,415,000 to effect a net saving on the operation of our physical plant over these four years of $873,000. This is a phenomenal record of accomplishment and gives concrete evidence that our University is operated in the interests of teaching and research rather than to burnish the gargoyles of our gothic.

State of the University, 14 October 1952

KIMPTON

We need first to recognize that the University of Chicago is now and will have to remain a small institution. Eight years ago the value of our endowment was $101,000,000. Today, after a hectic period of money-raising and after taking full advantage of the rising market in securities, the endowment stands at $200,000,000. This looked just dandy to me until I remembered that last year's *operating budget* alone for the Universities of California was $140,000,000. On July 1, 1951, we had an academic faculty numbering 788; eight years later the faculty numbers 830, an increase of 42 members. But during that same period our yearly budget increased $5,700,000, and I have yet to fear a faculty member complain of being overpaid. We have been running very hard and fast to keep even with the inflationary spiral, and some further running is indicated for the future. But the picture is not all bad. If we are to believe the recent figures of a survey made by the AAUP, our salary averages at the various ranks are equal to the very best, and this is the way they should be, only more so. Our ability to maintain and increase these salaries depends entirely upon our remaining roughly the same size as we now are. And this in turn means that only after the most careful consideration should we embark upon new activities, including, may I add, those new, innovating, "breakthrough" activities that so excite the imagination of the foundation officers. The very fact that we are a private university, accountable to the law and our own conscience, gives us a real advantage over our public sisters. We are not obligated to establish a school of engineering because there is a local need for it, or a course in harbor management because of the St. Lawrence Seaway. And there is good reason why we should take a long look at some of the things we are now doing to see if they are worth doing or if we are doing them well. Mediocrity is the single intolerable thing; when we find it, we must eliminate it if we are to survive as a great university.

State of the University, 3 November 1959

EVEN BEING EQUAL IS COSTLY

BEADLE

To a large extent size will be determined by financial resources. And there is an almost invariable tendency to grow in size more rapidly than resources permit. Collectively, everyone agrees that this should not occur, that the size of the place ought to be kept down and the quality up. At the same time each individual faculty member will argue eloquently that he could do so much better if he had a bit more space, another colleague, an increased budget for both research and teaching, an extra assistant or two, more secretarial help, and better equipment—not to mention a higher salary.

. . . I must speak of one undesirable trend in universities that is accentuated by increased government support for research in areas of science and technology. That is a trend toward greater and greater salary differentials between scientists, mathematicians, and engineers on the one hand and humanists and social scientists on the other. Such a trend would be nipped in the bud at the University of X. But in the here-and-now, many of us have responded to the competitive situation that exists by meeting market demands, rather than by establishing honest and equitable salary scales based primarily on academic competence. Almost all major universities in this country have succumbed to the temptation, some reluctantly and sadly, and some, I am afraid, without quite realizing what they have been doing. I hope we can take corrective steps at the University of Chicago. It will not be easy.

"The University of X: An Academic Equation"
Inaugural Address, 5 May 1961

418

BEADLE

It is a matter of both pride and regret that Chicago is a high-cost institution. The average salary of a faculty member at the University, figured on a nine months' basis, and with fringe benefits added, is $17,400. Last year it was $16,200. I realize there is no average faculty member with an average faculty salary, that hardly anyone understands what a fringe benefit is, and that public announcement of an average salary only leads to wives asking their husbands why they have been holding back on their paychecks. The fact remains that this appears to be the third highest faculty salary structure in the United States—considerably behind Harvard, and probably slightly behind Parsons College. Faculty salaries at Chicago have increased about 13½ per cent in the past two years. These increases have been essential to maintain the strength of the institution. They are not out of line. In fact, we wish the increases could have been even greater. We particularly wish the increases could have been greater at the junior levels, where the increase has been only slightly in excess of 11½ per cent.

Student Assembly, 18 November 1966

A DUTY TO DECIDE AMONG WORTHY CLAIMANTS

HARPER

If you wish me to tell you to-night the most pressing need of the University, I will do it in a few words. There are on the University grounds to-day three distinct heating plants, all of which are temporary. At great waste these different plants are conducted. Engineers, firemen and watchmen are required for all. No building on the grounds is adequately lighted. There is as yet no system of ventilation in our general lecture hall, nor can indeed the ventilation system of Kent Chemical Laboratory, the most perfect ever planned, be set in motion. What is it that we need? A central heating and electrical plant from which every building of the University may derive its source of heat and in which shall be located the electrical machinery which shall at

419

the same time adequtely light and ventilate the University build-
ings. This need cannot properly be classified under the head of
library or apparatus. It is, however, a necessary part of the mod-
ern equipment of a group of buildings. We need a chapel and
general library building, additional laboratories and additional
dormitories, but we need above all, and before all, the proper
facilities for heating and lighting the buildings that have already
been erected. Is there not somewhere a man who will appreciate
the great necessity of our case and render the needed assistance?

Convocation, 2 January 1894

HARPER

I desire to make the following suggestions:

1. The plans for the new Library to be located on Fifty-ninth
street in the main quadrangles should be completed at the earli-
est possible moment, and every effort should be made to secure
the erection of this building within the next two or three years.
No need of the University is greater today than that of the cen-
tral Library. The Library is, or should be, the very heart of the
institution. It will be impossible for the University to continue
its growth in any proper form if it shall be longer deprived of
this essential factor in the institutional life.

2. The time has come when the attention of the Trustees
should be given to the reorganization and higher development
of the Library staff. We may possibly be excused for the indif-
ference thus far shown to this important division of the Univer-
sity's work, but from this time forward there can be no possible
reason for lack of interest. The interest of every Department is
concerned, and now that the various Departments have been
placed upon a proper footing, their highest interest demands the
erection and further organization of the central Library.

3. Large sums of money are needed for the purchase of books
for the various Departments. The sum of $250,000 could be used
to most excellent advantage at once, and a permanent endow-
ment of $500,000, or even $1,000,000, is needed, the income to be
used in the purchase of books from year to year. It will be seen
from the figures given above that the University is even now
spending an aggregate of about $30,000 a year for books and
periodicals.

4. Some arrangement should be made by which, even before
the erection of the main building, better distribution of books

between the various Libraries may be secured. Some system of transmission may perhaps be found which will not prove to be too expensive. Investigation should be made at once in reference to the basis of this.

5. Whatever may be found to be true of the library instruction now being given, it seems quite certain that no better opportunity exists for the establishment of a School of Library Science than that which is connected with the library work of the University of Chicago. A good analogy is perhaps to be found in the Training Schools for Nurses associated with medical schools and hospitals. The University itself will be a great gainer by making use of the service of students in training for library work, and such training is more real and vital when actually connected with a large library.

6. The following Laboratories need to be added to the number already erected: (a) a Laboratory for the Geological and Geographical Departments, to be located north of Beecher Hall and east of Walker Museum, and to be connected with Walker Museum by a bridgeway; (b) a Laboratory for Physical Chemistry, to be erected on Ellis avenue directly west of Kent Chemical Laboratory; (c) Laboratories for the Departments of· Anatomy and Pharmacology, to be erected on Fifty-seventh street between Ellis avenue and Lexington avenue; and (d) a Hygienic Laboratory, to be erected on the corner of Ellis avenue and Fifty-seventh street.

7. The Museum erected by Mr. George C. Walker should be henceforth used strictly for the purpose proposed in its establishment, namely, for a museum. By the kindness of Mr. Walker, the University has been able to use a large part of the space of the Museum for class-room and laboratory work, but the time has come when this work should be transferred to some other building and the entire space of the Walker Building dedicated to its original purpose. It is true today the policy with reference to the development of museums is different from that which seemed to be approved in the first days of the University. At that time it was thought possible to bring together the material of all Departments, and to have what would be called a General Museum. Today it is apparent that each group of Departments desires to establish a museum and to have it located in the closest possible relationship to the lecture work of these Departments. In other words, the Departmental Museum seems to commend itself, after the fashion of the Departmental Library.

But, even from this point of view, it is possible to make use of the Walker Museum for several groups of closely related subjects. This matter should receive the immediate consideration of the Trustees.

8. The museum is as essential an element in educational work as is the library. It is these two factors which have revolutionized educational methods in the last quarter of a century, and yet it is these same two factors in the University equipment which are least fully developed. Our Faculties are strongly manned; the buildings are large and beautiful and numerous; the libraries are only half way developed; the museums have hardly begun. It is in respect to the libraries and museums that the greatest effort should be made in these coming years.

Decennial Report, 1 July 1902

BURTON

When so many departments of the University are in urgent need, it is difficult to discriminate. Yet it is safe to say that there is no division of the University whose need of development is more widely felt than that of the Libraries because they serve all departments and are a necessity to all. They are, however, an especially important adjunct of the Graduate Schools of Arts and Literature and of the Professional Schools which are closely associated with them. In these departments and schools the Libraries combine the functions which in the physical sciences are discharged in part by libraries and in part by laboratories. They contain the source material for research and are the work-shops of professors and students. Without adequate library facilities these departments are sorely crippled. Unfortunately, this is, in fact, the condition today in the University of Chicago.

From the founding of the University, the official term has been not "the library", but "the libraries." We have had not only a general administrative department for the purpose of purchase and cataloging of books, and a General Library for undergraduates and general readers, but a series of Departmental or Group Libraries especially intended for the graduate students in the various departments. These Departmental Libraries are located in the buildings of the various departments and schools, the School of Education Library in Emmons Blaine, Geology and Geography in Rosenwald Museum, etc. But since the erection of the Harper Memorial Library in 1911 it has housed not only the general administrative offices and the General Library, but the Library of the Modern Language Group, that of the History and Social Science Group, and that of the Schools of Commerce and Administration and Social Service Administration. This arrangement has indeed been a temporary one. With a view to providing class rooms, offices, and Libraries for those divisions of the University, as far back as 1902 it was planned to erect buildings for them in the spaces east and west of Harper. But the temporary arrangement still continues.

From the point of view both of the Libraries and of these departments, these additional buildings are urgently needed. The graduate work of the departments, all the undergraduate work, and the development of the libraries in all phases of their work are all seriously hindered for lack of this needed space.

The erection of these buildings will not, however, bring final relief to the libraries. Not long after their erection, and certainly within the period covered by this forecast, it will be necessary to decide whether a central library is to be built in which all the departments will have reading rooms, seminar rooms, and studies, the buildings of the Harper Group being devoted to the other uses of the department, or whether the plan which was approved in 1902 is to be carried into effect with the modifications which subsequent experience has shown to be necessary and a group of Library buildings united into one building and containing the General Library and departmental facilities for all the Humanities is to be erected around the Harper Memorial Library as the central unit.

Even before this question is settled and its answer embodied in buildings, the Libraries will need a large addition to their funds for the purchase of books and for the maintenance of a staff to purchase [and to] catalog the books and to serve the University public.

In the years 1911–1924 the annual expenditures of the libraries have increased from $60,446.00 to $234,486.00, the collection of books and pamphlets from about 400,000 to about 1,000,000. But even so the Libraries have not kept pace either with the great increase in the rate of salaries paid to the staff, or with the growing demands of the departments for more effective service, or with the growth of other Universities of the class to which Chicago belongs.

"The University of Chicago As It Should Be in 1940:
A Confidential Statement by the President," 1925

HUTCHINS

It would doubtless surprise you to learn that the first seven department heads I met on reaching Chicago all replied in answer to the question, "What is the most pressing need of your department?" "A new building." This does not mean that they wish to work in handsome Gothic structures. It means that departments sometimes reach a point where their work is so hampered by their accommodations that unless they improve them the department must go to pieces.

Obviously this is a question of emphasis and degree. It is as foolish to say that men should not be emphasized first of all as it is to suggest that no new buildings should be accepted. Men do come first at Chicago. They always have. They always will. We are at the moment subordinating everything to the improvement of the staff. We are again and again directing the attention of the public to the fact that funds for salaries are the one great overshadowing need of the university.

Student Assembly, 20 November 1929

KIMPTON

When a new chancellor takes office, I can assure you that the problems he is presented with soon approach infinity, and all of them are presented as equally pressing. But somewhere is *the* problem, or *the* two or three pressing problems, which may not even be among those that have been fervently presented. They may be the problems that none of us likes to face, those we thought would leave our door if we sat still and pretended we were not home. From the beginning I have regarded the problem of our community as one of our paramount problems.

State of the University, 10 November 1953

KIMPTON

But graduate education at our University also has its major problems. Our graduate training and research programs, particularly in the humanities and the social sciences, are beginning to be hurt by two serious inadequacies—our library and fellowships. The first is far more important and more costly. The University has always prided itself on weathering the depression of the thirties without cutting academic salaries, except in Medicine; but it cut every place else, and particularly the acquisition program of the library, since this was relatively painless. For reasons I do not altogether understand, the library budget was never really restored as times improved, and the cuts of the early fifties imposed a double liability. It is still a fine library, although more because of purchases in the first quarter of this century than in recent years, and the parsimony of acquisition has begun to have the cumulative effect of real deterioration. We were able to increase the budget of the Library 13 per cent this year over last year, and a further increase will occur next year. But this is by no means all our problem. At a structure to house the collection, Harper Library has come to the point where, almost literally, a book must be got rid of for a new book to be added. It is cold comfort to console ourselves with the fact that collections of other institutions are inadequately housed. The problems of obtaining a large capital gift for an expansion of Harper or a new building altogether and of providing an even more generous operating budget for the Library have become matters of major concern to the faculty, administration, and Board of Trustees. I am not without hope that some genuine progress will be made on these problems during the next several years.

The second inadequacy of our graduate program is the number and size of our fellowships, if we are seriously to compete with universities of comparable stature. A strange phenomenon of our times is that students pursuing the Ph.D. degree must be paid to pursue it, but there is no point in growing moralistic about this, since it is a fact. The sciences are reasonably well taken care of through federal and industrial fellowships and teaching and research assistantships. I am reliably informed that no graduate student in chemistry has paid his own way for years, but such is by no means the happy situation in the humanities and social sciences. Since there is nothing so frustrating to a faculty member as to lose a good graduate student or instruct a bad one, we must elevate our fellowship stipends to compete for the best.

State of the University, 11 November 1958

KIMPTON

Q. Well, I think that was a good question before—about the major problem facing your successor, whether we have one or what are the major problems?

A. I have difficulty in answering that question because really the problems of the new Chancellor are of his own making. Now what I mean by that is he selects the things that he feels need emphasis. If you take in my own case, and I have tried to outline those, you know I had a neighborhood problem and a serious one. I had also a problem with the College, I had the professional schools which were in bad case, I had the financial side of the institution which was in bad shape, and these were the things that demanded attention or so it seemed to me at that point. Moreover, I have to go on to say that they were the things that I selected as important. What my successor will select as important I really don't know.

Farewell Press Conference, 29 March 1960

BEADLE

I would next like to go to a high priority need, the library. We have a library of high quality but, for lack of financial support, it has fallen behind in quantity, in services and in its physical facilities. A new general library is the number one item on our priority of physical needs. This will necessitate an expenditure of some ten million dollars.

The tentative site is that of the tennis courts at 58th Street and University Avenue. I want to emphasize that this is tentative. There are some other possibilities.

In addition, it is recommended by the science division that a sciences library be constructed near 58th Street and Ellis Avenue. I want to say that given the meager financial support he has, Herman Fussler has done a remarkable job of keeping the library at the high level it now is.

State of the University, 6 November 1962

BEADLE

For decades the faculties and librarians have dreamed of an adequate library. It is without doubt the greatest single physical need of the University.

The plans, prepared under the dedicated, skillful and time-consuming supervision of Mr. Herman Fussler, University Librarian, are now made, and they are magnificent. They will be available for inspection following this report.

You will see plans for a truly great building—to be ideally located on Stagg Field. Incidentally, Stagg Field will be relocated diagonally to the four-block area to the north and west.

You will see a flexible plan that will house all graduate libraries except those of the natural sciences. Stacks and spacious reading rooms will be adjacent to one another on each of the five floors.

There will be a variety of study facilities, with seating capacity for 2,400, not counting the faculty wing that will include 260 private studies.

State of the University, 9 November 1965

LEVI

The pressure of budgets has its good side. It makes us not only count our blessings but set our priorities. Our priorities are clear. We have given most emphasis to faculty salaries, scholarships, and the needs of the library. Our faculty salaries on the average are second highest in the country. I wish they could be higher. Over the last eleven years the greatest increases in the regular budget of the university have gone, with the exception of one professional school, to the College, and then to the Humanities Division. This reflects the determination of the university at a time when greatly needed scientific support has been coming in part from governmental sources, but which in turn has been matched in considerable amounts by university funds, not to permit a distortion of university life and goals.

"The Shape, Process and Purpose of the University of Chicago." Class of 1971 Assembly
24 September 1967

LEVI

I almost hate to see a new building go up, because I suspect that all the students and many of the faculty think the way you get a new building is to have two old buildings get together.

Interview in Los Angeles *Times*, 6 July 1969

AGAIN: MONEY FOR PEOPLE

LEVI

Approximately 80 percent of the funds raised in this second stage will be used for professorships, programs and student aid, and for the maintenance of libraries and other essential facilities; approximately 60 percent of this amount, in turn, will be to provide supporting endowment for these purposes.

Thus a central focus of the second stage of the drive is to achieve sufficient capitalization so that the most essential activities of the University will not be left as vulnerable as they now are. This was the intention of the original endowment of the University. But Chicago is now eighth among the universities in the size of its endowment. In this sense it is an over-achiever. . . .

I must confess a constant worry as to the necessity for an enrichment of the quality of student life at the University.

. . . We have a magnificent library; the best in the country. Nothing like that can be said of our athletic facilities. They are woefully inadequate. The most recent athletic facility is the Field House which was dedicated in 1932. The women's gymnasium—in Ida Noyes—was built in 1916, the men's gymnasium in 1902. We do not have enough handball courts, enough indoor tennis courts, no adequate swimming pool, an insufficient number of basketball courts, and no good court. I should add that the complaints come not only from the students but the faculty as well, and they are continuous. Thus, in the second stage of the drive we propose to add to and upgrade these facilities. I believe it will be difficult to raise these funds. I suppose this is because Chicago, for many years, has been less well known for spectator sports.

I am sure the University has been correct in the priorities which it has given to the academic programs, but I hope the second stage of the drive will bring us a few more of the amenities which in fact, are helpful to the programs. The Joseph Regenstein Library, the Harper-Wieboldt College Center, and soon the Cochrane-Woods Art Center with the David and Alfred Smárt Gallery are indications that sometimes this can be done.

State of the University, 8 April 1974

MANAGING FOR MINDS

JUDSON

The gift of one million dollars made by the founder in January, 1909, has made it possible during the fiscal year just closed to administer the University without the need of providing for a deficit. It is the policy of the Board of Trustees to maintain this situation permanently. The many recurring needs of the University outside the lines of provision made by current funds should be met by specific provision made for the various purposes in question before any expenditures are incurred. It is the belief of the Board that in the long run this is the wise policy, and, further, that it is on the whole the honest policy. Of course this has no reference to unforeseen contingencies in the way of disaster either to investment or to plant. So far as foresight can provide, however, the University will expend money only when it has money to expend.

President's Report 1909–10 (Typescript Draft Version)

MASON

The financial problem is ever before the Trustees and administrative officers. It is a problem of reasonable and dignified education of people in the community as to the purposes and performances of the University, and that is the only lasting way in which we may hope to obtain the support for continued growth and continued intensification of effort.

This faculty has the complete confidence of the Board of Trustees. The Board of Trustees has the complete confidence of the faculty. What a happy combination! This faculty has the confidence of those great educational boards which are supporting work in productive scholarship. It has deserved it. I am sure that it will continue to deserve it.

But above all, let us never forget, as greater assistance comes and greater physical supplies are given, as new buildings are created and life becomes academically and scientifically easier for the worker, that there is a danger. Let us not forget that the greatest handicap of all is the lack of all handicaps; that great work in Chicago in the past has been done in attics or cellars.

Therefore, with the increase of physical facilities, I hope life will not become so easy that we shall forget that he who had to struggle against the greatest of disadvantages has often given the greatest discoveries to the world. So our hope is that as the physical plant grows, and as opportunities become greater, we shall gain in output, we shall not lose in enthusiasm, and we shall carry on with greater efficiency, in the same self-sacrificing spirit of the pioneer that has dominated this institution and that I hope always will.

Trustee-Faculty Dinner, 12 January 1928

HUTCHINS

The results of the year were remarkable. We began with an estimated deficit on the General Budget of $607,503 and ended with an actual deficit of $60,623. This deficit could be turned into a surplus by a few bookkeeping changes. The excess of retiring allowances over the income of the Fund was $71,435. If this had been charged to Retiring Allowance Accumulated Income instead of to the Budget we should have had a surplus of more than $10,000. To this could be added the income of Rosenwald Suspense, now accumulating at the rate of $19,000 a year. We could and I believe should add to this the earnings of the Press, $34,360, which has been tentatively placed in the working capital fund of the Press.

In March I said to the Committee on Budget that I expected the General Budget to be in balance by the end of 1936–37, assuming no further reduction in income. Actually it was in balance at the end of 1934–35. From one point of view this is highly gratifying. The University's financial position is almost incredibly strong. Since our expenditures were reduced $1,070,000 at the low point and were in 1934–35 almost a million dollars less than in 1930–31, we had to spend only $728,684 from reserves to balance the budget[1] in five years of depression. There is still $255,900 left in General Reserve, and Rosenwald Suspense, now amounting to $1,050,828, has not been touched.[2]

1. Including Athletics.
2. General Reserve should be further increased by the addition of $56,353 obtained from the sale of the Language Series published by the Press.

From another point of view the results of the year were not so satisfactory. When the budget was made up in March we expected a deficit of $200,000 to $250,000. If we had known that the actual deficit would be 10 per cent of the original estimate, we should have constructed quite a different budget for 1935–36. The estimates of income control the educational operation of the institution.

The estimated deficit for 1935–36 is $477,259. But the estimate of endowment income is $259,000 less than the actual income received in the year just closed. The Comptroller suggests in his admirable report that the actual deficit for 1935–36 may be as little as $115,000. In view of this remark other officers of the University, known to the Comptroller as the Foolish Virgins, confidently await a handsome surplus.

If we had known that the outcome of the year would be as favorable as it proved to be, we should have made some of the replacements mentioned above; we should have given attention to pressing needs for research assistance, and we should have raised a good many salaries, including those of the lowest administrative group.

Comparing 1930–31 with 1934–35 we find that the salary cost of instruction and research has declined 21.6 per cent. Research and laboratory expense has fallen 25.3 per cent. The item for publications is 44.7 per cent less than it was. Educational administration has declined 18.4 per cent, corporate administration 14.4 per cent, and buildings and grounds 10.1 per cent. The salary cost of instruction and research was only 43.6 per cent of our expenditures this year as against 45.8 per cent four years ago. Research and laboratory expense was 6.9 per cent as compared with 7.6 per cent in 1930–31.[3]

To indicate what our salary scale is I need only say that if we were to pay our instructors a minimum of $200 a month it would add more than $22,000 to our expenses. The situation is so serious that we should now, without waiting for a new budget, raise our good instructors to $2,000, assistant professors to $3,000, associate professors to $4,000, and professors to $5,000. Establishment of these dreadfully low minima would add about $10,000 to the budget. We should also restore at once the salaries of the competent administrative people who were getting

3. Athletics is omitted from the figures for 1934–35 in order to put the two years on a comparable basis.

$2,000 or less before the reduction in administrative salaries. That should cost $30,000.

In the budget for 1936–37 we should fill the most serious gaps in the faculty, raise the salaries of the best of our younger people, and give consideration to restoring the salaries of the competent members of the Administrative Staff who were getting $5,000 or less before the cut. In other words we should begin to rebuild the University, acting on the assumption that we are in a strong instead of a precarious financial position.

I realize of course that the Carnegie Corporation grant for the New Plan has expired and that the General Education Board grant for the same object expires next year. Because of the real estate in which it is invested Rosenwald Special may not be much longer available for the support of the budget. The redemption of many bonds and reinvestment at current interest rates may cut our income from bonds. On the other hand it should be possible to induce the Carnegie Corporation and the General Education Board to continue their assistance; the real estate in Rosenwald Special could be transferred to other accounts; and increased income from stocks, real estate, mortgages, and students should more than offset any decline in bond income.[4]

We may also expect some increase in gifts. The University has received $7,290,380 in gifts for endowment since June 30, 1930. The capital loss of $4,500,000 that we have sustained since that time can and should be wiped out by new money. The Birthday Fund, to which the Trustees alone have generously subscribed more than $40,000, suggests that we can do something besides reduce expenditures to secure a balanced budget.

I trust that we shall not be so preoccupied with the future that we shall sacrifice the present, and because of our desire to pass on to our successors an institution financially strong, pass on one that is educationally weak. With the tendency that we have occasionally exhibited to build up funds for all kinds of purposes, depreciation, amortization, replacements, working capital, and whatnot, we have sometimes seemed likely to starve to death with money in our pockets. Or as another officer of the

4. Some indication of the possibilities of recovery in student fees may be found in the fact that the Laboratory Schools produced $105,000 less than in 1930–31; the Law School $67,000 less, and room rents and Commons $35,000 less.

University has put it, we have threatened to carry so many life preservers that there would be no room for cargo. The future of the University, financially and educationally, will depend on the excellence of the faculty. For five years we have been compelled to ignore this fact. Now that we have come through the worst that can happen to us and still have fluid resources that must be the envy of any other institution, we should devote ourselves unremittingly to building up the staff and providing them with the facilities for their work. Recognizing the necessity of conserving our assets and aware of an obligation to make the community understand our aims, we must press on to achieve the essential purposes of the University, the development of education and the advancement of knowledge.

"Report of the President 1934–35" (Unpublished)

WE DO TRY TO UNDERSTAND HOW

KIMPTON

All these things are the result of the freedom, the flexibility, and the willingness to pioneer that mark the private, endowed institution. It is worth financing because it makes for progress, for constructive change, in precisely the same way that private enterprise as opposed to government monopoly makes for progress and for constructive change. And now let me pass on to this problem of financing private education.

The operating budget of the University of Chicago for the present year is 20 million dollars. Our gross operating budget runs about 48 million dollars a year because of a large project we currently conduct for the Atomic Energy Commission, but let me limit myself to our operating budget. Of this 20 million, roughly 5 million comes from income from our endowment which at book is valued at 70 million dollars, and at market at 100 million. Five million comes to us from the tuition paid by our students and five million from the patients in our hospitals, which, may I say in passing, are the chief marketable items we have. And if you have followed my arithmetic, you will note that I am five million dollars short, which is approximately the amount that we must raise each year from individuals, foundations, business, and the Federal Government. This is primarily the job of the head of the institution, and if you become annoyed at us poor college presidents of endowed institutions who so persistently rattle our tin cups in the marts of trade, take pity on us. The beggars in the streets do not know what trouble is.

This gives you a rough outline of our financial situation at the University of Chicago, and it is not dissimilar from that of the other large, endowed, independent educational institutions of the United States. Now, may I outline some of the problems we face, many of which as I mentioned before will have a familiar ring for you.

Under our present system of income taxation, very few are able to accumulate large estates which in the past have been used so generously to endow our universities. And with our system of inheritance taxes, such large estates as have been accumulated in the past are being dissolved. The day is rapidly drawing to a close when large capital gifts will come to an educational institution. The situation is not much happier with gifts from the income side. Gross incomes are currently high, but whatever the income, the take-home is small, particularly in the light of the present cost of living. The 15% deduction, offhand, sounds generous; it is a cheap dollar that is being given away, but too often the man needs whatever is left him of this dollar after taxes to live. This makes the problem of money-raising for educational purposes—in the words of an English friend of mine—difficult, not to say tough.

Along with the problem of raising money goes that of the purpose for which it is raised—and I can assure you that this very often miscarries. A dear and sweet old lady proposes to do something unusually generous for the University of Chicago, and we find that we are heir to a substantial fund to provide scholarship assistance to orphaned girls, residents of Brown County, Kansas, who have a farm background, and at least one of whose ancestors fought in the War of 1812, it being further stipulated that the entire fund shall be spent for the purpose indicated and none for the administration of the scholarships. If we accept the fund, we spend a dollar of our precious free money for every dollar of the legacy, trying to locate the appropriate girl in Kansas. This is obviously an extreme case, but you would be amazed to know how many buildings are given without an endowment to equip, heat, and light them; how many research funds are offered to investigate problems in which we have no interest and which would lead to an expansion of our staff and hence our out-of-pocket costs. A university can easily get itself into the paradoxical situation of going broke by accepting the wrong kinds of gifts.

Along with the problems of raising money and trying to make it, when raised, of real value to us, goes this bothersome matter of increasing costs. You are all too familiar with this present-day phenomenon in your own business for me to labor it in mine. But I would like to mention a few special curves that we in the University world have added to the spiral of inflation. There was a time when magnificent work in physics, for example, could be done in a barn with a few pieces of hand-made equipment for apparatus. The story has it that the great Sir Isaac Newton developed the theory of gravitation with nothing more elaborate than an apple falling on his head. We could afford to corner the apple industry in the United States for what it costs us to set up and operate a laboratory for modern research in physics. We have just spent 8 million dollars for a nuclear physics building, 2½ million for a cyclotron, a million for a betatron that was out of date by the time we got it built, and another 2 million for general equipment for the laboratory. May I casually mention that the cyclotron costs $1,000 a day to operate, without figuring in overhead. . . .

The last problem that I would like to mention is that the private university, unlike a business, has a very hard time passing its rising costs along to the consumer. It has only two commodities, teaching and research, and its research—at least for us at the University of Chicago—is not for sale. It represents in its progress the increasing body of human knowledge that properly belongs to all of mankind. If in our medical school we develop a new surgical technique or drug for the relief of human suffering, this belongs to the world. We cannot and should not sell it, and we don't. On the teaching side, we have doubled our tuition in the last ten years, and we feel we have now reached the breaking point. At a certain figure, the student goes to the State University or the local junior college rather than coming to us. And we are still spending at the University of Chicago almost three dollars for the student's one in the cost of educating him.

These are the problems of financing private education in the middle of the 20th Century. I believe that you will agree with me that they are tough problems. I hope that you will agree with me that the private university, free of political control and dictation, should continue to exist. If Harvard, Yale, Princeton, M.I.T., Columbia, Cal Tech, and Chicago, to mention only a few of our major endowed universities, should cease to exist, something of great value would go out of American life and thought. It is the tendency today when you get into trouble to turn to the Federal Government. I regard this as the most pernicious trend of modern times; it may solve our immediate problem, but it is building up problems on down the line that may force us at some point to change our entire way of life, and for the worse, in my opinion. I have been accused in this connection of behaving like a drunken sailor shaking his fist at a cigar store Indian, and I must admit, with a certain justification. We in the universities have accepted millions of dollars under the G.I. Bill of Rights, much of our medical research and training has been subsidized by the Public Health Service, our programs of research in the physical sciences have been underwritten by the Army, Navy, Air Force, and the Atomic Energy Commission— and we have been neither corrupted nor controlled in the process. All this I admit, but I remind you that in the final analysis, he who pays the fiddler calls the tune. Politics and bureaucracy move in slowly, but they move in. And the only justification for the existence of the private university is its complete freedom from this kind of domination. If you don't believe me, remember what happened under Hitler to the German universities, with all their magnificent tradition of scholarship, or view the universities of today behind the Iron Curtain. I do not mean to include in what I have said the relationship between the university and the Federal Government in a time of national emergency. We are good and loyal citizens, we have no communists on our faculty, we will do more than our part. It is a source of pride to us at the University of Chicago that the first nuclear chain reaction in the world occurred on our campus in December, 1942, proving the possibility of the atomic bomb and outlining the further steps necessary for its fabrication. But I earnestly hope that this state of national emergency does not continue so long that our halls of learning become indistinguishable from a corridor of the Pentagon Building.

In casting about for a solution to our problem that is consistent with our ideal of freedom, we at the University of Chicago have turned increasingly to American industry for encouragement and support. The relationship is not an unnatural one. Industry relies for its personnel increasingly on the universities. We are turning out skilled young people in physics, chemistry, biology, personnel management, law, accounting, and a hundred other fields. It is costing us far more than the tuition they pay as students to produce them, and why shouldn't American business, which receives the benefit of this training, help us with our load? There is an even more cogent reason, though harder to prove since it is less direct and immediate. The pure science of one generation is the applied technology of the next. It is the university scientist of today whose concern is only to extend the sum of human knowledge who is responsible tomorrow for a new development in the manufacture of steel, cloth, rubber, soap, gasoline, or food products. One of our chemists, for example, at the University of Chicago, in some work on free radicals laid the base for the current process of manufacturing synthetic rubber. The laws of pure science underlie the applications found in the industrial laboratory, and it is greatly to the advantage of industry to encourage the pure scientific research of the universities. Armed with these facts ·and arguments, we began talking with industry in 1945. The results at first were discouraging. "We can't give stockholders' money away; we don't need to support what the universities are going to do anyway; if we give to one, we shall have to give to all, and we can't afford it; money of this kind has to be spent in areas where we have plants, and we don't have any plant in your area; the universities are full of communists and left wingers, and we are not going to support any of those things." Interestingly enough, it was the very large companies, the ones who already had huge laboratories doing not only applied but even basic research, that first gave us a sympathetic ear. Standard Oil of New Jersey was our first contributor, and with the ice broken, some 26 other companies rapidly came along. In the years that have followed, we have extended our industrial support into the social sciences, the business school, law, and medicine, and we have sponsors of such diverse interests as du Pont, U. S. Steel, American Tobacco, Beechnut, Pittsburgh Plate Glass, International Harvester, and Union Carbide & Carbon. We are receiving at the present time over a million and a half dollars a year from

American business. I believe this is more money than any other educational institution receives from this source, with the possible exception of the Massachusetts Institute of Technology.

Our problem is still unsolved. We need more money. And perhaps even more important, we still have lots to learn about making our personnel, our facilities, and our work more available to industry. We are just beginning to build the bridge between the American university and American business so that both may easily and comfortably walk across it. Even so, much has been accomplished. American industry and the endowed university are the products of our system of free enterprise. It has become apparent to those who are willing to look, that they will stand or fall together.

"Financing Private Education." Mid-Continent
Trust Conference, 9 November 1951

KIMPTON

One of the urgent problems of private education today is money. The better the institution the broker it is, and as a result the University of Chicago is magnificently hard up. I hope we always are, because this means that we are spending all the money we can get our hands on and then some to keep our research and teaching program at the forefront among educational institutions of the world. On the other hand, it is a problem, and one which I have to solve as Chancellor of the University. We are, for example, spending during this current year $1,200,000 more than our income, and you can't go on this way indefinitely without the liquidation of the University, over which I do not propose to preside. One possibility is to boost tuition, and, if you have been reading the newspapers, you will note that other private institutions have done this. I am very loathe to do it, because it raises one more economic barrier to the serious student who deserves an education at the University of Chicago. A second alternative is to reduce our expenditure, and we are doing this in every way possible without jeopardizing the quality of our staff and program. A third alternative—and these are not exclusive—is to raise more money. The way to raise money is to have an institution of high quality and then interpret and explain this high quality to the community. This does not and cannot involve conforming to popular values and standards. A university which truckles to public opinion is unworthy of the

438

name. On the other hand, we deserve to be understood by the public and appreciated for what we are. I have tried as best I can to explain the nature and the contribution of the University of Chicago to all who will listen. Out of this, I freely confess that I hope a sympathetic understanding and appreciation will occur and support will follow. We will never accept money from individuals, foundations, or governments whose interest lies in controlling the policy of this institution. If anyone can show that we have changed our nature by conforming to public opinion, let him produce the evidence. I make no bones about my effort, on the other hand, to interpret and explain the nature and purpose of our great institution to the larger community of which we are a part. If you differ with this point of view, you can do so only on the basis that we are so odd, so different, and so out of step with the enlightened thinking of our time that we cannot be explained and appreciated. I hope this is not the case.

Student Assembly, 28 January 1952

KIMPTON

The bleak economic fact is that we cannot exist solely as a graduate institution. The cost of research, the cost of the training of the student for the Ph.D., must be borne in part at least by a substantial number of undergraduate students. There are only two sources of income that will make us secure in our precious academic freedom; one is endowment income and the other is tuition income. All other sources are precarious or corrupting or both. We cannot rely upon the whims of some fancy and illiterate fellow in a foundation who wants to titillate his board by financing some completely novel project that nobody ever thought of before. Such projects seldom have any real value. Nor can we place much more reliance on industry and government in their present state of education. They tend to buy gadgets to solve their problems, and a university is not a hardware store. I can think of one university in this country that became a second class institution by becoming almost exclusively a graduate school, and unless we are careful, we shall become a second. It is not without significance that the canny New Englanders of Harvard with three centuries and three hundred millions behind them insist that the heart of Harvard University is Harvard College.

Trustee-Faculty Dinner, 13 January 1954

KIMPTON

Our economic picture has even developed a few faint brush strokes of black to cover the prevailing color of red. The fiscal year ending on June 30, 1954, showed the black figure of $74,-895. This figure does not endanger our status as a not-for-profit institution, but as a symbol it has great importance to us all. We have balanced our budget for the first time since 1938 if we omit a couple of the war years. We have stabilized our economy, and we have righted the list in our financial ship. This has been accomplished through the efforts and patience of many people, both within and without the University. For example, our alumni in the year 1941–42 gave us $51,131, with 5,000 contributing; and in the year 1953–54, 11,000 alumni contributed $400,378. In other words, the number of contributors has more than doubled in twelve years, and the contribution has multiplied by eight. In this same connection I should mention our hospitals, including the new units that began operation during this year. Our total gross income—and, I hasten to add, our total gross expenditure—in our Medical School was the fantastic figure of $7,673,171; and I have not been aware of any diminution in the quality and quantity of research produced by our School of Medicine. But, most of all, this miracle of modern finance has been produced by all of you who with patience and a sense of high dedication have taken the bullying of the Chancellor's Office and have dispensed with services and facilities and acquisitions and salary increases. You have stabilized your University without losing your morale, your dignity, or your high sense of devotion to teaching, scholarship, and research. It is one thing, of course, to get a boat stabilized in high seas on a windy day, and it is quite another thing to keep it that way. We still have problems, but a monumental task has been accomplished.

State of the University, 23 November 1954

BEADLE

As everyone knows, government funds in support of research and training at the undergraduate, graduate, and postdoctoral levels have increased at a rapid rate since the war. Many academic people—trustees, administrators, and faculty members—fear that such support will lead to undesirable government control. There are indeed some grounds for this belief, but I am convinced there is no alternative to such support, and that if we use it intelligently it need not be feared. Increasingly, higher education contributes directly to national welfare. Though only the national government can and will support high energy particle accelerators such as the 47,000,000 dollar proton accelerator at Argonne, academic participation is essential in such a project. It is likewise essential in research related to space exploration. Right now we are proposing to the National Aeronautics and Space Agency (NASA) that it help support a large program in the natural and social sciences underlying space exploration. This effort would focus on training of the scientists and others who must be produced in larger numbers if we are to continue as a leader among nations—and such training is exactly what we are committed to, regardless of where we find support. Large programs of this type are essential if we are to remain in the forefront in important areas in which we already have deep and proper interests.

Trustee-Faculty Dinner, 10 January 1962

BEADLE

Now, the big question is where do we get the funds that we need to keep moving? The University of Chicago is different from some other institutions. We have a small alumni group, relatively. Forty-six per cent of them go into education, which means that they do not have too much money. Relatively many of the private sources of funds in this particular area have commitments to Eastern schools because of their being alumni or sending their children there. Alumni support, however, is increasing. I do not know what the figure is. It is not possible to say what it is because you have to say how you count it. I would say that it might be as low as $250,000 or as high as 2 million dollars, depending on whether you count bequests or whether you count trustee gifts when the trustees are alumni. Do those count as trustee or alumni gifts? Well, you can get any figure you desire within that range. However, we do expect that this will go up—we hope it will go up. We are working very hard on it. . . .

Foundations have been a large source of support for the university and we hope this will continue to be the case. For example, I was reading the history recently of the General Education Board. This board poured fifteen million dollars into the medical school, a going medical school of the kind that Mr. Flexner* thought it ought to be, and I am glad to say that he succeeded. I think we have certainly one of the very best medical schools in the United States.

Further, the Ford Foundation has invested some 29 million dollars in the university since it started operating and we have tried to use the argument with them that they now have so much, such a great investment in us that they cannot stop now. I don't know how persuasive we are going to be.

We receive a considerable amount of support from industrial sponsors and we are confident that this will increase. There is an increasing tendency for industry to support academic institutions and I am glad to say that the tendency is increasing to make this support unrestricted rather than restricted to special areas. This is in part in recognition of academic contributions to industry.

There have been a whole array of new highly sophisticated industries that have grown right out of academic institutions within the past few years. I can mention a few of them—Polaroid, Minneapolis-Honeywell, Minnesota Mining and Manufacturing, Raytheon, Hughes Aircraft, etc. The interesting thing about these is that most or all of them are either on the East or the West Coast. We produce plenty of academic talent in the Midwest but we do not have enough receivers in the Midwest and, therefore, something has to be done about this. Government, industry and the academic institutions are all worried about it but nobody has come up yet with the magic formula as to exactly how to break this trend. Somehow we have to provide a critical mass of receiving industry in this area if we are going to take advantage of the new developments that lead to sophisticated industries in contrast to the predominantly consumer product industries that we have in this area.

Government will certainly continue to be a source of support in many areas—physics, power reactors, space exploration, etc. Many people worry about government support. I don't know why they worry about federal government support when they

*Abraham Flexner was director of studies and medical education of the General Education Board 1913–28.—ED.

do not worry about state government support. They both look like tax dollars to me. In any case, it is perfectly clear that major academic institutions cannot continue to do what they are expected to do without massive government support. There are just too many things that cost too much money, like the kinds of instruments that go up in satellites for space investigations, at the basic science level. It is just not possible to support these mainly by academic budgets.

Take, for example, the high energy physics reactors. The reactor at the Argonne National Laboratory is a 50 million dollar installation. We cannot even build a 10 million dollar library with our own money and, therefore, we certainly could never build that reactor.

Therefore, we kind of see a triangle of industry, academic institutions and government that increasingly is working as a group. It is important that we in the university, if we are to do our part, facilitate communication here. This does not mean that we should get into applied research; it doesn't mean that we do work for the government that the government wants; it means we should do what we want to do—we should be academic institutions but, on the other hand, we should communicate with the recipients the discoveries of academic work which increasingly have rapid applications.

As you know, we have in the major stages, already almost completed in the plans, a national aeronautics and space agency science laboratory that will be constructed over by the Fermi Institute. We have increasingly come up with devices by which these massive facilities are used cooperatively. For example, the reactor and other facilities at the Argonne Laboratory are used by the members of the Midwest, the associated midwest universities, of which there are thirty-two. No one of them can support the facilities. However, collectively, they make use of these facilities. The Argonne Laboratory is indeed a national laboratory and it is a cooperative laboratory for the Midwest universities and colleges and, it is, of course, operated by the University of Chicago under contract.

Well, how will we get all the support we are going to need? Well, the trustees are going to have to do a great deal. The administration, obviously, is supposed to do it, through its development office and otherwise. Further, the alumni are going to help and, last of all, I would like to say the faculty.

I would like to say something about the role of the faculty because I think I have been accused by some of suggesting that the faculty ought to quit being faculty and get into the fund-raising business and that, of course, is absolutely not so. However, that does not mean the faculty cannot play and should not play an important role. Faculties have to say what they want, ... have to help sell what they want and many faculty members here have already helped a great deal in this respect. I think that academic areas that are successful in fund raising have been those that have been actively participated in by those therein saying what they wanted and then helping to get it. You can take some examples right here. Medicine most certainly is an example—law, business, education, the physical sciences, the social sciences and other areas to a lesser extent.

It is important that all of us understand our goals and our plans and take cognizance of them. In doing this, I do not mean that we must be one big happy family with no differences of opinion. God forbid that we should be so dull. Remember, it was recently pointed out by the Provost at Princeton University that, as a matter of fact, some tension between faculty and administration is actually desirable. I agree but there must be some effective communication and at least some mutual understanding.

Well, I would like to end up on a very minor point. A number of people have asked me, "Why do you spend all that money on tulips and petunias for the quadrangle?" Well, I would like to say that this is done for the purpose of improving morale of those who appreciate beauty as well as brains and brawn. The expense is taken care of by a special fund contributed to for this purpose by a number of friends of beauty. (Laughter)

This reminds me of a Dean of women of a well-known university with whom I was associated who said, in connection with the morale of her young ladies, "You know, the president once gave me a special fund to be used for helping discouraged and depressed coeds by sending them down to the beauty parlor to get a hairdo. I used to call that the 'Fairy Fund' until one day the president said to me that we ought to change the name of that."

Well, in honor of Miss Dean, we are unofficially calling the petunia fund the "Quadrangle Fairy Fund."

Thank you very much. (Applause)

State of the University, 6 November 1962

LEVI

There are some interesting, even though at times painful, consequences which arise from the shape of this university. Our alumni in teaching, despite the latter-day greater affluence of the teaching profession, have less money to give us. And the costs of education at Chicago are unavoidably high. A rough approximation of the cost per student per year, without including capital building costs at all, is $4,603. This is, of course, an average, but it understates the cost. The tuition, as you well know, is high, but happily not half that high. Recognizing the fact that income disparity among our students' families is probably greater at Chicago than at comparable institutions, Chicago returns in unendowed scholarship aid 32 percent of the tuition it receives. Special amounts for student support add greatly to this figure. Leaving out the Argonne National Laboratory, which the university operates for the U.S. Atomic Energy Commission and the Argonne Universities Association, and the Argonne Cancer Research Hospital, the budget comes to $117 million. If we leave out special endowed funds and funds for specific purposes, the budget becomes $62 million. Omitting the hospitals and clinics, it comes to about $45 million. Looking at the regular budget in terms of the amounts which can be allocated for the College, the divisions, and the schools directly, the figure becomes approximately $30 million. The fascinating point is that to support this budget, the university must not only count on $10 million in gifts which it assumes it will receive, but an additional $4 million to come from additional gifts or out of funds functioning as endowment. We could not possibly go at this pace were it not for the gigantic drive for funds which has been mounted by the Board of Trustees.

Class of 1971 Assembly, 24 September 1967

A LEAN PLACE ALWAYS

BURTON

It should be the ambition of a university—it *is* the ambition of the University of Chicago—to devote itself to the accomplishment of its duty within its field; to cooperate heartily with all

445

other institutions bent upon similar aims; to cast aside all materialistic aims and inferior motives; to give itself and its treasures of knowledge freely to the world. All that it seeks in the way of development is sought for this one end only: To do its part for the benefit and for the happiness of America and the world.

National Radio Address to Alumni, 24 March 1925

Harper

A university, although possessed of twenty millions of dollars, is, from a legal point of view, a charitable institution. Whatever may be its wealth or influence, its affairs are managed as are those of great charitable institutions. It does not hesitate to accept from any and every source gifts, large and small, with which to prosecute its work for the public benefit. It declares no dividends, but it gives to the public through its students every dollar paid by the students, and with each such dollar three or five in addition.

Decennial Report, 1 July 1902

Harper

The fact is, our very wealth is at once the source and the occasion of a poverty all the more difficult to bear because our friends cannot, will not see the exigencies of the case. The needs are very many and very great.

First Convocation, 1 January 1893

Harper

I desire to make the following suggestions to the public:

1. The impression which seems to have gained ground that the University, in view of the large gifts which have been made to it, is not appreciative of smaller gifts, is an entirely erroneous one. There are many ways in which a small gift can be used to the best advantage; in illustration I mention the following:

a) A gift of Twenty Dollars as a prize for marksmanship in the work of the Military Company.

446

b) Books, or money for the purchase of books, even in the smallest of sums.

c) The provision of pictures and paintings for the decoration of the many buildings.

d) The planting of a single tree.

e) The sum of $120 will pay the tuition of a poor student for one year.

f) The sum of $480 will carry him through his college course.

g) The sum of $3,000 will pay the tuition of one poor student as long as the University endures. There should be five hundred such endowed Scholarships in the Colleges of the University.

h) There should be two hundred and fifty endowed Fellowships in the Graduate Schools of the University. These endowments may be from $8,000 upward.

Decennial Report, 1 July 1902

BURTON

How are we going to do all these things, and not a few others that we have in mind but cannot state in detail, all looking to doing better work in research and giving you a better education?

For some of these buildings I am glad to say we have the money. But for most of them we have not the means, nor have we the large sums that will be necessary to provide equipment and better salaries and more instruction. For these sums we must look to our friends, and very largely to the citizens of Chicago.

A very old story was recently published in one of our Chicago papers to the effect that when President Harper was once referred to in his presence as asking people for money for the University, he replied that he never asked people for money. He only set before them the opportunity. I am not sure that we shall not ask people for money, but I am sure that we shall set before them the opportunity. And we hope that they will respond and that very soon we shall be able to begin that process of betterment that we hope will make the University of Chicago not necessarily bigger, but certainly better, not only than it is now but than any University in the country now is—indeed, the best that human skill and intelligence and money can make it.

Anniversary Chapel, 1 October 1924

THE BASIS OF THE APPEAL OUTLINED

BURTON

[Outline for Speech]

1. The University of Chicago is at a most interesting point in its history.

Avoid the word critical.

The two previous administrations admirably complemented one another and together constitute an ideal preparation for the future.

Dr. Harper a daring innovator.

Dr. Judson a conservative and constructive builder.

2. We have given much thought to what our policy should be. Now have a clear conception.

Colleges
   a) A policy of inclusion, not of exclusion.
      Wish I could lay the ghost of amputation.
   b) A policy of strengthening rather than expansion, of betterment rather than of bigness.
      No great gain in getting 1000 more students. Very great gain in making the school better.

Our great purpose should be to raise every department to the highest possible level. This will involve filling in gaps, perhaps actual creation of additional schools or departments. But this will be incidental to a policy of betterment.

Some discussion of a Slogan. The best possible University for our situation and our opportunity.

3. This policy will call

   a) First of all for increase of salaries. Competition. Increased cost of living. Have lost some men.
   b) Appointment of new men. In so doing we are looking for men of two classes and will take no others.
      1) Men of first rate ability who have already arrived. Wherever possible, the very best in their field. Mac-Lean, Keniston, Compton brothers, Craigie.

2) Young men who give promise of making good and whom we can try out.
c) Adequate Equipment.
   Swann's request for $100,000
   Manly's request for $10,000
d) Buildings
   Chemistry, Physics, Mod. Lang., Social Science etc.
e) New Departments and Schools
   Plans for Medical Schools
   A School of Politics
   Fine Arts
f) The Colleges
   Recent developments in college education not altogether satisfactory.

Ambition of the University to develop a new type of college which will have all the advantages of Oxford and Dartmouth, but also all the advantages of the new point of view in education.

4. Things already accomplished.

   a) The Medical Schools
   b) The Theology Building
   c) Athletics. The Field House
   d) The Chapel

5. Summary.

   Our ambition to develop a University.
   a) Including Colleges and Graduate & Professional Schools
   b) Of the highest quality that our wits can devise.
   c) Giving due attention to all elements,—not sacrificing one department to another.

To accomplish this will call for all the audacity of President Harper and all the wise conservatism of President Judson.

(Dated 7 November 1924)

BURTON

The Board of Education has strenuously insisted that every institution must appeal to the local constituency first and every region has responded loyally to the demand. There is no longer any occasion to fear that the West will seek to shift its share of the burden to the shoulders of the East. Our Western colleges are being endowed by gifts of prairie farmers of scanty income and meagre accumulation. In days past the men of the East have by their activity in Home Missions created bonds stronger than steel between East and West. The time has come when it should be done in education. We are one denomination East and West, with constant interchange of ministers and lay members. We cannot do our work effectively without high ideals of education and strong institutions in all parts of our land. If we would build for the future we must take not a narrow state-wide vision of our duty, but a vision from sea to sea, from the coasts to the mountains.

Nor is this a task that can be postponed. Whatever the war may demand of us by way of taxation or in gifts to the great cooperative relief agencies, we must face the fact that at the end of the war the need of Education will be greater than ever. We fight to create a new world. We must give to make the men who will build that new world. War destroys—God grant this war may destroy war itself—but to all the destructive work of war, necessary though it be, we must add construction—and for that work we shall need an army of educated Christian men and women. As we prize the future of the church, the future of the nation, the future of the world, now more than ever before must we work and give and pray for the cause of Christian Education.

> "Baptists and Education." Baptist Club of Philadelphia
> January 1918

MASON

Chicago is a free school. There were no restrictions attached by its founder to his generous gifts, the only thought being how he could best serve. So with all the men who have so wonderfully given of themselves to further the university. Let them be an example to you alumni so that you may help solve its great, its very interesting problems. All of us together will so continue in high emprise that no one need ever be ashamed of any branch of this wonderful university.

> Alumni of University of Wisconsin and University
> of Chicago (Milwaukee), 14 December 1925

MASON

The continued increase in efficiency of the University of Chicago is dependent upon its financial support, a large amount of which must come from the community in which it exists. This support cannot be obtained by pressure, but must come naturally and willingly as a result of the understanding on the part of citizens of Chicago of the aim and purposes of the University. The Citizens' Committee, under the chairmanship of Mr. B. E. Sunny, exists for the furthering of this understanding and, through its agency, recognition and appreciation of the University in the city have greatly increased.

Convocation, 12 June 1928

HUTCHINS

The departments are at present keenly alive to their responsibilities in this direction, and are anxious to improve the quality of their undergraduate work, as you are to have them.

To bring this about they will have to do more than bring more of the best of the existing staff into touch with undergraduate work. They must add in many departments, first-rate men who are interested in the problems of undergraduate education. This is entirely a matter of money. Unfortunately the method by which it has been proposed that we get this money is too simple to work at the moment, for it overlooks the donor and it overlooks the donee. The method proposed is that we should tell those who wish to give buildings to give their money for men instead. The difficulty is that this has been tried in many cases, here and elsewhere, with the results that the donor indicates that it is, after all, his money, and he knows what he wants to do with it. I have no hesitation in saying that the University has in every possible case presented this alternative to its benefactors. In some the suggestion has been accepted. In more it has been declined. But it is a mistake to assume that the University has been receiving unnecessary buildings. Every one of them, and notably the last great gift of the art building was essential to effective work. Presidents Burton and Mason found that they had to devote themselves to a building campaign in order to hold the men they had and have any chance at all of securing others. Because of their efforts the present administration does

451

not have to carry through an extensive building programme, but even at that one department of great distinction is disintegrating under our eyes because its working conditions are intolerable. One man has left it during the present quarter and we have no hope whatever of replacing him unless we can assure his successor of adequate facilities.

Student Assembly, 20 November 1929

ADJUSTMENTS FOR A NEW WORLD

HUTCHINS

The budget for 1944–45 was balanced, chiefly because a large proportion of the staff and facilities of the University was used and paid for by the government. Now that faculty members on leave are returning and the government is withdrawing from University buildings, the University will have to meet these costs, which cannot be less than a million dollars a year.

With great regret the administration recommended and the Board adopted general tuition and fee increases averaging 15 per cent effective with the opening of the Summer Quarter, 1945. The tuition charge is now $110 a quarter. There is in addition a University fee of $20 a quarter, which replaces the old special fees, such as those for registration, health service, laboratory, and graduation.

Gifts paid in during the year totaled $2,361,944, an increase of 28.9 per cent over the previous year. The striking fact about the gifts for the year is the continued decline in gifts of free money. It is perhaps inevitable that, as a university grows older, donors should regard its central work as established and should give, not to its central work, but to new enterprises representing their special interests. Such gifts place an additional drain on the general funds of the university by increasing the overhead which the central funds must bear, and the process, if carried far enough, must eventually impoverish the university. The seriousness of the situation at the University of Chicago is indicated by the fact that only 4 per cent of the gifts made to the University in 1944–45 were unrestricted. A large part of the year's unrestricted gifts came through the Alumni Gift, to which 5,405 former students contributed $122,664. Four alumni bequests, totaling $107,268, also were received by the University.

State of the University, 25 September 1945

KIMPTON

We raised over $13,000,000 this year, a million more than last. The alumni so appreciated talks from members of the faculty and administration other than the Chancellor that more alumni contributed more money than ever before except in the context of the campaign. And perhaps this is the place to mention the campaign, since this marked its third and final year. It closed quietly, chiefly because we were unable to make head or tail of the result.

We set out to raise $32,779,000 over a three-year period, and during this same period $64,655,508 in cash and pledges came to the University. But—and here we feel like the child under the lavish Christmas tree completely surrounded by presents but not the ones he asked for—the budget is still unbalanced, the book-acquisition program is unfinanced, the Law Building is not paid for, we do not have a cent for a men's dormitory or married students' housing, and our needs for the neighborhood, including a new high school, are still unmet. There is a happier side, however; if we did not get all of exactly the presents we wanted, we did still get an awful lot of presents. Sixty-six per cent of our faculty had salary increases this year of more than $385,000, and seventy-three per cent will receive increases next year of over $440,000. In addition to salary increases, there are four new endowed professorships. Since the last grim austerity year of 1955, the total budget of the University has increased $7,000,000, and $5,000,000 of this has been devoted to instruction and research. It was hard to part with such distinguished and beloved figures as Garfield Cox, Paul Cannon, Paul Hodges, Eleanor Humphreys, and Harold Urey—all lost this year through retirement—but we can hope that the 113 new people who joined us will in turn approximate them in scholarly and scientific stature.

More building is going on now along the Midway than since Rockefeller and Harper's plans coincided with the World's Fair of 1893. Some ten new construction programs have reached various stages of planning or completion during this year, and we now possess new facilities ranging from a very-low-temperature laboratory to a very-high-speed computer. During a period of business recession the value of our endowment increased by $11,000,000, and the canny Parker Hall managed to earn 6.2 per cent on the book value of our endowment through complex transactions ranging from United States government bonds to Havana Harbor. Even our enrollment increased this year, up 13 per cent at the undergraduate level and 7.1 per cent over all. In order to support all these buildings, activities, new appointments, and salary increases, we have been forced to raise our undergraduate tuition to $900 for next year, and our graduate tuition to the same amount, but by a lesser percentage. The fiscal-physical side of our house is in reasonably good order; we need more money, of course, but I gather from reading similar reports by heads of other educational institutions that *this* problem, at least, is not peculiar to the University of Chicago.

State of the University, 11 November 1958

BEADLE

To keep our top scholars and attract more, we must have dollars. These are needed for salaries, for libraries, for buildings, and for the machines that are of increasing importance in both teaching and research.

The budget of the current academic year is about $35,000,000, excluding the Argonne Laboratory and large government grants and contracts. That's ⅙ total endowment. For next year we will increase this by about $2,000,000. That is the income on fifty or sixty million dollars of endowment. Even so, it is only about a six percent increase, barely enough to keep up with minimal salary increases and general increases in costs. (We ought at least keep up with the Kennedy administration.) Obviously, we must look forward to greater increases than six per cent a year if we are to make significant advances.

In addition to such annual increases in operating budgets, we have obvious needs for buildings and major items of equipment. Even mathematicians, who traditionally need only paper and pencil, now say they must have computers, computer operators and programers. In fact, we are just ordering a computer that we judge will require some $700,000 a year to operate. If we add up the estimated costs of needed buildings, such as adequate library facilities (and I want to emphasize this as a high-priority need), a geophysics building, remodeling of Cobb Hall for the College, decent housing for music, an addition to the chemistry laboratories, a new home for psychology, college teaching laboratories in both the arts and the sciences, biology laboratories to replace those no longer suitable for modern experimental biology, and if we restore the magnificent old buildings on campus, and do all the other things we ought to do, the total comes to about $70,000,000.

Maintaining these additional buildings will entail an annual sum of five to six million dollars—equivalent to another $200,-000,000 of endowment. And this does not provide for putting any more scholars than we now have *in* these new buildings.

No doubt about it, we are going to have to raise money in larger amounts than most of us have been thinking about. What are the sources? Endowment income is about $7,000,000. It would be fine if that source could pay for everything. But, if everything the University of Chicago now does were financed through endowment income—government-supported work and all—we would need four billion dollars in investments. To do all we would *like* to do on the same basis would require pretty close to that ten billion figure Mr. [George] Stigler pulled out of a hat.

Much as we would all like to have that kind of endowment, we know we are not going to have it in any foreseeable future.

Trustee-Faculty Dinner, 10 January 1962

WALKING ON EGGS

BEADLE

What is our financial situation? The answer: becoming increasingly difficult for the reason most private universities are facing financial difficulties, namely, that costs of operation are rising faster than income increases. Our difficulty is accentuated to some extent because we live in a high-cost area—in housing, schooling, and so on. We also have a special expense in providing supplementary security—at a cost of some $600,000 annually, which is the income on about $15 million of endowment.

For all these reasons, and others, our salary levels must be relatively high. And they are rising fairly rapidly. We are now second to Harvard in the nation in faculty salaries. If corrected for age distribution, I strongly suspect we would be in first place.

Excluding income from hospitals and clinics, which is returned to the operation, regular expenditures budgeted for last year, 1966–67, totaled $41.3 million. Income to cover this was estimated to be $3.4 million short of doing so. At year-end the actual deficit that had to be covered from unrestricted campaign funds had been reduced to just under $1.8 million.

For the current year the comparable academic expenditures are budgeted at $45.9 million, up $4.6 million or 11.1 per cent. Income to meet this budget is estimated to be $4.2 million short of doing so. On the basis of past experience, this will be reduced, perhaps to $3 million. But there are two factors that will tend to work against such a reduction. Last year enrollments exceeded the estimates on which budgets were built. This year they fall short. The difference in student fees could be as much as half a million dollars—that is, that much less than predicted when budgets were drawn up.

Because of our special financial needs we are, as you are all aware, engaged in an extraordinary campaign to raise $160 million in three years to cover basic academic needs.

How are we doing?

Very well in many respects, thanks to the very effective work of an excellent Development and Public Affairs staff headed by Charles U. Daly, who stepped in to continue the good work Richard F. O'Brien had begun prior to his departure.

As of October 31, we have somewhat more than $104 million in receipts and pledges, counting only that fraction of the Ford Foundation challenge grant earned by cash receipts—about $11 million.

In addition to the magnificent work the Trustees are doing under Gaylord Donnelley's National Chairmanship in promoting the Campaign outside the University, they have demonstrated their confidence in a heart-warming and thoroughly persuasive way by pledging $12 million to the Campaign. Faculty members have also indicated their faith in a very tangible and generous way.

Chicago-based corporations have helped the cause in a gratifying manner. Some forty of them have pledged an average of $135,000 over the five-year period—that is over $5 million. Other corporations have increased it to $11 million.

We now have strong campaign organizations in major cities—thirty in all.

I am optimistic that during the next year we shall get the remaining $56 million. But I must add that success in that will not solve all our problems. As the campaign moves forward, two things happen. Costs go up. For example, the Library was carefully estimated to cost $18.6 million. The contract price is $1.9 million higher. Second, expectations rise faster than the projection anticipated.

Also, as happens in all such campaigns, many contributions are restricted in ways that preclude their use in meeting the needs originally specified in the campaign.

The conclusion is clear.

We must not be discouraged. We must also not relax.

When Edward Levi joined in persuading the Beadles to come to Chicago—he did so by challenging us to help solve a whole host of difficult problems. With his continued academic leadership assured, I know that all that are left at the end of the year will be in the best possible hands.

State of the University, 7 November 1967

LEVI

The planned second stage of the drive did not materialize in 1970. Major fund-raising efforts, even when they are part of a previous program, require intensive preparation and organization. But there were other distractions between 1968 and 1970 which made this impossible to achieve. Possibly 1970 was too early in any event; even donors may need some rest between extraordinary commitments. The two segments of the drive, however, were part of one plan. The failure to go ahead on the second segment has meant the University has not been receiving the endowment or expendable funds for faculty salaries, student scholarships or fellowships, or for the maintenance of buildings and libraries essential to retain the advances of the first stage.

457

The original ten-year plan by now, of course, is out of date. But over the last four years the plans have been twice revised and extended, based on new projections by the Deans and Officers. The objectives and assumptions have been subject to review by a special faculty committee, headed by Professor Chauncy Harris, who has accepted a continuing administrative role for this purpose. The Trustees of the University have considered these revised projections and goals with the Deans in two intensive retreats during the last four years. Under the leadership of Gaylord Donnelley and Robert E. Brooker, extensive preparations for the second stage drive are now under way. I have no doubt, whatsoever, that a campaign for funds, considerably larger than the first, will be launched and successfully completed, although, of course, this will not be easy. Approximately 80 percent of the funds raised in this second stage will be used for professorships, programs and student aid, and for the maintenance of libraries and other essential facilities; approximately 60 percent of this amount, in turn, will be to provide supporting endowment for these purposes.

Thus a central focus of the second stage of the drive is to achieve sufficient capitalization so that the most essential activities of the University will not be left as vulnerable as they now are. This was the intention of the original endowment of the University. But Chicago is now eighth among the universities in the size of its endowment. In this sense it is an overachiever. The University, in the past, has not required that new professorships be supported by endowment, that scholarships and fellowships be similarly supported, and that buildings not go up without maintenance funds. We probably should not be critical of this past experience which surely has shown that an extraordinary institution could be created, and which perhaps could not have been created in any other way. But our inability to start the second stage of the drive as early as 1970 is, itself, a telling warning that while private universities, if viable, will always require private funds, long-term obligations require arrangements for long-term support. And this in the broadest sense. A building is a long-term obligation. But so is a program which requires a continuation from one faculty member to another, and from faculty to students.

During this interval between the two segments of the drive, the Officers have recommended, and the Trustees have permitted and adopted, budgets with planned deficits or shortfalls between income and expense. There was a special payout from funds functioning as endowment of $1,826,000 in 1971–72, although this amount would have been covered as income if the total return concept adopted later by the Board had been retroactively applied. For 1972–73, there was a deficit of slightly less than $3 million, although if gifts carried forward for use in 1973–74 had been applied to this deficit, the amount would have been reduced to $992,000. The budget for 1973–74 was adopted with a projected $5.9 million shortfall, but it now appears—and I hope this is correct—the amount will be $4.5 million. Including all of these amounts since 1971, there will have been a cumulative shortfall of $9.3 million. I do not know whether this appears reckless or not. We have followed this course because we have believed that the high quality of the University was an important asset and a ground upon which the second stage of the campaign should be built. We wished to avoid the experience of the early fifties when drastic budget cuts helped to precipitate an academic decline. Having come back once, we did not know whether the University could accomplish this turnabout again. Against this payout from funds functioning as endowment, it should be noted that since 1969, the University has received about $9 million in gifts which the University, as a discretionary matter, applied to funds functioning as endowment. If the University had made the contrary choice and used these gifts as annual expendable funds, it appears there would have been no shortfall.

But it is clear we cannot continue indefinitely on this course which has been justified as a holding action between the two segments of the drive. We are now committed to eliminating this shortfall or gap between income and expense over a three-year period. The budget we have prepared for 1974–75 reduces the shortfall to slightly less than $4 million—a reduction of almost $2 million over the planned budget for this year—and this will have to be reduced further and substantially in 1975–76. The successful commencement of the second stage of the capitalization drive should make this possible with a minimum impairment of academic quality. If we are both fortunate and wise, there should be no impairment.

Among the factors adding to this shortfall was the decision to write down the valuation of certain securities held by the

Treasurer, and the almost simultaneous recognition that additional funds would have to be supplied to the Division of the Biological Sciences and The Pritzker School of Medicine beyond the budget allocations. The financing of the University's hospitals and clinics has been most carefully monitored over this period, greatly aided by an advisory Trustee committee, headed by Mr. Charles Brown. An important matter now and in the future with respect to the budget of The Pritzker School of Medicine and the Division of the Biological Sciences has been the continuing refusal of the State of Illinois, after three years of discussion, to pay the medical fees for the professional medical care rendered by our full-time medical faculty to in-patients in the University's Hospitals and Clinics who are beneficiaries of the Illinois Department of Public Aid. The consequence has been to force The Pritzker School of Medicine and the Division of the Biological Sciences and, therefore, the University as a whole, to subsidize the State of Illinois. The paradox of the refusal is that the State would pay if we hired a part-time staff to treat these patients. A part of the problem arises, I am convinced, from an unthoughtful, although perhaps popular, attempt to compel the University to segment its work, at the very time when the delivery of superior health care requires the closest coordination with ongoing research and instruction, unless, of course, the suggestion is that inferior care is to be given to those on welfare, or that the University should convey to the State the operation of special clinics so that it can do with them what it wishes.

Since 1969 the University has been on a policy which we have described as one of careful budget constraints. In 1969, with Vice-President William Cannon as Director, the University set up an Economic Study Commission, consisting of faculty, Deans, Trustees, and non-University representatives. Between 1969 and 1972 the staff of the Commission guided the assembly of analytic cost data on a University-wide but also on a departmental basis. The Commission also examined the management of the University in non-academic areas. Competing models for future University performance were developed. The Commission also encouraged valuable experiments, such as the steps taken toward automation in the Library. The work of the Commission laid the groundwork for continuing study and evaluation. As will be recognized, comprehensive reporting systems take a substantial time to develop. Considerable progress has been made in the rapidity with which data on operations are now made available. Using and extending the data and studies developed under the Commission's aegis, Professor D. Gale Johnson, Chairman of the Department of Economics, has carried forward studies to show the relationship between costs and income of individual departments, and on the economic consequences of academic decisions and practices. Out of this work—much of which has been sent to all Deans, and by Deans to Departmental Chairmen (who have reviewed the data on their department with Mr. Johnson)—have come analyses of the economic consequences which would follow the elimination or change in practices of particular projects and areas. Following the suggestion of the Economic Study Commission, an Office of Economic Analysis has been established in the Office of the President under the guidance of Professor Johnson. . . .

Including actual budget expenditures for 1970–71 and through the adopted budget for 1973–74, the cumulative increase in the amount of the regular unrestricted budget has been held to slightly more than three percent. With unrestricted non-governmental grants included, the percentage increase is 8.83 percent. The restricted funds, not including governmental grants, thus have increased almost 27 percent during this time on a comparable basis, perhaps in response to the programmatic inclinations of many foundations and donors. Since 1962, in fact, there has been an increase in the proportion of funds received by the University in restricted form, and this has placed a greater responsibility on individual departments and faculty members in particular programs. The result is not inevitable, but this can add to the centrifugal forces within the University—a pressure which federal government funds, in the form and for the purposes for which they have been given, have also augmented.

State of the University, 8 April 1974

7

EVER-WIDENING CIRCLES
OF RESPONSIBILITY

At the reception after the dedication of Haskell Hall in 1896 a
student went up to Mr. Harper, who stood beaming on the
crowd, and said, "How do you do it, Mr. President?" Mr.
Harper replied, "Chicago! Chicago! You couldn't do it any-
where else."

HUTCHINS

Any university which holds itself resolutely to its task runs
the risk of being misunderstood and disliked by a large mass
of the people. But I refuse to believe that this is inevitable
and unavoidable. It can avoid the irritation created by its ap-
pearance of aloofness and indifference; it can persuade people
beyond its walls that it is not neglecting the real needs of
men and women through basing its life on dreams; and it can
patiently explain itself and its high purpose, if necessary, over
and over again.

KIMPTON

"OUR UNIVERSITY"

HARPER

Today, as we recall the events of the five years, the strange and
wonderful elements in the situation are, not that so many mil-
lions have been given, for it must be recognized that the giving
has only begun; not that so many professors and students have
been gathered from the various divisions of the country, for
other institutions exist with larger numbers; not that it has been
possible to establish ideals of so high a character in this, a new
city and a new country, for with money and with men the highest
ideals may be realized; but rather (1) that the foundations of
an institution in Chicago have been laid by one who was not
himself a citizen of Chicago or of a neighboring state; (2) the
fact that of the many who have made gifts to The University,
every donor of any considerable sum is today living and able to
see the results accomplished through his gift; and (3) that in

462

so short a time and under circumstances so peculiar, the heart of this great city should have come to beat in such complete sympathy and harmony, with an institution which has so recently been planted in the midst of it. For does not the true citizen of Chicago, in speaking of The University, invariably call it "Our University?"

Quinquennial Statement, 1 July 1896

HARPER

It is fair to say that in the breadth of view which has characterized the work of the Trustees there is to be seen an expression of the spirit of the city of Chicago—a spirit to which the University is indebted for many of the important elements that have entered into its constitution.

. . . The charge of sensationalism has been made by some unthinking persons against certain instructors in the University. This has had its origin in the misrepresentations of professorial utterances which have appeared in the public press, having come from the pens of irresponsible reporters. An effort has been made in most of these cases to discover the basis of the newspaper statements, and it has generally been found that a remark, entirely innocent, has been twisted either by the reporter or by the editor to subserve a humorous purpose. . . .

The question next in importance to that of securing a spirit of unity in a Faculty made up of so many different elements was that of obtaining the good-will and support of the Chicago public. There was grave doubt whether the citizens of Chicago would rally to the support of an institution established so closely in connection with a single denomination and assisted so generously by one man. The history of other institutions organized wholly or in part along the same line was not encouraging, and the very fact that Mr. Rockefeller was understood to be able to furnish all the money that might be needed was a source of difficulty; but the people of Chicago exhibited in this matter great breadth of mind and intelligence. Moved by the example of a few men, known throughout the country for their large and generous consideration of important questions, the public at large soon came into friendly relationship with the University. This closer interest and sympathy was secured in part through the fact of the name, "The University of Chicago," and in part through Mr. Rockefeller's refusal to allow his name to be made a part of the main title of the University. It was really a source of considerable surprise that men of such character and in such numbers should within so short a time ally themselves in one way or another with the fortunes of the institution.

These three facts—namely, the sympathy of the public, the strength of the Faculty, and the character of the Trustees—furnish the basis for the progress thus far made. . . .

From the beginning the University has adopted the policy of making its affairs known to the public. This has not been done with the desire to advertise itself. A charge to this effect has frequently been made by those who, for the time being, were perhaps disturbed by the rapidity of the University's growth. Our feeling has been that the institution is a public institution and that everything relating to its inside history, including its financial condition, should be made known. Its deficits have been published as well as its surpluses, and we attribute largely to this policy of public statement, not only the interest of the public, but the confidence which has been shown on so many occasions. It is generally understood that everything relating to the internal history will be made known within a proper time; in other words, the books of the University, both financial and educational, the minutes of its Faculties, and even the record-book of the President are open to all. *Nothing is concealed.* Even that which at the first sight would seem to be disadvantageous is made known. The amount and character of its investments are published annually. Perhaps no other institution has shown a greater readiness to allow its internal affairs to be known and criticised.

The financial support accorded has been something phenomenal. In the course of ten years the list of donors to the University includes more than three thousand names, besides that of Mr. Rockefeller. The gifts actually received, ranging from one dollar upward, have aggregated (up to June 30, 1902) $17,417,-275, and of this sum, $5,978,371 has been given by friends of the University other than the founder. It is perhaps true that in the history of educational benevolence there is no parallel example. If account were taken of the wills which are known to have been made, this sum would be greatly increased. It is only fair to add that this interest has been largely a local one, inasmuch as the greater part of the $5,978,371 has come from Chicago.

The classes of society from which these contributions have been received are of every possible grade. It is also to be remembered that in the case of at least 90 per cent of these gifts the initiative was taken by the donor himself.

In no way has the University received more loyal support than in the great multitude of young men and women who have been committed to its care. When we reflect that there still exists a strong tendency in Chicago and the West, especially on the part of the alumni of eastern institutions, to send the children to the institution with which the parent was connected, and when we consider the great value of a period of residence entirely removed from the scenes of earlier life, we cannot be mistaken in interpreting the fact of the large number of students at work within the walls of the institution as an indication of interest and confidence on the part of the public. The moral support indicated in this and in so many ways has been a bulwark of strength in these early years—years necessarily full of difficulty and discouragement.

To the public press the University is more greatly indebted than it can adequately express; and while not infrequently statements have appeared which seemed to be injurious, it is certain that in no considerable number of cases have such representations been made for purpose of injuring the institution. The opinion of the newspaper public as to what is helpful and what is interesting often differs from that of the party concerning whom the statement is made. On the whole, it may be said that a fairly satisfactory representation of the work of the University has been presented through the press. It is at all events true that the interest of the papers has been greater than we could have wished, and that, in part, because of this interest, the University is known throughout the world in a way in which it would not otherwise have been known. The press will bear testimony that the University has not sought this prominence; that indeed much has been done by the officers of the University to avoid it; and that more than once official steps have been taken to persuade the press that the University would be just as well satisfied with a more limited share of its attention. It seems necessary to make this statement, since many people honestly believe that the University from the beginning has had a Bureau of Publicity, and that this Bureau has been conducted at great expense for the purpose of advertising the institution.

The University has occasionally accepted space in educational journals for the announcement of the opening and closing of its terms of work or for special announcements of special schools or divisions. It has also published similar announcements in the daily press of Chicago. But outside of these announcements its general policy has been not to expend money for advertising purposes except in the preparation of circulars of information which are sent out upon request.

. . . The fundamental purpose of the press of a city is surely to assist that city in building up its institutions, and not to injure it by tearing down institutions recognized as bringing credit to the city. In the spirit of the times, the newspapers of Chicago have permitted themselves too frequently to print statements utterly devoid of foundation, and to make representations of a humorous character equally hurtful to the University. The press is cognizant of the fact that eastern papers and eastern institutions lose no opportunity to take up these statements and use them to the injury of the University and of the city of which the University forms a part, and distinct and permanent injury is the result of such treatment. Because the daily press has not appreciated the nature and degree of the injury thus wrought, it has permitted itself to deal in this reprehensible way with institutions deserving only of assistance, and institutions which not only deserve but need such assistance. In other words, the press has with one hand greatly assisted the University and similar institutions, but with the other hand has torn down the very work it has sought to build up. This is not economical, nor is it on the whole a respectable treatment to accord an institution of the character of the University of Chicago. It is a degrading of the institution, and in such treatment the press degrades itself.

Decennial Report, 1 July 1902

JUDSON

It has from the first been the policy of the University to consider the scientific attainments of the members of the Faculty as subject to call for rendering such service as might be needed to the community at large, whether in Chicago, in Illinois, or in the nation. For some two years the Head of our Department of

Political Economy, Professor J. Laurence Laughlin, was granted leave of absence by the Board of Trustees in order that he might serve as Chairman of the National Citizens' League for the Promotion of a Sound Banking System, an organization which rendered a great service in connection with the reconstruction of our national banking system. The Head of our Department of Greek, Professor Paul Shorey, was Roosevelt Professor of American History at Berlin in 1913–14. Professor Charles R. Henderson, Head of the Department of Ecclesiastical Sociology in the Divinity School, who himself was one of the leading experts on criminology, held many important positions in the prison congresses both of the United States and of the world at large. The President of the University was given leave of absence for the greater part of a year in order to act as Chairman of a commission which investigated the needs of medical instruction and of hospitals in China for the Rockefeller Foundation. The University Auditor, Mr. Trevor Arnett, who is undoubtedly the foremost expert on university finance in the United States, has been able to give advice to numerous colleges and universities for the organization of their accounting systems—advice which I may say in every case has been accepted, and has been of great value in this important field of educational work.

Convocation, 6 June 1916

BURTON

Whatever of acquisition enters into its plans must come in solely as subordinate means to its supreme end, and that end service. The university must first of all serve its students, but not its students only. Its obligations are to the city in which it is located, from whose citizens it receives no small part of its support; to the state and the nation, to whose stability it owes the opportunity of continuing its work; to the world, from all parts of which its students come, to all parts of which its graduates go back.

This broad definition of its field of service is demanded, moreover, not simply by the extended character of the relationships of a university, but by the fact, which I hope to make clear a little later, that much of its work can be done successfully only as the university consistently maintains a breadth of horizon limited only by the possibilities of its outlook.

467

But it is obvious that this definition of the business of a university as service lacks something of definiteness and exactness. There are many other institutions that exist to serve. The church, the museum, the art institute; yes, and more and more, we are coming to recognize that even those corporations which the law defines as corporations for pecuniary profit are bound also to render service, and we are more and more claiming and confessing that the railroad, the street car, the packing house, the department store, while making for their stockholders a reasonable pecuniary profit, are bound to give service, and that their very right to exist is based upon their being serviceable. Moreover, individuals are more and more recognizing that to society, which furnishes that element of stability without which their efforts to promote their own business would be futile, they owe an obligation of reciprocal service. What then is the special type, or what are the special types, of service which a university is called upon to render?

To this question I should like to return a fourfold answer. The business of a university is discovery, dissemination of knowledge, training of men for service, and development of personalities: discovery of new facts and, by the collection and interpretation of them, of new truth; the dissemination of knowledge through oral speech and printed page, but especially of the results of the discoveries which the scholars of the university have made; the training of men to make practical use of their knowledge in the service of mankind; and the development of personalities capable of large participation in life and of large contribution to life.

> Chicago Association of Commerce and the
> University Club of Chicago, 1923

BURTON

We must maintain our friendly relations to our environment. We must cultivate Chicago not by following a wrong educational policy, but by doing thoroughly well that part of educational work which most strongly appeals to a community like that of Chicago. From this point of view the discontinuance of college work would be a fatal mistake.

> "The Future of the University." University of
> Chicago Senate, 24 February 1923

THE WORLD'S GREATEST LABORATORY

BURTON

In our own faculty, the group of social science departments has this year been engaged in a large piece of cooperative research with a view to determining the feasibility of using the City of Chicago as a laboratory for social and political research. The results have been so gratifying that an additional grant has recently been made for the prosecution of this work for a further three year period. The development of this research places the University in a wholly exceptional position as to facilities for this type of investigation, and affords an unsurpassed opportunity for pioneer work in the development of research in the field of Social Sciences.

Convocation, 17 March 1924

MASON

The great destiny of the University lies in this direction, in the serving of the community. Leaders in Chicago's great industrial force have demonstrated their willingness to devote a portion of their fortunes and energies to that end. It means that the University of Chicago, as the center of higher education of the middle west, will keep its growth in pace with the growth of the city.

In a smaller college town, the character of the community is affected to a startling degree by the university environment. In a metropolis like Chicago, the influence is less perceptible but no less certain. The lines of contact are always there and the intangible spread of ideas means the accomplishment of much good.

Certainly it is a source of great pride to its citizens that Chicago is keenly in quest of the higher things—look at the magnificent buildings where beauty is no longer sacrificed to efficiency. It means Chicago is devoting a portion of its wealth to cultural ideas.

Never before was there such a concentration of wealth and energy, brains and power, in the history of the world. The determination of Chicago is evident to reflect its own greatness in the greatness of its University.

Nothing can keep it from becoming the most potent force the world has ever known.

To my mind, one great thing is the development of contact and the closer meshing of city and university. With the prodigious wealth, resources, spirit and industries of Chicago and the specialized brains and intellectual power of the University in close cooperation, Chicago can become the most dominant power in the civilized world.

"Some Statements by President Mason"
Magazine, December 1925

HUTCHINS

Today, on the other hand, students of social problems have learned from students of the natural sciences that only by keeping in touch with reality can real life be understood. Students of government are studying the people who do the governing and those they govern. Students of business are studying it as it works instead of speculating about it; and legal scholars are examining the actual operation and results of the legal system instead of confining themselves to the history of phrases coined by judges and legislators long since dead. In this movement the University of Chicago has played an important part and must continue to do so. And naturally enough its work has been centered on this city and its surroundings. Through the co-operation of the Chicago superintendent of schools the Department of Education is working with teachers from three hundred public schools and conducting studies in seven of them. The School of Commerce and Administration is carrying on research in fifteen or twenty local industries. The School of Social Service Administration has revolutionized the treatment of the orphan in the city of Chicago. The Department of Hygiene and Bacteriology is in co-operation with the city health office. The Local Community Research Committee, representing the social science departments, is managing fifty studies of the community. If the focus of research is the world about us, the focus of research at this University should be primarily that part of the world about us called Chicago and the Chicago area. Research so focused is bringing up-to-date and giving a somewhat new accent to the University's traditional interest in its environment; it is going far toward bringing scholarship in touch with life as it is being lived today; and it may eventually lead to some slight advance in the life that is to be lived here tomorrow.

Inaugural Address, 19 November 1929

HUTCHINS

The University should make a conscious effort to remove the current distrust of the institution. I think this effort should be conscious, but not obvious. I do not believe that ringing declarations of patriotism have much effect except to raise questions as to why it was necessary to make them. Nor do I believe that the announcement of courses in Americanism or the requirement of an oath of allegiance from teachers or students would do more than amuse the public and the educational profession. The main thing is that the Trustees and the Administration should take every opportunity to make the community understand what a university is and in particular what this one is.

Outside this city Chicago is regarded as one of the great universities of the world. Mr. Edwin R. Embree, President of the Julius Rosenwald Fund, has lately published an article in the *Atlantic Monthly* rating Chicago the second university in the country. In view of its youth and the fact that it has about half the resources of Harvard, that is a very remarkable showing. Positive propaganda designed to show the people of Chicago what intelligent people elsewhere know, that the University is the chief ornament of the city, seems to me more profitable than defensive tactics.

The example of Harvard is instructive. For three hundred years it has concentrated on being the best possible university. It has ignored attacks upon it and has insisted on the most complete academic freedom. Although it has frequently been subject to criticism as severe as any the University has experienced, these attacks have quickly subsided, and Harvard is now the richest and one of the greatest universities in the world. The history of institutions that have compromised or given way before their detractors does not suggest that The University of Chicago should follow their example.

The greatest agency of propaganda a university can have is an active and informed board of trustees, who know all about the

471

university and believe in what it is doing. Our Board works harder than any I know. It manifests intense and intelligent interest in the institution. I believe the Administration has not done its full duty by the Board, in that it has failed to give it all the information it should have. This information has usually been supplied after or during a crisis instead of being furnished currently. In cooperation with the Committee on Instruction and Research, I hope to remedy this defect.

"Report of the President 1934–35" (Unpublished)

THE SOUL OF THE CITY

HUTCHINS

The University could have been established only in Chicago. It could have risen to eminence only here. Here alone could it flourish today. A great university requires a great community. It must not be so large as to lose all sense of being a community. It must not be so small that the currents of thought and imagination flowing through the world will pass it by.

Many colleges have performed creditably though they were situated in country villages. If their task is to transmit learning, and to do it according to the best custom of the times, there are no disadvantages and some advantages in having their charges removed from the excitements of the metropolis. Now that gasoline is to be restricted, the educational advantages of a rural situation may once more appear in practice as well as in theory. But if the function of an institution is to pioneer, to open new frontiers in education and research, it must be located in a center of the arts and sciences, in a city that commands a large territory, and a community eager to learn, to experiment, to press forward. Such has been the function of the University of Chicago. Such has been the character of this city.

The Baptists were right. They wanted a college in Chicago because they knew the city was the capital of the Middle West, and that the forces which would mould the life of that vast area would emanate from Chicago. Mr. Rockefeller was right. He decided in favor of Chicago, though he had never lived here and

472

had no sentimental connections with the place. He decided in favor of Chicago because he knew that the University would gain strength, power, and influence from it.

And so it has. The chief characteristics of the University are independence and courage. These qualities, as much as the vast sums it has received and as much as the educational and scientific excellence of the staff, have made the University great. If we ask ourselves why the University has shown the independence and courage which have distinguished it, we must ascribe it to two things, the attitude of the Founder and the spirit of the City. . . .

The spirit of the City has inevitably been the spirit of the University. Every year there are 4,183 young Chicagoans on the campus. In University College downtown and in Home Study there are 2,790 more. In the Chicago area live 18,000 alumni of the University. Whether they applaud or attack the policies of their Alma Mater, they retain a lively interest in it and form a connecting link between it and the community.

A newly forged link between the University and the community is the Citizens Board, whose loyalty and generosity have been displayed here this evening. Their interest in the University, their labors in its behalf, and their knowledge of its work will make these three hundred men and their successors a band of interpreters between the University and the community which it seeks to serve.

The classical channel of communication between the University and the City is the Board of Trustees. Twenty-six members of the group which legally is the University are residents of Chicago. . . .

. . . The commanding position of this city and its university means that the whole structure of education in the Middle West is built on the University of Chicago. . . .

The spirit of the University of Chicago, which it draws in from the City with every breath, is the spirit of independence and courage. It is the spirit of the pioneers. . . .

This is the principal, if not the sole, function of an endowed university, to establish ever-new frontiers of education and research. The state universities can and will carry on the bulk of the educational and scientific work of this country. The disappearance of distances and of denominational differences means that no institution can rest a claim for survival on its peculiar location or its peculiar religious flavor. You can now get to Urbana in about the same time that it used to take Mr. Harper to drive to the Loop. Few Baptist families insist on Chicago for their children because of its denominational ancestry. The state universities are excellent and are rising every year to new heights. But I believe that they would inevitably deteriorate if it were not for the example and the inspiration of a few strong, endowed universities. The influence of the University of Chicago on public education in the Middle West is a matter of historic fact. Its foundation transformed into universities state institutions that had been called universities because they were larger than colleges and had professional schools attached to them. It may be thought that these institutions are now so strong that they could go on from strength to strength without Chicago to support them. This is a vain hope. Even with the example of the endowed universities before their eyes the politicians of this country have halted and mutilated some of the finest state universities in the country. The University System of Georgia, organized, by the way, on a plan laid down by members of the faculty of the University of Chicago, is simply the latest victim of political rapacity. The standards set by the independent universities give the state institutions such protection as they have. If these standards were swept away, the destruction of every useful attribute of the state universities would be merely a matter of time.

> "The University and the City." University of Chicago Citizens Dinner (Fiftieth Anniversary) 26 September 1941

HUTCHINS

For the last fifteen years the University neighborhood has steadily deteriorated, until today, I am ashamed to say, the University has the unfortunate distinction of having the worst-housed faculty in the United States. The Board of Trustees, after an inspection of the current state of the University's environment, decided that renewed consideration must be given to a faculty housing project and authorized an appropriation for architectural studies.

> State of the University, 25 September 1945

A MESSENGER FROM US TO US

HUTCHINS

It is the program of the University, too, that must determine the public relations activities that in our time inevitably accompany any effort to raise money. The object of public relations is to interpret the University as it is and as it wants to be so that the public will understand and believe in it. It is not the aim to re-mold the University so that the public will like it. The most dangerous aspect of public relations work is its reflex action: we find that the public does not like something about the University; our temptation is to change this so that the public will like us. Our duty is to change public opinion so the public will like what the University does, and, if this cannot be immediately accomplished, to hold out against the public until it can be. Public relations work in a university is a phase of its efforts in adult education.

Trustee-Faculty Dinner, 10 January 1951

KIMPTON

Now, I should like to speak for a few minutes about the place of the University in this community. Let me say first that a university like this one can be and should be a tremendously valuable resource for this area. Our communication with our community always needs improvement. We are never asked to do as much as we might. And on our side, I suspect we are not as resourceful or ingenious or as informed as we ought to be in order to offer our services where they could be used. Perhaps we are too reticent. Let me merely illustrate a few of the kinds of things which we have been doing, many of which will be known to a few of you, but most of which have been done without any but the haziest public knowledge. The hospitals of our Medical School are uniquely prepared at a moment's notice to treat casualties on the South Side in the event of an atomic attack. The Executive Program of our Business School has for some years been preparing able young businessmen for leadership in our business community. Our Industrial Relations Center is rendering real service to Chicago industry on problems of management and labor. We constantly provide lectures and cultural events that bring to Chicago such figures as T. S. Eliot, Ralph Bunche, and Nehru. If I continue, I shall sound boastful, and I don't intend to. The fault is still ours that we do not do more for our community, and that we do not better communicate what we are already doing.

And this brings me to one more of my problems, which is the University's standing here in its own home town. I find that I enjoy travelling away from Chicago from time to time because, when I go to New York or California or into the deep South, or even into Missouri to sit on my farm for a few days, people are always telling me something good and great about this University. But, here in Chicago, when I read the newspapers and when I talk to citizens, I get quite a different view. I become almost persuaded that most of our students are either fresh from Russia or enroute there. I come to believe that our professors are marching about with smoking bombs in their hands and leers on their faces, with glittering eyes fixed on a shining target which is labeled "The American Way of Life."

The facts of the situation as I take a good long look at the inside of the University seem rather different. There is not, so far as I know, a single member of the Communist party on the faculty, nor anyone sympathetic to communism. I have not only my own rather extensive acquaintance among the faculty to rely on; but, in addition, two legislative investigations were unable to turn up a single communist. I am in the odd situation of having our Department of Economics written up by a recent issue of *Fortune* magazine as being one of the last strongholds of classical, free-enterprise economics, and we have been criticized for possessing no really adequate representative of the Keynesian view. . . .

Any University that holds itself resolutely to its task runs the risk of being unpopular and misunderstood by a large mass of the people. For the truth, indeed the search for the truth, is long, difficult and sometimes unpleasant.

But the University does need to be understood, in terms of its purpose and in terms of the means it uses toward that purpose; and misunderstanding is largely our fault. The University can do more than it has done to explain itself, perhaps over and over again. It can avoid the external irritations, the appearance of aloofness or indifference which sometimes characterizes the intellectual world. It can learn to communicate its purpose and its high dedication to the betterment of its community and the world. The University of Chicago has not lacked and does not lack for pioneering spirit. But it does not yet have the understanding, at least at home, which it needs.

It is partly because of Glen Lloyd's request that I came here today, but it is chiefly because I want to beg you to extend to us your sympathetic understanding. The role of a great university in trying to provide objective intellectual illumination in a world where the lights are very dim and even the stars wander is a most difficult one. And we have certainly failed in the past in communicating our purpose and our high dedication. This is my greatest problem, and one that I can solve only with your help.

> "The University and the Community"
> Commonwealth Club of Chicago
> 17 May 1951

KIMPTON

This morning, in the magnificent setting of Rockefeller Chapel, I became the sixth head of the University of Chicago. This evening, I have the privilege and responsibility of addressing the citizens of this great city which has lent its name to this great University. Whether the choice of the Board of Trustees was a wise one, only time will tell. I can only give you the dubious assurance that I approach the task with energy and humility. The energy is an accident of youth, and the humility stems from my conviction that in the work ahead I need the wisdom, counsel, and help of all of you. I do not say this lightly or with any intent to please or flatter. The Board has chosen badly if it sought one who knew all the answers. This is our University in our city of Chicago, and I look to you, its citizens, to give me the guidance and assistance I need. Cooperatively we can make the University even greater than it is today, and even more of an ornament to a city already rich in institutions of learning and culture. As a background for my plea for guidance, may I describe the University to you, name some of its problems, and try to indicate my conception of its purpose. . . .

The first problem, one which we share with the Illinois Institute of Technology, is the south side area in which our University is located. Sixty years ago, when the University was founded, it was the most desirable residential district in the city; the carriages of Chicago's elite moved sedately down Drexel Street, and nobody dreamed of the process of decay that would set in over the next half century. Now, I do not wish to run down our neighborhood too much. The area immediately adjacent to the University is certainly a pleasant and convenient place to live. It is the case, however, that it is no longer thought of as socially desirable, and this creates real problems in attracting both students and faculty. Oddly enough, if the area were a slum, it would be possible to get various kinds of assistance to clear it. When the problem is one of gradual decay, it is much more difficult to solve. It is one of the greatest problems of my administration to try somehow to reverse this trend. I admire the successful effort of Henry Heald and the Illinois Institute in this connection; we must go and do likewise. . . .

The problem that concerns me most—even more than our neighborhood and money—is the place and standing of our University in our community. I shall be very frank and even blunt about it. The city of Chicago does not like the University of Chicago very much. The University is thought of as a cold, aloof, and indifferent place, full of communist professors and students. One way of looking at this, I suppose, is to say that this is the city's tough luck; if it refuses to see what a jewel the institution is in its cultural crown, let the city go hang. I do not view the matter in this way. The problem is one of proper communication between town and gown, and if these lines have broken down over the years, it must have been partly our own fault; it is certainly our problem at the University to re-establish them. We must make ourselves understood and put an end to misunderstanding; we must make ourselves known that we may become favorably known.

Inaugural Banquet, 18 October 1951

IN THIS CITY, EMPIRES CAN STILL BE BUILT

KIMPTON

A university which truckles to public opinion is unworthy of the name. On the other hand, we deserve to be understood by the public and appreciated for what we are. I have tried as best I can to explain the nature and the contribution of the University of Chicago to all who will listen. Out of this, I freely confess that I hope a sympathetic understanding and appreciation will occur and support will follow.

Student Assembly, 28 January 1952

KIMPTON

The need for understanding the University of Chicago by its own community is not a problem that has just developed. I think there is an impression that the founding of the University was an enterprise that enlisted the enthusiasm of the citizens of Chicago in the nineties, a sort of civic enterprise that reflected the desire to add culture to the rapidly growing commercial, manufacturing, and railroading enterprises that centered here. That is not the case. The city, even at the start, regarded the University with indifference or, at best, with mixed emotions. As you probably are aware, there had been a University of Chicago, under Baptist auspices, which had originated in 1856 in the gift of ten acres of land, near 35th Street and Cottage Grove Avenue, from Senator Stephen A. Douglas. This institution collapsed in 1886, foreclosed by an insurance company, after a long series of vicissitudes including the Civil War, the Chicago fire, and the wild financial gyrations that marked the progress of the region in those times. But it was allowed to sink without any noticeable regret on the part of citizens and with no response to the desperate efforts by its supporters to raise the comparatively modest sums that would have kept it afloat.

The present University of Chicago owes its origin to the zeal of a relatively small group of enlightened men, motivated by the desire to see the Baptists have a college in the city as an outpost in the expanding west. It must be confessed also that another motivation was to rival those heretical Methodists up in Evanston. For the impetus to get this project started, they turned first not to Chicago but to the east and to the almost legendary figure who was lighting the lamps of the world, John D. Rockefeller. . . .

Mr. Rockefeller's initial gift left the smaller share of the beginning to others; his subsequent contributions, ultimately totalling over 35 millions, enabled the University to develop into a world-famous institution with a rapidity without parallel. Only after they had Mr. Rockefeller's participation did the proponents of the new undertaking turn to Chicago. The response was generous; the Baptists of Chicago, and indeed of the entire country, made contributions that were large in relation to their means. And a small group of Chicago's leaders supplied the balance of the money to match Mr. Rockefeller's conditional founding grant.

The University was an exciting project, because of Mr. Rockefeller, and even more because of the man who accepted the task of organizing it and leading it. William Rainey Harper had big and original ideas, and because of notions that seemed fantastic to some, he provoked considerable ridicule and attack as well as enthusiasm. The University was described as "a foreign intrusion in the life of the city," and as "Harper's folly." But there was no folly about it, as the succession of new buildings and the acquisition of distinguished members to its faculty rather quickly demonstrated.

Without Mr. Rockefeller, there could not have been a University of Chicago, at least as we know it. But even the magnificence of Mr. Rockefeller's gifts could not have established a truly successful university as a part of Chicago and the middle west. The University required the support of influential citizens, and these rallied to it. They were the men who were the pioneers in the effort to create the city itself. Among them were Charles L. Hutchinson, Marshall Field, Andrew MacLeish, E. Nelson Blake, Leon Mandel, Martin A. Ryerson. Interestingly enough, many of these first citizens of Chicago and first supporters of the University were emigrants from the east, particularly New England, who brought with them the tradition of learning. From the first, the University has consistently enjoyed the active participation and help of its outstanding citizens. Its Board has always included the ablest and most public-spirited men of Chicago, and, as Harold Swift has said many times, it is undoubtedly the hardest working board in the country. They are devoted trustees, who take the time to know the University in detail and to give their energy, intelligence, and influence to its welfare. The chairmen of the board through the years testify to its distinction and devotion: Martin A. Ryerson, Harold H. Swift, and Laird Bell have all made the welfare of the University their primary concern. In addition to the trustees and alumni, who have given large sums, many thousands of Chicagoans have in the last sixty years donated millions for buildings, endowment, scholarships, and research. In a very real way, then, the University has through the years enjoyed the confidence and support of important elements of the city. . . .

The origin of the University, the speed of its expansion, the quality of its leadership, and its environment all combined to give it unusual characteristics. Like Chicago, it was adventuresome, confident, boisterous, dissatisfied with things as they were, and always striving to be better. An institution that started out to create the concept of a university, a place where discovery of new knowledge would be emphasized, in a country that had barely recognized such a development as possible, certainly was confident, and it had to be venturesome. It had none of the usual reticences of older institutions; if it wanted to do something new, it obviously could not be cautious and traditional. But what must be recognized is that the University was not trying to be new and different simply for the sake of novelty. It had goals that were clear and defensible. It had the ability to demonstrate that its aims could be achieved and that they were worth achieving. The University has always been a pioneer, striking out into new country, and, like the pioneer, often with little or no company until it had cut new paths. If the University has faults, they are the errors of commission rather than of omission. . . .

In Chicago, you can hardly escape the influence of the University. Its social scientists have analyzed many aspects of the city's life and organization. Whether the problem be housing, race relations, governmental efficiency, or the mobility of labor, faculty members are on constant call from official and volunteer agencies concerned with meeting the problems of urban civilization. The medical and research center of the University is known for its work on cancer; its Lying-in Hospital has been the model for obstetrical care; and more is known on the Midway than anywhere else about the effects of radiation hazards such as atomic bombs might present. Several hundred companies come to the University's experts to learn about such things as the latest methods of industrial relations, selecting their potential executives, educating their employees in the basic facts of economics. And so it goes; wherever you turn, you find the influence of the University.

You find the influence of the University exerted, too, on an even broader scale. The combination of scientific skill and flexibility of administration made the University the center of the work on the development of the atomic bomb. The University was chosen as the contractor to operate the great Argonne National Laboratory of the Atomic Energy Commission. The Army, the Navy, and the Air Force bring difficult problems in national defense to the University scientists and even to scholars in the social sciences. Just from the standpoint of the University's contribution to the defense of the country, then, it is an asset of incalculable value.

All these things I list by way of illustration of the influence of the University and its direct and indirect relations to the community. What the University does has enormous practical implications in making our life better, easier, and more secure. But I would not justify the University in terms of more efficient atomic bombs, or even in the cure of diseases. Nor am I interested in justifying the University of Chicago only. Naturally, knowing it, knowing the scholars and scientists who comprise it and for whom the University exists and knowing, too, their achievements, I am proud of it and zealous in its interest. The other day Mr. Samuel Goldwyn of movie fame visited the palatial mansion in Pasadena now occupied by the Ford Foundation. He beheld the beautiful furniture, the rugs on the floors, the pictures on the walls, and the swimming pool in the back. "Well," he remarked gravely, "If you have got to give money away, this is a nice place to do it." And that's the way I feel about the University of Chicago. If you have to be chancellor of a university, this is a nice place to do it. But an understanding of the University of Chicago in the Chicago community has implications beyond its own advancement and progress. All good universities—and we have many of them in this country—need understanding and the sympathetic support of the American people. For all universities are trying to do something that no other institution is equipped to undertake. They are the conservators of the values of our civilization. In them, men and women with a detachment and selflessness that does not ordinarily characterize human effort, are concerned with the aspirations of mankind. I remind you that we must cherish and cultivate these higher aspirations as the foundation for ultimate triumph over materialistic philosophies of social organization. Without understanding, and without the conviction produced by understanding—that universities are uniquely necessary—they cannot flourish and make their contributions. Without the universities our world would be desolate, for the hope, the security, and the confidence they create would be lost.

"The University and the Community." Women's Club (Chicago), February 1952

IT MAY BE A FIGHT, BUT WE ARE HERE TO STAY

KIMPTON

Police protection has improved, we are organized to prevent further deterioration of housing. The University has played a leading role in the organization of the South East Chicago Commission. We are prepared to contribute $55,000 for the support of that commission's work. We are giving liberally of our time and energies to start it on its way. This problem is by no means ended, but at least we have begun and we are determined to see this fight through.

One encouraging aspect of the formation of the commission has been the welcome and support given the University when it entered the fight against crime. There has grown a definite feeling among our neighbors that once the University began to act, things were bound to happen. We cannot be grateful enough for the encouragement and support of our neighbors in the campaign to improve Hyde Park. Without the co-operation of the entire community, we could not even have begun our fight against crime.

This recognition given our present struggle against crime in Hyde Park gives me encouragement in the next step of our relationship to our community, the broader community in which both the university and Hyde Park exist. Perhaps we could sum up this problem by saying we need to know Chicago better. We need to take our proper role in seeing to it that Chicago knows us better, through actions which are reflected in the daily experience of our community. . . .

. . . We must be prepared to take a more active, constructive role in Chicago affairs than before.

This is essential, and it can be done without sacrificing a single one of the freedoms vital to the existence of the university, without diverting ourselves from our basic tasks of teaching

483

and research. There is a wide chasm between interest and help-fulness on the one hand, and subservience and going along simply for the sake of going along on the other. While we are not to be considered a mere community-service service station, in doing our basic job, we accomplish much that will inevitably benefit the community. The city of Chicago has been good to us.

It has become fashionable in certain unexplainably smug pub-lications to speak of Chicago as a "tired" city, a city whose fu-ture lies wholly in its past. Chicago may complain more about its aches and pains than any other city, but it is by no means tired. And neither is the university. Both the city and the uni-versity have problems, some of them in common. By establish-ing better relations between the community and the university, it may become easier to surround these problems and annihilate them.

Re-establishing our communication with the community, while a task that must be constantly borne in mind, presents to us no insurmountable barriers. The facts are on our side. We are in a very real sense an ornament to Chicago, to the judgment of those pioneers who aided in our foundation.

Alumni Gathering (Chicago), 4 June 1952

KIMPTON

The neighborhood surrounding the University has come to oc-cupy an increasing amount of concern and energy on the part of both faculty and administration. It is extremely important that we maintain a community in which our faculty desire to live and in which our students will be secure. In order to combat the forces of uncertainty and deterioration at work in the neighbor-hood, the University has taken the initiative in the organization of the South East Chicago Commission. It is concerned to or-ganize the total community in order to stabilize it and prevent further flight from the area. Its more specific program is to fight crime, prevent illegal conversions, organize the citizenry within each block, and begin a long-term project of neighborhood plan-ning and improvement. This program is designed to supplement the existing activity of the University in making loans to faculty members for housing within the area and in buying up and re-habilitating deteriorated property.

State of the University, 14 October 1952

KIMPTON

The danger is that we can become merely a service and repair station, but it is within our power to become The American Research Center. . . .

Within the great freedom and breadth of America, where is the place for the American Research Center? Where else if not in the center of America—the center of its natural resources, its transportation, its industry, and its social problems? And where else if not in the City of Chicago? Small towns and suburbs are for evening strolls, and for male and female colleges, and for early faculty retirements that start about four o'clock every afternoon. But what I see is The American Research Center, and I see it in the city described by Carl Sandburg as the "tall bold slugger set vivid against the little soft cities."

Trustee-Faculty Dinner, 7 January 1953

KIMPTON

Our fundamental problem in the universities is that we are not generally understood; and it is our fault as well as that of the public. We need to come out from behind our ivy and say what we are like and what we stand for. Most of all, we need to play a more significant role in the concerns of our nation, our state, and our city. We have too long stood remote from the affairs of the world and the real needs of men and women. If we are the storehouse of knowledge and of wisdom we purport to be, let us increasingly translate these things into action for the benefit of our fellow man. But above all else, we need to be known and understood. In principle, at least, I welcome these investigations of the universities by Congress, though I am dubious about the motives and competence of the men who are making them. If there are real Communists lurking within our faculties, let us know about them. But we are entitled to a full investigation. Let appropriate public bodies investigate other things about the universities—their contributions to freedom, to the progress of civilization, to the increase of human knowledge, and to the training of our youth. If the whole picture were assembled through appropriate investigation, I would not fear the outcome or the judgment of our times. It is for all these reasons that I want to talk today about the responsibility of the universities to the welfare of our country, and specifically I wish to talk about the City of Chicago and the University to which it lent its name.

. . . This is our problem, and it is the problem of the large metropolitan areas of the United States. This combination of a migration into the cities and a flight to suburbia has in turn produced two phenomena which are as inevitable as they are undesirable. With the increasing population pressures, apartments and houses have been cut up and crowded until they have become slums. With the growth of slums goes an increase in juvenile delinquency and crime. This is the problem of the City of Chicago. The leadership to solve this problem has been lacking for three decades, mainly because the leaders lived some place else. From the comfort and security of suburbia the problem lacked reality. I am happy to say that increasingly the great men of our city have come to recognize this problem for what it is and are seeking through appropriate organizations a solution to it.

I am not very proud of the role—or lack of one—that the University of Chicago has played in this situation over the last quarter century. If our civic leaders ignored it, the University's social scientists surveyed it, and this is almost as bad. Half of our Library must be filled with surveys of Chicago, an exercise that has kept our graduate students busy and has strengthened our firm grasp upon the obvious. The area which surrounds the University—the neighborhoods which are called Kenwood, Hyde Park and Woodlawn—is typical of much of the City of Chicago. There was a day when the fine old homes and beautiful apartments of this area were lived in by those who built them and did much to establish the commerce and culture of our city. Gradually over the years these people have moved north or west or farther south, and these dwellings have been accommodated to the population pressures of our day. When I took over as Chancellor of the University just two years ago, I decided that the problem of our area is one of the most important I have. The area has to improve, because we will not join the flight to suburbia. We are here to stay, and for reasons more weighty than the two hundred million dollars it would take us to move. In many ways our location is an ideal one. It is close to the Lake. The I.C. provides magnificent transportation to the Loop, and the area includes the best park system in the City of Chicago. There are many fine churches and synagogues, and such outstanding institutions as the Museum of Science and Industry and the University of Chicago. All these things make it an ideal place in which to work and live. But more than anything else is the fact that there is only one location for us if we are to continue our dream of being the research center of the Middle West. More and more, enlightened industry, far-seeing Government bureaus, and intelligent associations of professional men are realizing that basic research must go on, and it must be conducted by a university. By a natural affinity translation centers are being built around our University to bridge the gap between the search for basic knowledge and its application in the world of action. The Institute of Meat Packing took up its residence on our campus a number of years ago; the United States Weather Bureau has just located in our neighborhood to be adjacent to our distinguished Department of Meteorology; the American Bar Association proposes to locate its national headquarters in a three-million-dollar building on the south side of the Midway. This is the dream we have of the future of the University of Chicago, and this dream plays an important part in our thoughts about our community. It is for all these reasons that the University of Chicago feels a strong responsibility for its community and has entered upon its problems with the weight of its knowledge and its prestige. Moreover, as we solve these problems, it is conceivable that we may be able to establish a working model for the solution of similar problems elsewhere in our own city and in other cities of the United States. We have the facilities through our University Press to publish the results of our successful and unsuccessful experiments. Perhaps we can make a contribution to human knowledge in one of the most important problems of our times—the rehabilitation and conservation of the American city. I cannot imagine any more important contribution that a university can make.

Well, what did we do? We saw first that the community must be organized. This was not easy. We had chosen for study and action the area from Thirty-Ninth to Seventy-First, between Cottage Grove and the Lake; and the area contained economic and social levels varying all the way from Thomas E. Wilson, who still lives in a stately old mansion on Woodlawn Avenue, to a flophouse bum, who, incidentally, lives just two blocks away from Tom. There were some six neighborhood groups already functioning within the area described, all doing rather different things and all cordially hating one another. One group of real estate owners was groping for a substitute for the restrictive covenant; and a group of believers in the brotherhood of man was organizing welcoming parties for families of minority groups that entered the area. It was not a happy combination of citizenry to try to organize.

We used a rather sensational kidnapping and attempted rape case to bring the community together and announce a plan for the organization of the South East Chicago Commission. It was to include a board of some seventy-five members, since increased to ninety, who represented a cross section of the community; a small, working, executive committee; and a full-time executive director of the Commission with his staff. The budget was set at $30,000 a year, and the University of Chicago offered to put up $15,000 the first year if the community raised a like amount. The enthusiasm for the organization is perhaps best expressed by the fact that the community raised over $20,000. The Commission had and has three objectives: (1) to do something about crime; (2) to do something about illegal conversions, those existing and those contemplated; and, finally, (3) to do some hard-headed, long-range planning for the area. It was understood from the beginning that the Commission was an action group.

The S.E.C.C. did not propose surveys or dreamy-eyed plans to build another community out into the Lake. It proposed to work with everyone who lived, worked, or had influence in the area, and it had no hesitation in seeking and obtaining the cooperation on a voluntary or involuntary basis of tavern keepers, policemen, hotel owners, and ward heelers. It was fortunate in obtaining as Executive Director one Julian Levi, the grandson of Rabbi Hirsch and the son of Rabbi Levi, who had made a fortune by age forty in the practice of the law and business. He is exactly the kind of man we want. He is as dedicated and as idealistic as his forefathers and as shrewd and tough as the city in which he was brought up. I have admired him ever since the day when he was asked by an uplift, strength-through-love group what they could do to help the neighborhood. He suggested they paint the Hyde Park Police Station and offered to pay for the paint out of his own pocket. That was the end of that.

Well, what did we do about crime? The Captains of the Sixth and Seventh Police Districts miraculously resigned or were transferred immediately after the Commission was established, and two tough, able and completely honest trouble-shooters were placed in charge. We engaged as a full-time staff member an expert on police affairs, and our effort centered upon demanding that the established authorities do their job. We have kept for over a year a statistical table showing from day to day how many police we have in the area and what they are doing. We check several nights a week to be sure that squad cars' crews are cruising and not at rest in a warm and cooperative garage. We have kept a detailed map showing where crimes are committed in the area and we have demanded special protection in these bad spots. In ways that may sound trivial but are quite important, we have worked to improve the morale of the police in our districts. We have obtained for them through special donations from our residents adequate lockers and typewriters for the stations, and we have congratulated our Captains and their men for jobs that have been well done. Our objective has been to demand that the police do their duty and to provide every assistance that we can in helping them do it. The statistics begin to speak for themselves. In Hyde Park we are, for example, now averaging 43.5 fewer offenses per month than at this same time a year ago; and there are 39.8 more clear-ups of offenses than a year ago. In Woodlawn the report shows a decrease of 94.4 offenses per month and a clear-up record which is double that of a year ago. In the Hyde Park area we have been leading the city for some little time in terms of offenses which have been cleared by arrests.

Let me give one example of a technique which we have used with considerable effectiveness and which goes under the euphemistic title of "voluntary compliance". There is a hotel in our area—it shall be nameless since it is now under new ownership and management—which was the center of the narcotics traffic on the South Side. Last year it had over a hundred raids, and the owners had the temerity to file an injunction suit against the police department to stop it from raiding them. We addressed a letter to the owners asking that they clean up their shop, and received no reply. We then called on their insurance company and asked them if they cared to insure this kind of property and operation. The insurance company was properly appalled and promptly cancelled the insurance. The owners were unable to obtain other insurance and the bank that handled their mortgage of some $75,000 immediately called its loan. The owners threatened to sue us and we urged them to do it. But the hotel is now in new hands and operating in a very satisfactory manner.

Another success we have had where the compliance was somewhat more voluntary has been with the tavern owners of the area. They have organized under our stimulation and have drawn up a list of undesirable characters whom they decline to serve or have around. The taverns of our area now conspicuously display a sign to the effect that they have been approved by the South East Chicago Commission.

The real estate problem has been a far tougher one upon which to make an immediate dent. The population pressures in Chicago, and particularly on the South Side, have proved a bonanza to unscruplous speculators who have carved up the fine old houses and apartments of the area without any regard to zoning, health, and fire ordinances. The legal machinery for taking action against these characters is hopelessly creaky and out of date. A citizens' group files suit against such a landlord, and two thousand dollars' worth of attorney's fees and two years later the property owner is fined $200. I speak with some degree of authority when I say that if you want to make a fortune currently in the City of Chicago, illegal conversion is the way to do it. And so great are the needs for housing that even the most honorable and decent of our City officials close one eye and sometimes two to this problem, simply by way of attempting to meet the housing needs of the hordes of people who have flocked to our city. There can be no solution to this problem without new legislation. One piece of legislation that we are currently pushing will entitle the plaintiff to attorney's fees if judgment is obtained on an illegal conversion against the defendant. If the bill passes, it will help in dealing with a bunch of ruthless speculators who have no hesitation in ruining our city if they can make a fast buck in the process.

Another activity in this same field that we are currently engaged upon is a fairly elaborate campaign of prosecuting two real estate operators in the area. Each of them owns three properties which have been illegally converted. We now have detailed internal photographs of all of these properties, photostated rent receipts from the tenants, and an iron-clad case is being built against the owners. We plan to move on them with the full knowledge and consent of the Building Commissioner and the Mayor, and in about a month you will see some sparks fly out

490

of the South Side. It is our hope that from an activity of this kind we may be able to discourage other such enterprising speculators from entering our area.

In all these activities we have had the full cooperation of the legitimate real estate operators in our community. They have recently organized and have prepared a brochure for property purchasers describing what can and what cannot be done to property purchased. These real estate dealers will display within their windows the sign of the South East Chicago Commission.

On the long-range planning for our area, the progress has been necessarily slow. We have been too busy putting out brush fires, allaying panic and arresting flight from the area to have been able to work out in detail the shape of things to come; but we have been cooperating with the Metropolitan Housing and Planning Council of the city in formulating a plan specifically for the area. As we dream our dream of the future of the University, we work hard to attract new institutions to our community, and we are greatly neartened by the plan of the American Bar Association to establish its national headquarters on our campus. And, as our community turns the corner and starts uphill, we hope to catch the glitter of investment capital venturing out to meet us.

The job is not done—in fact, it has barely begun—but the bare beginning is full of promise. A community has been organized and has actually done something to remedy its ills. It has worked with other organizations and the appropriate municipal authorities to do something about our city. It is conceivable that within several years we can stand as a model of what almost every city in the United States ought to do to save itself. I am very proud of the fact that the University of Chicago is playing a significant role in this movement. In so acting it is taking a direct and immediate responsibility for the community of which it is a part. Along with the great scientific and cultural values which it symbolizes, the University of Chicago is merging its needs with the real needs of the men and women who surround it. Under the West Stands of Stagg Field ten years ago the University of Chicago produced the first nuclear chain reaction, which may result in saving the free world. In our work today with our community, we hope that we are starting another chain reaction which may prove the salvation of our cities.

"Responsibilities of a University to Its Community"
Union League Club of Chicago, 16 April 1953

KIMPTON

I come finally to the third of our component parts—our physical properties and those that closely surround us. And I should like to begin with the problem of our community. When a new chancellor takes office, I can assure you that the problems he is presented with soon approach infinity, and all of them are presented as equally pressing. But somewhere is *the* problem, or *the* two or three pressing problems, which may not even be among those that have been fervently presented. They may be the problems that none of us likes to face, those we thought would leave our door if we sat still and pretended we were not home. From the beginning I have regarded the problem of our community as one of our paramount problems.

Two years have done much to change the face and character of our community, thanks to the vigorous leadership of the South East Chicago Commission, in which the University has played an active role. Since many of these improvements are visible to anyone who has lived here for some years, I shall concern myself with some of those that are about to come. New state legislation has been procured whereby neighborhood corporations can organize and through control of 60 per cent of the property of an area can obtain eminent domain rights over the remaining 40 per cent. For the first time, we have a tool with which we can force the improvement of run-down structures or the demolition of properties that have become slums. Of equal importance is the interest of the Land Clearance Commission in our area. The Commission, operating with federal, state, and city funds, is empowered to condemn as slum a part or the whole of any selected urban area. After condemnation it proceeds to demolish the buildings at public expense and to sell the cleared land at a fair-use value or convert it to some public purpose. The Commission is now in the process of surveying our area, and selective demolition shortly will follow that will eradicate the pockets of blight and decay. The South East Chicago Commission has been able in its work to maintain a nice blend of idealism and practicality which precisely fits the problems of our environment and the character and personality of Julian H. Levi, the Executive Director of the South East Chicago Commission.

From our community let us turn to our University. I ask you from time to time—as I ask myself frequently—not to forget its distinctive purpose amid the pressure of its problems. As a great university in the great industrial city of America, we have the opportunity, such as no other educational institution has, to advance knowledge and to translate it into action that will affect all aspects of our way of life. This was the dream that Harper had both day and night, and we should see that each year brings it closer to fulfillment. Our long-range plan of surrounding ourselves with organizations which build a bridge between our pure research and the world of practical affairs has moved forward with the rising walls of the national headquarters of the American Bar Association on the south side of the Midway. Other organizations are seeking out the University community as an appropriate place for their national and international headquarters. We shall encourage those which are worthy and reject those which do not serve our high purpose.

State of the University, 10 November 1953

OUR ROOTS IN THIS PIECE OF EARTH

KIMPTON

But there are certainly some things we can do that will not dismantle the place and will help us in meeting the problem of the day. First, we should capitalize on the magic that we have for the minds of all thoughtful men and women. And we should approach them with more warmth and less remoteness, with more humility and less arrogance. For most people in the world of education the University of Chicago is the city in the sky. But we must do more than lie suspended somewhere between heaven and earth. We must end the separation from our earthly roots if we are not to wither away and die. Secondly, we must fracture this stereotype that exists in the minds of those who can send us students.

Trustee-Faculty Dinner, 13 January 1954

KIMPTON

Even our neighborhood begins to have a new look. The first of a series of plans for the demolition of old and outmoded buildings and for the construction of new and more appropriate housing and commercial areas has been completed over the past year. The plan has been viewed with approval and even enthusiasm by a political hierarchy beginning with the President of the United States. It is hoped that within a year no one will recognize Fifty-fifth Street. New single-family residences will replace the World's Fair walk-ups on the south side of the street, and an efficient and modern shopping center will take the place of the seedy structures on the north side. These things will be accomplished by a combination of government resources and private capital, and already the hope of the new look has stabilized and brightened the community. The new and beautiful headquarters of the American Bar Association has grown up during the year and is an ornament to our community. The National Council of Churches, full of wisdom and Rockefeller resources, located the heartland of American Protestantism in Morningside Heights of New York City, whose total population, it is interesting to observe, contains only 10 per cent Protestants. But other plans are afoot for the location near us of large national associations whose work and ideals are close to our research at the University of Chicago. The neighborhood, like the budget, the curriculum, and the enrollment, is not yet saved, but at least we are on the road to salvation and with propriety can give vent to a mild hallelujah.

State of the University, 23 November 1954

KIMPTON

The most substantial donation to date comes from public funds, with the Federal Government, the State of Illinois, and the City of Chicago among them putting up over $10,000,000 to acquire and demolish some forty-seven acres of deteriorated property in the center of Hyde Park. The machinery of government moves slowly, and the area has suffered through the time lag; but, even so, through constant needling the program has moved faster than any government clearance project in the history of the country. Perhaps more important than anything else, our community has earned the reputation among dubious characters of being a poor place in which to commit a crime or operate a slum. The crime statistics in our district show a sharp decline over the last two years, and there is no enterprising landlord of deteriorated properties who would not gladly move his wretched business, if he could, to another part of the city. Redevelopment corporations are being organized all over the area by which debilitated properties can be acquired under eminent domain. It is a large and carefully calculated gamble, and the stakes are very high. At stake is the nature of our University and indeed the pattern of urban life in America for the balance of the twentieth century.

State of the University, 1 November 1955

KIMPTON

Mayor Daley, you present an inspiring picture of a great city that is destined to become even greater under your strong and imaginative leadership. For sixty-five years our University has been a proud part of this great city. As this community fathered us, named us, and has generously supported us, so we have dedicated ourselves to the service of our city and of our country.

A great university is a strange and complex organization, and, at first glance, its place and function in the life of the community are not evident. It is a storehouse of the accumulated knowledge of the ages, and its purposes are, first, to increase this knowledge, and second, to transmit it in an ordered, disciplined way to the next generation. As we work on a more accurate description of the solar system, the composition of the atom, the shadowy origins of our western civilization, the original folios of the texts of Shakespeare's plays, we seem very remote from the affairs of men and the real needs and problems of our community. And yet, as this knowledge increases, as men learn the fundamental secrets of the physical world, explore the nature of man and increasingly apprehend and appreciate the beautiful, these things become applied to the problems of our civilization to enrich and prolong our lives. A great University only seems to be remote from the affairs of man because it attacks our problems at a more fundamental level than most are conversant with.

But as this enormous knowledge is gradually turned to practical account, we obtain a vision of its significance for our community and our country. It was, for example, the late Edwin Oakes Jordan, a professor of biology at the University of Chicago, who, by his testimony before the Supreme Court, proved

495

that the water from Chicago's drainage canal would not pollute the water supply of St. Louis and thereby saved the city some thirty-three million dollars. And to turn from the local and immediate to the cosmic, it was the University of Chicago that undertook the enormously difficult and dangerous task of gathering scientists from all over the world to explore under the stands of Stagg Field the possibility of a controlled chain reaction that would produce in turn the uncontrolled reaction that became the atomic bomb. It is appropriate that a university in our community should usher in the atomic age.

. . . We are honored this evening by the presence of representatives of some of the other leading institutions of our area, and I know that I speak for them too when I say that we are proud of being a part of this great metropolitan area. There are universities in this country, and good ones at that, that reside in sleepy little towns. I feel sorry for them. It is right for a great university to be deeply a part of a great community, to share its triumphs, its problems, its immediate plans, and even its dreams. It has been America's destiny to produce the greatest cities of the world, and America's great universities should share this destiny.

It is a natural association. As our American civilization has become increasingly urban, the needs of the city and the university have increasingly drawn together. A city is a collection of men, and as cities have grown, men in them have developed a greater need both for more general knowledge and more specialized knowledge. The general knowledge is essential if a man is to be a good citizen, discharging his moral, political, and religious obligations to his community. And the specialized knowledge is essential if he is to discharge his business and professional obligations to his community. The training of men to meet both the general and the highly specialized responsibilities of urban living is the business of the universities. As we do it well or badly, our cities will flourish or decay.

And as our cities grow, there is a corresponding need for a growth in new knowledge of all kinds. How do we meet the problems—economic, racial, physical—of an enormous city that is growing all the time, how do we make the wheels of industry turn faster and in new directions, how do we train the business and professional man of tomorrow for new and creative leadership, how do we build and support a great center for music, art, and literature, and how in a great material metropolis do we keep uppermost the spiritual needs of men? These are the questions that we in the universities are struggling with, and it is through correct answers to such questions that a city is made and kept great. Our universities bring to bear upon these questions the wisdom of the past, a profound knowledge of the present, and an informed prevision of the future. Our great city and its great universities are partners in a total enterprise. If either fails, we both shall fail; and if we both succeed—and succeed we shall—we shall build what to our fathers at Old Fort Dearborn and even to us today will seem to be the heavenly city, the city in the sky.

Trustees' Civic Dinner, 12 March 1956

KIMPTON

Finally, there is the ever present threat to students, faculty, and the very life and future of our University—the neighborhood. As I gathered my thoughts on this topic in July when this report was composed, I found them dismal thoughts indeed, and if I now repeated what I then wrote I would not only depress but mislead you. At that time we had gained some new, powerful, and unexpected enemies to our gigantic urban renewal program, and our friends still had to rise and be counted. Mr. Zeckendorf seemed hopelessly bogged down in difficulties with zoning regulations and the Redevelopment Plan, and our local wasteland stretched out bleak and unrelieved.

In these circumstances, you will forgive me, I hope, if I peek beyond the shroud of gloom that enveloped us at the end of the last academic year and behold the sun that even then was trying to break through. Mr. Zeckendorf, with the aid of the remarkable Julian Levi, somehow cut through his red tape, and houses, apartments, and shopping centers are springing up all over the place. After a series of bitter local and city hearings that seemed to stretch out world without end, the City Council unanimously approved the Urban Renewal Plan that will bring $40,000,000 of public money into our area and an equal amount of private financing. There will be new parks and playgrounds and schools, new dwellings and traffic patterns and shops; and out of slum and blight a new city will arise. There remain problems, of course, but these also will be solved; the tide has turned for us, and out of our success will emerge the pattern of rebuilding Chicago and indeed much of urban America. Surely this is the place and time to pay tribute to the leaders of our community, to the newspapers of our city, and particularly to our Mayor, Richard J. Daley, who have remained, amid all the frenzy of opposition, steadfastly loyal to the ideal we ourselves have had of rebuilding a great and stable community that may provide a model for our city and for our nation.

State of the University, 11 November 1958

KIMPTON

One of our chief difficulties, of course, is the neighborhood, but I am less worried about it than I was eight years ago. An obvious reason is that much of it is being torn down and rebuilt. But there are other reasons too. The deterioration of our surroundings has brought our faculty community closer together, both literally and figuratively. The vast majority lives within a mile radius of the University, and it is as pleasant and happy a community as you could find in the most bucolic of our sister institutions. More than that, most of the other major universities are in trouble too, and I discover that their troubles are even more acute than our own. Faculty who have actually lived in Hyde Park–Kenwood like it, and I seriously doubt that it now constitutes a major factor in the decision of a faculty member to leave the University. But bringing a new and distinguished faculty member to our campus is a different problem. Here I believe the difficulty is the city of Chicago itself. Broad shoulders, freight-handlers, and hog-butchers are not everyone's dish of tea, if you will allow me to mix a neat metaphor. You will recall the story, probably apocryphal, of the child of one of Mr. Harper's early appointments drawn from Harvard. As the youngster ended his bedtime prayer the night before they left Cambridge, he said, "Goodbye, God, we're going to Chicago." I happen to love the city myself, with its vitality, its culture, and its beauty, but the fact remains that Chicago—and even the Midwest—does not constitute a lure for some people.

State of the University, 3 November 1959

WE HAD TO DO IT

KIMPTON

Again, the involvement of our universities, our faculties, and our students in the world of action stems from nobility of purpose. It is no longer sufficient to be a spectator, an aloof scholar, a simple learner. Government is not just to be studied, it is to be participated in; injustice is to be corrected not contemplated; learning for its own sake is meaningless unless it is put to work for some worthy social purpose. William Rainey Harper once observed that "the university was the prophet, priest, and sage of democracy."

It is now far more the protagonist than the prophet and priest, and less sage than a combination social laboratory and consulting service. And who can deny the value of these things? The University and its learned and committed people are a powerful force for good in the world of action. Nobody should be more aware of these things than I, for I injected the University and its people, its power and prestige into the practical problem of helping to create about us a stable and racially-integrated community.

But I confess to you a certain uneasiness about the new model of higher education in America that has spread its enormous influence throughout the world. In committing ourselves to educate everybody, we have spawned some pretty bad education in a lot of our institutions of higher learning. We are not clearly aware of it at Chicago, with our distinguished faculty and our highly selected student body, but you would be amazed at what passes under the name of higher education in the boondocks.

Convocation, 16 December 1966

BEADLE

One of the questions about the University of X that had to be answered was, "Where should it be located?" We, its builders, thought of a scenic setting—hills, woods, a lake; perhaps it should be near the mountains. It should, we thought, be near a fair-sized city but not in it. It should be in an area in which it

499

would have social impact on its community. It would be a residential university, with good faculty and student housing, but it would be separated from the "outside world" by thousands of acres of surrounding land.

When my wife and I were first being "looked over" for the University of Chicago, we could not help thinking, "How different from the University of X." Perhaps, we thought, it might be possible to move the University out of its crowded, smoky surroundings to the oak-covered hills to the south and west— near the Argonne Laboratory, for example. The cost would be great, but think of the problems that would be left behind!

What a mistake! We are not at all sure now that even the University of X should be isolated in the country. Certainly the University of Chicago would be a far less interesting place and a far less significant institution *if it were* so isolated. The problems it faces in helping to rebuild a section of a great city are not only challenging in themselves, but they are also of the greatest national importance. Until we Americans have learned to rebuild and prevent slums, restore beauty to our cities, and provide education and social opportunities to people who have not had them—largely because of the color of their skins—we will not have justified the faith of those who laid the foundations of our nation. We cannot do it by running away or by burying our heads in the sand.

If a great university will not stay and use its knowledge, wisdom, and power to help solve a critical problem, who will do it? There is talk of a Peace Corps and of other grand schemes to help underdeveloped nations in far parts of the world. We should, of course, do everything possible in that direction—but in doing so we should not forget that we must somehow learn to cure the sickness of poverty, unemployment, and racial discrimination that blights the hearts of our great cities.

In our own surroundings, a magnificent start has been made through the combined efforts of the University, the local community, the city, the state, and the federal government. We owe a deep debt of gratitude to Lawrence A. Kimpton for taking the lead in this enormously difficult and often discouraging undertaking. We must keep up the effort, for if we succeed, we will have established a pattern for the rest of the nation to follow. This is a noble goal for a noble university.

Our mythical university will never come to be, for real universities will always be as imperfect as are the real men and women who conceive and build them. Still we must never forget the power of an ideal. While our imaginations are continuously constructing new specifications for our perfect university, let us do the best we can with what we have right here—The University of Chicago.

"The University of X: An Academic Equation"
Inaugural Address, 5 May 1961

BEADLE

As for plans for campus expansion, I can say that the South West Hyde Park four-block area is about three-fourths purchased and half cleared. The remainder will be acquired within a year.

The South Campus project is moving along. Initial City legislation has been passed by the City Council.

These two developments will provide for University land needs for at least the next twenty-five years.

Not everyone appreciates fully the importance to a university of the community in which its students and faculty live. A professor recently returned from a visiting semester of teaching at a sister university with the comment that it was great to be back in an intellectually stimulating community. He meant more than the University. He meant to include the two square miles to the north of the University in which seventy per cent of our faculty members and most of our students live.

Many of you may not realize what a marked change has come about in that area within the past few years, thanks to the efforts of leaders in the community, organizations such as the South East Chicago Commission and the Hyde Park-Kenwood Community Conference, and the University.

Within the past two years the University has completely modernized nine apartment houses between 51st and 61st Streets for the use of single students, married students or nurses. Two more are now under way. The improvement in those completed is almost unbelievable, thanks to the efforts of Ray Brown, Winston Kennedy, and others working on these projects. . . .

The renovation of buildings about which I spoke has had a remarkable catalytic effect. Recently the head of a highly successful firm of builders and operators of large apartment buildings told me his firm would now consider purchasing, modernizing and managing the Piccadilly Hotel as an apartment building, but only because of the modernizing of nearby buildings by the University. Otherwise, he said, they would not have given this project even the slightest consideration. Other buildings in the area have also been upgraded. The housing vacancy rate is now lower than in any other comparable area of the city.

Many of you will have noted in Monday's papers that the attractive new Draper and Kramer high-rise buildings on South Shore Drive at 48th Street are being given the Federal Housing Authority Award of Merit for superior design, the only such award in Illinois for 1963, I understand. The firm's head, Ferd Kramer, is about to set another record as Chairman of our national Alumni Fund drive.

Trustee-Faculty Dinner, 8 January 1964

BEADLE

The University is very much aware of the problems of the inner city, and the opportunity offered to be a good neighbor. Over the years, since 1950, the University has given more than $30,000,000 to urban redevelopment. What this has meant to the University in the depletion of its resources can be seen when it is realized that a substantial part of the funding for the Blum village residential plan for students, the music, art, theatre buildings, the Science Library, and key units of the Science Center would have been provided by these funds. Put differently, each one of the collegiate divisions could have the endowment of $5,000,000 which we are seeking for them, and funds would be left over. We are now spending $525,000 annually to provide supplementary policing for the University area. This is the annual income on about $13,000,000 of endowment. As can be seen, much of the $160,000,000 drive is made necessary because of the funds which this University gave and is giving in the struggle to stay in an urban environment. The contributions made by this University to urban redevelopment will bring to the City of Chicago in matching Federal grants $42,000,000, to be used for urban renewal anywhere in the city.

At this time I want to point out that, contrary to a rumor sometimes heard, the University owns almost no neighborhood property that is not used for student-faculty housing or strictly academic purposes.

Student Assembly, 18 November 1966

BEADLE

We have a special problem with housing in the South Campus area scheduled to be cleared. It is often rented at very low rates to keep appraisals from dropping as they tend to do for vacant buildings. These are, therefore, attractive to some students. This practice accentuates the University's security problem, and we are expected to provide protection in almost impossible situations.

In the 1950's, when major University resources, both intellectual and financial, were directed toward various neighborhood problems, and students were at an all-time low, relatively little could be done in adding needed facilities or properly maintaining existing ones. . . .

What is our financial situation? The answer: becoming increasingly difficult for the reason most private universities are facing financial difficulties, namely, that costs of operation are rising faster than income increases. Our difficulty is accentuated to some extent because we live in a high-cost area—in housing, schooling, and so on. We also have a special expense in providing supplementary security—at a cost of some $600,000 annually, which is the income on about $15 million of endowment.

State of the University, 7 November 1967

STABILITY, DIVERSITY, CHANGE

BEADLE

Erroneous conceptions of the University of Chicago are many and widely held—that it is large, that it is wealthy, that it is City- or State-supported, that it has no athletic program, that teaching is largely done by graduate assistants in large classes, that its campus is densely crowded and that the area near the University is an intolerable one in which to live. I trust you here know all of these are largely false.

About the last of these, the neighborhood, there is still much lack of knowledge and understanding, even among faculty, students, alumni, and staff of the University.

I wish I had time adequately to summarize the complete story of Hyde Park-Kenwood—the two square miles to the north of the University in which live some 6000 faculty, staff and members of their families, more than 6000 University students—and 33,000 other people who are attracted to the area for a variety of reasons, not least among them the presence of the University.

For almost half a century, Hyde Park-Kenwood and the section of Woodlawn between Sixty-Third Street and the Midway were in large part white communities. During the forties and fifties they began seriously to deteriorate—through age of buildings and influx of poor people, largely Negro, in search of inexpensive housing. By 1956 the population of Hyde Park-Kenwood had increased about fifty per cent over its capacity, defining capacity as legal occupation of dwelling units. Thirty-eight per cent were Negroes. On the basis of all previous experience of neighborhoods in such transition, the process would continue until the total area was an overcrowded, deteriorated slum, inhabited by Negroes with less than minimal financial resources.

It didn't happen in Hyde Park-Kenwood. Why? Because the community organized and acted effectively to resist the trend.

It is often said this was done through Negro exclusion or Negro removal. The fact is that between 1956, when the total population was 76,000, and the present, when it is 55,000, less than a third of the reduction in population was the result of Negroes being displaced or voluntarily moving from the community. The percentage of non-white is now almost the same as it was twelve years ago, namely, thirty-eight per cent.

It is a fact that the community early accepted the concept of racial integration and took effective steps to establish a stabil-ized and attractive interracial community. As just one example, a group of Kenwood housewives some dozen years ago took it upon themselves to welcome new families, Negro and white, who elected to move into the large, single-family residences of that area, and to help them enter fully into community life. The annual Kenwood Ball, multiracial and strictly limited to Kenwood residents, continues to this day as a recurrent symbol of the success of the effort.

Not only is the present population of Hyde Park-Kenwood diverse racially, it is also highly diverse economically, religiously, intellectually and socially—almost a cross section of the population of the nation.

In a real sense, Hyde Park-Kenwood renewed itself. The effort was grass-roots inspired. But many factors were essential to its success. There had to be a critical mass of people to remain and make the effort. Those with ties to the University formed a stable nucleus. The University's resources—intellectual and financial—were essential. The City of Chicago played an indispensable role. City, State and Federal legislation had to be drafted and passed. Private capital had to be attracted.

It is now more than fifteen years since the effort began. Some $300,000,000 in private capital has been invested. Deteriorated buildings were demolished. Town houses and apartment buildings were constructed. Sound buildings were upgraded. Fifty-fifth Street was widened and more than two dozen saloons along its mile removed. Crime was reduced. Neighborhood parks were built. Some of the local merchants who were "urban renewed out" have moved into three cooperative shopping centers and are encouragingly successful. The co-op Supermarket is said to gross more than $6,000,000 annually.

A number of hotels and apartment houses no longer financially tenable for their original purpose have been renewed and converted into married student housing by the University—at a cost of many millions of dollars. There are now about 1000 such apartment units available. These and other expenditures by the University in the Urban Renewal area—some $14,000,000 —have earned more than $42,000,000 in Federal Urban Renewal Credits for the City of Chicago—to be used for renewal projects elsewhere in the City. Much of it will go into the Woodlawn renewal effort now in progress.

After much discussion and deep soul-searching, Hyde Park accepted as part of its urban renewal program the concept of public housing in small, architecturally diverse units scattered through the urban renewal area. The social theory was that residents of public housing under such circumstances would conform to the community and become a part of it. There are now thirty-six such units, out of a total of 100 in the original plan. The future may well bring superior alternatives to additional such units, but those that already exist confirm the prediction. The existing units are integrated racially and they are so successful that many persons familiar with the community, including interested and concerned students, are either not aware of their existence or do not readily identify them. I know of no other community in the nation that has succeeded so well in such an effort. If all others were to do so, there would be no national public housing problem.

Several institutions have left the community. For example, the George Williams College, which trains inner-city YMCA and YWCA workers, paradoxically moved to the new luxury community of Oak Brook in the western suburbs. But others have been attracted to Hyde Park. One, the new Lutheran School of Theology, to which some students object because they say it displaced low-cost housing for students and others, approximately replaces George Williams College in student and staff population. What these students and some others do not fully appreciate is that the very survival of the Hyde Park-Kenwood area as a community in which academic people and others responsible for its stability will want to live depends on a certain critical mass of residents with strong commitments to remain in it. Students collectively are an important part of the community, but individually their commitments to remain a part of it are minimal. They also often fail to recognize that, had not such a critical mass been maintained over the past two decades, the area would surely have become untenable for the continued existence of the University in its present form and place. It is likewise true that, without the University's dedication to the preservation of the community, Hyde Park-Kenwood would long since have deteriorated beyond recovery, short of far more drastic measures than those taken.

The University is involved more or less directly in solving other inner-city problems. In Woodlawn, for example, there are student tutoring projects, job-training evaluation studies, a child care center, a mental health center, and an experimental school program supported by the United States Office of Education, in which the Chicago Public School System, The Woodlawn Organization, and the University collaborate in an all-out effort to find new and more effective patterns for inner-city education.

Through the Mandel Legal Aid Clinic, the Law School faculty and students provide legal advice to those otherwise unable to afford it.

Medical students have corresponding programs for those who cannot otherwise get proper medical aid.

This summer eight faculty-student task forces set up by the Center for Urban Studies will work with an equal number of committees of The Woodlawn Organization. They will deal with mental health, youth, welfare, employment, housing, legal rights, physical planning and legal planning, as a prelude, it is hoped, to a model cities program for Woodlawn.

One hundred eighth- and ninth-grade students from Wood-lawn and similar schools will participate this summer in a sup-plementary educational and recreational program at the Uni-versity.

These examples by no means exhaust the ways in which the University interacts with its neighboring communities.

I could also point out that the University is one of the City's very large employers. In addition to faculty and students, the non-academic staff of the University numbers 6800. A high per-centage of these live in nearby communities. Approximately a third are non-white.

Some of our students think the University has not put enough emphasis on the solution of inner-city social problems. There are also doubters as to whether Hyde Park-Kenwood is the successful interracial community I have made it out to be. They may be right—but if there are other Universities or other com-munities that have done as well in handling their fair share of the nation's social problems, I have yet to hear of them.

Convocation, 7, 8 June 1968

AND WE DID IT, IN SOME WAY

LEVI

We did in fact play a major role in restoring and maintaining an integrated community, and the university's work has given leadership through example as well as study in urban affairs. And while our college is surely not free from the pressure of the discipline of learning, the combination of a research-oriented institution with a small undergraduate college has given us the opportunity for many of the qualities sought—and frequently sought in vain—by the small liberal arts institution. But these results are in fact dependent upon the university's self-limiting goals; its recognition that its only uniqueness ultimately arises from the power of thought, the dedication to basic inquiry, the discipline of intellectual training. Even the university's role with other citizens and institutions in reestablishing its com-munity—an emergency response, which might be thought to be an exception—would have been impossible without the recogni-tion by the faculty who lived in the area that the continuation

507

of the community was important because of the intellectual interdisciplinary values this proximity helped to support. That was basically why they wanted to live there. It would have been impossible also without the background of training, recognition of problems, and creativity which followed from the university's pioneering role of many years in the study of urban society. It is perhaps pardonable to say that a different kind of university could not have saved the community. The university's role is not based upon a conception of neutrality or indifference to society's problems, but an approach to the problems through the only strength which a university is entitled to assert. It is a conservative role because it values cultures and ideas, and reaffirms the basic commitment to reason. It is revolutionary because of its compulsion to discover and to know. It is modest because it recognizes that the difficulties are great and the standards demanding.

University of Chicago Citizens Board
16 November 1967

LEVI

These are serious service programs. The University of Chicago's work with the community is extensive at its best, unspectacular, and dedicated. Research is involved, but one must not work with people without primary concern for them. Service in these programs is therefore primary. These activities impose a heavy cost upon the university and its faculty. They require and reflect preferences and choices—the allocation of precious resources of time and energy. Moreover, they involve considerable administration and almost total involvement in day-to-day practical affairs. Of course there are many other programs relating to public policy at all levels in which individual members of the faculties participate.

A prominent journalist and author, after interviewing fifteen faculty members at a luncheon, and being, I trust, duly impressed with them, expressed his regret that Chicago was an ivory tower university, concentrating on the theoretical rather than the practical. All faculty in the room agreed that Chicago's role should be theoretical, basic, and long-term, rather than immediate and practical. Unknown to the author, and perhaps to some of the faculty themselves, was the fact that every mem-

ber present in that room was a member of one or more govern-
mental task forces or had recently been on a similar advisory
assignment. The theoretical university has responded through
its faculty to the challenge to attempt to apply its knowledge
to the practical order. It always has. . . . Reference is sometimes
made also to the major funds now going to universities from the
federal government. But again these funds either recognize, or
are intended to increase, the strength of the universities. And the
question remains: What strength and for what purpose? We
need guidelines, and it is natural that your university, which has
always been introspective and self-critical, and which has always
sought a central unity among all its activities, should wonder
about the relationship between this central unity and these new
service community functions. But there is another side to this
scrutiny of the place of service functions within a university.
This other side asks what the relationship is between these ser-
vice functions and responsible government social action.

The service functions are enormously varied. While research
and education have a wide range, many of these enterprises have
little relationship to any special skill of the university. They
range from running a security force—the university spends
twice as much as does the city policing the Hyde Park-Kenwood
area—to urban redevelopment, with the mixed bag of questions
which that raises, to particular operations such as clinics, where
the university, initially as least, clearly has something special
to contribute. But there is a long-term question even as to the
special clinics. Dr. Albert Dorfman, who is chairman of the De-
partment of Pediatrics at Chicago and responsible for the crea-
tion of the Woodlawn Child Health Center, has commented that
almost every medical school is planning or participating in some
community health program. "The enthusiasm for such pro-
grams," he goes on to say, "is based on novelty and naïveté.
Eventually their weaknesses will appear no matter how en-
thusiastic their present reaction." He enumerates some of the
weaknesses. "The portion of the population that can be served
is only a tiny fraction of the need. The medical personnel avail-
able to medical schools is only a small fraction of the national
pool. Almost all of the faculties of medical schools are chosen,
quite properly, because of abilities as teachers and investigators.
No medical school will survive if it requires highly skilled
faculty to perform the routine tasks required for the perfor-

mance of a successful community health program." Furthermore, "society is unlikely to finance such programs in the long term at levels of costs now being encountered." Dr. Dorfman justifies the present role of medical schools in community medicine as an attempt to "use their talent and inventiveness to examine the nature of the problem and discover solutions. Universities should not and cannot become administrative instruments of public or private services, but rather must be designers and innovators."

Undoubtedly a similar defense could be made of the University of Chicago's role in urban redevelopment. The university took the lead in collaboration with other community groups and with a responsive city administration. It drew upon the enormously talented yet varied ability within the university, including that of the chancellor and of the professor of urban studies. It had the advantage of a long tradition of the study of urban matters. An important result of that undertaking is to be found in the clearer vision and isolation of those urban problems which should not be dealt with on any long-term basis by universities as operating mechanisms. These are matters which must be worked out through the creation of new governmental structures within the network of local, state, and federal government, by a frontal attack on the unsolved problems of the relationships of cities and suburbs, by a much more determined and effective use of public facilities to establish proud communities. Our cities are in desperate need of replanning and rebuilding. The governmental problems far transcend any solutions which can be operated by a single private institution or group of institutions. There is something singularly sad about a New Deal or a Great Society which can only find the way and the means for an integrated society when there is a private institution available to give enormous funds before the government can respond, and even then is unable to respond in such a way as to build upon the natural assets of the community including the institutions within it. It is as though school systems, park systems, and police departments were to be had only on a matching basis. The cities cannot be saved in this way. There are simply not enough universities to go around for this purpose. And their powers quite properly are too limited in any event. A university is not a government. It is not good for the university, the community, or the government to think that it is.

The point then is quite simply that it is inappropriate for universities to be in charge of many of these services for more than an innovative and pioneering period—inappropriate because the universities are not the best means to carry through these programs effectively. Better means simply must be found.

University of Chicago Club (Washington, D.C.)
3 May 1968

CLEAR VISION OF THE GOOD PURPOSE

LEVI

The issue raised is central to what a university should be and what it should stand for. It is of course quite true that the ideas of individual scholars in universities are not likely to immediately sway the world, although some have had considerable effect. The tasks which university faculty have undertaken, sometimes within, sometimes without the universities, should not obscure the fact that universities exist for the long run. They are the custodians not only of the many cultures of man, but of the rational process itself. Universities are not neutral. They do exist for the propagation of a special point of view: namely, the worthwhileness of the intellectual pursuit of truth—using man's highest powers, struggling against the irrevelancies which corrupt thought, and now standing against the impatience of those who have lost faith in reason. This view does not remove universities from the problems of society. It does not diminish, indeed it increases, the pressure for the creation and exchange of ideas, popular or unpopular, which remake the world. It does suggest that the greatest contribution of universities will be in that liberation of the mind which makes possible what Kenneth Clark has called the strategy of truth. "For," as he says, "the search for truth, while impotent without implementation in action, undergirds every other strategy in behalf of constructive social change." One would hope that this liberation of the mind would result from a liberal education at Chicago at both the undergraduate and graduate level.

I know this speaks against a popular wind. Let me make clear what I am not saying. I am not saying that controlled exposure

511

to problems of the society cannot be important for education and for research. This exposure has given great strength to professional schools; but it is controlled exposure. There is a duty upon all institutions, including education, to do their part to unify the society in which we live and to help fulfill the openness of that society, including most particularly the paths of the intellect. But undue reliance upon universities as handy agencies to solve immediate problems remote from education can only end in the corruption of the universities. And the danger is greater because corruption is easy and attractive, particularly when it is dressed up as a relevant response to the problems of our day. The danger is greater, not because we should be against these activities, but on the contrary because we must be for many of them. The burden upon the universities is particularly heavy because they know they must relate to and indeed must help create those professions and other institutions in our society which will transmit and put into service the basic knowledge which flows from our institutions of higher learning. We must, for example, create networks of medical care, of adult educational enterprises, of new kinds of education for primary and secondary schools, and new channels for the social sciences, so that the ideas of the academy can be tested, rejected, corrected, and put into use. The universities must be related to these networks. But the risk is great that in doing so the universities will lose their protected remoteness, their freedom to be objective, their determination to seek intellectual truth on its own terms. This would be the greatest disservice. The problem is how to create these networks and, in part, to create them for the very purpose of preserving the inner strength of the universities.

What then are the guidelines? I have done little here except to stir the questions. Surely among the guidelines is a continuing awareness that universities are not governmental agencies; that universities do not speak for communities, but that communities must speak for themselves; that university service operations must not become so routinized and habitual that they are continued in this way when others could do them just as well or better. Beyond this, a university must know its own character. It is not enough to say it is dedicated to education and to the cultivation of intellectual pursuits. It must be able to see itself as a whole in spite of diversity. To see itself as a whole requires a recognition throughout the entire enterprise of the primacy of the commitment to teach and thus preserve the cultures of many civilizations—of the primacy of the commitment to basic inquiry and to the candor and discipline of reason. Perhaps the answer is that the limits of the institution's growth must be compatible with these commitments. The continuing strength and unity within will measure that growth. Perhaps all this means is that one must work harder to build up the central strength if there is to be growth at the periphery.

We can, I hope, be proud of the contributions which the university is making to service in the community. I hope also that we are strong enough and confident enough of our ability to preserve our central purpose to continue these commitments, to be a good neighbor and not the great house on the hill, to help our troubled society return to health, and to preserve that proper power which is the power of the reasoned word.

Inaugural Address, 14 November 1968

LEVI

In a similar vein, in 1967 Professor Franklin Ford, then Dean of Arts and Sciences at Harvard, looked at the shape and diversity of American higher education in an article in *The Virginia Quarterly Review* on the national and regional roles of our universities. Professor Ford urged that universities consider their specific locations if they are to appreciate all their tasks and opportunities. He wrote that it was "inconceivable that any one kind of institution could discharge for this immense country all the parts of the tasks" of higher education. He recognized with admiration the enormous and changing role of state-supported institutions in the Midwest which have become academic centers of national and international importance. Then he went on to describe The University of Chicago as "clearly a giant, a 'world university,' " but which, in addition, "has a special role as the largest, richest and most prestigious of private institutions in the Midwest." I am not sure of the accuracy or appeal of these adjectives, so graciously intended, and in any event I trust the following sentence, from Dean Ford's article, will not be misinterpreted. Dean Ford wrote about The University of Chicago: "Thus its regional leadership must at times consist in challenging what might otherwise be the total domination of that sector of the country by the mighty engines of state-supported education."

Professor Ford concluded his article—and one must remember this was in 1967—with a plea that in allocating support to higher education, care be "taken not to damage the few dozen places which have already achieved some sort of critical mass in terms of intellectual standards and experience." In this last plea, he remarked he was speaking in part for Harvard. "There is no point," he wrote, "in trying to sound so statesmanlike as to become anonymous." He was, of course, speaking for Chicago as well. As he correctly emphasized, however, this final claim was "too vital to be dismissed as selfish." It concerned a quality, the presence or absence of which could have widespread effects on higher education in the United States.

State of the University, 8 April 1974

THE LAST WORD

KIMPTON

The second apology that I have to make is that I am talking to you for a second time this year and you may be led to suspect that there is nobody else on the campus at the University of Chicago that has anything to say. This I can assure you, is not true. [Laughter] Sometimes I wish that it were true. [Laughter]

University of Chicago Citizens Board
25 June 1953

LIST OF SOURCES

WILLIAM RAINEY HARPER

Convocation, 1 January 1893. MS Harper Papers.

Convocation, 1 April 1893. University of Chicago *Calendar*, May 1893, pp. 21–26.

Convocation, 2 January 1894. University of Chicago *Weekly*, 11 January 1894.

Convocation, 1 July 1896. University of Chicago *Record*, 3 July 1896, pp. 224–28.

Quinquennial Statement, 1 July 1896. University of Chicago *Record*, 17 July 1896, pp. 253–59.

University of California Charter Day Address, 1899. University of California *Chronicle*, April 1899, pp. 65–82.

Decennial Report, 1 July 1902. *The President's Report: July, 1892–July, 1902.* Chicago: University of Chicago Press, 1903.

"The College President," 1904. University of Chicago *Magazine*, November 1938, pp. 5–7, 20.

HENRY PRATT JUDSON

Association of American Universities (Chicago), 27 February 1901. "The System of Fellowships." *Association of American Universities: Journal of Proceedings and Addresses of the Second Annual Conference.*

Harper Memorial Student Body Meeting, 15 January 1906. University of Chicago *Record*, March 1906, pp. 34–35.

Convocation, 12 June 1906. University of Chicago *Record*, July 1906, pp. 12–17.

Washington Education Association (Seattle), 1 January 1908. "The New Education." University of Chicago *Alumni Magazine*, February 1908, pp. 399–404.

Association of American Universities (Ithaca), 7 January 1909. "Discussion of Mr. Wilcox's Paper." *Association of American Universities: Journal of Proceedings and Addresses of the Tenth Annual Conference.*

Association of American Universities (Ithaca), 8 January 1909. "Discussion of Mr. Kinley's Paper." *Association of American Univer-*

sities: Journal of Proceedings and Addresses of the Tenth Annual Conference.

"President's Report 1909–10" (Typescript draft version). MS Presidential Papers.

The President's Report 1909–10. Chicago: University of Chicago Press, 1911.

"The Idea of Research." University of Minnesota Presidential Inauguration, 18 October 1911. University of Chicago *Magazine,* November 1911, pp. 14–18.

Convocation, 11 June 1912. MS Presidential Papers.

Convocation, 6 June 1916. University of Chicago *Record,* July 1916, pp. 132–40.

"University Ideals." Date and occasion unrecorded. MS Judson Papers.

ERNEST DeWITT BURTON

"President Harper—The Educator." *Monthly Maroon,* January 1906, pp. 142–47.

"In Association with His Colleagues." *Biblical World,* March 1906, pp. 220–22.

"Baptists and Education." Baptist Club of Philadelphia, January 1918. *The Positive Note in Christianity.* Philadelphia: American Baptist Publication Society, 1918, pp. 189–209.

"The Future of the University." University of Chicago Senate, 24 February 1923. MS Presidential Papers.

Convocation, 12 June 1923. University of Chicago *Record,* July 1923, pp. 177–96.

Board of Trustees. Acceptance of the Office of President, 31 August 1923. MS Presidential Papers.

Anniversary Chapel, 1 October 1923. MS Presidential Papers.

Football Dinner, 15 November 1923. MS Presidential Papers.

Chicago Association of Commerce and the University Club of Chicago, 1923. University of Chicago *Record,* January 1924, pp. 43–54.

Alumni Gathering (New York), 1923. MS Presidential Papers.

Convocation, 17 March 1924. University of Chicago *Record,* April 1924, pp. 115–20.

Anniversary Chapel, 1 October 1924. University of Chicago *Record,* January 1925, pp. 18–22.

Outline for Speech. Dated 7 November 1924. MS Presidential Papers.

"Business and Scholarship—What Have They to Do with One Another?" Executive Club of Chicago, 27 February 1925. *Exec-Club News,* 3 March 1925, pp. 4–8.

Alumni Dinner, 26 February 1925. MS Presidential Papers.

Fund-Raising Campaign (Chicago), 18 March 1925. MS source unknown.

National Radio Address to Alumni, 24 March 1925. MS Presidential Papers.

Alumni Gathering (Chicago), 24 March 1925. MS Presidential Papers.

Alumni Gathering (Los Angeles), 1925. MS Presidential Papers.

LIST OF SOURCES

"The University of Chicago As It Should Be in 1940: A Confidential Statement by the President," 1925. MS Presidential Papers.

CHARLES MAX MASON

Alumni of University of Wisconsin and University of Chicago (Milwaukee), 14 December 1925. MS Presidential Papers.

"Some Statements by President Mason." University of Chicago *Magazine*, December 1925, pp. 65–66.

Convocation, 15 June 1926. University of Chicago *Record*, July 1926, pp. 173–82.

The President's Report 1925–26. Chicago: University of Chicago Press, 1926.

Wieboldt Cornerstone Ceremony, 14 December 1926. University of Chicago *Record*, January 1927, pp. 17–19.

Trustee-Faculty Dinner, 12 January 1927. University of Chicago *Record*, April 1927, pp. 136–40.

Convocation, 20 December 1927. University of Chicago *Record*, January 1928, pp. 58–59.

Trustee-Faculty Dinner, 12 January 1928. University of Chicago *Record*, April 1928, pp. 95–98.

Farewell Address to the Faculties, 1 June 1928. University of Chicago *Record*, July 1928, pp. 150–52.

Convocation, 12 June 1928. University of Chicago *Record*, July 1928, pp. 141–46.

ROBERT MAYNARD HUTCHINS

Inaugural Address, 19 November 1929. University of Chicago *Record*, January 1930, pp. 8–15.

Welcome. Student Assembly, 20 November 1929. MS Hutchins Papers.

Trustee-Faculty Dinner, 8 January 1930. University of Chicago *Record*, April 1930, pp. 104–9.

Alumni Dinner (Chicago), 22 January 1930. MS Hutchins Papers.

Alumni Meeting, 7 June 1930. MS Hutchins Papers.

Convocation, 23 December 1930. University of Chicago *Record*, January 1931, pp. 1–9.

"Education and the University of Chicago." Radio Address (WGN/Chicago), 2 January 1931. MS Hutchins Papers.

Association of American Universities (Chapel Hill, North Carolina), 13 November 1931. *Association of American Universities: Journal of Proceedings and Addresses of the Thirty-third Annual Conference* 33(1931):137–42.

"The Characteristics of the University." Convocation, 20 December 1931. University of Chicago *Record*, April 1932, pp. 77–81.

Trustee-Faculty Dinner, 12 January 1933. University of Chicago *Record*, April 1933, pp. 120–23.

Convocation, 13 June 1933. University of Chicago *Record*, July 1933, pp. 182–84.

Undergraduate Assembly, 12 December 1933. "All about Consolidation." University of Chicago *Magazine,* January 1934, pp. 91–95.

"The Future of the University." Trustee-Faculty Dinner, 10 January 1935. MS Hutchins Papers.

"Report of the President 1934–35." MS Presidential Papers.

Alumni Club of New York, 6 April 1936. MS Hutchins Papers.

New England Church Club of Chicago and Fortnightly Club of Chicago, 3 March 1937. "Ideals in Education." *American Journal of Sociology* 43(1937):1–15.

Maroon Banquet, 19 May 1937. MS Hutchins Papers.

Alumni Dinner (Chicago), 16 October 1938. MS Hutchins Papers.

Undergraduate Assembly, 12 January 1940. *Football and College Life* (Broadside). Hutchins Papers.

Alumni Meetings (Illinois), 25 March 1940, 10 April 1940. "Eighteen Points about the University." MS Hutchins Papers.

Chicago Association of Commerce, 29 January 1941. *Higher Education and National Defense* (Chicago Association of Commerce pamphlet).

Alumni Assembly, 24 September 1941. "Owls to Athens." MS Hutchins Papers.

Fiftieth Anniversary Dinner, 26 September 1941. MS Hutchins Papers.

Assembled Faculties, 7 January 1942. "The University at War." University of Chicago *Magazine,* January 1942, pp. 1–7.

State of the University, 25 September 1945. Chicago: University of Chicago, 1945.

Trustee-Faculty Dinner, 9 January 1946. MS Hutchins Papers.

Modern Forum Inc. (Los Angeles), 19 April 1950. MS Hutchins Papers.

"About Research at the University of Chicago." Dedication of American Meat Institute, 3 October 1950. MS Hutchins Papers.

Parents' Association of University of Chicago Lab School, 1 November 1950; Hillman Lecture (Columbia University), 21 November 1950. MS Hutchins Papers.

Farewell Address. Trustee-Faculty Dinner, 10 January 1951. *Faculty News Bulletin,* Winter 1951, pp. 1–2.

Farewell. Student Assembly, 2 February 1951. *Tower Topics,* March 1951, pp. 1–4.

Alumni Assembly (Chicago), 9 June 1951. MS Hutchins Papers.

LAWRENCE ALPHEUS KIMPTON

Commonwealth Club of Chicago, 17 May 1951. MS Kimpton Papers.

Order of the C Dinner, 7 June 1951. MS Kimpton Papers.

Inauguration Banquet, 18 October 1951. University of Chicago *Magazine,* December 1951, pp. 15–20.

Mid-Continent Trust Conference, 9 November 1951. MS Kimpton Papers.

Trustee-Faculty Dinner, 9 January 1952. MS Kimpton Papers.

Hillel Foundation (Rockefeller Chapel), 13 January 1952. MS Kimpton Papers.

Student Assembly, 28 January 1952. University of Chicago *Magazine*, March 1952, pp. 18–21.
Women's Club (Chicago), February 1952. MS Kimpton Papers.
Alumni Gathering (Chicago), 4 June 1952. MS Kimpton Papers.
State of the University, 14 October 1952. Chicago: University of Chicago, 1952.
Trustee-Faculty Dinner, 7 January 1953. MS Kimpton Papers.
"Responsibilities of a University to its Community." Union League Club of Chicago, 16 April 1953. MS Kimpton Papers.
Convocation, 12 June 1953. MS Kimpton Papers.
University of Chicago Citizens Board, 25 June 1953. MS Kimpton Papers.
State of the University, 10 November 1953. Chicago: University of Chicago, 1953.
Trustee-Faculty Dinner, 13 January 1954. MS Kimpton Papers.
State of the University, 23 November 1954. Chicago: University of Chicago, 1954.
Order of the C Dinner, 2 June 1955. MS Kimpton Papers.
State of the University, 1 November 1955. Chicago: University of Chicago, 1955.
Trustees' Civic Dinner, 12 March 1956. MS Kimpton Papers.
Alumni Meeting, 9 May 1956. MS Kimpton Papers.
Order of the C Dinner, 31 May 1956. MS Kimpton Papers.
Convocation, 7, 8 June 1957. MS Kimpton Papers.
State of the University, 5 November 1957. Chicago: University of Chicago, 1957.
Trustee-Faculty Dinner, 8 January 1958. MS Kimpton Papers.
Convocation, 13, 14 June 1958. MS Kimpton Papers.
State of the University, 11 November 1958. Chicago: University of Chicago, 1958.
State of the University, 3 November 1959. Chicago: University of Chicago, 1959.
Trustee-Faculty Dinner, 14 January 1960. MS Kimpton Papers.
Farewell Press Conference, 29 March 1960. MS Kimpton Papers.
Convocation, 10, 11 June 1960. University of Chicago *Magazine*, October 1960, pp. 10–12.
Convocation, 16 December 1966. MS Kimpton Papers.

GEORGE WELLS BEADLE
Inauguration Luncheon, 4 May 1961. MS Beadle Papers.
Inaugural Address, 5 May 1961. "The University of X: An Academic Equation." University of Chicago *Magazine*, June 1961, pp. 3, 6–10.
"Thoughts of a New President." Trustee-Faculty Dinner, 10 January 1962. MS Beadle Papers.
State of the University, 6 November 1962. MS Beadle Papers.
Trustee-Faculty Dinner, 9 January 1963. MS Beadle Papers.
State of the University, 5 November 1963. MS Beadle Papers.
Trustee-Faculty Dinner, 8 January 1964. MS Beadle Papers.
State of the University, 10 November 1964. MS Beadle Papers.
Trustee-Faculty Dinner, 14 January 1965. MS Beadle Papers.

521

LIST OF SOURCES

State of the University, 9 November 1965. MS Beadle Papers.
State of the University, 1 November 1966. MS Beadle Papers.
Student Assembly, 18 November 1966. MS Beadle Papers.
Trustee-Faculty Dinner, 11 January 1967. MS Beadle Papers.
State of the University, 7 November 1967. University of Chicago *Record*, 21 December 1967, pp. 1–7.
Convocation, 7, 8 June 1968. MS Beadle Papers.
State of the University, 5 November 1968. MS Beadle Papers.

EDWARD HIRSCH LEVI

Association for General and Liberal Education (Chicago), 25 October 1963. *Point of View: Talks on Education.* Chicago: University of Chicago Press, 1969, pp. 3–19.
"The Role of a Liberal Arts College within a University." Liberal Arts Conference (Chicago), 4 February 1966. *Point of View*, pp. 87–99.
Class of 1971 Assembly, 24 September 1967. *Point of View*, pp. 123–34.
University of Tulsa Presidential Inauguration, 10 November 1967. *Point of View*, pp. 31–40.
University of Chicago Citizens Board, 16 November 1967. *Point of View*, pp. 3–19.
University of California Legal Center Dedication (Berkeley), 2 January 1968. *Point of View*, pp. 57–73.
University of Chicago Club (Washington, D.C.), 3 May 1968. *Point of View*, pp. 41–56.
Inaugural Address, 14 November 1968. *Point of View*, pp. 175–86.
Life Insurance Association of America (New York), 11 December 1968. *Point of View*, pp. 135–49.
American Law Institute (Washington, D.C.), 23 May 1969. *Point of View*, pp. 151–62.
Interview in Los Angeles *Times*, 6 July 1969.
Class of 1975 Assembly, 26 September 1971. *An Adventure in Discovery.* Chicago: University of Chicago, 1972.
Trustee-Faculty Dinner, 12 January 1972. *The Common Endeavor.* Chicago: University of Chicago, 1972.
Trustee-Faculty Dinner, 10 January 1973. MS Courtesy of the Office of the President.
Twentieth Anniversary Celebration of Hebrew Union College, Los Angeles, 12 February 1974. *The Integrity of Universities.* Chicago: University of Chicago, 1974.
State of the University, 8 April 1974. *Record*, 13 May 1974, pp. 83–95.
Interview in *Maroon*, 26 April 1974.
Campaign for Chicago Dinner (Chicago), 14 November 1974. MS Courtesy of the Office of the President.
Farewell. Faculty Reception, 8 February 1975. *A Celebration of Kate and Edward Levi.* Chicago: University of Chicago, 1975.

INDEX

Abe (paperman), 286
Administration. *See* Faculty, and administration
Allen, Francis A., 379
Alumni, 226, 441, 445
American Bar Association, 487, 493–94
American Meat Institute, 129
Angell, James R., 358
Architecture and physical plan, 19–20, 126, 368, 373, 507–8
Arnett, Trevor, 318, 416
Arnold, Matthew, 55
Athletic facilities, 206, 208–9, 213, 216; Bartlett Gym, 205, 208, 216–18, 228–33; financed from athletic funds, 219; Field House, 208, 218, 228, 233; gym for women, 216; Ida Noyes Hall, 205, 208, 233; and intercollegiate athletics, 233; Marshall (football) Field, 213; proposed, 232; Stagg Field, 218–19, 229, 232
Athletics: and alumni, 226; and Brown University baseball team, 212; and education, 212–13, 217–18, 231, 313; football and program in, 229; and health, 213, 215–16; and intellectual life, 212, 217; intercollegiate, 205, 212, 214–17, 219, 221–24, 228, 232–33; intramural, 205, 215, 217, 227–28, 232; and moral character, 212, 214–15,

231; outdoor, 214; participation in, at UC, 206, 227, 232; participation of UC chief executives in, 216, 219, 225–27; recruitment for, 212–13; scholarships for, 228; and student life, 211–12; UC policy on, 211, 217, 231, 309; UC and proper role of, 228; UC success in, 213; women in, 214, 231. *See also* Athletic facilities; Football
Avery, Sewell L., 412

Baptists and the University of Chicago, 36, 41, 44, 240, 473–74, 479–80
Beadle, George Wells: and biology comprehensive exam, 306; choice of, as president, 284–85; continued interest in UC, 287; decision to come to UC, 457; mentioned, 286, 289; quoted, 68, 155
Beadle, Muriel (Mrs. George), 284–87
Bell, Daniel: *The Reforming of General Education* quoted, 304–6
Bell, Laird, 247, 250, 480
Blackwood, Easley, 407
Blake, E. Nelson, 480
Board of Trustees, 216; and academic freedom, 124; and community, 471–72; contribution

523

183–84, 302, 308–9; Chapel Assembly of, 293; courses versus examinations in, 5, 29, 294, 305–6, 308, 320, 322, 338–39; degrees in, 293, 295–98, 338; Division Lecture plan in, 293; educational aims, of, 24, 38, 99, 187–89, 313, 317–19, 322, 326, 333; enrollment in, 166–68, 174, 332–33; experimentation in, 29, 307, 320–21; general education in, 319, 322, 326, 333, 341, 347; graduate teaching assistants in, 304, 340–41; and high schools, 12, 333–34; Junior College, 292, 295–301, 304–5; need for unity in, 294–95, 301; New Plan for, 304–7, 320–21, 327–30, 334–35; opportunity and compulsion in, 29, 187–88, 220, 300, 319, 330; as part of University, 1, 12, 29, 97–98, 292, 299, 304–6, 310, 312–15, 336, 346, 370; quality of work in, 308–9, 318, 332–33; question of abolition of, 19, 101, 301, 304, 307, 312, 448; Senior College, 292–95; size of, 301–2, 448; specialized education in, 99, 322, 326, 332–33, 347, 373; standards of performance, 183, 294, 301; and student's goals, 188, 305–6, 308–9, 313, 322, 326; student's rate of progress in, 294, 309, 323–24, 328, 330–31; transfer students in, 293–95, 329. *See also* Athletics; Education; Faculty; Research; Students; Teaching; University of Chicago

College history 303–7; under Burton, 274; under Harper, 292–301; under Hutchins, 38, 277, 339; under Judson, 274; under Kimpton, 306, 337–39; under Levi-Booth, 288, 341

College teachers, education of, 12, 58, 109, 320–21, 371–72, 374–75

Colwell, Ernest, 252

Compton, Arthur Holly, 448
Compton, Karl Taylor, 448
Convocation, 4
Coulter, John M., 355
Cox, Garfield, 453
Craigie, William A., 448
Crisler, Herbert O., 227
Cuppy, Hazlitt Alva, 386
Curriculum: completely prescribed, 305; limited importance of, 347; need for organization of, 189–90; specialization and generalization in, 190–91; and student opinion, 221; too many courses in, 318

Daley, Richard J., 495, 498
Daly, Charles V., 456
Deans: duties of, 89; responsibilities of, 323; weakness of, 144
Denneny, Michael, 340
Depression, 117, 119, 430–33
Dickson, Leonard E., 355
Disruptive demonstrations: and academic freedom, 156; UC policy on, 196–98; UC vulnerability to, 197–98
Dissemination of knowledge, 58, 96, 136, 393–408
Divinity School, 365–66, 379–80
Dodd, William E., 358
Donnelley, Gaylord, 456
Donnelley, Thomas E., 245
Donohue, Maurice F. X., 403
Donors and University of Chicago freedom, 82
Dorfman, Albert, quoted, 509–10
Douglas, Stephen A., 479
Du Bridge, Lee A., 284

Eckhart, Bernard A., 368
Education: and Christian, 449–50; importance of, to UC, 32, 101–2, 121; methods of, in the College, 317; outside the classroom, 20–23, 203, 205–8, 212–13, 217–18, 231, 309, 313; outside

Education (*cont.*)
UC walls, 26, 402; by participation in research, 99, 103, 155, 187–88, 316–19; study of, at UC, 18–19, 121, 291, 307, 320–21, 363–65. *See also* Dissemination of knowledge; University of Chicago Extension
Eliot, Charles W., 303
Eliot, T. S., 476
Ellis Hall, 401
Embree, Edwin R., 471
Endowment, 34, 428, 439, 458
Engineering, provision for work in, 357–58
Existence of the president, 277, 291

Faculty: and administration, 10, 128, 144, 146, 149, 248, 263, 444; administrative roles of, 10, 78–79, 85, 127–28, 140, 144–45, 157, 242–43; appointment and promotion of, 60, 77–78, 116–18, 127–30, 139–41, 143–45, 411–12; and Board of Trustees, 245, 247–48, 250–51; characterized, 141; and Communism, 476; community service activities of, 306, 466–67, 481–82, 495–96, 508–9; contracts and mobility of, 89; cooperation among, 19–20, 79–80, 106, 370; and communication with students, 88, 204; division of, into collegiate and graduate, 80, 98, 139, 147–48, 298, 302, 314, 333, 451; and Extension Division, 397–98; failings of, 87–88; and football, 229; full time plan for, 111, 137–38, 141–42, 150; fund-raising role of, 444; housing of, 149, 177–78, 474; importance of, 44, 57, 77, 104–5, 114, 116, 149–51, 374, 409, 424, 433, 451; intra-communication of, 21, 33, 51, 54, 57, 61, 74–75, 102–3, 139, 146, 149, 290, 335, 444, 507–8; material needs and wants of, 87,

132–33, 409–10; needs for space of, 298–99, 315, 348; and New Plan, 330; organization of, 78–79, 85, 88–90, 113–14, 126–28, 144–45, 292–93, 298; and Quadrangle Club, 95–96; recruitment of, 151–52, 409, 478, 498; and research, 85–87, 90–91, 99–100, 359, 508; salaries of, 86–87, 105, 110–12, 132, 150–52, 169, 355, 431–32; — competitiveness of, 413–14, 416–17, 419, 456; — importance of, 57, 409–11, 416–17, 448; — and related questions, 95, 413, 417, 451; — variations in, 77, 87, 418; size of, 110–11, 117, 146, 412, 416–18; strength of, and the Depression, 119; as teachers, 88, 139; tenure, 84, 112, 119–20, 413. *See also* Research; Teaching
Faith of the founders, 152
Federated Theological Faculty, 379–80
Fermi, Enrico, 139
Field, Marshall, 248, 480
Filbey, Emery T., 252
Finances: endowment and, 454–55; and faculty quality, 414–16; faculty salaries and, 412; financial information and, 460–61; and freedom, 126–27; fund-raising and, 438; importance of, 415–16; increasing operating costs and, 435; overall situation of, 455–56, 503; planning, 432–33; problem of government help with, 436, 513–14; and research, 135, 436–38; tuition and, 435, 438, 445–46, 452, 454. *See also* Budget; Depression; Gifts; Money; Tuition
Flexner, Abraham, 442
Flood, Ned Arden, 386
Flophouse bum, 487
Flynn, Frank, 380
Football: alumni and, 220; amateur, 228–30; compared with other sports, 222; and educa-

INDEX

Harper-Wieboldt College Center, 428

Harris, Neil, 407

Hass, Walter, 230–31

Heald, Henry, 478

Heiserman, Arthur, 405

Henderson, Charles R., 186, 467

Hildebrand, Roger, 341

Hirsch, Emil G., 488

Hixon, Frank P., 412

Hodges, Paul, 453

Hopkins, Mark, 186

House System, 10, 176, 210, 299

Huggins, Charles, 153

Hulbert, Eri B., 366

Humphreys, Eleanor, 453

Hutchins, Robert Maynard: attitude toward American undergraduate education, 138–39; and College, 277–78; contribution to UC, 264, 277; existence established, 277; experience of, 278; fresh look at education, 264; goals of, for UC, 276–77; invoked, 63; mentioned, 287; paraphrased, 69, 289–90; quoted, 153; and students, 277

Hutchinson, Charles L., 243, 480

Income and freedom, 439–43

Inghram, Mark, 341

Institute of Sacred Literature, 401

Institutes, 376–78

International House, 206

International Relations, program in, 322–23

Izzy (laundryman), 286

James, Henry, *What Maisie Knew* alluded to, 118

Jewish participation in founding of the University of Chicago, 7

Johnson, D. Gale, 461

Jones, George Herbert, 367

Jordan, Edwin Oakes, 495–96

Judd, Charles H., 364

Judson, Harry Pratt: achievement of, 270, 273; activities of,

271; and the College, 274; conserved UC strength, 272; consolidated gains made, 263; mentioned, 252, 304, 448–49; personal qualities of, described, 271; service of, to community, 467; stabilized UC, 270, 272

Katzenbach, Nicholas, 379

Keniston, Ralph H., 448

Kennedy, John F., 285, 454

Kennedy, Winston, 501

Kimpton, Lawrence Alpheus: accomplishments of, 281; decision to retire, 283–84; elevation to Chancellorship, 477; goals of, set and achieved, 283; mentioned, 68, 282, 285–87, 289, 306; and neighborhood problems, 499–500; owed a debt of gratitude, 281; parts of, in Revels, 281; personal qualities of, 280; picked by Hutchins, 280; quoted, 290; role in urban development, 510; tough jobs of, 280

Knowledge for its own sake, 72, 133

Kramer, Ferdinand, 501

Laughlin, J. Laurence, 358, 467

Law, Robert, Jr., 412

Law School, 342–47, 366–67, 379

Leon Mandel Assembly Hall, 8

Leveling trend among universities, 513–14

Levi, Edward Hirsch: and Beadles, 457; contributions to UC academic strength, 287–88; existence asserted, 291; faculty recruitment by, 288, 289; feelings at inauguration, 289–90; mentioned, 304, 339, 379; personal qualities of, detailed, 289; plan for College, 288; quoted, 57; rare talents of, detailed, 288; as talent scout, 151–52

Levi, Gerson B., 488

528